EATING DISORDERS
ANONYMOUS

EATING DISORDERS ANONYMOUS

The Story of
How We Recovered from
Our Eating Disorders

The General Service Board of
Eating Disorders Anonymous

2016

Eating Disorders Anonymous
The Story of How We Recovered from Our Eating Disorders

EDA's program of recovery is adapted from the first 164 pages of *Alcoholics Anonymous,* the "Big Book," with permission from Alcoholics Anonymous World Services, Inc. Permission to reprint and adapt this material does not mean that AA has reviewed or approved this or any other EDA material. AA is a program for recovery from alcoholism only. Use of AA material in the program of EDA, which is patterned after that of AA but which addresses other issues, does not constitute endorsement by or affiliation with AA.

Published by Gürze Books, Carlsbad, CA (gurzebooks.com)
as a service to:

Eating Disorders Anonymous
www.4EDA.org
info@eatingdisordersanonymous.org

Library of Congress Cataloging-in-Publication Data

Names: General Service Board. Eating Disorders Anonymous.
Title: Eating disorders anonymous : the story of how we recovered from
   our eating disorders / the General Service Board of Eating Disorders
   Anonymous.
Description: Carlsbad, CA : Gürze Books, [2016] | Includes bibliographical
   references.
Identifiers: LCCN 2016038763| ISBN 9780936077857 (trade pbk.) | ISBN
   9780936077864 (ebook)
Subjects: LCSH: Eating disorders--Treatment.
Classification: LCC RC552.E18 | DDC 616.85/26--dc23
LC record available at https://lccn.loc.gov/2016038763

Printed in the United States of America.

1 3 5 7 9 0 8 6 4 2

CONTENTS

PERSONAL STORIES
PART I
Pioneers of EDA

Part II
They Stopped in Time

PART III
They Lost Nearly All

APPENDICES

PREFACE

*W*e, the members of Eating Disorders Anonymous (EDA), acknowledge our huge debt to the founders and Fellowship of Alcoholics Anonymous (AA). EDA has deep roots in the Twelve-Step program of AA and the Twelve Traditions of the AA Fellowship.[1] Although recovery from an eating disorder is not identical to recovery from alcoholism, we wish to convey that we have only adapted the AA program as necessary, ensuring those with eating disorders can readily grasp and apply the AA founders' concepts.

In truth, some of these adaptations have been significant. The founders of EDA recognized an "abstinence first" approach to recovery from eating disorders to be ineffective. Thus, EDA's focus on balance and perspective, rather than abstinence, distinguishes it from most other Twelve-Step fellowships. EDA *fully* embraces the Twelve-Step concept that "recovery is a process not an event." When recovery entails dealing with food, something we need almost as much as air and water, any rigid approach to food-related behaviors—including thinking of food as "an addiction"—simply did not work for us. We think our approach is effective because it focuses our attention on changes that lead to long-term success.

---

[1] EDA's program of recovery is adapted from the first 164 pages of *Alcoholics Anonymous*, the "Big Book," with permission from Alcoholics Anonymous World Services, Inc. Permission to reprint and adapt this material does not mean that AA has reviewed or approved this or any other EDA material. AA is a program for recovery from alcoholism only. Use of AA material in the program of EDA, which is patterned after that of AA but which addresses other issues, does not constitute endorsement by or affiliation with AA.

While this volume is not intended to be a supplement to *Alcoholics Anonymous,* we highly recommend that the reader become familiar with the original text.[2] Much guidance and inspiration can be found there. Note that the chapters in both books are arranged similarly to accommodate easy cross-reference.

The solution we outline here is based on our personal experiences of having and recovering from our eating disorders. For members of EDA, this typically means gaining perspective (Step One), gaining hope (Step Two), preparing to make changes (Steps Three and Four), becoming accountable (Step Five), surrendering to a new approach without fear of self-recrimination or judgment (Steps Six and Seven), recognizing and repairing damage done (Steps Eight and Nine), maintaining integrity and trust (Step Ten), and building a foundation for, and then expanding on, a purpose-driven life (Step Eleven). As a result of working these Steps, we experience a transformation that enables us to gain—and maintain—a healthy perspective. This enables us to break free, and stay free, from eating-disordered thoughts and behaviors. Most EDA members recognize this transformation as a spiritual awakening,[3] yet the transcendent experience of full recovery is not limited to those of us who adopt a spiritual or religious faith. In Step Twelve, we share our experience,

[2]   Early members of EDA successfully used the AA "Big Book" and the AA "Twelve and Twelve," translating the words "alcohol" and "drinking" to "acting out" and the word "alcoholic" to "eating disordered." Sponsors may, of course, still do so. An online, English version of the 4th edition of the AA "Big Book," *Alcoholics Anonymous,* is available here: *http://www.aa.org/pages/en_US/ alcoholics-anonymous,* and an online, English version of the AA text, *Twelve Steps and Twelve Traditions,* is available here: *http://www.aa.org/pages/en_US/ twelve-steps-and-twelve-traditions.*
[3]   The term "spiritual awakening" can refer to an event—a vital spiritual experience—or to a gradual change. Those of us who are atheists also experience a transformation, enabling us to place service before selfishness.

strength, and hope. We apply the principles of the program to all we do: this way of looking at life and our place in it works under all conditions.

EDA has no opinion on the current scientific, medical, and humanistic debate about whether an eating disorder is an addiction or whether an addiction is a disease. We want no one to be distracted by academic arguments about labels. The founders of AA made a serious effort to clarify the complexity of the various manifestations and forms of alcoholism: theirs was not a "one-size-fits-all" definition, and neither is ours. Our stories show a great diversity in type and severity. Some of our members conceive of their eating disorders as an addiction and a disease, while others do not. In the end, we find it matters very little what labels we apply, if any at all; our solution is not contingent upon any specific conception of what an eating disorder may or may not be.

Some medical professionals have been critical of Twelve-Step groups for denigrating the value of medical treatment. They are concerned that viewing an eating disorder as an addiction or disease absolves the individual of responsibility for addressing their condition, prevents them from recognizing that their condition is treatable, creates a culture in which patients believe they are unable to fully recover, and requires a cult-like dependence on a spiritual power as a marker of recovery.

We certainly hope that anyone with a genuine understanding of the Twelve-Step programs of AA and EDA will immediately recognize the flaws in these objections. For those who are less familiar with these programs, we address these points one by one.

First, EDA members typically work closely with medical professionals. EDA recognizes that many people need, and greatly benefit from, the support of the medical community. Most EDA members are eager to help newcomers find and leverage *whatever* support is available.

Next, in all Twelve-Step programs, the individual is ultimately held accountable for their behavior. Rather than using "the condition" as an excuse for failing to exercise one's own agency to recover, all Twelve-Step programs require members to recognize that they alone must make the decision to change; they alone must take action for the decision to be effective. Those who object to the Twelve-Step approach on the basis that it is a "culture of powerlessness" should recognize that the first step is but an admission of perspective gained; the rest of the steps are all about *gaining* the power needed to build and sustain recovery.

Those who object to Twelve-Step programs on the basis that they foster dependence on a spiritual entity should understand that for most EDA members, spiritual dependence produces independence from fear, self-pity, despair, myriad forms of obsession, and freedom from mortal peril. For others, working the Twelve Steps need not entail reliance on any spiritual source at all. The choice of how to work the Steps is up to the individual. "God" in EDA literature can mean the Deity, a deity, a spiritual entity of one's own understanding (a Higher Power), or a non-spiritual conception (a higher purpose). Reliance on any one of these conceptions confers a perspective that transcends our immediate physical, social, and emotional circumstances and allows us to "keep calm and carry on" with what really matters. All Twelve-Step groups encourage members to "take what you can use and leave the rest." This is not a statement to be found in any cult.

Finally, while AA maintains a position that can be described as "once an alcoholic, always an alcoholic," EDA's stance is that people can and often do recover fully from their eating disorders. In EDA, we recognize that our responses to life are conditioned by how we have reacted in the past. And while life-long patterns can be changed, it is hard work. EDA provides support for those who are ready to engage in the work of recovery.

In early recovery, we learn to take small risks to build trust with ourselves and others. We soon discover that this takes time and patience, so we do our best to follow the guidance we hear in EDA meetings:

- Eat when hungry, stop when moderately full. Consistent nutrition is essential for recovery. Recovery is about feelings, not food, but we can't reason or build trust when bingeing, purging, or starving.

- Get basic needs met first. If hungry, eat. If angry, find a safe outlet. If lonely, reach out. If tired, sleep. If ashamed, talk about it.

- Ask others for input, then make your own decisions.

- When anxious or troubled, do something that focuses attention on your physical senses, get outside, pray, or meditate. Then deal with the problem head-on.

- Get open with others. Honesty restores integrity.

- Develop willingness to look at things differently. Recovery is not rigid.

- Go to Twelve-Step meetings, read the literature, and work the Steps with a sponsor.

- Be proactive and plan your recovery.

Following such suggestions, and relying on others' experience, strength and hope, we may do well for days, weeks, or months—only to find ourselves right back in tired, old habits that don't serve us or anyone else. Indeed, a "normal" recovery often involves what can seem like a distressingly long period of back-and-forth, as we learn more about what changes are truly required. But mistakes that lead us back to old behaviors should not be feared: they can be powerful tools for building a solid foundation *if* we are consistently open and honest about our expectations, resentments, fears, self-pity, shame, guilt, confusion, frustration, and despair—all the messy emotions that drove us into our eating disorders in the first place. This then opens us up to the difficult process of changing the thoughts that underlie these emotions. To maintain progress, we need as much support as we can get.

We in EDA don't find it helpful to count numbers of any sort: we don't weigh or measure anything, including days or years of freedom. Instead, we recognize what we call "milestones of recovery," which are self-defined markers on our journey. Even on our worst days, it is essential to recognize that we are doing things that are right and good, and supportive of our success. In meetings, we encourage everyone to claim as many milestones as they can. As we resolve our underlying thinking problems and become more positive and proactive, our recovery grows stronger and more flexible. By practicing the habits of thought and behavior we learn through working the Twelve Steps, we find we can rely on them to bring us durable peace and freedom: we need never return to our old patterns.

We still have normal life challenges, of course, and we experience emotions just as deeply as before—though there are differences. In full recovery, many of our most powerful emotions are positive: love, joy, delight, satisfaction, and a sense of wholeness and happiness. When we experience distressing emotions, we no longer seek escape; we know what to do and generally do it automatically. When troubled, we take stock, seek to understand where our thinking has gone awry, make amends where needed, and immediately turn our attention to how we can use our experience to serve some good purpose. Full recovery is resilient. We are able to do all sorts of things that used to "trigger" obsessive thinking and eating-disordered behavior. We can go anywhere and do anything that normal people do, without re-engaging our eating disorders: we are restored to sanity.

Our EDA groups include members who are religious, spiritual, agnostic, and atheist. Though our ideas about God, Higher Power, and higher purpose may be very different, this creates no great friction among us. We are allied in our common struggle to establish reliance on something greater than ourselves. Rather than debating theological differences, we grow in tolerance and humility as we share our experience, strength, and hope with each other. We cherish the diversity of our ideas and our stories, for these offer fresh hope to the newcomer.

We respect each individual's journey. We encourage members who have a strong faith in God to continue to seek God with all their hearts. We support members who seek to grow along different spiritual lines, and we respect members who seek peace in service to the greater good. In EDA, we celebrate everyone in recovery.

We acknowledge that EDA has no monopoly on recovery. Many people recover from an eating disorder without any intervention, while others benefit from medical, social, and psychological support. We appreciate and respect that a combination of support is often desperately needed by those who find themselves as profoundly helpless in their eating disorders as we once were.

We know our solution—the program of EDA—relieved us of our eating disorders. Our main purpose in writing this text is to share our accumulated experience, strength, and hope so that others might also find relief. We hope that you, the reader, will find guidance you can use in the following pages. And we wish that everyone might be happy, joyous, and free.

DOCTORS' OPINIONS

*E*DA members encourage everyone seeking recovery from an eating disorder to work with qualified medical professionals. For the most severely afflicted, a trained and experienced team—usually including a physician, a psychiatrist, a psychologist, and a registered dietician—can mean the difference between life and death. Even in relatively mild cases, caring and trained professionals can be essential to sustained change.

We think everyone engaged in eating disorders recovery will be interested in what medical professionals themselves have to say about the process and about our organization. It is a great honor to offer the following letters of support from three such individuals who have dedicated their time, talent, and energy to helping people with eating disorders develop strong foundations for recovery.

Our first letter is from Dr. Ray Lemberg, PhD. Dr. Lemberg is a clinical psychologist in practice in Arizona since 1977. He received his doctorate from the University of Maryland and is a pioneer in the field of eating disorders, having formed the first psychiatric inpatient program in Arizona in 1980. Dr. Lemberg has made over one hundred presentations on this subject; is Associate Editor of: *Eating Disorders, The Journal of Treatment and Prevention*; is the author of forty-five papers and publications; and editor of three books on eating disorders, the most recent, co-edited with Leigh Cohn: *Current Findings on Males with Eating Disorders* (NY/London, Routledge Press, 2014).

Dr. Ray Lemberg's Opinion

To Whom It May Concern:

When the "Big Book" of Alcoholics Anonymous was published in 1939 no one could have dreamed of its monumental impact. AA is now over 2,000,000 members strong. Eating Disorders Anonymous (EDA), which was founded in 2000 in Phoenix, Arizona, is modeled on the same Twelve-Step philosophy, respecting and preserving the major tenets of AA. The Twelve-Step model has been powerful in promoting recovery through support and fellowship as well as by demonstrating the success of those who were able to escape the grip of obsessive thought and compulsive behavior.

Years ago, Dr. Scott Peck, psychiatrist, wrote the bestselling book, *The Road Less Traveled,* which had a significant impact at that time. Dr. Peck conveyed that the pursuit of happiness was misguided, as happiness is a fleeting emotion. Instead, fulfillment in life is achieved, in part, by delaying gratification and overcoming obstacles that inhibit growth and transformation.

The EDA philosophy has many parallels to these teachings. A major contribution by EDA is an aim to broaden the understanding and conceptualization of a "Higher Power." In essence, finding meaning in life is often dependent on finding purpose outside and beyond self-preservation and self-interest.

Typically, the process of recovery is arduous and characterized by backward and forward movement that ultimately is necessary for creating a fundamental life change. It involves internalizing the belief that each person's journey is uniquely individual, and that personal transformation is possible. It also involves the sense of belonging to a fellowship that empowers a person with the strength of knowing that he/she is not going it alone.

Within the EDA text that follows, it is proposed that the concept of a Higher Power can be embodied by the idea of a higher purpose. This allows those who do not embrace religious convictions to empower themselves with a higher level of life's meaning, and enables them to evolve into more complete and resilient people. Recovery is much less about one's relationship with food and much more about one's relationship with oneself, others, and a higher purpose.

In this context, for some people the concept of faith is in a Higher Power, for others it is in a higher purpose. Both embrace a deep commitment and reliance on believing that someone or something is of much greater importance than self.

The work that follows is innovative, significant, and groundbreaking.

Raymond Lemberg, PhD
Clinical Psychologist

Our second letter is from psychologist Dr. Sumer Aeed, whose guidance was critical in EDA's identification of balance and perspective as goals of recovery. Dr. Aeed holds a doctoral degree in Educational Psychology/Counseling Emphasis, a master's degree in Counseling Psychology, and a BA in International Relations. She has worked for over twenty years in the counseling, consultation, and education fields helping individuals and families create healthier relationships. As the founder of *What's Your Story Experiences*—experiential workshops that support transformation and healing—Dr. Aeed guides individuals to explore the power of their unique stories. An adjunct faculty member at Northern Arizona University, she has developed prevention programs for youth, serves on several boards with a focus on healing and prevention work, and writes

articles in the field of mental health for numerous magazines and websites. Dr. Aeed's work helped EDA embrace
the idea that consciously taking care of our own basic needs
is essential to establishing relationships of trust. This idea
is central to EDA's message of recovery, and we are grateful
for her contribution.

Dr. Sumer Aeed's Opinion

To Whom It May Concern:

Our identity is forged by our story; that story deter-
mines our emotions, behaviors, relationships, possibilities,
and truth. People conquer their eating disorders in many
different ways. Yet we often seek "the" answer, or "the"
story, rather than looking for our own. Thankfully, there
is a way out.

As a psychologist and educator with twenty years of
experience working with eating concerns across the spectrum, I am passionate about individuals having access to a
broad base of tools and solutions on their road to recovery.
I have not only witnessed the devastation that eating disorders can play out in people's lives, I have seen the stories of
hope and new beginnings that can be forged from the pain.

Research shows us that eating disorders stem from bio-
psycho-social-spiritual roots, and my experience is that
a resilient recovery allows for tools in all of those areas.
Through the power of the group, the power of shared stories, and the power of others speaking into our lives, we
can co-author our recovery stories, borrowing pieces from
each other's chapters and weaving them into our own.

What I often see in my clients are patterns in which they
go 100 mph, get inspired, dig in and fall back down, see
the breakthrough, and then end in yet another breakdown.
They decide it's all a waste of time and then think, *I can't*

keep living like this. They are determined to find "the" answer and get it exactly right, while ensuring they don't risk or let go of anything. They are stuck in not being willing to change the questions they ask, which are still all about body, food, and control. This is all that they know and all that they trust, even though it is gradually killing them day by day. They watch others recover and feel hopeless, sometimes wondering if people "in recovery" are all just lying. Then they see hope in their eyes and peace as they sit side by side, realizing they aren't lying, and wanting what they have. Clients then become willing to listen—even when it does not make sense and challenges all that they are doing—desperate to find some other way to live and weary of the despair, disgust, and shame weighing them down.

Although my experience stems from the varied stories that people struggling with eating challenges bring to their "table," aspects of the following might sound familiar to many readers. The more things spin out of control inside, the harder you work to keep the outside looking "fine"—not realizing there is any other way to live, certain everyone feels this way, while at the same time afraid you are alone and broken in some unspeakable, unfixable way. Others see possibilities that you are not yet ready to claim; you let go of old ways of thinking and create new habits; you get to the "end" and then start all over again. You hide, you are seen, and you feel certain you would be the one person that the tools would not work for. You have slow chapters of great effort with seemingly little benefit—journaling, meditating, yelling at the fridge, not wanting to look in the mirror. You face the devastation of the eating disorder, still not able to tell the truth. You live with your body cut off from the head down, refusing to connect in any way to this horrible thing you are stuck in, with which you must "do life." You push your body past any logical or healthy limits, seeing what you are doing, and still not being able to stop. You feel like someone else's foot is on the accelerator, racing you towards an unhappy ending.

The story shifts as you begin slowly hearing, seeing, doing something different for a page or two of your story, being willing to do the writing, and finding the magic of the Twelve Steps when you truly work them. You become able to look back into the eyes of others as they see you— truly see you. You are able to take a deep breath into your body. You rediscover how to play, how to laugh and be silly. You decide to put your trust in just one person, however small a step. You feel a tiny bit of control being released and try not to be discouraged by how badly most of you wants it back. You become able to sit still with your body, with food, with emotions. You start being able to lean in to your story, even the scary chapters. You begin to understand some of the pieces you have read, heard, or written about, and you feel hope for the first time. You see that there are many more chapters yet to be written, and feel daunted, but excited, about what's to come. You learn to be in the moment, which is completely foreign. You truly hear the Promises of EDA and the Twelve Steps: a new freedom and a new happiness, not regretting the past nor wishing to shut the door on it.

Professionally I am so grateful for the many possible paths to recovery. But whether you are young or old, have this symptom or that, this label or that, this body or that, I find the following to be universally helpful in stories of recovery and hope: developing a relationship with our body by reconnecting or sometimes connecting for the first time; a sense of gratitude which can sustain hope as we walk through the tough parts of our chapters; a willingness to do whatever it takes; a sometimes blind trust in the process and in whatever group and/or therapist we are allowing to support us and speak into our lives; an ability to get back up and move along the path after falling down for the seemingly impossible hundredth time; the willingness to speak the truth however ugly, scary, or shameful; finding a way to move in our bodies that works for us; letting go of the old rules that created a certainty of failure; and being willing to face and work with the unknown, a step at a time, until it becomes the known.

Stories in recovery also involve being able to feel all our feelings, knowing they won't kill us, and knowing they have absolutely nothing to do with food; learning when we are full of feelings versus full of food; learning how to get still, whether through meditation, spiritual practice, or being duct taped to the chair to start; learning how to listen to our own intuition, beliefs, and truths and to let go—piece by piece, message by message—those that no longer serve us; writing our own non-fiction story and being willing to rewrite our old "perfect" ending with the "perfect" body, finding instead one we can sustain and that can sustain us: our own groove. This is the rough, inelegant, challenging road to recovery—and not for the faint-hearted.

I have heard recovery stories from atheists, people of all walks of spiritual life, ten-year-olds, seventy-eight-year-olds, people with stories of painful, hard-to-imagine childhoods, those whose bodies have been ravaged by eating disorders, those of all genders and sexual persuasions, those who had just started down the path to disconnecting from their body, those with generations of family who struggled with food and body issues, those with a myriad of other physical and psychological challenges to overcome, those to whom the idea of "sharing" was horrifying, and those who thought they simply did not fit or belong in any category that made sense. To any of you in this paragraph and those who still don't see yourself here, there is hope.

So, the "right" path? That is part of the recovery myth, along with the "right" diet, exercise program, and all the rest. "Your" path? That will be a unique combination of program tools, your own truth picked up and dusted off, and a hope and confidence in the chapters yet to come—knowing you are not alone. EDA offers the power of fellowship and a sense of faith, however you may define it. Trust the process, be willing to do the hard work, find others who support you and can hold the places for you that you can't yet see, and be gentle with yourself—this is a whole book and not a short story.

Warmly,
Sumer Statler Aeed, EdD
Licensed Psychologist

Our third letter is from Dr. Lacresha Hall, MD, FAPA. Dr. Hall is Board Certified in Child, Adolescent, Adult and Forensic Psychiatry, and Addiction Medicine. She has served as the Medical Director for an addiction treatment center and as the CEO and founder of a residence supporting women with eating disorders and addictions. Since 2003, she has worked as a psychiatrist supporting eating disorder and addiction recovery in California, Florida, and British Columbia. We are very grateful for her support.

Dr. Lacresha Hall's Opinion

To Whom It May Concern:

I am happy to have this opportunity to share my experience treating patients with eating disorders to increase the awareness and understanding of this disease as well as the process of recovery. I was fortunate to gain experience working at a well-known eating disorder center and to own a transitional living facility for women with eating disorders and addictions, both in South Florida. I have also had the pleasure of treating many individuals as they work a

Twelve-Step program through fellowships such as Eating Disorders Anonymous (EDA).

I had my first encounter with a patient who had an eating disorder around 1993, while still an undergraduate. I was working as a mental health technician at a residential treatment facility for adolescents. I can still remember her frail but muscular frame sitting on the porch with a Thigh-Master squeezed between her legs. At that time, I had no experience with eating disorders, but could somehow feel her pain and despair. I remember telling her that I did not want her to die, sensing even then that death was a possible outcome. I saw her for the last time before I returned to University. She had a vacant look of sadness about her— one that has become all too familiar to me over the years. I felt that she somehow knew that I had "seen" her, if only for a moment, despite her attempts to remain invisible.

After that, I completed my undergraduate studies, attended medical school, and had years of additional psychiatric training. Still, I was not adequately prepared to do this work. Eating disorders have the highest morbidity and mortality of any psychiatric disorder,[1] and are both widely misunderstood and feared. I have witnessed this combination of misunderstanding and fear lead to feelings of shame, judgment, and failure on the part of both the patient and provider during attempts at recovery.

An eating disorder is not about food, the body, or weight; it is an ineffective solution to a problem that has become concealed to the point of being unrecognizable. In effect, an eating disorder successfully distracts everyone from focusing on the true problem underneath. Therefore, since food and weight are not the real issues, no amount of bingeing, purging, or restricting will solve or change any-

[1] Arcelus, J., Mitchell, A.J., Wales, J., Nielsen, S. (2011) Mortality rates in patients with anorexia nervosa and other eating disorders. A meta-analysis of 36 studies. *Archives of General Psychiatry*. 68(7), 724-31.

thing. Yet, individuals with eating disorders often persist in thinking they can perfect these faulty solutions.

Once a patient begins the quest for recovery, they often find themselves caught in a powerful dance between control and will. The more control a person experiences from an eating disorder the more control they will ultimately lose, making it difficult for the person to will themselves out of a position of self-deception. In my opinion, recovery occurs through the exposure of this deception and acceptance of the underlying truth

Many uncomfortable truths accompany an understanding of the function of an eating disorder. When those truths are discovered and accepted, space is created and the mind is free to focus on alternative solutions. When this space can be held without judgment from self or other, the person is free to exercise their power of choice. Seeing that means not only freedom of choice, but also freedom from fear-based decisions. Insight and change come along with the responsibility to make choices and to accept the consequences of those choices: good, bad or otherwise.

I wish I had a simple answer for every patient who has asked me, "How do I recover?" The fact is that recovery comes differently for different people; one person's path cannot be compared to that of another. However, I have found there to be two common denominators in those who do recover: truth and trust. In my experience, every person who has been successful in recovery has had at least one person somewhere along their journey with whom they could be totally honest—someone who, without judgment, behaved as if success was a viable option—despite previous setbacks. It is the presence of a trusting relationship that allows people to accept their truth, no matter how painful it may be. This gives them the freedom to change, if they so choose.

We must also accept that, for a multitude of reasons, many people may not want to recover. If that is their truth at that time, we must accept them as they are and allow them to make that choice. What I say to my patients is, "You will give up your eating disorder when you no longer need it." Until then, their behavior makes sense in the context of its actual function. All truths have to be embraced for recovery to be an option. That is real freedom: the ability to choose and to choose not. Choosing not to recover, however, is different than giving up. This subtle distinction is important. Making a conscious choice—even if not in one's best interest—means there is hope of making a different choice.

I feel that my ability to practice psychiatry is a gift—something that I was meant to do. Anything that any of my patients have ever seen in me that they may consider good or inspiring, I believe is a reflection of God. The shortcomings are all mine. God is a difficult topic for some and a concept that many will never accept or believe. Therefore, I may not bring up God directly with my patients, but I am unconditionally accepting of whatever faith—or the absence thereof—they bring into the room. However, I often find that those who have chosen God as their Higher Power generally feel less alone. This provides them with a stable foundation to rely on as they finally realize their eating disorder can no longer be trusted.

In my opinion, two conditions must be present when helping someone on their path to recovery: the belief that recovery is possible, and the strength to stand up to the eating disorder. This is basically a definition of faith, and without faith the eating disorder can convince anyone that recovery is not possible. Although belief in God has helped—and will continue to help—millions of people, it is not a prerequisite for recovery. However, faith in the process of recovery is required.

In my experience, both loved ones and those with the desire to recover need something to hold onto. The more stable and consistent that something is, the more effective it will be. Therefore, I believe that faith-based programs, including EDA, offer perfect opportunities for providing important conditions for recovery such as: unconditional acceptance, belief that recovery is possible, and examples of how people apply real solutions to life problems.

One of the reasons I continue to do this challenging work is that I have had the unique opportunity of seeing many patients recover from their eating disorders using Twelve-Step programs, therapy, community support, spiritual support, and various combinations of these and other methods. Few experiences are more rewarding than bearing witness to the changes that allow someone to see themselves as God intended. It is also a privilege to celebrate the victorious moment when a patient is able to look back and no longer recognizes the person who once suffered from an eating disorder. I write this letter to encourage you to never give up hope, to never stop believing, and to assure you that recovery is not a luxury for a select few—it is available to all who choose it.

Dr. Lacresha Hall, MD, FAPA

LETTERS OF SUPPORT

*I*n the previous section, three medical professionals in the field of eating disorders treatment provided support for EDA's approach. In the interest of providing further assurance that our ideas are sound and well-respected, we are including two letters from leading voices in the field of eating disorders recovery research and advocacy—Jenni Schaefer and Robyn Cruze. A third letter, from a pastor in recovery through AA, affirms that EDA's message of recovery through reliance on God remains the central theme of our text. A final letter of support comes from the editor of a respected AA forum, AA Agnostica, backing EDA's expansion of the 12-Step approach to all who wish to recover, whether they follow a spiritual, religious, or secular path.

Jenni Schaefer, bestselling author of *Goodbye Ed, Hello Me*, conveys such warmth and humor through her writing that her ideas have brought hope to millions, inspiring us to change the way we think about eating disorders. As Chair of the Ambassadors Council of the National Eating Disorders Association, Jenni carries the message of recovery to a wide array of audiences, including treatment professionals, individuals seeking recovery, and their loved ones. She speaks via national broadcasts as well as presentations in schools, conferences, and treatment centers. Jenni leverages her position and influence to help advance research in the field of eating disorders recovery and recently teamed up with Harvard Medical School and Jennifer Thomas, PhD, to co-author the book *Almost Anorexic*. We are delighted and grateful to have her support.

Jenni Schaefer's Letter of Support

To those who courageously fight eating disorders:

One of the most helpful books in my eating disorder recovery was the "Big Book" of Alcoholics Anonymous. I'm not an alcoholic, but that didn't matter. While reading AA's basic text, I replaced the word "alcohol" with "food" and "alcoholism" with "eating disorder"—or simply the initials E.D. Personifying my illness as an abusive partner named "Ed" was a therapeutic technique I learned that allowed me to separate from the eating disorder. Let's just say that Ed hated the "Big Book."[1]

Despite Ed's kicking and screaming, I highlighted pages and inserted sticky notes throughout, marking places where I felt particularly understood and inspired. I related to the stories of overcoming adversity and gained hope that maybe one day I, too, could triumph over my illness. Upon the suggestion of a friend in AA, I made a point to read certain passages from the "Big Book" every day. I am happy to see that some of these sections are quoted directly within this book.

What you hold in your hands is the heart and soul of AA's "Big Book" exquisitely linked with experience, strength, and hope related to your struggle with an eating disorder. Unlike me, you won't have to worry about swapping out words as you read. This book was written just for you. I wish a text like this had existed when I was lost in my illness. I am thrilled that the founders of Eating Disorders Anonymous began their life-saving work, which eventually made this book a reality.

---

[1] If you decide to utilize this personification technique, you might choose to refer to your eating disorder by another name. Like some, you might view your illness as a female. The key with this technique isn't the specific name or even whether you name your illness at all, but rather that you begin to think about yourself as being separate from your eating disorder.

I am also grateful that the founders started Twelve-Step meetings. A couple of years into my recovery, I attended the first-ever EDA meeting in Nashville, Tennessee, where I lived at the time. Each week, a group of us squeezed into a small room in a local church. Back then only one EDA meeting took place in the community per week, so I supplemented my program by attending open AA meetings, where non-alcoholics are welcome as observers. Inspired by the release of this important book, I believe that one day, as with AA, Eating Disorders Anonymous meetings will happen regularly, throughout the day, every day, in cities across the globe.

EDA meetings and the Twelve-Step approach were keys to my ultimately reaching full freedom from my eating disorder. I have always valued EDA's message that a complete recovery is, in fact, possible. I didn't know this when I wrote my first book, *Life Without Ed*, but I did know it—and actually lived it—by the time I wrote my second, *Goodbye Ed, Hello Me*. In the time between these two books—and my being "in recovery" and "fully recovered"—I embraced something pivotal, and that was spirituality. I learned, again from a friend in AA, that there was a hole in my life that needed to be filled with spiritual substance. To me, this meant letting go and having faith in a Higher Power, which I call God. I began to regularly recite the Serenity Prayer, words commonly heard in Twelve-Step meetings:

> *God grant me the serenity to accept the things I cannot change; courage to change the things I can; and wisdom to know the difference.* [2]

But spirituality, for me, wasn't about just believing in a Higher Power. It was also about connecting with music, nature, and people. Spirituality is anything that connects

---

[2] Often attributed to American theologian Reinhold Niebuhr, the Serenity Prayer in its current form is used within Twelve-Step groups worldwide.

me back to myself in a real, authentic way. So, if you have trouble relating to a spiritual framework, don't worry. This book is for you, too. EDA has found a way to relate to all people, whether they embrace spiritual concepts or not. The "Big Book" of Eating Disorders Anonymous creates no boundaries, but instead reaches out to help everyone who suffers with these insidious illnesses. EDA makes room for every type of eating disorder.

Many of us, at least initially, try to disqualify ourselves from getting help. Ed might say, "You don't binge, purge, and restrict enough," or simply, "You don't have an eating disorder." Our eating-disordered culture supports this notion, too, as some of us actually receive accolades for having a life-threatening illness (e.g., "I wish I were as thin as you.") Despite my being underweight at the time, I remember walking into my first eating disorder therapy group, scanning the room—analyzing body shapes and sizes—and hearing Ed yell, "You're not thin enough to be here!" But eating disorders don't look a certain way, and how often you binge, purge, or restrict is irrelevant. What matters is pain and suffering. No specific eating disorder diagnosis—or lack thereof—can adequately measure the torture that is an eating disorder. If you are miserable because of food and weight, or if negative thoughts about eating and your body take away from your quality of life, EDA's "Big Book" is for you. Eating disorders may look and manifest differently, but the agony of the disorder is the same.

Many of us also need professional help, and I appreciate that EDA supports reaching out for assistance from eating disorder experts. I don't think I could have recovered from my own eating disorder without the help of a qualified therapist, dietitian, and doctors. I needed continued, professional care in order to stay on the recovery path. Gratefully, my treatment team encouraged me to attend

Twelve-Step meetings. My recovery was like a big jigsaw puzzle. It took years and lots of sustained effort in order for me to find all parts of the puzzle, and even longer for me to see how the differently-shaped pieces fit together. I do what I do today—speak and write about recovery—so that others won't have to spend as much time looking for puzzle pieces as I did. I am guessing you will find that this book, and the EDA fellowship, are essential pieces of the puzzle of your life.

As you read, you are likely to experience resistance. Maybe you already feel some—or a lot. Consider that Ed might be the one encouraging you to put this book down. Ed doesn't want you to get better, and it is likely that he will become very angry—and loud—when you first start making changes. Ed's goal is to continue to control your every move, and this book is about breaking free. So, of course, he will say that these pages lie. But, within this book, you will read one true story after another about people who never believed they could recover—but they did.

It is surreal to me now that I am writing a letter of support for the "Big Book" of Eating Disorders Anonymous. Years ago, when I was reading my tattered blue copy of AA's "Big Book," I wouldn't have even considered that one day, I'd be a small part of a similar effort aimed at helping people overcome their eating disorders. Back then I believed I could not possibly get better. Maybe you feel the same way. But I assure you: when you continually add pro-recovery actions to an eating disorder, your life can come full circle in the most amazing ways.

If you follow the guidance in this book, stay connected with support, and never give up, you can find independence from your eating disorder. And, one day, when you are working your 12th Step—carrying the message of hope to those who still suffer—you will look back and clearly see how your life has come full circle. Seemingly impossible things happen when you make the decision to recover in each moment, one day at a time. Even if you are in the middle of a relapse right now, you can choose recovery with the turn of this page. As they say in Twelve-Step meetings, "Do the next right thing."

This beautiful book will show you how.

Sincerely yours,
Jenni Schaefer
Author of *Life Without Ed* and *Goodbye Ed, Hello Me*
www.jennischaefer.com

Robyn Cruze is Eating Recovery Center's National Recovery Advocate. She is a member of the National Speakers Association, a certified life and corporate coach, and has published several books, including *Making Peace with Your Plate* (co-authored with Espra Andrus) and *Lovely Dreams*. Robyn writes and speaks on topics that promote eating disorder recovery and the building of healthy relationships with food, body, and beauty. The letter that follows reflects Robyn's experience of recovery and supports many of EDA's core tenets: that shared stories of strength and hope can pull us through the hard times, that we need to take care of basics and develop trust before we can make headway in recovery, and that happiness and safety are found not at the dramatic extremes to which some of us gravitate, but instead emerge somewhere in the middle area—in balance. We are grateful for Robyn's insights and are delighted to present her letter of support.

Robyn Cruze's Letter of Support

As a recovery advocate, certified coach, and author, I spend my days educating professionals as well as helping those who struggle with an eating disorder—and their loved ones—claim recovery. The messages I share are a combination of research, nuggets of hope freely provided to me, and lessons learned via my personal journey to and in recovery. The power of story, together with research, is a magnificent tool. It evokes identification and inspiration, which bring about awareness—and often significant change—on how we treat and recover from eating disorders, a distorted body image, and other comorbidities.

Many of us who struggle with an eating disorder have found that it's like being in quicksand—the more we fight, the further down we go. We've also found that recovery is a combination lock that is unique for everyone. There is no one right way to do it, and what works for some may not work for others. I found recovery by applying the Twelve Steps, finding balance and perspective, taking care of basics, and learning to trust—first others, then a higher purpose, and then myself. Much of my own recovery process is reflected in the approach suggested by the text you are about to read, the "Big Book" of Eating Disorders Anonymous.

In my experience, a common belief keeping many people from recovery is that without the eating disorder they would find themselves out of control, both physically and emotionally. This fear is crippling and has them either running away from food or towards it for relief. Ironically, the very act of surrendering and giving up the fight becomes their saving grace, providing them with the ultimate empowerment. And within the surrender comes a connection many of them have longed for and needed.

There are two sides to recovery that are equally powerful, yet neither is as successful alone as when coupled with the other. On the one hand is treatment for and education about eating disorders (and comorbidities), and on the other, is inspiration and identification. Just as we benefit from appropriate treatment for our mental, emotional, and physical concerns, we also need good people to identify with, who inspire us through the ups and downs of ongoing recovery.

While the Twelve Steps of EDA, adapted from Alcoholics Anonymous, provide strength and hope, the program is not easy. In the beginning, we can expect to experience difficulty with new concepts and verbiage that ask us to "admit powerlessness" and surrender to something other than the eating disorder—something outside ourselves. Don't be alarmed; you wouldn't be the first to have concerns about such ideas. My course of action whenever I have been in doubt about anything in my life, is to ask whomever or whatever may be in the universe supporting me for the willingness to try something new. It is this surrender and willingness that sets me free, not the label I use. The truth is, believing in a power outside of ourselves often has nothing to do with religion or spirituality, but rather with trust.

Recovery, in its early stages, can be messy, scary, and hard. Many of us who advocate and educate in recovery fail to tell you that. We get so busy cheerleading for recovery, because we know it is so very possible. But there is work to be done. Recovery can feel like you are being told to jump off a cliff not knowing that anyone will be at the bottom to catch you. "Oh no, no, no!" we cry. "We need a harness, a rope, hiking boots, and a clear map to get down! We need to take baby steps and we require lots of hand-holding!" Well, good news: the people that we find in Twelve-Step meetings are our rock climbing tools. They are holding our hands, making this journey with us—one step at a time.

Many of us who struggled in the isolation of the illness, desperately crave connection. Our eating disorders closed us off from the outside world, promising that they would set us free once we fulfilled their demands. Well, they lied. Recovery is not achieved in seclusion. After all, "a sick mind can't treat a sick mind." Recovery takes a village; it grows on support and love. Knowing that we are not alone and that others are on the same journey are healing tools freely offered in Twelve-Step meetings. Eventually, we discover that we begin to trust others and later ourselves. And that, my friends, is the gift of recovery.

Those of us who have had eating disorders have the propensity to live life at the extremes. We are either "perfect" or "useless," "good" or "bad," "elated" or "suicidal." When we come to recovery, the extremes of the illness have exhausted us. But by beginning to work through the Steps, we find balance. Who knew that the gray area of life, the patch between the polar extremes, is where we discover safety, comfort, and true happiness? Finding balance is not about food or the way our bodies look—though these are part of the equation. More importantly, it is about discovering a sense of clarity and a profound sense of self that has been concealed within our illness, waiting to be reclaimed.

In recovery, we can begin to explore our truth and feel our feelings without fear that they will destroy us or make us insane. Working on the Twelve Steps gives us the courage to question our beliefs about ourselves and our purpose in the world. I promise you, every one of us has a purpose, and you will surely discover yours on your recovery journey. Just like the promises from AA's "Big Book" affirm,

> If we are painstaking about this phase of our development, we will know a new freedom and a new happiness. We will not regret the past nor wish to shut the door on it. We will comprehend the word serenity and we will know peace. No matter how far down we

have fallen, we will see how our experience can benefit others. That feeling of uselessness and self-pity will disappear. We will lose interest in selfish things and gain interest in our fellows. Self-seeking will slip away. Our whole attitude and outlook upon life will change. Fear of people and of economic insecurity will leave us. We will intuitively know how to handle situations which used to baffle us. We will see that our service to God, our Higher Power, or the greater good has done for us what seemed humanly impossible. Are these extravagant promises? We think not. They are being fulfilled among us—sometimes quickly, sometimes slowly. They will always materialize if we work for them.[3]

My hope for you, dear Readers, is to make way for the miracle that recovery offers and boy oh boy, dream big—so very, very big.

Remember: hope is found in surrender, and recovery is found in action.

I believe in you!

Robyn Cruze
Author of *Making Peace with Your Plate* and *Lovely Dreams*
www.robyncruze.com

Balancing EDA's acceptance of secular ideas about recovery with the idea of finding peace and freedom through reliance on God, the General Service Board (GSB) of EDA is happy to include a letter of support from someone vested with religious authority. We respect that a letter from one

---

[3] *Alcoholics Anonymous.* (2001) New York, NY: AA World Services, Inc., 84. Substituting "we have fallen" for a phrase that is inappropriate for the current context, and substituting "service to God, our Higher Power, or the greater good" in place of language that is less inclusive.

such person cannot possibly speak for all of us with religious conviction, yet Pastor John's letter emphasizes three important points: that reliance on God remains at the core of Twelve-Step recovery, that our Fellowship reflects a plurality of positions of faith, and that this book is not just for people wanting a secular path.

The author of the following letter is the Community Life pastor at a church in a region of Florida recognized for its strong support of addiction recovery.[4] Pastor John is a married father who holds a Bachelor of Science in Psychology with a minor in Communication. He is currently pursuing a Master of Divinity in Biblical Studies and has a newborn son. Sober through the Fellowship of AA for sixteen years, he is grateful for the candor and authenticity that Twelve-Step community brings. He is also passionate about seeing people discover and enjoy a new capacity for freedom through intimate relationship with God and authentic relationships with others.

Pastor John's Letter of Support

My name is John and I am a recovered alcoholic. I am also a person who has struggled with disordered eating and body image issues my whole life.

These struggles used to be a source of serious discouragement for me. Left to my own devices, I was next to defenseless against my habits of acting out. Prior to taking action I was no match for the titanic struggles generated by the allure of my cravings. I turned to food for comfort and pleasure, for a reward and an escape. When I was bored I

---

[4] Cross, J. (2007, November 11) In Florida, addicts find an oasis of sobriety. *New York Times*. Retrieved from *http://www.nytimes.com/2007/11/16/us/16recovery.html*

turned to food. If I wanted a diversion food was always there. If I was pissed, food helped. I felt so out of control.

This was confusing to me.

Why was it that I had been able to achieve sobriety in one area while I continued to struggle so intensely in this one?

Wrong question.

By asking "why" without facing and admitting my problem, I was preventing myself from recognizing and embracing a solution.

Eventually I realized I needed rescue.

I needed rescue from myself.

Further, I needed the reassurance that there would be an ongoing rescue for me and a promise of soul-satisfying, life-giving restoration and beauty to enjoy. I needed companions and camaraderie if I were ever to make a lasting change.

How would I sustain that commitment to change? I needed hope. I needed hope embodied by those who had found it themselves. I needed a community around me that could understand the perils of disordered eating and the distorted thinking about body image that accompanies it.

I am pleased to say that just such a community awaits you in the pages that follow.

This is where the unifying power of the Twelve Steps comes in. I have long held a deep love for the Twelve Steps. They give me a framework for reorienting my heart and mind when I am struggling. Unlike my alcoholism, I cannot just be abstinent from food. With the grace of perspective that I gain from the Steps, however, I am able to manage my various struggles with self and temptation successfully.

What's more, I need a simple, ongoing program of action if I am to protect the freedom I've begun to experience. Here the Twelve Steps come to the fore again. They are a continual source of direction that helps me to reorder my priorities for effective action. The four main movements in the Twelve Steps help me to remember the shape of the journey before me: (1) remember and admit my problem (powerlessness), (2) embrace and adhere to the solution (for me, enjoying and exalting God), (3) know which strategies will reinforce my commitment to growth and change, and (4) live for a purpose greater than myself by putting God and others before myself. Through following this repeated process I get to increase my collaboration with God in His mission to impart hope and restore beauty to the world.

The four basic outcomes of working the Steps can be thought of as (1) peace with God vertically, (2) peace with self internally, (3) peace with others horizontally, and (4) peace with the world around me externally. I begin the process self-imprisoned and self-obsessed and finish outward-oriented and other-centered. Along the way, my aims and desires are purified to maximize my usefulness to God and others. I begin the journey weak and double-minded and discover traction and momentum as I persist in fighting the good fight. I get stronger over time. I've tasted freedom and do not want to forfeit it or lose the accompanying agility and power that come from protecting my sobriety from disordered eating and self-consumed thinking.

For me, resolving the spiritual malady resolves and uproots the other two issues: the obsession of the mind and allergy of my body to acting out in eating-disordered behaviors. I'm thankful for books like this one that enhance my understanding of how to grow and change in my relationship to food and body image so I can be free to live for—and serve—God and others. This book reminds me that freedom is possible and achievable through working the Steps; they encourage and motivate me. They make me thankful to have such resources and companions. They boost my confidence in increasing my self-mastery and self-efficacy through continued dependence upon God. I am enabled to be a blessing to others. What more can I ask for?

It's my joy and humble honor to commend EDA's "Big Book" to you and invite you to join us in this journey toward increasing enjoyment of and capacity for freedom from disordered eating and body image issues.

You are not alone.

Learning from each other we can continue to rely upon God and continue to fight the good fight.

An imperiled and embattled journeyer with you,

John O.

While the previous letter affirms that reliance on God remains central to Twelve-Step recovery in EDA, our General Service Board (GSB) wishes to further reassure readers that EDA's seemingly radical ideas about secular recovery have a long and deep history within AA. The idea that Twelve-Step groups should reach out to and embrace everyone—regardless of their position on matters of faith—finds support in statements by AA's co-founder, Bill Wilson, and members of AA's GSB.

The reason we have chosen to adapt the message of spiritual recovery to reach out to atheists, agnostics, and others with an alternative approach is twofold. First of all, there is no doubt that men and women can recover from their illnesses by applying the Twelve Steps in a secular way: one of the founders of our organization quietly did so, and remains in recovery after many years. A secular approach to working the Twelve Steps is broadly applicable, and secular groups in the Fellowship of AA are growing rapidly. Yet perhaps the most compelling reason for expanding our perspective is that that men and women die of their eating disorders every day. Some who died might have found recovery had it not been for the insistence of Twelve-Step groups on proffering an exclusively spiritual or religious path. We think it is time to clear up any confusion on this point. If EDA's main purpose is to carry the message of recovery to all who suffer, then we must carry the message that one can build and maintain recovery by working the Twelve Steps as an atheist or agnostic: it absolutely does work.

That said, EDA does not insist that everyone adopt or embrace the secular approach! Nothing could be further from the truth. The spiritual solution is and always will be at the core of Twelve-Step recovery. Instead, we have added guidance and support for those who simply cannot work a program that requires dependence on spiritual aid. As "roomy" as the traditional Twelve-Step view of spirituality may be, any approach that requires reliance on something a person cannot trust is not going to work for them. An honest atheist is never going to be able to form a deep personal connection to, faith in, or reliance upon, any "realm of the Spirit." An atheist can, however, form a deep personal commitment to, and reliance upon, the idea of service to the greater good.

Our key point is that recovery need not depend on the intercession of any spiritual entity. The AA text itself makes clear that *reliance on the idea of something more important than ourselves* is what we need to provide the peace and perspective to think and act unselfishly. We could not recover on the basis of moral and philosophical convictions, nor on the basis of religious faith alone[5], nor on the basis of

---

[5] *Alcoholics Anonymous.* (2001) New York, NY: AA World Services, Inc., 76, 88, 93.

anything else that was grounded in a limited, self-focused perspective, until we were willing to let go of preconceived ideas and began to rely absolutely on ideas that we could trust—whether these ideas were of God, or of a higher purpose. The original AA text is absolutely correct about that point: *Reliance on something greater than ourselves is a solution—one that anyone can apply.*

The lived experience of atheists and agnostics in EDA and other Twelve-Step groups is that secular recovery using the Twelve Steps as a foundation is absolutely possible. Many have walked free of eating disorders, alcoholism, and other issues by following the same process as their more spiritually-inclined, fellow Twelve-Step group members. It is not an easier, softer way.

The idea that people with secular views can work the Twelve Steps is supported in the following letter from Roger C—author, editor, publisher, and administrator of the AA Agnostica website. AA Agnostica provides support and inspiration for non-religious seekers of recovery through their website and publishing company. They have released six books over the past several years, including *The Little Book: A Collection of Alternative 12-Steps*, which contains twenty mostly secular versions of the Twelve Steps with concise interpretations of each Step by well-respected authors Gabor Maté, Stephanie Covington, Allen Berger, and Thérèse Jacobs-Stewart. Roger's letter invokes AA co-founder Bill Wilson in support of the idea that Twelve-Step groups ought to embrace anyone with a desire to recover.

Roger C's Letter of Support

To whom it may concern:

I would like to tell you a bit about the secular movement within our fellowship, one that is becoming an increasingly important part of Alcoholics Anonymous. Let me be clear that while there has been some resistance within AA, opposition has been the exception and not the rule. Fortunately, most people understand AA in much the same way as Bill Wilson expressed it at a General Service Conference in 1965:

> In AA we are supposed to be bound together in the kinship of a universal suffering. Therefore the full liberty to practice any creed or principle or therapy should be a first consideration. Hence let us not pressure anyone with individual or even collective views. Let us instead accord to each other the respect that is due to every human being as he tries to make his way towards the light. Let us always try to be inclusive rather than exclusive. Let us remember that each alcoholic among us is a member of AA, so long as he or she so declares.

Bill Wilson had no problem with secular versions of the Steps. When presented with one rewritten by Buddhists, which replaced the word "God" with "good," he wrote:

> To some of us, the idea of substituting "good" for "God" in the Twelve Steps will seem like a watering down of AA's message. We must remember that AA's Steps are suggestions only. A belief in them as they stand is not at all a requirement for membership among us. This liberty has made AA available to thousands who never would have tried at all, had we insisted on the Twelve Steps just as written.[6]

---

[6] *Alcoholics Anonymous Comes of Age.* (1957) New York, NY: AA World Services, Inc., 81.

The previous quotes from Bill Wilson are from the 1950s and 60s. What about today? In February of 2016, the AA General Service Office (GSO) wrote the following:

> We are aware that many AA's feel that by using an unauthorized version of the Twelve Steps a group so removes itself from AA that it should call themselves by another name, while many other AA's feel that this fellowship allows unparalleled freedom...

> A quick look at our AA directories indicates that the GSO lists atheist and agnostic groups, and some appear to have been listed for many years. In describing an AA group, the directories use the long form of Tradition Three:

>> Our membership ought to include all who suffer from alcoholism. Hence we may refuse none who wish to recover. Nor ought AA membership ever depend upon money or conformity. Any two or three alcoholics gathered together for sobriety may call themselves an AA group, provided that, as a group, they have no other affiliation.

For many of us, this issue is all about moving forward and being respectful of a contemporary reality in which polls and research over the years—Pew Research, in particular—have shown that more and more people describe themselves as agnostics or atheists. When asked about their religious affiliation, the answer is increasingly "none."

I am happy to report that within the fellowship of AA our secular movement is growing fantastically. When AA Agnostica was first established just a few years ago, there were two agnostic meetings in the Toronto area. Today there are a dozen. At the same time there were less than eighty agnostic meetings worldwide. At last count, there were over 300, with new ones starting up every day of the week.

In November 2014, the first international Convention

was held for agnostics, atheists, and freethinkers in Alcoholics Anonymous in Santa Monica, California. Over 300 people attended. Great talks were given, one by Ward Ewing, past chair of AA's General Service Board and another by Phyllis Halliday, then General Manager of the GSO of Alcoholics Anonymous. There have been other regional conferences since, including one where I presented a talk on "The History of Secularism in AA."

What is it all about?

As Bill Wilson put it in 1965, we need "to accord to each other the respect that is due to every human being as he [or she] tries to make his [or her] way towards the light." In that same talk Bill discussed the people—he specifically mentioned "atheists and agnostics...people of nearly every race, culture, and religion"—who came into the rooms of AA and "did not stay." He asked, "How much and how often did we fail them?"

Later that summer, at AA's 30th anniversary International Convention at Maple Leaf Gardens in downtown Toronto, more than 10,000 delegates, trustees, and AA representatives from twenty-one countries rose to their feet, joined hands and, led by Bill, for the first time ever recited the new AA responsibility declaration: "I am responsible. When anyone, anywhere, reaches out for help, I want the hand of AA always to be there. And for that I am responsible."

That's what it's all about. That's how I understand the mission of any Twelve-Step organization, and the inclusive language it must therefore employ: we are committed to "anyone, anywhere" in recovery.

Best wishes to all of you in Eating Disorders Anonymous,

Roger C
AA Agnostica
Hamilton, Ontario CANADA
http://aaagnostica.org

Chapter 1

GISELE'S STORY OF HOPE

*O*ur first story is from Gisele B., the founder of EDA. In 1999, after years of trying to recover on her own, Gisele sought help for her eating disorder at a treatment center in Phoenix, Arizona. Inpatient treatment was not an option for a single mother who lacked insurance, but a resource at the center suggested that Gisele attend one of their facilitated self-help groups for eating disorders recovery. Annette, EDA member number three,[1] began attending that same group in November 1999, and she and Gisele bonded over their experiences. Though still struggling with her eating disorder, Annette was grateful to be sober through Alcoholics Anonymous (AA) and she encouraged Gisele to give AA a shot. Gisele soon found sobriety and became inspired to start a group like AA for people with eating disorders. Annette wasn't too keen on the idea at first, having just arrived at the conclusion that abstinence-based approaches to eating disorders recovery were ineffective. But Gisele was determined: she started the first EDA group in February 2000 with practically no support at all.

Gisele's courage and determination—and her willingness to be true to herself—created EDA. Never let it be said that you cannot make a difference; Gisele's example proves

---

[1] Joanie, a friend of Gisele's through AA, was EDA member number two. Joanie stayed with us for the first few years then moved to a state that did not have any EDA groups, at a time when EDA did not have phone or online meetings. At last contact, Joanie was doing well with the support of her AA group.

you can. EDA exists because of her bravery. We are honored to present the story of her journey in recovery.

My story starts out pretty much like everyone else's. I came from a dysfunctional family and all that it entails. My recovery began when I realized I was becoming exactly like my mom. It was my worst nightmare. I felt lost.

My mom was often violent; I pictured her as a monster. She controlled every aspect of my life and I grew up feeling like *I did not exist.* From the outside, I guess we looked like a normal family, but later I discovered all sorts of skeletons in the closet. My dad was a "don't make waves, don't rock the boat" kind of man. He would stuff his emotions inside, except every now and then, he would just *explode.* Looking back on it now, I can laugh at some of the horrible things that happened in my family, but at the time it was a miserable existence.

Until I was seven years old, we lived on a ranch in Colorado. I had two older brothers. That sounds a bit like the setting for a great Western novel, but it was not the idyllic *Bonanza* family my dad wanted. It took me a long time to accept that my parents did the best they could with what they had. I was told I did not speak until I was five years old. I thought I just had nothing to say to these people, but there were some actual reasons for that: I was raped by a babysitter and molested by my oldest brother before we left the ranch. This caused, shall we say, a few problems.

When I was seven, we moved to Olympia, Washington. I thought we moved because my dad lost the ranch, but the real reason was because my mom was having an affair and would not stop. Now I can see that the dysfunction in my family was a cycle my parents both inherited from their own families, but this insight was no help to me as a child! My strongest memory of those early years is that I was alone—and I mean really alone with no one around— much of the time. The only one who paid me much attention was my oldest brother, who teased me a lot.

When I got to school, I did not fit in for a couple reasons. First of all, I went to a special speech class that made me feel dumb and different. Throughout the years I've had a stammer and problems with speaking. Now I know this wasn't because I was stupid; I'd had problems from not talking or learning how to communicate at an early age. I also didn't fit in because of the way I thought about myself: from as far back as I can remember I just wanted to die. I have had to turn thoughts of suicide, which I called my "safety net," over to God: I had to ask for the obsession to be taken away.

Growing up, I did everything I could to escape my home life. I'm sure we looked normal from the outside— my brothers and I were well-behaved church-goers. The church was very legalistic and controlling. What people didn't see was what happened at home if we misbehaved. I was always involved in sports, which allowed me to eat as much as I wanted. But later I realized that I had always had a horrible image of myself and tried to escape in every way I could. I believe my eating disorder and my alcoholism started when I was in my early teen years. Which appeared first really doesn't matter; I had the "isms," which meant for me, everything I touched would turn on me.

I left my parents' house at age seventeen, while in a screaming fight with mom. I guess I thought that leaving would make my life finally start and that I would somehow know what to do next. But for the next few years, all I did was to jump from place to place, and party to party. I had *absolutely no plan* for my life at all. A lot can happen to a single, young female—and it did, including three more rapes.

I moved to Alaska because I found a job that paid well. I didn't know at the time that moving to get away from my problems was what they call "a geographic" in AA, but I discovered the same thing everyone else does: wherever you go, there you are! In Alaska, when I wasn't working I was drinking and smoking pot, and my bulimic behavior started. Then, about three months into my Alaska "adventure," I received a call. Drew, the only person I thought knew me and loved me had committed suicide. I went home for the funeral, but I couldn't stay and "deal," so I went back to Alaska to finish my contract.

Soon after, I went through what I think of as my first psychotic break. I drank more, smoked more, and binged and purged more. I was a wreck! I began hallucinating. My behavior changed. I stole from work and from the store where we all shopped. Another gal and I were hanging out with a bunch of safe guys, but then I decided to pick out this long-haired, blonde guy for myself—a guy my age (all of nineteen!) that everybody seemed to want—and he played along. I also remember getting into fights with other women at that time, but I don't remember much about that period. I would "come to" with blood on me, my hands swollen and beaten up. We were all just a bunch of misfits.

Then, when I left the bar after one of my nights spent partying, I was followed and raped by the bouncer. I did not report it because I figured no one would believe me. Not long after, I got caught stealing, was fired from my job in Alaska, and reluctantly returned to my hometown.

I stayed with a friend, who took me to see a doctor. I don't remember the purpose for the visit, but I sure remember the news: I was three months pregnant. I was scared and didn't know what to do, but I decided to keep the baby. I had been drinking and smoking in that first trimester and I wasn't sure if the baby's father was the rapist or the blonde guy. To say the least, my pregnancy was hardly a happy time! But having my daughter was a blessing, even though I did not know it yet. I know God gave me my daughter so I would slow down and stay alive long enough to "get it." I still continued to party a bit, though I did my best to be a good mom. I tried to do and be what everyone thought I should do and be.

The first choice I made entirely on my own was when my daughter was still in diapers: I decided to fix my problems by doing another "geographic" to Arizona. I just could not stay around my family any longer. My insides would twist when my mom held my daughter, and I knew things would end up horribly if I stayed. There was one family I knew who moved to Arizona and they said I could stay with them. So I packed up the two of us, sold everything, gave my car (a white-with-red-interior Maverick) to my dead friend's little sister, and moved to Arizona. I continued to do my best as a mom and take care of us. I even tried individual therapy and medications, but I was not making much headway—my addictions were starting to rule my life.

My parents drove truck for a living at that time, and sometimes when they came into town on a delivery we would go to dinner together. Once, because I thought it would help, I confronted them about my brother molesting me. They told me I was crazy and swept the secret back under the rug, stomping it down for good measure to be sure no light or air could get underneath! I lost hope of ever resolving my issues. My drinking and my eating disorder both got worse and began to affect every aspect of my life.

When I tried to slow down the smoking and drinking, I got out of control with my bulimia. It ended up in a vicious cycle. It got so bad I thought I would be found dead hugging the toilet, my heart given out.

I know this all sounds horrible, and it was, but I bring up the past because I want people who are as desperate as I was to *have hope*. I have learned no matter what background you come from or what you have been through, there is hope for change. I had to do two things: keep talking about it and find someone or something to change my perception of myself and my life. When I started doing the best I could in my recovery, my life did change. It was slow going, but life did get better!

My recovery began when I realized I was about ready to start beating my daughter. My anger and rage got so bad! Up to that point, I had always buried my feelings, my life, and who I was. And now I was exploding, turning into the monster I had feared in my mom. I didn't realize how miserable I was. My grand idea was to send my daughter away, and probably die with the direction I was going. That made no sense because I loved her more than life—but I was so confused! I called a local treatment center and went in for a consultation.

I could not be admitted because I had no insurance and no one to watch my daughter. However, they did get me into a group meeting of other people with eating disorders, which is where I met Annette. The group itself was not very productive, but Annette and I got to talking, and she invited me to my first AA meeting. I was high when I went; it was the best I could do at the time. I have to say, my connection with Annette was not an accident, and I will forever be grateful for her.

I continued with AA and found recovery from my alcoholism, but it wasn't helping me with my eating disorder. I kept struggling! Although I started to recognize the different addictions to be all one disease, I could not seem to make the AA program work for my bulimia. I knew that other groups for people with addictions were sprouting off of the AA "Big Book," so I decided to go ahead and start a group for my eating disorder.

I went to the Board at the AA fellowship hall where I went to my AA meetings, and I picked a name, a room, a time, and a format. I put up signage and started announcing EDA—Eating Disorders Anonymous—at AA meetings. I was scared, but I figured, *I can't be the only one struggling with this problem.* I needed to try *something,* because I felt like I was dying from my disease. Turns out, I wasn't alone. People did start coming in, though slowly at first. We used a format adapted from my AA meetings with some changes in wording. The group started getting regular attendees. Annette was very supportive, and together we started discussing where it might go from there.

Our support for each other— not being alone in our disease—made a big difference. Annette has a business background and she really took off on the organizational end, getting our own Board set up and recruiting members to start more EDA groups. Even as we were figuring out how to get recovery we were assembling EDA from nuts and bolts. I was a little scared the organizational side of things was growing too fast while we were still struggling with building and maintaining recovery, although I look back now and can say it happened just like it was supposed to. At the time, however, I was scared EDA was running away from what I wanted it to be. I was still unhealthy in my disease and I couldn't speak up or say what I wanted because, frankly, I still didn't know what that was. Nor did I know what would work for recovery, but I believe God was with us through the entire process.

Our program actually started growing. I was excited; we had pamphlets, formats, and new meetings sprouting up. It was slow, but I did start getting recovery from my bulimia. The first time I remember bingeing and throwing up was in Alaska, so I had been bulimic for about fifteen years. I never thought in a million years I would be able to stop! It was hard, because with my alcoholism, I could abstain from alcohol, but when it came to food, I still had to eat! I stayed with EDA for a long time, but because of resentments and warped thinking, I walked away for a while. I focused on my daughter, Alcoholics Anonymous, and tried more therapy. Before I knew it, I had not practiced my bulimia for about ten years. But I was still having trouble with feelings and emotions and not knowing who I was or what I wanted to be when I grew up!

When my daughter graduated high school and joined the Air Force, I had to take a good, hard look at myself. She had been my rock and the reason I was in any kind of recovery at all. But I know now that whatever the reason was for *starting* in recovery, I *stayed* because life was better with it than what I knew I would fall back into without it. Without recovery I had no value or purpose but now I thought, *Wow. I might actually have a chance; life might be ok.* There is such timing in what happened in my life; I can see how God has used everything to get me where I am today!

I didn't understand it at the time, but my mom's death a few years ago is an example of how God keeps showing me what I need to learn. I had a choice: I could continue living in the past, *or I could do something different.*

Through the years I kept trying to have a relationship with my mom. I just wanted explanations for why she treated me like she did. I felt hated, and I wanted her to apologize. My expectations were *nuts* given who she was and how she saw things, but I could not see this yet. So when she died, I was left with a big pile of resentments and no answers. When I went back for the funeral, I got in a big fight with my dad and left with even more resentments than I came with. I was handling things the best I could, but got caught off guard and went into a tailspin. My eating disorder returned, only this time I was using anorexia to deal with my emotions. It was a gradual process, and by the time I realized what was happening, I was extremely underweight and stuck in anorexic thinking and habits.

Then someone from EDA came back into my life, which, again, I am sure was God-inspired. We were able to be honest with each other about where we were in our lives and with our eating disorders. By talking to her and getting honest with myself, I could see the truth, and it was not good. I certainly was not dealing with emotions and feelings well at all! Despite my shame and anger, I did eventually accept help. I had some wonderful friends who wanted me to get better and who were very supportive. I got out my toolbox from what I had learned, but I needed more. So I went back to EDA meetings and also to an eating disorder therapist, who put me in touch with a nutritionist. It was difficult to go to meetings because I had not been involved for so long. But I was more scared of my disease than ever because of how it snuck up on me.

Even though it was a difficult process, I am glad now that I went through my disease a second time. There were things I was missing in my recovery that I discovered by experiencing that joy all over again. I was still a victim, wanting someone or something else to blame. I kept hearing the voice of a southern woman in AA who would say, "Nothing happens in God's world by mistake." She was right! When I look back, I see God working all the way through my life, in good times and bad. As a result of getting honest and working through the thinking habits that led me back to my eating disorder, I gained a stronger recovery—and so much more!

It was no longer good enough to be a *survivor*; I wanted *freedom!* I got into service and took a group of ladies through a "Big Book" study. I got so much more out of it that way: I gained recovery from my eating disorder and a new friend who is now my life partner. I also started seeing another therapist who was perfect for me. I was finally ready—desperate enough to want to get out of my denial. This was the hardest time in my recovery, because I was looking at the real me. Between my therapist and my friend, I was able to process differently, and could see exactly who I was. In my desperation I would ask, "Why ME?" My friend answered me quite simply, "Why not!" This made something inside click, and I suddenly had a choice.

When I was seven and we moved from Colorado to Washington, my parents decided to find a church. This is where man's interpretation of God put some warped ideas and legalistic views in my life. When I was in my teens, I had a crush on a friend who was a girl, but I denied it because our church condemned homosexuality. I tried to be "normal" and have boyfriends, but those relationships never worked out. In my late twenties, I tried a few lesbian relationships, but I was still so unhealthy that those didn't work out either. One of my partners was committed to working for LGBT rights, but that wasn't the fight I wanted at the time. I just wanted to be myself and be in a relationship. I continued to question. I would wonder if I felt the way I did because of the rapes and molestation, or because of who I was. In therapy, I finally worked it out when my therapist said, "Why does it matter? Just be who you are. It doesn't matter if the chicken or the egg comes first." When I finally did come out, people weren't surprised. My daughter just said, "Well, that makes sense!" and ended up being really supportive. She just wanted me to be happy and find someone to love.

Accepting my sexuality, which had been a struggle since my teenage years, has been a huge freedom and load off my back. Because of how the church made God out to be a hateful, condemning, vengeful God, and my own worries about what people were going to think—there was an enormous barrier between me and God. Now that I have accepted myself for who I am, my relationship with God has changed completely; my perception of Him has totally changed. I used to picture Him as this judgmental, black-and-white presence that commanded what I should be and do. I am so grateful I've been able to let God out of the box!

I started exploring different ideas about God and forms of spirituality, and now I believe that God—the same God I knew as a child—isn't just one Being, defined by one group of humans. Some of my readings have helped me come to an understanding that God is a term for a special kind of energy. Native American cultures also have this unifying idea: that natural things—the sky and rocks and trees—have value in a spiritual sense. My relationship with God is still evolving, and I want it to evolve. Just like my recovery, I want my relationship with God to grow.

I also believe that everyone is on their own journey and that we explore and grow in our own perfect time. I wish people could see God, or spirit, or whatever with open eyes. I think we are all spiritual beings living a human existence. I believe religion is manmade, and that God didn't intend for us to get bogged down, but to seek Him spiritually. Having happiness and freedom and sharing this with each other is a great place to be. But when we get stuck on details about what we should be and do, we are going to have trouble. Recovery can't be built on top of a rigid, fear-based foundation: we have to break free from it!

When we started EDA, we discovered it was going to be about finding balance and perspective, not abstinence, in the midst of life. That takes time and patience; it is not going to come together all at once. During my day, I would start having little moments where I thought, *It might be ok!* You may have some "Aha!" moments and probably see some thinking patterns begin to shift long before you see your eating-disordered behavior change in a major way. This is ok, because it's part of the foundation on which recovery is built. You may not even recognize that you are in recovery until you begin to notice you are responding differently to the things that used to set you on edge. For me, I'd be working on some major issue, then realize all of a sudden that lots of little issues had worked themselves out just fine. Don't waste energy on things that aren't that important, like quibbling with yourself about what you ate for breakfast or worrying about what others think of you. If you get stuck on the little things, you might not work on the big things. That's exactly where your disease wants you: it knows what each of your little things are, and it is going to use those to prevent your recovery. Don't let it fool you: you've got a choice!

The big things that need and deserve attention include: finding the positive, focusing on gratitude, and having respect for what actually may be going right with us, the people in our lives and—let's go even bigger—*the world* (because it does not revolve around me!). That is something I had to learn along the way. If I focus my attention on the negative, that is what I am going to get. If I focus my attention on the positive, I can find the power to do things that matter. Gratitude is an action word: I have to act on it! If I am focusing on the positive, I am going to get more gratitude, more power, and more joy.

When I started respecting myself more, I started wanting better for myself. I got a decent job. I have good, healthy relationships in my life, including a partner who loves and respects me—amazing! My daughter and I have a good relationship and I get to decide what type of relationship to have with the rest of the family. I don't have to have a relationship with everyone: I can pick and choose. We can't be all things to all people.

It takes time to decipher what we really need to fully recover. What works for others may or may not work for you. Be patient! Keep things simple and keep moving. Respect yourself and your efforts to find recovery. Keep taking small risks, building trust with yourself, and focusing on the bigger picture: you will walk free if you work at it.

Some ideas that help me find balance and perspective, and maintain my recovery:

- **Do first things first.** Take care of basics and prioritize by what matters in the long run.

- **Do one thing at a time.** A day at a time is too much for us, especially in early recovery!

- **Be true to yourself, be honest, and be kind.** Integrity builds recovery.

- **Be at peace.** Recovery is not a box that you fit your life into: it is open and free. That doesn't mean everything is grand in your life, it means you can live in peace *no matter what*. Get past the idea that things are happening to you or because of you—they are just happening!

- **Forget about counting days and years of recovery.** Recovery is not about days, or months, or years. You can have years of "recovery" and still be rigid and stuck. Recovery is an inside job: you know you are there when you are at peace with food and in balance in other areas of your life.

- **Do what is in front of you. Keep it simple!** Remember we have to take care of basics before we can do much else: if hungry, eat; if angry, find a safe outlet; if lonely, reach out; if tired, sleep; if ashamed, talk about it.

- **Lighten up—don't take life so seriously!** In our eating disorders, we spent so much time afraid and alone—lost in ourselves—that we lost the joy in life. Recovery means finding humor. Laughing at myself reduces shame and puts things back in perspective. It's not all about me, which is easier to see when I laugh and find joy. Everybody has insecurities. We get so busy looking at ourselves and our deficiencies we forget how good it feels to share our experience of life.

- **Do the work.** In the "doing" comes the understanding and the recovery: we have to do the work. We take the Steps to change the way we think. When we change the way we think, we get options to change what we do. When we take the right actions, we start getting the right results. Not feeling "up to it" today? Ask yourself what you would do if you felt better—and then do it.

- **Focus on the positive, and seek balance in everything.** Balance to me means asking, *Where am I focusing my energy?* Then, I work on putting my energy where it matters. For instance, at work recently, I was using up way too much energy on the negative by arguing with people. It was draining! I had to remember that whatever I give out is what I get back. So I changed my attitude and perspective, which changed the dynamic completely—and I got my peace back.

- **Keep taking stock of where you are and respond accordingly.** I sometimes forget to take care of the simple things. I have to recognize that when my food and sleep get sideways, I have to change what I am thinking and doing to make sure I take care of myself so I can focus on the positive: going to church, going to meetings, talking with my partner and support people, and just doing what's in front of me.

- **Stay accountable for your thoughts and actions.** Once I got to a point where I did not want my disease to keep me stuck any longer, I started keeping myself accountable for my eating-disordered thoughts and behaviors to my partner and support people. Annette and I used to call this "telling on ourselves," which can sound like self-shaming, but we laughed a lot. It is amazing how silly our responses to life can be. I mean, there is humor in admitting that, *Somebody didn't respond like I thought they should when I said something completely stupid, so now I want to shove food in my face. That will totally make it all better!* Come on, people: lighten up! We are only as sick as our secrets!

- **Find gratitude for what you have.** Gratitude is what makes it possible for me to do the things I need to do with love and compassion. I used to pray for the willingness to be willing. Now that comes easily because I experience the Promises; I experience joy every day. It's the simple things.

- **Get into service: it is an important aspect of balance!** When I am too absorbed with myself now, I can usually catch myself and laugh. Sometimes it is easy to forget that there is a whole other existence out there! When it's all about me, life can get awfully miserable. When it's all about what I can do to help others, it's amazing. When I found recovery, I also found empathy. My eyes opened up. Now I can see where people are hurting, and usually there is something right in front of me that I can do to help.

Service doesn't have to mean doing big things; it means being open to see the confusion and pain of others and being willing to take the time to help them. Being open to service may leave you vulnerable, but when I close myself off from others, I miss out on some of the most magical moments. When I put myself on the line, willing to be of service, I get the strength and power to be genuinely helpful. I can help a little old lady find the husband she lost in the airport. I can talk to the person in the wheelchair who is sitting all alone. It is so much better to have heart! Being of service brings me joy. The more I do even little things to be of service, the more gratitude I have.

For me, seeking balance means reaching out to regain perspective when I am all caught up in negativity. Connecting with people is hard when I'm in physical or emotional pain, but when I speak out loud about my problems with my partner, I can more easily break my issues down into what they usually are: expectations and old thinking. *Then* I can see where I can be helpful.

My life today is by no means a perfect picture, but it does not have to be. The difference is, now I have choices! I have a few physical problems and I sometimes have issues with people where I work. Recently, my adult daughter came home to stay with us for a while, and at first I got caught up in fear. *How were we all going to interact? How would things go with my partner and me? Was my daughter going to live with us the rest of her life? Holy hell!* In the end, I looked at it from her perspective in order to see how to be useful to her—instead of making it about me. Breaking it down, I was able to find gratitude that I could just do the necessary next steps to get things going: setting up a room, finding connections, helping line things up for her.

I have to remember that I can't do it alone. We don't know how to do things until we learn how to do them. It is almost laughable that we have so much shame about things we've never done before. I used to think: *Here I am, thirty years old, I should know how do this!* But if we've never done something before, no matter what age we are, there is no reason why we should expect ourselves to know how to do it. It takes an adult perspective to have humility and admit when we need help.

It is important to remember we are examples to others in our lives. When I accepted shame from my church and mom, and hung onto it, I ended up passing it down to my daughter even though that was the absolute last thing I ever wanted. I kept thinking, *Things are the way they are because of my horrible failures*, instead of thinking—and showing my daughter how to think—about the positives. Now that I am more focused on the positives, I hope that example will carry over!

All I can do right now is what is right here in front of me. I am grateful for the peace and freedom that comes from focusing on doing the next right thing, one thing at a time. I am still powerless over situations in my life today, and if I don't use the tools my life will again become unmanageable. But when I use the tools—the Steps—I can be at peace. I have worth today, and my life has meaning, because it isn't all about me anymore.

If you are just starting on your journey in recovery, work with a sponsor on the first three Steps, the basics of which are, "I can't, He can, and I think I'll let Him." *We have to keep it simple and keep moving.* Finding a Higher Power or purpose will help you jump into the rest of the Steps, which will bring the Promises into your life. Don't worry about doing things the right or wrong way; just do the next right thing and trust that more will be revealed as you move forward. Don't wait for the "perfect" time. There is none! But you can *make* the perfect time: that time is *right now*.

Chapter 2

THERE IS A SOLUTION

*W*e, the members of Eating Disorders Anonymous (EDA), have found a solution to the problem of our eating disorders. We who were once very alone, miserable, and hopeless are now happy, joyous, and free. We are eager to share with you what worked for us.

Though we are "normal" folks in most respects, we are not united by the things that commonly bind people together. We share no common political or religious position and we come from all walks of life. Every ethnicity, gender, and sexual orientation can be found among us. We are young and old, muscular and frail, affluent and far from it. And our eating disorders were as varied as we are. Some of us binged until very severely obese; some of us starved until very severely underweight; others appeared normal while engaged in very abnormal eating practices. Some of us experienced only one type of eating disorder, while others adopted various patterns over time. What joins us together is not our illness—our eating disorders drove us away from the people who loved us the most! The bond we share is a *common problem* (a seeming inability to regain health and sanity on the basis of self-knowledge and desire alone) coupled with a *common solution* (the Twelve Steps of EDA).

Finding Hope

In order to find hope of recovery, we first had to admit we had a problem. Then we had to take action to put ourselves on a different footing with life and a different understanding of our place in it. Admitting we had a problem was hardly sufficient by itself, but it was a good first step.

Most of us had no real issue admitting we had a problem to ourselves. Yet it was difficult, we found, to fully open up to a friend or someone in the medical profession. Typically, we minimized the severity of our situation. We wanted a solution without fully divulging the truth of our daily lives, lest we be labeled crazy. We did not want to acknowledge just how damaging our obsessions had become. In any case, our reluctance to deal honestly with reality usually led to more years of suffering despite the best efforts of those who wanted to help us. Unable to trust ourselves to get out of the situations we had created, we could not seem to trust others, either. This was a huge block to progress.

Having an eating disorder is not like most other chronic conditions that people can objectively understand. To outsiders, we imagine it must look as if we are dispassionately choosing to be ill and stay ill. Not surprisingly, we cannot easily discuss our condition with others, even helpful professionals. We ourselves find it hard to comprehend how we became so ill, let alone how we could possibly have stayed ill for so long. We discover that it's easier to talk with people in recovery, who understand first-hand what we have been through. We can be open and free with each other with very little effort. No one can inspire trust, confidence, and hope in an eating-disordered person like someone who has "been there."

We do not profess to have the only solution, nor do we think our solution is necessarily better than any other. There are many paths to recovery. Our main hope is that you find one that works for you. We certainly never discourage anyone from taking any action that feels like the right road. But we are here, should other means fail.

We are equals, regardless of the manifestation of our eating disorders or our current circumstances. Those in recovery do not have a "superior" attitude with respect to those who have not yet found relief or taken action. You will find neither pity nor shame in our rooms. Some of us have advanced degrees and some of us work with eating-disordered clients. But in EDA, we are all peers.

The good news is that no matter how sordid and miserable your story, how mild or severe your symptoms, we have been there. We are confident you can recover, because we were able to recover ourselves. Were you molested? Were you ridiculed and berated? Many of us were, too. We felt as you felt. Perhaps you can find no clear and obvious reason why you developed an eating disorder, or the reasons seem trifling compared to the severity of your illness. Many of us fit that description, too. Did you create needless pain and misery in your life and in the lives of those who cared about you? We certainly did. Yet despite the damage we caused, we found that even the most awful truths about ourselves, and our lives, could be turned to good purpose.

Perhaps you want to quit doing things you know are problematic, but think your case is not as hopeless as some of ours. We hope you are right. If you are not sure whether your condition is serious enough to merit a dive into the Twelve Steps of EDA, we urge you to read the next chapter, "More About Eating Disorders."

Our main purpose in this book—as in our groups—is to share our experience, strength, and hope with others who struggle with eating disorders, so that they might hear the message of recovery and find it for themselves. We will be bringing up controversial topics, including mental illness, religion, spirituality, atheism, psychological and psychiatric treatment, and sex. We want to be clear that we are addressing these topics not because we wish to stir things up, but because they are important to recovery. In this chapter, we discuss how many of us got so ill and introduce material that explains how we got better.

Assessing Severity

All forms of eating disorders are dangerous. Electrolyte imbalances caused by over-exercise and other forms of purging can lead to heart failure. Health effects associated with binge eating include obesity, sleep apnea, and diabetes. Anorexia is associated with the highest mortality rate of any mental illness.[1] Regardless of type, eating disorders exist along a spectrum of severity, which, for brevity's sake, we will divide into three categories:

Inconsistent (irregular or intermittent): People with inconsistent symptoms of an eating disorder may occassionally become obsessed with weight or body image, and sometimes engage in one or more behaviors that are hallmarks of a classic eating disorder: restriction of intake, bingeing, use of laxatives, enemas, exercise, or other forms of purging. Such people may or may not develop a full-blown eating disorder or be aware that their behavior is dangerous. People with occasional symptoms are usually able to maintain something that looks like a normal life and may be relatively unconcerned about changing.

[1] Arcelus, J., Mitchell, A.J., Wales, J., Nielsen, S. (2011) Mortality rates in patients with anorexia nervosa and other eating disorders. A meta-analysis of 36 studies. *Archives of General Psychiatry.* 68(7), 724-31.

Consistent (regular and persistent): People who routinely engage in eating-disordered thoughts and behaviors may be very ill, but many respond favorably to one or more modalities of treatment such as nutritional counseling, individual therapy, intensive outpatient therapy, or inpatient treatment.

Resistant (obsessive and intractable): People who become obsessed in their engagement with eating-disordered thoughts and behaviors often report feeling hopeless about their condition; many get to a point where a normal life seems impossible. Most have tried one or more forms of treatment, yet despite progress toward recovery, patterns of negative thinking (thoughts that lead to anger, resentment, fear, self-pity, shame, guilt, confusion, frustration, and despair) seem impossible to escape. When such thoughts occur, people with more severe eating disorders revert to restricting, bingeing, and/or purging no matter how dire the consequences. People thus situated have lost faith in the idea that they can walk away from their eating disorders; they have fundamentally lost trust in themselves.

Somewhat ironically, the person whose eating disorder meets the more severe description may be best situated to benefit from the means we have laid out in this text. If they are able to find hope and develop even a modicum of trust, such individuals are often willing to go to any lengths to build a solid recovery. However, our goal in this text is to try and help *everyone* develop the willingness to change— especially those who have not yet reached the point of desperation—so that they, too, might be free.

It is important to mention here that over time all of us in EDA, including those who are the most ill, discover that the source of our eating-disordered behavior is not our body, but rather our *thoughts and the mental and emotional states they produce*. Certainly, severe malnourishment and electrolyte imbalances can render us physically incapable of rational thought and action; such issues require immediate attention. Yet we need to be very clear about this point: In our experience the issue is never a physical allergy or addiction to any food. People can certainly treat food like an addiction, but food is not addictive in and of itself. If you believe that a diet or disciplined program of eating will cure you, you will find no support for this idea in EDA meetings or literature. Once we are nutritionally stable, food is completely beside the point—even if it does not feel that way at first.

Hitting (or rolling around on) the Bottom

After months or years of living with eating disorders, we who are writing this text arrived at a point where we urgently wanted to stop. We wanted to be rid of our destructive behaviors and obsessions once and for all! Many of us had physical consequences and extreme emotional disturbances, and some contemplated suicide. At times, we felt there was no hope; we were condemned to patterns of thought and behavior we desperately wanted to stop. We were sick of the endless thoughts about food, weight, and our bodies. We struggled with a sense of not belonging and never feeling "all right." No matter how much we acted out, obsessed, or tried to control our fixation on food, it was never enough. *We* were never enough.

Rarely were we able to achieve any kind of serenity or peace when active in our eating disorders. Some of us were told that we would never recover unless we changed, yet we persisted in trying. We promised ourselves that if we just weighed a certain amount, looked a certain way, experienced horrible consequences, or if our disorders ever affected our relationships or our jobs, we *would* change. Long after ample evidence to the contrary, we continued to think that if we could muster enough willpower, self-restraint, and discipline, we could and would bring our eating disorders "under control" at last. But no matter how great our willpower seemed to be in other aspects of our lives, or how dire the consequences of our behavior, our eating disorders were unstoppable.

Most of us had the idea that if we could "manage" our weight, food, and bodies well enough we could still act out in some form or another—at least from time to time. Early on, most of us were able to stop, control, or moderate our obsessions temporarily when we really made an effort. But as time passed, this became increasingly difficult. The more we allowed the eating disorder to be part of our everyday lives, the more entrenched our negative thinking and behavior became. Eventually, we came to the realization that our disorders were more powerful than we were. Even those of us who had near-death experiences found the *desire to stop was not enough to fundamentally change our thinking or behavior.*

Many of us suffered a litany of health problems, ranging from weakness and dizziness to electrolyte imbalances, suicidal thoughts, seizures, ruptured organs, and hospitalization. Of course, we had issues before the negative thoughts and behaviors became habituated; most of us had been anxious or depressed long before developing our illnesses. But in our experience, pre-existing conditions only worsened over time as a result of engaging in eating-disordered patterns.

Even just a few consequences should have been enough to scare us into recovery, but they weren't. When we attempted to moderate or control our behaviors, our eating disorders came back—often with a vengeance. When we attempted to assert control over our lives, we found ourselves "giving in" just to get relief from our obsessive thinking. Consequences, self-disgust, and humiliation were never enough to stop us in our tracks. When the option to think or behave differently presented itself, we sometimes thought about changing, but most of the time we were too frightened to change. We felt anguish and despair, not trusting that small changes could result in the big shifts we knew we needed to make. Sometimes we were so numb that we did not recognize opportunities to change. We reacted to most situations as if on auto-pilot, without any premeditation at all. Ultimately, whatever manifestation of eating disorder we had, we just did it: nothing seemed able to get in our way.

In desperation, we sometimes placed ourselves under the care of medical professionals and even loved ones in hopes that outside support could help us. We tried to follow suggestions and plans of action exactly as directed, but most made little progress. From the outside looking in, others could not understand us; from the inside looking out, we could not explain ourselves. Sometimes normal eating and health was restored with the assistance of a medical facility, but even when freed of the physical consequences of our behavior, the thoughts persisted and we ended up back where we started. It began to dawn on us that our eating disorder issues must be rooted in our minds after all. Medications often helped, but despite our hopes and those of our medical teams, nothing seemed to work reliably in the long run. Sometimes our symptoms grew even worse after we sought outside support.

Although a few of us remained convinced that we just needed to "hit bottom" to find the motivation to recover, many of us began to realize we had been rolling around on "the bottom" for years on end: we were simply unable to find the footing needed to come up for air. It dawned on some of us that an eating disorder could be a progressive illness, in the same way that alcoholism is described in the book *Alcoholics Anonymous*. That is, the more we practiced our behaviors, the more we seemed to need them.

Some of us came to believe that if outside support and prescribed medications could not remove our negative thoughts—or stop those thoughts from forming—then maybe being active members of a religious organization would work. We immersed ourselves in attending services, praying, participating in support groups, volunteering in outreach programs, hoping that if we got closer to God through these commitments, we would recover. We did not. Our obsessive thoughts continued to wash over us, tugging on us as we struggled to reach the bright shore of recovery. No matter how much service we performed, lasting relief seemed beyond our reach. Many of us got to a point where we thought the only way we could ever gain complete physical freedom was if we gave ours up—and were hospitalized.

Many EDA members attempted to recover through abstinence-based Twelve-Step programs. However, following a disciplined plan of eating, perhaps refraining from certain foods or food groups as is often suggested, generally afforded us little, if any, reprieve. Much to our horror, many of us experienced an explosion of eating-disordered thinking and behavior in response to such programs. Rigidity around food seemed to fuel our obsessions, which led to an even more powerful illness. In many Twelve-Step programs, we did find comfort knowing that we were not alone, and that the crazy ideas we had about ourselves, food, weight, exercise, and our bodies were quite common. Unfortunately, knowledge that we had company, and the understanding and insight that comes from empathy, did not—in and of themselves—provide for significant or lasting change.

Confronted with mounting evidence from our individual experiences, most of us concluded that there was simply no way out of our misery. We felt condemned to live with our eating disorders forever. We could see that our illnesses ruled our thoughts and actions. In essence, they controlled our lives. That was a bleak realization.

A Way Out

Fortunately, we found recovery from this seemingly hopeless state of mind and body. How is this possible when many of us had been declared incurable—and believed it? Lucky for us, we have a way out—*there is a solution.*[2] While we were out looking for the "one thing" that would make it possible for us to stop acting out by removing the constant thoughts about food, our weight, and our bodies, that one thing—the key to our freedom—turned out to be the *spiritual awakening or transcendent transformation we achieve as a result of working the Twelve-Step program of Eating Disorders Anonymous.* Not all EDA members consider their "transcendent transformation" to be religious or spiritual in nature. Anyone uncomfortable with the idea of a spiritual awakening is welcome to substitute "transformation" wherever the phrase occurs.

---

[2] *Alcoholics Anonymous.* (2001) New York, NY: AA World Services, Inc., 25.

How do we go about this awakening or transformation? Some early members of EDA did it by working straight from the original text, *Alcoholics Anonymous,* substituting the words "acting out" for "drinking" and "eating disordered" for "alcoholics."[3] We found this approach effective even for those suffering from the most severely disordered thinking and behavior patterns. The changes we experienced sometimes came quickly, sometimes slowly; sometimes we were aware of them, and sometimes not. There came a point, however, when we began to notice that we had a new outlook on life and new reactions to life events.

We found that an essential part of this transformation was a shift from self-centeredness to constant thoughts of others and how we might help them. We began to see how the truth of our experiences before and after recovery could serve to benefit others. We were floored to realize that the simple process of working the Twelve Steps of Eating Disorders Anonymous resulted in gradual improvements in our lives, until we no longer had to deal with eating-disordered thinking or behavior except when supporting newcomers—work that continues to remind us just how fortunate we are.

Day by day, as they work the Steps, newcomers in EDA find their eating disorders weakening: the stranglehold gradually loosens. Our recovery grows with our increasing reliance on ideas that hold more power to provide peace and perspective than our eating disorders ever did. As

---

[3] While this volume is not intended to be used merely as a supplement to *Alcoholics Anonymous,* we highly recommend that the reader become familiar with that original text. The chapters in this book are organized in concordance with the chapters in the AA text, so the reader may readily refer back to the original material.

we learn to trust these ideas, our consciousness or awareness of a Higher Power or higher purpose deepens and expands. Our deliberate and thoughtful efforts to align our actions accordingly begin to engage us more and more. It does not matter whether our Higher Power or purpose—*God or a greater context of our own understanding*—agrees with anyone else's conception. What matters is that we, individually, come to a point of acceptance that there *is* a Power or purpose greater than we are, and that we can trust it to help us overcome our eating disorders.

Many are happy to find their idea of a Higher Power aligns well with that of an organized religion; others are content with a conception that does not fit into any specific creed. Some find that making a commitment to serve a higher purpose—outside of and greater than themselves—works well. While the specifics matter a great deal to us individually, collectively we can see that our differing ideas all work to bring peace and freedom from our eating disorders. As we surrender our thoughts and actions to better serve either God or a higher purpose of our understanding, remarkable things begin to occur: our thinking becomes less disordered, our acting out becomes less frequent, and we begin to see our emotional lives develop a breadth and depth we had never before imagined. We are restored to sanity as a result of working the Steps. While many of us describe our transformation as a miracle, we can all be glad that recovery is a rational and perfectly logical outcome of deliberate thought and action. Recovery, and joy in what we are able to do once we are free of the bondage of our eating disorders, brings tremendous satisfaction and deep gratitude.

We invite you to embark on the journey of recovery with us, and see for yourself: *there is a solution that will work for you.*

How to Use this Book

In Chapter 3, "More About Eating Disorders," we explore in greater detail what it means to have an eating disorder, and we explain why *programs and practices addressing our mental and spiritual states make more sense than diets and disciplined programs of eating*. Through a few examples, we examine the strangely ineffective mental state that precedes a return to eating-disordered behaviors. We discuss how, *even after we have made a solid start on our journeys into recovery*, we can remain vulnerable to "triggers" and prone to "going on auto-pilot" when circumstances invoke old patterns of thought and habit. We show how our simple program of action—what AA describes as a "design for living that really works"[4]—goes beyond addressing these "strange mental blank spots,"[5] enabling us to move past the concept of simple "recovery" or "restoration" to something greater than we could have imagined: a happy and purposeful life in which we are connected to others and to the universe in ways that feel complete and fulfilling.

In Chapter 4, "We Agnostics, Atheists, and Believers," we bring up the challenge that having a "spiritual solution to a spiritual malady" poses for those who are atheist or agnostic. Although we take a different approach than the chapter "We Agnostics" in AA's "Big Book," we show why objections to the concepts of a "Higher Power" and a "spiritual awakening" need not pose a barrier to recovery. The good news is that a fundamental transformation, on the order of what Dr. Carl Jung described as the "vital spiritual experience" necessary for the hopeless to recover,[6] is acces-

---

[4] *Alcoholics Anonymous.* (2001) New York, NY: AA World Services, Inc., 28.
[5] Ibid., 42.
[6] Ibid., 27.

sible to everyone through working the same Twelve Steps. The reality is that atheists can work the Steps successfully with a few accommodations. We think AA's founder, Bill Wilson, would have found these adaptations acceptable. When presented with the idea that Buddhists in Thailand wanted to use a version of the Twelve Steps that substituted "good" for "God," Bill responded, "*To some of us, the idea of substituting 'good' for 'God' in the Twelve Steps will seem like a watering down of AA's message. We must remember that AA's Steps are suggestions only. A belief in them as they stand is not at all a requirement for membership among us. This liberty has made AA available to thousands who never would have tried at all, had we insisted on the Twelve Steps just as written.*"[7]

Chapters 5, 6, and 7—"How It Works," "Into Action," and "Working with Others"—lay out the Twelve-Step program of recovery as it works for us. Those of us with a solid religious practice may find it somewhat easier to take the Steps than those of us who do not, yet we must stress that even those who are totally comfortable with their understanding of God may find the process quite difficult. As the saying goes, our solution is simple but not easy. The AA "Big Book" chapter, "There is a Solution," makes clear that religious conviction by itself does not guarantee recovery.[8] We have to do the work.

Regardless of our approach—religious, spiritual, or secular—we members of EDA take essentially the same program of action and obtain the same results on our path to recovery. Our conceptions of a Higher Power and higher purpose are as varied as we are, yet we do not debate these concepts amongst ourselves. Our task is to carry the mes-

<hr />

[7] *Alcoholics Anonymous Comes of Age. (1957)* New York, NY: AA World Services, Inc., *81.*
[8] *Alcoholics Anonymous.* (2001) New York, NY: AA World Services, Inc., 27.

sage of recovery as it has worked in our own lives, not to direct the lives of others. Each person is responsible for their own thoughts and actions; each person is responsible for their own recovery.

In the latter portion of this book, we present individual stories that describe what we went through and how we recovered. Here you will find evidence of the diversity in our backgrounds; distinctions in the manifestations of our eating disorders; variations in our conceptions of God, a Higher Power, or a higher purpose; and differences in our experiences with recovery in EDA. We hope no one is repelled by the desperate circumstances to which some of us were reduced. We surely hope that those of you reading this have not arrived at a comparable state, but we think that only by being completely transparent will we connect with the truly desperate. We hope our stories will serve to reassure you that you are not alone and convince you that you, too, can recover.

Chapter 3

MORE ABOUT EATING DISORDERS

No one wants to be labeled "eating disordered," but we think everyone ought to know what the label means. For brevity's sake we will not list all the clinical eating disorder criteria in detail, however a limited overview taken from the American Psychiatric Association's *Diagnostic and Statistical Manual of Mental Disorders*, Fifth edition (2013), is provided below.[1]

Anorexia Nervosa: Those of us with anorexia struggled with obsessions over weight and body shape. Weight loss became of primary importance to the exclusion of most everything else. Weight and shape concerns often led to: frequent weight checking, body-checking behaviors such as looking in mirrors, having slight fluctuations in weight result in a dramatic impact on mood, and/or excessive exercise. Characteristics may have included persistent restriction of energy intake leading to significantly low body weight (in context of what is minimally expected), intense fear of weight gain or becoming fat, or persistent behavior that interfered with weight gain (e.g. self-induced vomiting; misuse of laxatives, diuretics, or other medications; fasting; or excessive exercise). We typically experienced disturbances in the way we related to our bodies and shapes, and we persisted in not recognizing the seriousness and risks associated with low body weight. For more informa-

---

[1] For more detailed information, see: "Types and Symptoms of Eating Disorders." National Eating Disorders Association. Retrieved from *https://www. nationaleatingdisorders.org/types-symptoms-eating-disorders*

tion please see "EDA on Anorexia" under the Literature tab at *www.4EDA.org.*

Bulimia Nervosa: For many of us, bulimia started as a weight-control technique that quickly became a stress management tool when we discovered it suppressed unwelcome emotions. Once a pattern of bulimic behavior was established, it was incredibly difficult to stop. Common characteristics included: recurrent episodes of binge eating with a sense of lack of control during the binge episode, and inappropriate compensatory behaviors (e.g. self-induced vomiting; misuse of laxatives, diuretics, or other medications; fasting; or excessive exercise) to prevent weight gain. Symptoms included: self-evaluation that is unduly influenced by body shape and weight; rigid dieting followed by binge eating; hiding/stealing food; frequent over-eating, especially when stressed; disappearing after eating to purge; use of laxatives, vomiting or over-exercising to control weight; swelling of the glands in throat, face, and neck. For more information please see "EDA on Bulimia" under the Literature tab at *www.4EDA.org.*

Binge Eating Disorder (BED): BED is characterized by compulsive overeating, in which we consumed a huge amount of food while feeling out of control and powerless to stop. Those of us who were binge eaters often felt highly distressed about our inability to control food intake; however, we did not usually over-exercise or purge as might a person with bulimia. Warning signs included: eating large amounts of food without purging, a sense of lack of control with respect to eating, eating until uncomfortably or painfully full, feeling guilt or shame about our eating patterns, self-medicating with food, and hiding food. For more information please see "EDA on Binge Eating" under the Literature tab at *www.4EDA.org.*

Other Specified Feeding and Eating Disorders (OSFED): OSFED may be a catch-all category, but don't be fooled: it is just as serious as any other eating disorder and the ambiguity can be misleading. We who did not meet all the clinical criteria for one of the above diagnoses might have suffered just as badly, and deserved as much help, as someone with any other diagnosis.

Examples of OSFED:

- All the criteria for Anorexia Nervosa are met except that our weight remained within or about normal range, despite significant weight loss.

- All criteria for Bulimia Nervosa are met except the episodes of binge eating and inappropriate compensatory behaviors occur less frequently.

- All the criteria for BED are met except the frequency of binges.

- In Purging Disorder, purging behavior aimed to influence weight, shape, or emotional state is present, but binge eating is absent.

- Those of us with Night Eating Syndrome have recurrent episodes of eating at night (i.e. eating after awakening from sleep, or consuming excess calories after the evening meal).

For more information please see "EDA on OSFED" under the Literature tab at *www.4EDA.org.*

Not one among us aspired to any of these designations![2] Most of us started out quite innocently, never imagining the condition we would find ourselves in further down the road. If you told us back when we thought we did not really have a problem just how desperate and hopeless we would become, we would not have believed you; we would have been offended and would have rejected the idea as preposterous. But over time, our eating-disordered thoughts and behaviors gradually progressed from something we engaged in only occasionally to something that we relied on to get through daily life. Some of us, faced with near-death experiences or total responsibility for the lives of others, were able to moderate our behaviors somewhat. Some of us were able to stop, sometimes for extended periods. But when we picked up old patterns, we soon became as ill as ever.

When most people first realize they have a problem with eating, they don't think it is particularly severe. We certainly didn't. If eating-disordered thoughts and behaviors are not yet well-established, you probably think you can recover on your own. We hope you can! We would not wish anyone the misery we endured. But understanding the true nature of an eating disorder before trying to work a program of recovery can be critical, so it may be worthwhile to conduct an experiment to see if you are really one of us. If you find yourself bingeing and want to stop, try some controlled bingeing. See if you can stop abruptly halfway through a normal binge, and stay out of bingeing

---

[2]   There are many other eating disorders not covered above. Compulsive overeating, for instance, is not a diagnosis in the *DSM-5*, yet many of our members were struggling with the thoughts and behaviors associated with this form of disordered eating. Whether your situation is covered by the *DSM-5* or not, you are always welcome to attend an EDA meeting if you have a desire to recover from patterns of thought and behavior that feel like disordered eating to you.

behaviors altogether for the next week or two. Did you find that to be no big deal? If you are anorexic, try eating what and when everyone else is eating for a week or two. Can you do it? If you purge, try to limit your purging to just once over the next week or two. In all honesty, without resorting to any excuses, were you able to do it? If you are like us, you will not be able to manage eating normally, at least not without suffering serious emotional repercussions (such as anger, resentment, and self-pity) over any extended period of time.

If you see yourself in the above descriptions, you have probably already tried one or more of the following to address your eating issues: eating three wholesome and nutritious meals a day, eating five small meals a day, eating only in the company of other people, eliminating specific foods or food components labeled "problematic," eating only vegan food, eating according to a specific food plan, working with abstinence-based Twelve Step groups, seeking guidance from religious leaders and spiritual mentors, seeking resolution with the support of medical professionals and medication, surrendering to an intensive outpatient therapy program, and/or committing yourself to an inpatient treatment program.

Some people with eating disorders find lasting relief through one or more of these approaches, and many regain physical well-being under medical supervision. Let us affirm: *we strongly encourage everyone to make full use of every resource they can to support their recovery.* Many people do recover from their eating disorders through individual therapy, and almost everyone can benefit from working with a skilled and well-trained team of medical professionals, including a registered dietician. Such people can often shed much-needed light and provide valuable direction.

Yet, many in our fellowship were unable to make full use of available resources, disappointingly finding only temporary relief. Unable to let go of the patterns of thought that led to eating-disordered behaviors, we ultimately resorted to old ways of coping. How can this be? Some of us were privileged to work with some of the very best medical professionals in the field. Others had amazing spiritual guides and mentors. Some were able to work with renowned therapists at highly sought-after treatment centers. But despite our best efforts and the dedicated work of well-trained and caring people, many of us did not *fully* recover. Even though we had made progress, we returned to old patterns that we by then understood were injurious to mind and body. Why does this happen?

We can provide answers, of course, but they are trivial compared to the frank and urgent mortal peril we face when engaged in our eating disorders. We should note here that anorexia has the highest mortality rate of any mental illness, with bulimia and OSFED (formerly ED-NOS) not far behind.[3] Obesity—a not-infrequent side effect of disordered eating—is implicated in approximately 300,000 deaths per year in the United States and may be second only to smoking in preventable causes of death.[4] Sadly, we came to the conclusion that our minds were so warped by entrenched patterns of thought and action that we lost the power of choice: we behaved as if compelled by stark insanity.

[3] Arcelus, J., Mitchell, A.J., Wales, J., Nielsen, S. (2011) Mortality rates in patients with anorexia nervosa and other eating disorders. A meta-analysis of 36 studies. *Archives of General Psychiatry*. 68(7), 724-31.
[4] Flegal, M., Williamson, D.F., Pamuk, E.R., Rosenberg, H.M. (2004) Estimating Deaths Attributable to Obesity in the United States. *American Journal of Public Health*. 94(9), 1486-1489.

Michelle's "Strange Mental Blank Spot"[5]

Let us consider the case of Michelle. Michelle had been severely bulimic in her teens and early twenties, and had undergone inpatient treatment for depression and anxiety. She had a good working knowledge of how to address these issues through cognitive behavioral approaches. She was sober in AA and was working a program of abstinence in another Twelve-Step group where she had an excellent sponsor who was taking her through the Steps. Michelle was making good progress in her recovery and had been free of her eating-disordered behaviors for quite some time. At this point, the family kept only "healthy" food in the house. Home life was stable. Michelle's husband had a good job, money was no issue, and everyone was moderately happy and healthy. Michelle was not anxious or depressed.

Michelle's small children kept her busy, active in the community, and engaged with friends and neighbors. One day, after an enjoyable visit to the zoo with her own and several neighborhood kids, Michelle made dinner as usual. The children were not especially fond of vegetables, though these were a staple at evening meals. Dinner was unremarkable. Once the meal was over, the kids went out to play, her husband excused himself to watch television, and Michelle began to clean up as she had many times before without a problem. The neighbor children had not eaten their share of vegetables, and Michelle thought nothing of helping herself to an extra portion; wasting food that could not easily be reheated did not make sense. It tasted good. She had another serving. Though vaguely aware that this behavior was a red flag, Michelle did not take any of the obvi-

---

[5] *Alcoholics Anonymous.* (2001) New York, NY: AA World Services, Inc., 42.

ous steps to stop, to understand what was happening, or to prevent what happened next. Once the vegetables were gone, she searched the refrigerator for something else that would soothe what now felt like a case of jangled nerves. There was absolutely nothing in either the refrigerator or the pantry that would be of any interest to a normal person thinking of eating "binge food," but it did not matter. Within half an hour, Michelle managed to consume enough perfectly innocuous, "healthy" food to lead her to want to purge.

Even at that point, disaster could have been averted had Michelle called her sponsor, sought relief through the Steps, or been willing to divert her attention long enough to wait out the uncomfortable fullness. But she did none of those things, and so began a weeks-long return to the very behaviors that led Michelle to seek recovery in the first place. Despite having a good understanding of where a few wrong moves could take her, and despite having a good support network that might have changed the outcome had she leveraged it, Michelle had no effective mental defense against the return of her eating-disordered behaviors. Though she well understood that bingeing and purging had formerly put her life in jeopardy, and could well do so again, there had been no premeditation whatsoever before starting the binge, little consideration at several points during the binge, and only a few seconds of indecision before purging. At the time, it made no sense—least of all to Michelle. Nothing was obviously wrong at any physical level. Nutrition and electrolytes were not a factor. The types of food involved would not have been considered "problematic" by anyone, not even Michelle's sponsor at the time. Yet Michelle seemed to have experienced what the AA text calls a "strange mental blank spot"—a seemingly inexplicable return to old patterns after new ones have been established.

It may come as a relief to know that no matter how unpredictable a return to old behaviors may seem at first, there is always some warning, and—while it may seem completely obscure at first—an underlying cause. When we become willing to look at our issues and attitudes (a daily 10th Step practice) and look for ways to leverage our experience, training, time, talent, and energy to serve a higher purpose (a daily 11th Step reflection), our recovery gradually becomes more resilient. We stop reacting automatically to triggering situations and start making deliberate, conscious choices with ever-increasing ease and reliability. Sanity is restored so long as we remain willing to do what is needed for recovery. It takes a while to figure this out!

Though initially baffled by the return to bulimic behavior, Michelle later reflected that more was going on with her than she had originally thought. When asked about what she had been thinking, she eventually told us,

> I was vaguely upset that the neighbor children who joined us at dinner had not eaten their vegetables. That set a bad example for my own children, and I thought I should have talked with them about the importance of eating their veggies. Those kids had dinner with us fairly often and they never ate their veggies, so this was nothing new. I didn't think it was proper to correct other people's children at the dinner table unless they were doing something really terrible, so my response wasn't new either. The neighbor family's circumstances, however, had recently taken a turn for the worse. I started thinking how unprepared I was to take over caring for these children, and I immediately became overwhelmed.

Now, no one had asked me to "take over" the care of three additional children. The children needed support, but I was blowing my part all out of proportion. Even though I had been in Twelve-Step programs a long time, I did not recognize that I was making the situation all about me—my inadequacies and my feelings. Rather than doing the right things that would have put the situation back in perspective, I did all the wrong things. I barely thought about what I was doing at all! Rather than relying on my Higher Power to help me through the immediate situation so I could turn my feelings to some good purpose later, I turned to old habits to relieve my feelings within a few heartbeats of feeling overwhelmed. Because I hadn't been practicing reliance on my Higher Power, I lost my daily reprieve from my eating disorder with no thought about the consequences at all.

You may think Michelle is a ridiculous or extreme example, yet every one of us has experienced something disturbingly similar. We may have reflected more than Michelle did before engaging in old patterns, but there was always something going on with us—in tandem with perfectly rational thoughts—that blinded us to our issues and left us prey to insanely trivial reasons why it would, suddenly, be perfectly fine to sabotage our recoveries. Our good lives, our love of all that is just and right, and our ability to think rationally about our situations did not save us from insane thinking and behavior.

Once re-engaged with our eating disorders, we were filled with remorse, guilt, and all manner of other emotions that served as additional justification for continuing the insanity. We became shockingly immune to concerns regarding the potentially terrible consequences for ourselves, our families, and anyone else who depended upon us for emotional, moral, social, or financial support. On an emotional level, we were unable to be genuinely present for ourselves or anyone else, abandoning our families, friends, co-workers, and communities. Things may have looked normal from the outside, but we knew better.

Despite knowledge of what she could have done instead, Michelle remained vulnerable *precisely because she had not been relying on practices that would have revealed what she was* really *thinking, which would have given her an opportunity to turn the energy of her emotions to some useful purpose.*

Self-Will and Self-Knowledge Are Not Enough: Marla

In the story of the jaywalker in the AA chapter, "More About Alcoholism," the authors pose a hypothetical case in which a fellow has a penchant for jaywalking. For whatever reason, the fellow gets a thrill from "skipping in front of fast-moving vehicles."[6] He does this sporadically and experiences no significant consequences for quite a while. Up to this point, people are inclined to write off his behavior as foolishness. Then the fellow's luck deserts him, and he is hurt, though slightly, a few times. Normal folks would, after a few consequences, stop doing things that result in injury. But not this chap. He is soon hospitalized with a more severe injury. When people go to see him, he is adamant that he has changed his ways and will not return to his old behavior. When he is released from the hospital, he pulls another stunt and is almost immediately in much worse condition than before. He is rushed to the hospital for a long stay, since the time required to recover is far more

---

[6] *Alcoholics Anonymous.* (2001) New York, NY: AA World Services, Inc., 37-38.

extended. This time he means business and is sure he will never dart in front of cars again, yet upon release, he is nearly killed in yet another jaywalking incident. This man would be considered crazy, wouldn't he? The AA text points out that if we substitute alcoholism for jaywalking, the story is a perfect fit for alcoholic behavior. People with eating disorders, too, may recognize the pattern of promises, broken trust, and physical damage. Even if our behavior has not been so extreme, we have usually been just as untrustworthy—and just as crazy—as the hypothetical jaywalker.

Some people who are temporarily engaged in fad diets, obsessed with their weight or body image, or prone to using food for emotional reasons, can stop obsessive and disordered patterns of thought and behavior without too much difficulty—all on their own. We think such people may be the norm rather than the exception. Many others who seek guidance and support can and do learn to recognize and effectively address their issues through hard work in individual therapy, intensive outpatient therapy, or inpatient treatment.

Many of us, however, were not able to recover on the basis of self-knowledge alone; eating disorders can be fiendishly intractable and obstinate. Let us consider another example. A young woman named Marla joined one of our EDA groups while also in an eating disorder treatment center for anorexia. Marla was a delightful person who seemed to catch on to new ideas very quickly. She soon made a full recovery in treatment. Marla returned to college and was immediately caught up in the fun and excitement of a national engineering team competition. Appreciating what we said about the importance of working with others, Marla continued attending our EDA meeting for a month, despite a busy schedule. She sounded great, bringing hope and fresh courage to many who were still in treatment. Then Marla's schedule changed, and the EDA meeting was no longer possible for her. But she assured us that there was no chance she would ever return to an eating disorder; her newfound understanding just wouldn't permit it.

We heard no more from Marla for over a year. Then one day, a nurse wheeled a completely emaciated woman on intravenous support into the EDA meeting room. None of us recognized the exuberant and delightful person we had known in the sunken-eyed, shrunken visage sitting before us in a wheelchair, but it was Marla. Despite youth, good health, a brilliant mind, an engaging personality, a great sense of humor, a host of people who would do anything for her, and full knowledge of herself as an eating-disordered person, Marla had returned to the treatment center utterly defeated. As she later explained it, she had fallen madly in love with a young man who initially seemed to reciprocate her feelings, but who then took up with someone else. Almost involuntarily, while she was trying to sort out her feelings, Marla had started restricting her food intake. Eating made her feel ill. But rather than seek out people she knew would help her, Marla depended instead on the least trustworthy companion she had to help her cope: her eating disorder. Marla later confirmed what we were all thinking: self-will and self-knowledge had provided no defense whatsoever against the return of her symptoms. Like Michelle, Marla succumbed to the undertow of her eating disorder *because she stopped relying on practices that would have helped her regain perspective.* Happily, Marla was able to make a full recovery after her physical condition returned to a near-normal state. She worked the Steps, learned to apply more aspects of the program, and adopted a daily practice that keeps her safe.

We hope our stories bring home to you, the reader, that we of the "hopeless" variety are absolutely unable to stop engaging in eating-disordered behaviors on the basis of need, desire, self-will, and self-knowledge. We can be full of confidence, but when caught off guard, we can be reduced to human wreckage with astonishing rapidity. Despite having fully functioning intellectual capabilities, a reasonably well-developed amount of common sense, and ample motivation to want to remain fully engaged in life, we were prone to being caught off guard.

There Is a Solution

Yet, as you have read in the previous chapter, there is a solution. We have shown how we seem to have no effective mental defense against a return to old patterns—especially that "strange mental blank spot" described in AA's Big Book.[7] The defense must come from reliance on God, a Higher Power, or from daily commitment and surrender to a higher purpose, each of which provides perspective and opportunities to turn even the most troubling emotions into a form of energy we can use to make lives better for others. We repeat: our proposal is simple, but not easy. To be effective, we have to willingly give up our old relationship to life and our place in it. We have to take specific actions that humble us and restore us to sanity every day. We help others to remind ourselves why we need to remain disciplined about our daily practice. Working with others keeps us actively working the Steps and living in recovery. The self-sacrifice required to give freely of our time and energy helps keep us out of selfishness (self-centeredness),

[7] *Alcoholics Anonymous.* (2001) New York, NY: AA World Services, Inc., 42.

and safe from losing sight of what matters. Such work not only provides perspective, it keeps us honest and humble: we quickly learn we cannot be effective if we are not! With a daily practice of surrender and service, we become flexible and strong. Without it, we become brittle and vulnerable. The results of working the program are simply amazing. Rather than merely having "life restored" we found freedom, peace, camaraderie, enjoyment, and adventure beyond our wildest dreams.

The chapter "More About Alcoholism" in the original AA text, cites medical professionals' support for the Twelve-Step approach: Dr. William D. Silkworth, director of a treatment center, wrote, "Though not a religious person, I have profound respect for the spiritual approach in cases such as yours. For most, there is virtually no other solution."[8] In the next four chapters, you will read exactly what we did to recover. Whether you consider yourself religious, spiritual, agnostic, atheist, or someone who does not embrace any such label—you will find others like yourself in our Fellowship. We believe there is a solution that will work for you, too. In the next chapters, we show how we can work the Twelve Steps to find recovery from *every* position on the spectrum of faith.

[8] Ibid., 43.

Chapter 4

WE AGNOSTICS, ATHEISTS,
AND BELIEVERS

*E*arly on in our practice of the Steps, we members of
EDA are required to establish a foundation on which
we can begin to build a durable and resilient recovery, one
that does not leave us vulnerable to triggers or easily blindsided by unexpected "mental blank spots."[1] For many of
us, this means a growing reliance on God. For others, it is
a willingness to consider our own conception of God—a
Higher Power—with which we can feel comfortable. Still
others must find something else—a higher purpose, such
as service to the greater good, that is more important to
us than we are to ourselves. Any of these can provide a
context for the development of objectivity about ourselves
and our place in the world—a perspective that enables us
to respond and act rationally regardless of circumstances.
In order to recover, all of us need to find something greater
than ourselves on which we can consistently rely. The purpose of this chapter is to help you find a way to get started
on this vital and necessary step.

Clearly, we are a diverse group of people with differing views, so it is critical to emphasize that we follow
a *shared process* (working the Twelve Steps) to a *shared
goal* (recovery from our eating disorders). Accepting that
there are many ways to describe the power or purpose as
we have come to know it, we wish to point out differing
paths that some of us have taken. Any one of them can,

[1] *Alcoholics Anonymous.* (2001) New York, NY: AA World Services, Inc., 42.

and will, lead to recovery if you follow the process outlined in this book.

First, we present a statement from our members who
consider themselves to be atheist or agnostic. We recognize
that many of our readers struggle with the spiritual orientation found in Twelve-Step fellowships. We hope to show
that this needn't be the case!

From Agnostics and Atheists in EDA:

In defining the Twelve Steps as we know them today,
the founders of AA adapted and expanded the premises of
the Christian Oxford Group to ensure that as many people as possible would be able to grasp and apply the solution they had found. The authors of AA's "Big Book" stress
again and again that the message of recovery extends not
only to people who can readily grasp and apply spiritual
principles, but to those for whom a spiritual experience
seems utterly impossible: the atheist and agnostic. The
entire fourth chapter of the AA text, "We Agnostics," is
devoted specifically to such individuals. Our main purpose
in writing this statement is much the same: to carry the
message of recovery to those who still struggle, regardless
of what they currently believe, or can believe.

Authors of the AA chapter "We Agnostics" advance a series of arguments for why one ought to have faith. We will
not refute, dispute, or disparage anything you may have
read there. On the contrary, atheists and agnostics in EDA
should have profound respect, appreciation, and gratitude
for the spiritual approach employed by so many people in
recovery, including the authors of the seminal text, *Alcoholics Anonymous*. Without the AA and EDA programs as
written, many of us would never have found recovery at all.

If you have not yet read the AA chapter "We Agnostics," we encourage you to do so.[2]

We want to make clear that we are not here to convince anyone that atheism or agnosticism are goals to which one should aspire. Without a shadow of doubt, having such a position does complicate and strain efforts to work the Twelve Steps. Yet, many who fully understand the reasons why the AA text declares one should have faith remain fundamentally unable to agree with the underlying premises that the universe needs a God to explain it, or that any problem, no matter how big or overwhelming, requires a deity or spiritual force to solve it. We are neither "evil" nor inherently different from others in recovery, yet we cannot find evidence of what the AA text refers to as "the fundamental idea of God" deep within ourselves.[3] Our statement is dedicated to those for whom no arguments for the existence of a spiritual entity make sense. If our many years of recovery in Twelve-Step programs have taught us anything, it is the value of honoring our own truth.

For those who have found a spiritual connection that works for them and are reading this section out of interest in helping others who suffer from an eating disorder (such as sponsees who are struggling with Steps 2, 3, 5, 7, or 11), please understand we atheists and agnostics in EDA and other Twelve-Step programs take no issue whatsoever with anyone's faith or spirituality. We admire and applaud those who are able to work the program without accommodation. We ask your forbearance. We are not attempting to "water down" the power of the spiritual approach; we are pushing the envelope so it can encompass more of those who suffer as we once did.

[2] An online version of the chapter (published by the General Service Office of Alcoholics Anonymous) is available here: http://www.aa.org/assets/en_US/en_bigbook_chapt4.pdf.

[3] *Alcoholics Anonymous.* (2001) New York, NY: AA World Services, Inc., 55.

Our main purpose in writing this is to convey to non-believers a message of recovery that will work for them, exactly as they are. We are convinced that no one need take anything on faith alone: we can recover using an approach that is based solely on logic and common sense.

As described in *Alcoholics Anonymous*, the famous doctor, Carl Jung, explained to Rowland H. that the only antidote to lifelong, chronic alcoholism for someone of his description must entail "a vital spiritual experience."[4] Dr. Jung is quoted as saying, "To me these occurrences are phenomena. They appear to be in the nature of huge emotional displacements and rearrangements. Ideas, emotions, and attitudes which were once the guiding forces… are suddenly cast to one side, and a completely new set of conceptions and motives begin to dominate them."[5] The Twelve Steps are designed to produce exactly the type of "vital spiritual experience" described by Dr. Jung.

Step Twelve begins, "Having had a spiritual awakening as the result of these steps…," clarifying that the founders of AA laid out the Steps to produce exactly the kind of "huge emotional displacement and rearrangement" that Dr. Jung understood to be necessary for the hopeless alcoholic to recover. The good news for atheists and agnostics is that while the Twelve Steps are defined as a path of "spiritual progress," they serve equally well as steps to growth of perspective and to recovery—regardless of one's position on God or spirituality. Thankfully for people like us, the principles of love, tolerance, gratitude, humility, and service are not exclusively religious or spiritual. The attitudinal and behavioral changes that are the hallmark of recovery need not depend on faith and prayer, but rather on changes from irrational to rational thinking, and especially on daily action based on self-reflection and service to others.

[4] Ibid., 27.
[5] Ibid.

To help those who trip over the word "God" in Twelve-Step literature, we are pleased to share our experience, strength, and hope. As we have noted throughout EDA literature, it does not matter whether you use the word "God" to mean the Deity, a deity, a spiritual entity (a Higher Power), or a non-spiritual conception (a higher purpose). The fact of our recoveries demonstrates that reliance on any one of these conceptions confers a perspective that transcends our immediate physical, social, and emotional circumstances and allows us to "keep calm and carry on" with what really matters. Our advice is to honor your own truth. And although your understanding will necessarily grow and change over time, you only need to focus on whether or not your actions honor that truth in the here and now.

We have found that working the Twelve Steps is a discipline much like the practice of yoga: one does not have to be especially spiritual for it to be profoundly effective in reducing pain and stress. The benefits we experience as a result of working the Twelve Steps go much farther, however. The joy we feel at being able to turn bad experiences to good, the delight we know as we become happily useful, and the exhilaration and connection we feel as we appreciate the deep bonds we establish with others, all serve to remind us how much we have to offer.

Allow us to make clear that our approach is grounded in the same actions one finds in the Twelve Steps with very few changes. Note that this is no easy alternative to the hard work required for recovery. In the following chapters, "How It Works (Steps One through Four)," "Into Action (Steps Five through Eleven)," and "Working with Others (Step Twelve)" we have attempted to provide guidance not only for those who are able to apply a religious or spiritual solution, but also for those who cannot. We trust no one finds this unduly offensive. We hope that those who have taken the principles of the Twelve Steps to heart will take what they can use and leave the rest, understanding that our approach reflects our best effort to carry the message of recovery to all who may need it.

The message provided in this book—that one may find recovery without needing to consider another's conception of a Higher Power—is sure to bring "luster to tired eyes and fresh courage to flagging spirits."[6] Those who would otherwise have avoided Twelve-Step recovery altogether may be encouraged to know that their own conception of a greater good is all that is needed to commence a journey towards recovery from an eating disorder.

But what about those who have faith, yet find it lacking in terms of healing from their eating disorders? As is mentioned elsewhere in this book, what had been missing from our faith was action, specifically *spiritual* action working towards the removal of eating-disordered thoughts and behaviors. Our purpose in writing this EDA text is to show other people with eating disorders precisely what spiritual action we took, in agreement with the AA text which reads: "To show other alcoholics precisely how we recovered is the main purpose of this book."[7]

Some of our more spiritually inclined members would also like to emphasize the "Big Book's" other stated purpose: "…that's exactly what this book is about. Its main object is to enable you to find a Power greater than yourself, which will solve your problem."[8] Let us hear from them.

---

[6] Ibid., 53. Spelling of "lustre" Americanized for readability in the US.
[7] Ibid., xiii.
[8] Ibid., 45.

From Believers and People of Faith in EDA:

When faced with the proposed writings of the EDA "Big Book," we who are more religiously inclined could not accept many of its secular precepts without mentioning some of our thoughts on the matter. Those of us with a deep love for God didn't like the thought of downplaying the importance of faith and reliance upon a Higher Power. We had our faith and we loved it. As stated in the AA book, "When we became alcoholic (eating-disordered), crushed by a self-imposed crisis we could not postpone or evade, we had to fearlessly face the proposition that either God is everything or He is nothing. God either is, or He isn't. What was our choice to be?"[9] We chose that He was.

Further, how could we ignore believers who consider God to be the most important aspect of their lives, or casually reduce this power down to a "greater good?" We feel so strongly about faith and our love for God or our Higher Power that we proposed that this response be included in the EDA volume for the believers and for the way of faith.

Interestingly, some religious enthusiasts find the "Big Book" of Alcoholics Anonymous to be too secular, believing that it allows you to choose your own God. We who study the AA "Big Book" do not hold this to be true. It doesn't state you can choose your own God, but rather that you can choose your own conception of God—whatever that may be. And often that turns out to be God, with a capitol G. After we commence our spiritual growth, "we found ourselves accepting many things which then seemed entirely out of reach. That was growth, but if we wished to grow, we had to begin somewhere. So we used our own conception, however limited it was."[10] It also states in the AA book, Twelve Steps and Twelve Traditions, "Relieved of

---

[9] Ibid., 53. Parenthetical element added.
[10] Ibid., 47.

the (eating disorder) obsession, their lives unaccountably transformed, they came to believe in a Higher Power, and most of them began to talk about God."[11]

It has been our experience that no matter what faith a person comes into the Fellowship with, that faith will grow. The AA "Big Book" discusses the many avenues through which people come to faith in AA when they accept their need for a Higher Power. Some had no faith, some had faith and found it lacking, some had resentments against faith or against people of faith, and some thought they had evaded the God idea altogether. We find no problem working with individuals (such as during sponsorship) who have a different faith than we do. We do our best to share what has helped us, and hope they adopt a similar way of life—whether or not it includes the same conception of God. We who are more religiously inclined are happy to work together with those who are more secular for the common purpose of recovery from an eating disorder. But it is no secret that those of us with faith wish for others to experience what we experience—although we push this on no one. We only serve to be helpful and share our hope and our stories of recovery. Ours is a program of attraction, not promotion.

We would like to point out that some of us who have a strong faith didn't always have it. Many of us acquired faith—or went back to it—when we got sober from our eating disorders through working the Steps of EDA. Many of us had some level of faith and some had none at all, yet we found that without seeking our Higher Power—God as we understood Him—we could find no recovery. Since our eating disorders deal with food, which is necessary to life, many of us found that we had to draw even nearer to God than we had previously. And our relationship with God has

---

[11] *Twelve Steps and Twelve Traditions.* (1981) New York, NY: AA World Services, Inc., 28. Parenthetical element added.

indeed become the most important aspect of our lives. That is why we wish to share the Great Reality, the great wonder that is our faith, and why we feel uncomfortable when it is reduced to a level of "greater purpose." Many of us have come to feel that conscious contact with God is something that we cannot ignore or evade if we wish to maintain recovery. While respecting that others find recovery through reliance on other conceptions, we think it critical to share our personal understanding with newcomers.

Those of us with faith believe that anything is possible with divine inspiration, though God does require our participation. We need action, for "…it is only by action that we can cut away the self-will which has always blocked the entry of God—or, if you like, a Higher Power—into our lives. Faith, to be sure, is necessary, but faith alone can avail nothing; we can have faith yet keep God out of our lives."[12] Thankfully for us, no matter where we are spiritually, "God does not make too hard terms with those who seek Him."[13]

We people of faith want to highlight how deeply rooted we are in our reliance upon a Higher Power and we encourage everyone to seek out and explore their faith. As it says in the Eleventh Step section of both the AA "Big Book" and our EDA text, many of us return to religious practices we may have held in the past. We are encouraged to be quick to make use of what religion offers.[14]

Many of us took comfort from the story in the AA book, *Twelve Steps and Twelve Traditions,* about the sponsor who explained that he "took it (meaning spirituality and Step Two) piecemeal"[15] himself. In fact, none of the Twelve Steps can be taken or understood all at once. But

---

[12] Ibid., 34.
[13] *Alcoholics Anonymous.* (2001) New York, NY: AA World Services, Inc., 46.
[14] Ibid., 87.
[15] *Twelve Steps and Twelve Traditions,* (1981) New York, NY: AA World Services, Inc., 26.

if we are doing what is suggested, a new way of life starts infiltrating our lives and slowly we shift our way of thinking and doing.

We who have recovered and found our faith in God want to share that which is the deepest reality for us, the core of our being, our inspiration for life, the giver of life, the one who makes all things possible. We wish to honor Him in all our endeavors and give credit to Him where we feel credit is due. We encourage those of you with faith not to be dismayed, and not be downtrodden by anything in this book you may find is not in line with your own conception of God; know that we, too, are out there, and we pray for all of you to recover from your eating disorders and grow closer to God.

We hope that you do not find these statements offensive in any way. We wish to give all sides equal representation, not wanting to divide or make recovery seem too daunting of a task for those who struggle with faith. Most of us struggled with faith ourselves. However, we in EDA believe that, as reflected in the AA text we must all "hang together or die separately. We (have) to unify our Fellowship or pass off the scene."[16] Faced with the thought of excluding any of our fellowship from finding hope in EDA, we embrace common ground. We do not want anyone to miss out on this journey of recovery; that is our primary purpose.

Some of you may be troubled by the secular tone of this text, while others, hoping to find a more secular experience, may be dismayed by what seems like constant references to God. In either case, you are not alone! So we emphasize again that even though we EDA members have

---

[16] *Alcoholics Anonymous.* (2001) New York, NY: AA World Services, Inc., xix. Verb tense changed from "had" to "have."

divergent positions on faith, *our common ground is obvious*: the fact of our recoveries and the process through which we achieve peace and freedom.

Our strength lies in our diversity. We acknowledge that your experience may lie anywhere along the spectrum of faith. Whatever it is, EDA welcomes you, embraces your position, and cherishes your recovery. Regardless of your beliefs concerning God or a greater good, you will find yourself reflected in this text. We encourage you to take what you can use and apply it. Trust your truth, respect others as you would like to be respected, and remember that your example counts. If we are open, honest, and empathetic, we can effect real changes in ourselves *and* we can help one another.

In summary, though we may have differing ways of faith, there are two things we absolutely agree on: life with an active eating disorder is no life at all, and the Twelve Steps show a way out that is so powerful we need never return to the dark days. In the next three chapters we describe exactly what we did to recover from our eating disorders. We hope you find the courage to carry on: recovery is worth the effort!

Chapter 5

HOW IT WORKS (STEPS 1—4)

*I*n our experience, the Twelve Steps outlined in the chapters "How It Works," "Into Action," and "Working with Others" in AA's text, *Alcoholics Anonymous*,[1] define a process that works as well for those with eating disorders as it does for alcoholics. So, in the next three chapters, we present EDA's version of these Steps and clarify exactly how we recovered from our eating disorders. Those acquainted with similar programs will find EDA's approach reassuringly familiar, yet distinct.

While the EDA approach demands rigorous honesty and integrity, it does not insist on "abstinence first." We recognize that recovery from an eating disorder is usually a gradual process and that establishing a foundation for a different kind of life takes time and commitment. Through continuous, daily practice, we slowly learn to rely on new ideas and perspectives that work, as we let go of old ones that kept us stuck in a cycle of misery and hopelessness. As the AA text declares:

> Rarely have we seen a person fail who has thoroughly followed our path. Those who do not recover are people who cannot or will not completely give themselves to this simple program, usually men and women who are constitutionally incapable of being honest with themselves. There are such unfortunates. They are not at fault; they seem to have been born that way. They are naturally incapable of grasping and developing a manner of living which

[1] *Alcoholics Anonymous*. (2001) New York, NY: AA World Services, Inc., 58-71.

demands rigorous honesty. Their chances are less than average. There are those, too, who suffer from grave emotional and mental disorders, but many of them do recover if they have the capacity to be honest.[2]

Let us be completely clear: we think anyone *can* recover from having an eating disorder, though not everyone does. We would like to assure all readers that it is completely normal for someone with an eating disorder to continue to engage in old patterns of thought and behavior until they have—through repeated and determined practice—learned to rely more heavily on a new foundation created through working the Twelve Steps. As the saying goes, recovery is a process, not an event. Just as in the AA text:

> Our stories disclose in a general way what we used to be like, what happened, and what we are like now. If you have decided you want what we have, and are willing to go to any length to get it—then you are ready to take certain steps. At some of these we balked. We thought we could find an easier, softer way. But we could not. With all the earnestness at our command, we beg of you to be fearless and thorough from the very start. Some of us tried to hold onto our old ideas, and the result was nil until we let go absolutely.[3]

Whether or not we are members of a religious organization, we have to find a different way of relating to the world, a brand new way that enables us to find peace, power, and perspective we formerly lacked. We are not able to change by focusing on ourselves directly. It is too much

[2] Ibid., 58.
[3] Ibid.

for us![4] Instead, we have to allow change to happen within and through us by doing two things:

1. **Removing ourselves from the center of our own attention by placing our focus on something greater than ourselves that we commit to serve without reservation.** All people in Twelve-Step recovery find their new freedom, peace, power, and happiness comes directly through steady reliance on God, manifested as a Higher Power of their own understanding, or on the idea of serving a higher purpose. To provide perspective and meaning to our lives, we replace self-centeredness with God-centeredness or service to the greater good. It is that simple.

2. **Recognizing that serving God and/or the greater good requires us to first take care of our own basic needs for air, water, food, sleep, clothing, shelter, and physical safety**. We remember the old adage, "God helps those who help themselves." We found we could not reliably turn our attention to a higher plane until our basic needs—not wants—were met. We must first take care of these basics, and it is *our responsibility*—not anyone else's—to do so.

These ideas are simple, but not easy to implement![5] Here are the steps we took, suggested as a program of recovery, through which we allow the needed changes in ourselves to occur:

[4] Ibid., 59.
[5] Ibid., 14.

The Twelve Steps of EDA

1. We admitted we were powerless over our eating disorders—that our lives had become unmanageable.

2. Came to believe that a Power greater than ourselves could restore us to sanity.

3. Made a decision to turn our will and our lives over to the care of God *as we understood God*.[6]

4. Made a searching and fearless moral inventory of ourselves.

5. Admitted to God, to ourselves, and to another human being the exact nature of our wrongs.

6. Were entirely ready to have God remove all these defects of character.

7. Humbly asked God to remove our shortcomings.

8. Made a list of all persons we had harmed and became willing to make amends to them all.

9. Made direct amends to such people wherever possible, except when to do so would injure them or others.

10. Continued to take personal inventory and when we were wrong promptly admitted it.

11. Sought through prayer and meditation to improve

---

[6] "God" in EDA literature can mean the Deity, a deity, a spiritual entity of one's own understanding (a Higher Power), or a non-spiritual conception (a higher purpose). Reliance on any of these conceptions confers a perspective that transcends our immediate physical, social, and emotional circumstances and allows us to "keep calm and carry on" with what really matters.

our conscious contact with God *as we understood God,* praying only for knowledge of God's will for us and the power to carry that out.

12. Having had a spiritual awakening[7] as the result of these steps, we tried to carry this message to others with eating disorders, and to practice these principles in all our affairs.

Many of us first reacted to this list like those who first encounter AA's Twelve Steps: "What an order! I can't go through with it!" And, in the same way that AA members comfort newcomers, we in EDA are happy to reassure, "Do not be discouraged. No one among us has been able to maintain anything like perfect adherence to these principles."[8] The point is that we are willing to grow along the lines we have set down. We aim for *balance,* understanding that "our real purpose is to fit ourselves to be of maximum service to God and the people about us."[9] We claim progress, never perfection.

Our description of the eating-disordered mind in Chapters 3 and 4, coupled with our personal adventures before and after finding recovery, make clear three pertinent ideas:

- That we had serious problems—eating disorders—that we could not solve despite our best efforts.

---

[7] The term "spiritual awakening" can refer to an event—a vital spiritual experience—or to a gradual change. We who are atheists also experience a transformation, enabling us to place service before selfishness.

[8] *Alcoholics Anonymous.* (2001) New York, NY: AA World Services, Inc., 77.

[9] Ibid., 14.

- That no accessible human power had relieved our eating disorders.

- That reliance on God, a Higher Power, or a higher purpose could—and would—restore us to sanity and set us free.

We now present a discussion of each of the Steps. The current chapter, "How It Works," covers Steps One through Four. The next chapter, "Into Action," provides a review of Steps Five through Eleven, and the following chapter, "Working with Others," discusses Step Twelve.

Step One: *We admitted we were powerless over our eating disorders—that our lives had become unmanageable.*

Before recovery, we could not stop "acting out" in ways we knew caused harm. We were miserable. Even when aware that there might be a way to get and stay better, we were stricken with the same "mental blank spots"[10] as people suffering from alcoholism. We persisted in repeating the same behaviors even though what we were doing was irrational considering the possible physical and mental consequences. We remained ill despite our best efforts and the efforts of others who wanted to help us.

Yet, we think it normal for people with eating disorders to take issue with the idea of powerlessness. Most of us had the same difficulty! The key point is not about being "powerless" in the overall context of our lives, but about *having* **insufficient** *power to overcome our eating disorders*

---

[10] Ibid., 42.

specifically. Everything we tried—up to the point where we considered taking this important 1st Step—had obviously failed, or we wouldn't have gotten to this juncture at all.

There is a reason why the founders of AA chose the word "powerless" for Step One. The whole point of the Twelve Steps is to enable the person who takes them to *find the power to recover*. If the First Step had said "helpless" or "insufficient" instead of "powerless," then the 2nd Step—which is all about finding one's own hope, strength, and *power* to change—would not have made as much sense.

Perhaps you are also struggling with the second clause of Step One, "…that our lives had become unmanageable." Most likely, your life appears fairly manageable on the surface. A lot of things might be going smoothly; that was the case for most of us. But let us explore a bit further.

- Do you use your eating disorder to help you manage your emotional states in one way or another so your life *feels* more manageable?

- Do you feel completely *safe within yourself*, able to rely on yourself to do all that is required of you, without having to resort to behaviors that you know cause harm?

Reflecting on these questions makes clear that the two clauses of Step One are actually parallel: *If you have an eating disorder that you cannot control, by definition that part of your life—which will doubtless be a central part of your life—is not manageable, at least not by you.* Step One is an admission of defeat: despite our best efforts, we could not recover on our own. This is all that is required to make a solid beginning.

The remaining Steps outline techniques to help you let go of old ideas that did not work and lay a solid foundation of ideas that do. Then you will be given directions for building on the foundation you have put in place. You are in charge of all of that, and you are not going to be asked to build on anything that you cannot trust. Steps Two through Twelve are all about finding the power to gain and then retain the sanity that enables you to lead a happy and purposeful life.

If you are reading this, you have probably already admitted you are powerless over your eating disorder and are willing to try almost anything that sounds reasonable in order to recover. You are ready to move to Step Two.

Step Two: *Came to believe that a Power greater than ourselves could restore us to sanity.*

Many of us had no problem with the fundamental idea of God. Our main issue was that we doubted our ability to recover, since we had not yet found lasting freedom *despite our belief.* Others of us had always believed in God, yet we couldn't figure out how to allow God into our lives to a greater degree, especially when we knew that meant we would have to lay aside our eating disorders. Some of us who had faith had grown up with a kind of negative fear or resentment towards God that needed to be overcome in order to build a deep and meaningful relationship.

Those of us who are atheist or agnostic struggled to find a conception of a Power that we could reconcile with our ideas about how the world works. Some of us tried using a conception that aligned well with the "Spirit of the

Universe" described in the AA chapter, "We Agnostics,"[11] while others used the power of our EDA group as our Higher Power. People were clearly getting better through reliance on these sources of hope and guidance, yet many of us remained skeptical.

We all agree that some fundamental force or forces seem to be able to create life in the most inhospitable places. Not only do these forces generate life, they regularly triumph over adversity. Trampled plants often renew themselves, lost lizard tails grow back, flesh wounds heal, and broken bones knit back together over time. We accept this as part of the natural world. How wonderful it would be if we who are afflicted with eating disorders could allow ourselves to tap into this fundamental healing power and get well!

Just like the processes through which broken bones heal, we do not need to understand all the details of the recovery process to trust that it works. If we adopt a conception of a fundamental healing force in nature, we will have no doubt about the force being greater than ourselves. Not one among us thinks themselves immune to the forces of physics and chemistry. If we can believe that we are not immune to fundamental healing forces, and if we can believe that surrender to the healing forces of nature can restore us to sanity, we are most of the way through Step Two.

If you have read through all the Twelve Steps, you will have seen that Steps One and Two are laying a foundation. We need to *open ourselves up to a relationship with something greater than ourselves* to get through the remaining steps and fully recover. We urge you to be flexible about this point specifically. Opening up to a relationship with a

[11] Ibid., 46.

God of one's own understanding —whether a Power, purpose, or both—can be difficult. The process requires profound honesty and a daily practice that includes both self-reflection and appreciation for all that is good and right. Whatever conception we choose, we will need to *draw upon* it as we move forward with the next Steps. In Step Three we turn our will and our lives over to the care of God as we understand God. To do so, we must find a concept we trust to provide perspective on our lives. In Step Seven, we humbly ask God to remove our shortcomings. We will need a Power or purpose that helps us move past current limitations so we can make good use of our time, energy, skills, and talents. In Step Eleven, through prayer and meditation we "seek knowledge of God's will for us and the power to carry that out." In this Step, as in all the rest, we need a connection to a Power or purpose that provides us with the strength and perspective to keep calm and focus on what really matters.

It is helpful to remember that all of us—religious, spiritual, agnostic, and atheist—are in the same boat. Whether we believed in God or not, our dependence on our eating disorders demonstrated that *God would not relieve our condition without our explicit permission, cooperation, and ongoing action.* The situation is the same for everyone: we commit our lives to God as we understand God and then live out that commitment on a day-to-day basis. *Faith alone is not enough.* We see people of faith struggle mightily with their eating disorders every day. As the AA text makes very clear, *only reliance on something greater than ourselves—combined with action—sets us free.* "Faith without works is dead."[12]

By this point, those of us who are atheist or agnostic

were prepared to declare the Twelve Steps impossible: we had had enough of all this "God talk!" Then, it dawned on us that the idea of serving a purpose greater than ourselves—anything in which we solidly believed (perhaps the ideas of fairness and justice) could work, if *we fully relied upon the idea of service* to bring us the needed perspective. We could then develop a relationship with this conception that would put our lives in context.

Those of us who are in recovery—regardless of whether we adopted a religious, spiritual, or non-spiritual solution—are all emphatically in agreement:

- *We needed a different way of looking at the world and our place in it,* because our old way left us vulnerable and prone to acting out.

- *We needed to rely on this new way of looking at the world*—instead of our old patterns of thought and behavior—to provide a perspective that brought us peace.

- *We found we could not rely on anything that we were not willing to trust,* and "the result was nil until we let go absolutely."[13]

Our job in Step Two is to identify or define something greater than ourselves that we can open ourselves up to and trust, for we need to rely on it.

We all had major issues with trust. In Step One, we admitted we could not fully trust ourselves to manage our own lives. We demonstrated repeatedly that we experienced

[13] Ibid., 58.

"strange mental blank spots"[14] pertaining to our eating disorders; we could not trust our own minds to keep us safe! Yet, even at our very worst—unable to depend on ourselves, struggling to trust those around us, caught up in any number of forms of acting out—we often found we were still able to understand what was fair and just, true and worthwhile. *Except when it came to ourselves.* When it came to ourselves, we seemed unable to maintain anything like a reasonable perspective.

Let us take ourselves out of the picture altogether for the moment and reflect on what we *can* truly trust. We find it helpful to consider the causes we care deeply about. For some of us, these are revealed through our relationship with God: we find peace and purpose to the full extent that we rely upon God (or a Higher Power) to help us. For others, a higher purpose—revealed through our thoughtful response to life as we see it—gives us perspective and peace.

We wholeheartedly believe that *every one of us can find something or some cause besides ourselves that matters just enough for us to be willing to set aside our issues,* one day at a time, to serve it. Our purpose should be something we care deeply about, or our commitment to serve will surely falter. Some of us have chosen to carry the message of recovery as our higher purpose. Others have chosen to advocate for victims' rights, civil rights, and animal rights. Still others have worked to solve the global problem of access to clean water. We need not look far to find inequitable and unjust conditions or problems to which we could reasonably turn our time and attention. As long as we are earnest about growing stronger so we can better serve our higher purpose,

---

[14] Ibid., 42.

any will do.[15] If you choose a higher purpose that reflects your core values and about which you feel deeply passionate, you can rest assured that you are well on the way to a durable recovery.

We need not worry whether we have identified a "correct" conception as the focal point for our new frame of reference. Once we get to Step Eleven, our daily practice will help us refine and enlarge our understanding, whether it be of God's will for us or how to best serve the higher purpose which we have taken to heart.

Once we find something we can use as our new focal point and begin to arrange our lives accordingly, peace and power start flowing into us. With this shift in orientation a new perspective appears almost automatically. Our emotional struggles take on a different meaning when "our main purpose is to fit ourselves to be of maximum service to God (our Higher Power/higher purpose) and the people about us."[16] Rather than resisting, judging ourselves, and getting caught up in the drama of our lives, we find we can now use our experiences and responses to help us grow into fully aware, deeply empathetic, and genuinely helpful people. Although we are in no way free from having emotions, we no longer need be mired in them: we do not suffer needlessly. We experience pain—sometimes a lot of pain—but we now intuitively know that we can use our pain to some good purpose, such as helping others or making much needed changes in our lives. We know that

---

[15] A note of caution: if you are atheist or agnostic, we suggest you find a higher purpose other than or in addition to service to family as a starting point. It can be challenging to maintain calm perspective at times when family tension is high.

[16] *Alcoholics Anonymous.* (2001) New York, NY: AA World Services, Inc., 77. Parenthetical phrase added.

running from pain means still more pain, so we begin to accept life on life's terms with grace and dignity; as we do so, we gain peace and power. When we stop running from our emotions, we find ourselves free to experience the many delights that come with being fully alive.

The second part of Step Two asks us if we are now willing to believe that reliance on God or our higher purpose can restore us to sanity. We are here to tell you that our experience bears this out: *We grow to care more about serving our Higher Power/higher purpose than about the things that stand in the way.* Once we have adopted and practiced reliance on this new perspective for even a short while, the desperate urge to sidestep emotional difficulties eases and the aching black hole of neediness begins to fill up. We become less dependent on old habits and we can more easily see life's emotional challenges for what they are:

- *Signals* that we may be neglecting something that needs to be dealt with first (i.e. taking care of the basics)

- *Reminders* that we are only human

- *Challenges* to our commitment to place service to the greater good ahead of our self-generated emotional states

- *Opportunities* to build bridges of empathy and understanding with others who struggle with similar issues and challenges

- *Means* through which we grow more resilient, strong, and flexible in our recovery

- *Impediments* to fully serving others in the here and now

Everything hinges on whether we can find a Higher Power or higher purpose that we trust enough to be willing to set aside our fears, self-pity, and resentments. If you believe that reliance on your Higher Power or higher purpose can help keep you from acting out—even just for one day—you have just completed Step Two. You are on the road to recovery!

Step Three: *Made a decision to turn our will and our lives over to the care of God as we understood God.*

Until we reached Step Three, many of us were working toward recovery with the idea that we "must" have it, because living with our eating disorders was untenable. We were frightened of what our lives might look like without them, but taking Step Two signaled that we developed hope that change was actually possible for us. We were encouraged to see others having an easier time when they actively sought and maintained recovery as something valuable they wanted in its own right, not because they were running from their eating disorders or felt obligated to "follow the rules." We wanted the kind of recovery that looked and felt like real freedom. This is where Step Three came in.

For those of us with a deep and abiding faith and trust in God, Step Three makes tremendous sense; our main difficulty lies in following through on our commitment. For the rest of us, Step Three may present a serious obstacle. Some of us get what the AA text describes as "mental gooseflesh" with respect to the idea of worship.[17] Let us be clear: there is no need to get hung up on the word. We ask you

[17] Ibid., 54.

to consider the following rewording of Step Three: *"Made a decision to commit our will and our lives to the service of our Higher Power/higher purpose as we understood it."* We believe this to be the logical equivalent for those who struggle with the idea of God, and somewhat easier to understand and apply.

No matter how we approached this step, when we looked back over our lives, we could readily see that we had been struggling to get ourselves—and sometimes those around us—to conform to our ideas about how things "should" be. Rather than adapting ourselves to reality as it presented itself to us each day, appreciating the beauty and diversity of experiences this world had to offer, and searching for the best way to use our time and talents, most of us spent a great deal of energy trying to make life match our expectations. It's natural to want the people around us to share our hopes and beliefs, but more than most, we who struggled with eating disorders wanted parents, teachers, classmates, partners, spouses, bosses, co-workers, employees, children, friends, relatives—even institutions and society as a whole—to behave in certain ways, even when this sometimes meant the loss of relationships we cared about. Toward the end of our eating disorder "careers," some of us insisted only on being left alone in our misery. We hope you have not yet reached this level!

We should point out that we were usually quite virtuous in our efforts to "manage" things. Our motives were generally excellent: we earnestly wanted what was best for all concerned. We worked hard and usually set a good example. We could be patient, kind-hearted, and generous. Many of us were modest and self-sacrificing. We were often delightful company, but at heart we were not satisfied unless, as the AA text describes it, "the lights, the ballet, the scenery, and the rest of the players" were arranged to our liking. When our arrangements worked well, we were happy and assumed everyone else was, too. When things did not work out so well, we applied ourselves still harder to ensure our expectations were met. Surely if we were just more determined or more gracious, things would work out the way we wanted. When they didn't, we admitted we were partly at fault, but often blamed others more than we blamed ourselves. We gradually became "angry, indignant, and self-pitying."[18]

Although we often did not realize it, our perspective revolved around the idea that we ourselves were of central importance. We tended to think our ideas were inherently right and were sometimes dismissive of other views. In retrospect, we can see how unreasonable this was. We inadvertently hurt others while making sure we got what we wanted; sometimes they retaliated. We were also hurt when others refused to accept our direction or failed to validate our ideas. *Couldn't they see we just wanted what was best?* Without ever consciously meaning to be selfish or self-seeking, our thoughts and behavior solidly reflected the idea that we privileged our own thinking above that of others. We were busy "directing the show." The AA text calls this "playing God."[19] We had to admit we somehow made everything all about us, our beliefs, and our expectations of how things should be. All Twelve-Step programs make clear that this type of thinking simply does not work. As long as we persisted in forcing our will—our ideas about how things ought to be—on others (and ourselves!), we needed

[18] Ibid., 6.
[19] Ibid., 62.

to act out in our eating disorders to assuage the hurt, anger, indignation, and self-pity we suffered as a result.

Remember that we are dealing with eating disorders, which are complex, life-threatening illnesses.[20] By the time we arrive at Step Three, we need to find a new frame of reference that provides the objectivity and power to address our condition with all the urgency we can muster. As discussed in Chapters 3 and 4, full recovery from an eating disorder requires a complete emotional displacement and rearrangement, a *transformation* as profound as any known to human experience. This isn't easy for anyone. We have to place service to God, our Higher Power, or higher purpose ahead of our worldly wants and desires. Can you do it? Of course you can!

Within Twelve-Step programs everywhere, millions of people have been able to achieve exactly the type of transformation we have been talking about. These people are living happily and completely free from their illnesses. The AA text tells us, "People of faith have a logical idea of what life is all about" and that "…we might have observed that spiritually-minded persons of all races, colors, and creeds were demonstrating a degree of stability, happiness, and usefulness which we should have sought for ourselves."[21] This is absolutely true! We are happy to add that many atheists and agnostics are also quietly living lives of sane and useful purpose. They too have a logical idea of what life is all about and are demonstrating a degree of stability, usefulness, and happiness we ought now seek for ourselves.

[20] Arcelus, J., Mitchell, A.J., Wales, J., Nielsen, S. (2011) Mortality rates in patients with anorexia nervosa and other eating disorders. A meta-analysis of 36 studies. *Archives of General Psychiatry.* 68(7), 724-31.
[21] *Alcoholics Anonymous.* (2001) New York, NY: AA World Services, Inc., 54.

The AA text declares, "When we saw others solve their problems by a simple reliance upon the Spirit of the Universe, we had to stop doubting the power of God. Our ideas did not work, but the God idea did."[22] This statement is certainly true for those who are able to apply the concept of a Higher Power, and the key element, we find, is actually the concept of *reliance*. Those of us with religious convictions as well as those without them find that our ideas failed *not because they were inherently "soft and mushy,"*[23] *but because we had not **relied** upon them*. Religious, spiritual, or neither, we were busy using our eating disorders as a crutch to get through our day-to-day existence, with no clue that a sense of purpose or duty could carry us through life's challenges instead. Perhaps because we had not taken full responsibility for meeting our own basic needs, we had somewhat childishly allowed ourselves and our emotional condition to take center stage in our lives. When we did so, no matter how strong our religious convictions, philosophical ideas, or moral principles, we simply could not seem to live by them. In the eye of the storm of our emotions, dependent only on ourselves, we were hopelessly stuck, trying to fix something broken within us with tools that were also broken. It didn't work. We must have something more durable, more powerful, more permanent, and ultimately *more important than we are to ourselves* to serve as our foundation.

In Step Two, we discussed the idea that God, a Higher Power, or a higher purpose could restore us to sanity. Do you trust God, or were you able to define a Higher Power or higher purpose greater than yourself, whom or which

[22] Ibid., 52.
[23] Ibid., 53.

you are open to serving? Some of us are such skeptics that this question gave us a significant pause! But once we began to put these ideas into practice we soon acknowledged that *humble and anonymous work is exactly what we (and the world) most need.* No matter how we conceive of God or purpose, the question is whether we are now willing to consider putting everything we have—our time, energy, thoughts, and actions—into being of greatest possible service.

Suppose you have identified a Higher Power or higher purpose with which you feel comfortable, but you are far from confident in your ability to serve anything without reservation. Perhaps you have a family to support. Surely, you cannot be expected to sacrifice time, energy, and money that your loved ones desperately need so you can contribute towards some "greater good." That would be adding insult to injury, would it not? Haven't our families already sacrificed and suffered long enough?

If this is an issue, we ask you to think about long-term impacts on your loved ones; it makes no sense to cause them greater injury. They need us to be real and authentic, solid and dependable. It may be hard for a family to accept that their lives will be better if you are working for a higher purpose, but we assure you, *we are better able to support our loved ones once we are in recovery.* If you were to ask them sincerely about the bigger picture, you would almost certainly learn that your restoration to health and sanity is their greatest concern. They are likely to understand that everything else will fall into place once you are well.

We should also think of the example we are setting for others. If we are able to successfully establish a purpose-driven life, we stand a much better chance of supporting those we love in their own pursuit of the same. Do you find it scary that your life partner might decide to pursue a higher purpose, or live in service to a Higher Power (activities that might not include you)? Do not be discouraged. Some of us had the same fears, and our family members felt the same way. But our experience is that if we are considerate of our family, attentive to their needs, include them in our efforts, and work hard for their benefit, they generally respond by being similarly considerate, attentive, and inclusive.

Perhaps you doubt if you can find the strength and power to carry out the decision you are being asked to make in Step Three. Your experience may have demonstrated that you cannot completely trust yourself to honor commitments of the sort required of you here. We truly understand and agree that this is a serious concern. We recognize your hesitation and respect your willingness to be honest with yourself about it. But please be assured that the point of Steps Four through Nine is to sweep away any barriers to your sanity and integrity so you *will* be able to honor your commitments. Once you are able to maintain balance and perspective through some emotionally challenging situations, you will begin to see that *reliance on your idea of a Higher Power or higher purpose does for you what you could not do for yourself.* You can trust this process; it works for us and it can work for you, too.

In Step Three, our job is to resolve—decide—*to be open to committing ourselves to serving God, a Higher Power, or the greater good: something that inspires and enables us to transcend our current limitations.* Step Three is a jumping-off point into recovery. Are you now willing to give up the old ways and try some new ones? If so, we ask you to repeat the 3rd Step prayer, or the alternative statement below, or both. We emphasize that there is nothing magical about either one. Your decision to change your frame of reference is the logical, correct, and practical next step on your path to recovery.

Original form of the 3rd Step Prayer

God, I offer myself to Thee—to build with me and to do with me as Thou wilt. Relieve me of the bondage of self, that I may better do Thy will. Take away my difficulties, that victory over them may bear witness to those I would help of Thy Power, Thy Love, and Thy Way of life. May I do Thy will always![24]

Alternative 3rd Step Commitment

I, [state your name], am now willing to commit myself to serving the greater good and be of cheerful service to those around me. I am willing to make my service to a higher purpose more important than any desire for recognition or reward. When filled with fear and self-doubt, as I am sure to be at times, I resolve to remember my willingness and do the next right thing that prepares me to be of better service. I gratefully embrace this opportunity to turn my will and my life over to serve a useful purpose.

We encourage you to write the 3rd Step prayer or alternative statement down on paper. Your commitment is your new foundation. Honor it. Repeat it every morning before you start your day. Repeat it throughout the day. Read it before you start your 4th Step, and read it before providing sponsorship guidance to others. Be unashamed. If you have taken this step, you are on solid ground in your recovery!

---

[24] *Alcoholics Anonymous.* (2001) New York, NY: AA World Services, Inc., 63.

Step Four: *Made a searching and fearless moral inventory of ourselves.*

We think Step Four is crucially important, because it uncovers all the thoughts and emotions that fuel our insane behaviors and helps identify new ways of thinking and feeling that we can use in recovery. This prepares us for the rest of the Steps, which restore us to sanity.

In Step One, we admitted we were untrustworthy and unreliable in taking care of ourselves. If we are honest with ourselves, we will see we haven't been truly available for others, either. We did not allow ourselves to mature and grow as human beings while we were busy acting out and numbing ourselves emotionally. Since we can never be fully effective in serving God, our Higher Power, or higher purpose if we are operating from a place of instability and unreliability, we can hardly hope to be successful in honoring the commitment we just made in Step Three *unless we are willing to expose and let go of the fears and issues that caused us to want to use an escape in the first place.*

As long as we refuse to address our needs and our issues, and as long as we allow ourselves to remain prey to volatile emotions—no matter how good our intentions or how deep our desire to be of service—we are not going to be as effective as if we are truly free to think and act without the encumbrances of an eating disorder. The purpose of Step Four is to help us find, and prepare us to let go of, everything that has been keeping us from being able to handle life on life's terms with dignity and grace.

When we examined our lives closely, we saw that much of our misery and paralysis could be chalked up to durable habits of thought and behavior. Underlying these habits were ideas that we needed to bring out into the open so we could define a clearer and more reasonable way to think. First, we had to accept that as independent adults, we were each responsible for our own well-being. We needed to meet our basic physical and safety needs before much, if any, progress could be made. In order to establish relationships of trust, including reliance on God, a Higher Power, or a higher purpose, we had to do the initial hard work of taking care of ourselves.

A reference to Maslow's hierarchy of needs seems appropriate here.[25] His theory of human motivation is built on the premise that people have four basic needs (physical, safety, love/belonging, and esteem), which must be met or they are *too anxious* to achieve "self-actualization" or transcendent, altruistic goals. While some take issue with the idea the one need might supercede another (observing that all needs coexist simultaneously), there can be little doubt that human beings *must* get their physical and safety needs met (such as for water, sleep, food, clothing, and shelter) before they can readily form relationships of trust and interdependence with others. It is only reasonable to suppose that we might not be able to develop a relationship with a Higher Power or honor a commitment to a higher purpose while neglecting to take responsibility for our basic needs for food and safety. First things first!

Why didn't we take responsibility for getting our basic needs met? We cannot be sure, and the answers will vary, but it is clear that engaging in eating-disordered thoughts and behaviors satisfied a set of emotional needs. We needed escape. We needed comfort. We needed soothing. We

[25] Maslow, A.H. (1943) A Theory of Human Motivation. *Psychological Review,* 50 (4), 370–96.

needed momentary release from anxiety or depression. We needed to handle our rage and indignation. We needed a way to express ourselves. Our eating disorders somehow covered a lot of these bases, and yet it was never enough. We were never satisfied.

Why couldn't we be satisfied? In Step Four, we have to confront a basic truth about ourselves: somewhere along the way, for whatever reasons, we took a wrong turn in our development. We might not have been fully responsible for this wrong turn; it may have been made during the innocence of childhood. It doesn't matter. We need to be responsible for ourselves *now*—regardless of how we got here.

Most of us recognized that at least some of our issues were tied to our sensitivity. When we were children, before we developed an eating disorder, we remember having had genuine concerns about serious causes, including questions about the "human condition." Some of us remembered having a pure and unencumbered love of God. Most of us cared a great deal for our friends and families. Our ability to attend to these deep concerns and cares, however, was much diminished by our emotional sensitivity. When hurt, threatened, angry, resentful, or frightened, we were too overwhelmed to serve the causes we cared about. We lacked the peace and power to stay focused on what really mattered, because we were caught up in our emotional reactions to life: people, places, situations, and things. We also lacked an objective, empathetic perspective that would have made our normal, human problems seem manageable. As adults, we find little has changed. While we were often quite good at helping our friends diagnose and solve their issues, *we were easily overwhelmed and unable to address our own problems, because we had no objectivity and no context.* We were stuck in the center of the storm.

We can be grateful that we are now on more solid footing. In Step Three, we made a decision to create a new focal point for our lives through service to God, our Higher Power, or higher purpose; we embarked on the fundamental and vital journey toward the "emotional displacement and rearrangement" Dr. Carl Jung described as critically necessary for recovery in his discussion with Rowland H.[26] This idea lies at the heart of all Twelve-Step recovery. With Step Three, we made a decision to shift our context, so that we could understand and address our problems with a degree of objectivity and maturity that was previously unattainable. Now when we look at our problems, we can see them from a different frame of reference: *they affect our ability to work for what really matters.* And problems that stand in the way of our service have to either be solved or put aside. Having just completed Step Three, which established a new perspective, we now need to put it to practical use. The phrase "use it or lose it" has very real and urgent meaning at this point!

Before starting our journey to recovery, we had been fearful of self-examination, concerned that if we took our pride and ego out of the picture there would be nothing left of us.[27] Once we regain a sane perspective, though, we begin to see how we can put our existing traits and talents to good use. Even so, we may still be a bit afraid. We have failed many times before, and it has been painful. But we must explore what has been blocking us from real progress all this time, so we can overcome any vestiges of our old ways and prevent a return to them in the future. That is what Step Four is all about: *uncovering and beginning to*

---

[26] *Alcoholics Anonymous.* (2001) New York, NY: AA World Services, Inc., 27.
[27] Ibid., 36.

*address the real reasons for the emotional distress that fueled
our eating disorders.*

Ironically, the very feelings that we repeatedly experienced as a *result* of engaging in our eating disorders—what the
AA text calls the "hideous four horsemen": Terror, Bewilderment, Frustration, and Despair[28]—also *reinforced* them. These
kinds of emotions (and others such as resentment, fear, self-
pity, shame, guilt, and confusion) regularly overwhelmed us
and rendered us unable to work or focus effectively—*unless we
found escape.* Somehow a reliance on our eating disorders enabled us to cope while slowly strangling and displacing nearly
everything that was healthy in our lives.

The AA text reminds us that, just as drinking is for
alcoholics, our eating disorders were only a symptom of
more fundamental problems. To address these, we had
to get down to causes and conditions. We needed to take
stock of ourselves to understand what we were *really* dealing with, so we could identify appropriate solutions. Step
Four is exactly that: a fact-finding and fact-facing inventory
through which we identify ways of thinking and acting we
want to stop, keep, and start.[29]

How can we ensure success in conducting our "searching and fearless moral inventory?" The answer is simple:
by following the prescription laid out in the AA text[30]—or
something very much like it. Convinced that our self-focused sensitivity had been the source of much of the pain
that drove us to find relief in our eating disorders, we asked
ourselves what we had been so sensitive about. We do this
by examining in detail the sources and causes of our most
challenging and troubling feelings.

---

[28] Ibid., 151.
[29] Ibid., 64.
[30] Ibid., 64-71.

Below we offer suggestions from the AA "Big Book" and an exercise to help with this Step. This might seem like a lot of work, but let us assure you, it can be completed in a relatively short time. You probably spent more time in escapist engagement with your eating disorder *each week* than is required to complete this exercise. We are convinced you will find it extremely useful, because you will refer to your inventory in all remaining Steps.

The main points of the 4th Step exercise outlined below are twofold:

1. *To establish a list of flaws in our thinking*—areas where we have been caught short in the past—so we can address these squarely and effectively.

2. *To define a new plan of action* for how we would like to respond to each familiar provocation in the future. We are planning exactly how we will "Act, Not React."

4th Step Inventory

For this exercise, we need an empty notebook that opens in such a way that both left and right pages are blank, and a few separate pieces of paper for brainstorming purposes.

We remind ourselves that our purpose in Step Four is to find what has been causing our emotional disturbance, so that we can use our new frame of reference to define a sane response or resolution to life's inevitable challenges.

The AA "Big Book" suggests we start our inventory by reviewing our resentments and provides instructions on how to address them.[31] Next, we are asked to review our fears. We are reminded that our fears arise from the problems with our perspective, and we are provided guidance on how to address them.[32] We are then asked to review our sexual conduct, looking for areas where we had caused harm, or aroused jealousy, suspicion, or bitterness. We are to look at our own behavior, especially where we had been selfish, dishonest, or inconsiderate.[33] Then we are asked to define a sane and sound ideal for future conduct.

Focusing on these areas works well for many of us. However, EDA suggests making worksheets for the eight topics below, because these can continue to plague us until they are addressed directly:

Eight Topics for Exploration

1. **Resentment**: people and institutions with which we have an old anger that was never fully resolved (same as in the AA text).

2. **Fear**: things that frightened or still frighten us (same as in the AA text).

3. **Self-pity**: reasons we felt or feel sorry for ourselves.

4. **Shame**: things about which we felt or feel ashamed, despite not being responsible for them.

5. **Guilt or "harms done"**: wrongs we had done or are doing to others.

6. **Confusion**: situations where we felt or still feel abandoned or bewildered.

[31] Ibid., 64-67.
[32] Ibid., 67-68.
[33] Ibid., 68-70.

7. **Frustration**: things that made or make us angry, even if we have no resentment in connection to them.

8. **Despair**: reasons for hopelessness, past and present.

The AA text suggests creating a table with columns covering the *sources* of the emotional disturbance, the *causes or reasons* why we were disturbed, and *aspects of our lives that are at risk or threatened* by the behavior of others. Later, we are asked to consider *our own part* (errors in thinking) to define a better way to think about the situation, and to create a response or *resolution*. While the AA "Big Book" describes this method specifically for addressing resentments, EDA members have found it helpful to apply this same approach to each of the areas of exploration above.

Basic Guidelines for an EDA 4th Step Inventory

On a separate sheet of paper for brainstorming, we pick a topic to explore from the list above and go back through our lives, writing down every person, principle, and institution we can think of in connection with the emotion (the sources). Next, we rank-order these sources by which cause the most intense or most frequent instances of the emotion we are considering. Then, in our notebook on a pair of facing blank pages, we create and complete a table with **five columns** (see example in Appendix D):

1. **Source**: who or what caused the emotion.

2. **Reason/ Cause**: why we felt the emotion.

3. **At Risk/Affects My**: which part of us was threatened or hurt.

4. **My Error/My Part**: the error in thinking that led us to be sensitive or vulnerable in ways that prevented us from growing stronger.

5. **Resolution**: what we are willing to do about it, both now and the next time we feel this way.

If you are like most of us, this exercise probably seems overwhelming! Let us reassure you that an essential part of the 4th Step exercise includes beginning to establish and reinforce a practice of *moderation*. Some sponsors find it helpful to limit their sponsees's writing to the top ten or fifteen sources of trouble in each topic. Limiting an inventory in this way might feel a bit concerning to those familiar with other Twelve-Step programs, yet will certainly qualify as a "good enough" searching and fearless moral inventory. Recall that we are dealing with eight topics, not just three.[34] The keys are to find patterns of problematic thinking and solutions to them that we trust, so we can start to apply those solutions in daily life. It is very important to stay focused and keep moving! Step Ten also gives us a daily opportunity to address anything that might have been unintentionally overlooked. Of course, if anything is really bothering us and could interfere with our recovery, we write it down.

Appendix D provides an example of a 4th Step Inventory. Have a look at it, and then create your own. Merely reading is insufficient!

---

[34] Not all sponsors recommend limiting entries, nor does the AA source material, which suggests an inventory covering resentments, fears, and sexual conduct. AA does not include a separate inventory for self-pity, shame, guilt, confusion, frustration, and despair; however, many of us found ourselves unable to progress in recovery until we addressed each of these topics specifically.

4th Step Inventory Example: Resentment

To start, we brainstorm on a separate sheet of paper. We will use this information to fill in our five-column worksheet later. In the discussion below, we offer resentment as an example, but the approach works well for each of the topics we recommend exploring: resentment, fear, self-pity, shame, guilt/harms done, confusion, frustration, and despair.

1. First, we brainstorm about sources of resentment. A resentment is usually an old, unresolved anger that lurks in the background of our minds, ready to jump out whenever an opportunity presents itself. Thinking back, we list anyone or anything that causes us to feel resentment.

- To list people, think of family members, former relationships, past and current friendships, jobs, etc. It might be useful to look at cell phone, email, and social media contacts.

- We do the same with institutions. Institutions can be groups of people, organizations, or places such as banks, credit card companies, magazines, police departments, cities/states/countries, restaurants, colleges, universities, and organized religions. If thinking about them makes us angry, we put them down on our list.

- We brainstorm for principles we might resent, such as: the idea of love at first sight; racism and other forms of prejudice; and sayings such as "honesty is the best policy," "you live under my roof, you follow my rules," and "fake it 'til you make it."

Then, we go back through our list and mark the top ten people, top two institutions, and top three principles that we feel the most "hot emotions" about.[35] Finally, we take the first person from that list, and put his or her name on our inventory worksheet in the first column on the left, under **Source**.

2. In the second column, **Reasons/Causes,** we list the reason(s) why we were upset, leaving a few empty lines between each one (we will need the space later). When listing reasons, we are specific. We do not say "they treated us badly," we list exactly what they did or said, or in some cases what they didn't do that we thought they should have done.

We repeat this process—listing sources in the first column, and reasons in the second column—for the top ten people, top two institutions, and top three principles. *Once done with these, most EDA sponsors recommend their sponsees stop.* We recall that we are looking for *patterns* in our incorrect thinking. We want the inventory to be fearless and thorough, but if we list every person from our brainstorming list who has ever wronged us (and how), we might never finish! We cannot afford to get bogged down now. *We are not looking for other people's errors, only our own.*

We keep these brainstorming lists to use when we get to Step Eight. Our daily Step Ten inventory can be entrusted to pick up anything important that we might inadvertently miss.

3. In the third column, **At Risk/Affects My,** for each *reason* (not just for each source), we write if the cause of resentment affects or threatens any of the following: self-esteem, pride, ambition, finances, security, sexual or intimacy needs, and family or social relationships.

---

[35] Not all sponsors recommend limiting entries, nor does the AA source material.

- **Self-esteem** reflects the way we feel about or value ourselves: self-respect or self-regard. Our dignity and composure, as well as our self-esteem, can feel threatened when people or institutions disrespect, discredit, or undermine who we are (or what we are trying to do.)

- **Pride** is taking pleasure or finding joy in one's achievements, possessions, or character. Pride can feel like self-esteem, but it contains the seeds of arrogance—a hard, brittle humorlessness—that interferes with our ability to connect empathetically with others. People and situations that threaten our pride appear to compromise or diminish the way we want others to see us.

- **Ambition** includes the desire for reward, recognition, or validation. Ambitions can be long term, such as dreams and goals for our future (jobs, finances, relationships), but they can also be short term desires or wishes (wanting to be respected or included in conversations, events, and friendships). Anything that reduces the chances that we will get what we want is a threat to our ambition.

- **Finances** mean our economic base: our bank accounts. Much that we depend on for our stability, including hopes for future opportunities, may be tied up with our sources of income.

- **Security** involves anything we need—or think we need—for health and safety, such as food, clothing, home, job, and transportation. For some of us, the possibility of any change initially felt like a challenge to our security!

- **Sexual or intimacy needs** include relationships of trust and mutuality that enable us to care for ourselves and others at a physical, emotional, and (for some) spiritual level. Whether or not we are able to recognize it before recovery, part of being human involves the need for physical connection and intimate touch. Threats in this area can include attitudinal problems, unreasonable expectations, health issues, lack of trust, and things that lead to and include infidelity.

- **Family and social relationships** cover connections with members of our current families, families of origin, friendships, and coworkers—on the job, in the community, and in organizations and institutions. Threats to such relationships can include issues with integrity and trust (as with sexual relationships), but may involve external factors, such as institutional or cultural bias, societal expectations or prejudice, and slander.

If we feel **any other emotions** in addition to resentment when we review the sources and reasons columns, we list them.

At this point, we stop and review our worksheet so far. It should be obvious that there is quite a lot going on with us! Our most important relationships are usually quite messy, and while other people involved are not necessarily blameless, we must keep in mind that the inventory is ours—not anyone else's. We need to stay focused on our own thoughts and behavior. Anything that interferes with our ability to see our issues clearly leaves us vulnerable to the familiar comfort of irrational, old ways of thinking and behaving. We have to be rid of resentment or risk backsliding!

4. Next, we brainstorm for the fourth column, **My Error/My Part,** in which we consider each instance where something we care about has been put at risk and reflect on whether *we ourselves might have contributed* to the situation in some way. We have to find out where our thinking left us vulnerable. In most cases, we discover that we had been *selfish, self-seeking, dishonest,* or *afraid.* We did the wrong things, because self-focused thinking prevented us from understanding—and then fear prevented us from doing—the right things, even when we objectively knew what we should do. We suffered as a result, sometimes a great deal. Many times, we found we had relied on other people, institutions, or principles to solve our problems, to validate us, or to reward us in some way. We had expectations that were neither realistic nor reasonable.

Before listing our errors, however, we find it useful to consider the idea that the other people involved are quite likely to have been suffering, too. For each person against whom we have resentment, and for each reason we have resentment, *we think about the suffering of the other person involved.* As the AA text states:

The Resentment Prayer

We asked God to help us show each person, in each situation the same tolerance, pity, and patience we would cheerfully grant a sick friend. When a person offended, we said to ourselves, "This is a sick man. How can I be helpful to him? God save me from being angry. Thy will be done." [36]

---

[36] *Alcoholics Anonymous.* (2001) New York, NY: AA World Services, Inc., 67.

Now that we have considered the suffering of others involved in each reason for resentment, we can fill out the fourth column, My Error/My Part. We resolutely consider where we had been at fault, disregarding the other person's errors altogether. Exactly how had *we* been selfish, self-seeking, dishonest, and/or afraid? What, exactly, prevented *us* from doing the right things?

Common Errors to Consider

- **Self-seeking** behavior is when we act out in ways that draw attention to ourselves or to gain advantage over others. It is always selfish! It can be as subtle as saying to someone, "I look fat" when we are looking for them to say that we *don't* (because fat is supposed to be a bad thing). In most cases we are seeking comfort, validation, and reassurance that we exist and are noteworthy or remarkable in some way.

- **Selfishness** is being concerned with our needs while ignoring the needs of others. Being inconsiderate of others is always selfish, but not necessarily self-seeking. Thinking we know how other people should live their lives reflects a selfish perspective, but is not necessarily self-seeking if we do not share or impose our opinions.

- **Dishonesty** comes in many forms including outright lying, dishonesty through omission, dishonesty with ourselves, cheating, infidelity, untrustworthiness, unreasonable expectations of self and others, arrogant and ungrateful attitudes, and blaming others for what ails us.

Anything that shields us from the truth about ourselves is a form of dishonesty.

- **Fear** is a complex emotion that can prevent us from seeing the truth about ourselves (and others) in the context of our lives as a whole. When we perceive a threat to any of the aspects of life that matter to us (the list above), we are likely to respond in ways that do not reflect the person we want to be. When we are afraid of losing what we already have, afraid of not getting what we want, afraid of not being good enough, or afraid of the unknown, we typically react from a place of selfish protectiveness rather than a place of empathy and compassion. This is self-limiting, for it prevents us from growth and from creating the relationships of trust we need to recover. (We discuss fear as it relates to eating disorders in more detail below.)

We do not necessarily limit our errors to self-seeking, selfishness, dishonesty, and fear. Please refer to Appendix D for examples.

5. Now we are ready to reflect on the idea, "We admitted our wrongs honestly and were willing to set these matters straight."[37] In each situation, we ask ourselves what helpful attitude we can now assume, what "kindly and tolerant view" of other people might now help us take appropriate action—instead of an inappropriate reaction—the next time we experience a similar feeling of resentment or anger. We write all this down in the fifth column, **Resolution.** Please

[37] Ibid., 67.

note that we are not yet planning for, or making, amends. Instead, we are using our new frame of reference to define a way of looking at each situation that takes away the pain and power to hurt us.

When done with our exploration of resentment, we can breathe a sigh of relief. We may not yet feel very different, but we know we are making progress. Now we tackle each of the remaining topics, first brainstorming on a separate page of paper, and then, using the same pattern we used for resentments, completing our "searching and fearless moral inventory" worksheets.

Remaining Inventory Topics:

- **Fear:** We list things that frightened or still frighten us. We consider death, illness, insanity, abandonment, loneliness, aging, the unknown, losing what we have, not getting what we want, financial insecurity, body image, sex and intimacy, not being good enough, and fear for others' safety and security.

- **Self-pity**: We identify reasons we felt or feel sorry for ourselves.

- **Shame**: We name things for which we felt or feel ashamed, even though we are not responsible for them. We include situations where we were bullied or abused, and anything for which we feel embarrassment (but which we did not cause), such as childhood poverty, basic personality (i.e. introverted/extroverted), gender, race, ethnicity, sexual orientation, and other peoples' issues.

- **Guilt or harms done:** We are explicit about wrongs we had done or are doing to others. We include lies, cheating (including infidelity), manipulation for recognition or reward, theft (including non-payment of taxes), property damage, and any emotional or physical damage done to others.

- **Confusion:** We identify situations where we felt or feel abandoned or bewildered.

- **Frustration**: We list things that made or make us angry, even if we have no resentment in connection to them.

- **Despair**: We outline reasons for hopelessness, past and present.

Exploring Fear

One emotion that we examine thoroughly is fear, because it features so prominently in our lives. We ask ourselves what fundamental issues give rise to not only specific fears, but also our pervasive anxiety. The AA text suggests that we were afraid because self-reliance failed us,[38] and indeed, many fears seemed to stem from our lack of control. We cannot control whether we get old or sick, even though we can influence things a bit. We cannot control whether people like us or leave us, even though our attitudes and actions may influence these outcomes. Even when we are in complete control, or think we are in control, we may still be afraid, because we have not always been able to do what we know we need to do.

[38] Ibid., 68.

All of us—whether we suffered from orthorexia, anorexia, bulimia, compulsive overeating, BED, OSFED, or other disorders—found balance and moderation with food challenging. Most of us were afraid of gaining (or losing) weight. Our thoughts tended to go back to old patterns whenever we were anxious. For some of us, even the *idea* of recovery was scary; what a cycle of misery that created!

Learning to listen to and trust our bodies takes time and patience. It is easy to second-guess decisions regarding food, and hard to let things go by trusting in the bigger picture. Mindful eating is a goal for many, yet others find the more they focus on food the more obsessive a concern it becomes. It may be helpful to know that everyone's weight fluctuates within a relatively narrow range over the course of a month or a year, varying with hormonal cycles and seasons. This applies to men as well as women. Other factors may also play a part; we try not to worry too much about it. We reassure ourselves that we *can* make conscious decisions and then make an effort to be aware when "hunger" pangs signify emotional needs. Our connection to God, our spiritual connection, or our focus on serving a greater purpose may require more attention. Perhaps we are neglecting sleep or need to pay attention to a significant other. Perhaps we are facing a fear that we have not yet given ourselves time to consciously address.

We think of the healthy example we want to set for other people in our lives and do our best to avoid modeling behaviors that are rigid, restrictive, or excessive. We make a conscious effort to remind ourselves that what is most loveable and precious about us has nothing to do with our body size. No one who truly loves us is going to care how big or small we are unless we are hurting our health. People who love us certainly are going to care if we are healthy, but we do not want anyone to worry about whether we are taking proper care of ourselves. That is our job, no one else's. We want to be sure we have enough energy, focus, and balance to do what needs to be done every day. If we focus on how we can be of service, we can let go of fear, let go of the past, and trust that we will be safe.

Many of us were afraid of our bodies. We thought of them as entities separate from our minds, when in reality our minds and bodies are integrated and inseparable. We struggled to control our impulses. We imagined that our bodies had needs—primal, instinctual needs—that were impossible to manage. Some of us were afraid of the intimacy of sex; others were frightened at the intensity and/or impropriety of our sexual urges. Awkwardly, some of us were all the above. Here we must remind ourselves that we are fundamentally no different than anyone else. Sexual release and physical intimacy are important components of human experience, yet few of us have an uncomplicated history when it comes to sex. In working Step Four, just as we consciously work to define a sane and reasonable response to other aspects of life, we define an ideal for our sexual conduct that respects the power and importance of sex while enabling us to care for ourselves and others in a safe and authentic way. In full recovery, living out our ideal is a source of great joy and satisfaction.

As with food and sex, physical exercise was another area where many of us went to extremes, either through avoidance or by overdoing it to the point of damaging our bodies and our relationships with others. In recovery, we need to be ever mindful of balance and moderation. We think it best to follow rational guidelines. Medical authorities suggest that about an hour of mixed activity every day is healthy.[39] Walking is perfectly good exercise; gardening and household chores count. Aerobic exercise is important for optimal health, but we should be cautious about overdoing it: consultation with a doctor is recommended. Rigidity and fear around anything, including exercise, generally signal a weak connection with our Higher Power or higher purpose. If you are focused on service to others, however, you will probably be too busy to overdo it with exercise!

Most of us were frightened that we would be even more miserable, anxious, and unhappy if we stopped engaging in all forms of our eating disorders. Such self-concerned fears kept us stuck in old patterns for a long time. But when we become willing to face our fears so we can recover, we start to see that *a focus on food is only a distraction*.

Though at first we were frustrated and afraid that letting go of control might mean we would suffer from even worse body image issues, we had to learn to stop "playing" with our food and body weight. Food is nutrition and energy; our bodies let us know what they need. If we eat more than we need, we will be uncomfortable, but we will not be hungry again for a long time. If we skip a meal because something distracts us, we will eat more—perhaps more than usual—at the next meal. But overeating or undereating on a regular basis are red flags that we are not taking care of basics, or are ignoring something that needs to be addressed.

If we are to work the Steps and walk free, we have to establish trust with our Higher Power or higher purpose, so we can be present for the things that matter in a larger context. The specific details of what we eat will balance out if we are *making an earnest effort to eat for the purpose of*

[39]   Centers for Disease Control and Prevention. (2008) Physical Activity Guidelines for Americans. Retrieved from *http://www.cdc.gov/physicalactivity/ resources/recommendations.html*

building our capacity to be useful. We eat healthy food when we can; and, when we do not, we recognize that our bodies may need things our minds may not fully appreciate—and let it go. We ask God or we turn to our Higher Power or higher purpose for help in keeping our thoughts on what we can do to be of useful service.

If we trust in our Higher Power or higher purpose and we are doing everything we can to set aside our fears and do what we think is the right thing, *we will have to trust that the outcome will be okay*—even if it terrifies us or feels wrong at times. When we are working to make life better for others, we need not worry about ourselves as much, provided we are taking care of basics. At the most rudimentary level, *taking care of basics means: If hungry, eat. If angry, find a safe outlet. If lonely, reach out. If tired, sleep. If ashamed, talk about it.* We learn to be accountable to ourselves and to others because this restores our integrity and objectivity. We need these to break free of our old patterns. We take care of ourselves so we can move beyond our immediate concerns to things that matter in the long run. As we gradually come to rely on something greater than ourselves to bring peace and perspective, we are able to eat when hungry and stop when moderately full. We can find peace with food. We can enjoy it and we can leave it alone when we are not hungry. Our bodies will not punish us; they will be restored to health and balance.

When considering the errors in our thinking with respect to all forms of fear, we identify attempts to control what is not ours to control. We list where we have allowed our thoughts and actions to be ruled by fear when we knew we should have done something else instead. Relying on the perspective now provided by our Higher Power or higher purpose, we remember that *our fears exist for a good reason: to help us focus our attention on what really matters.* In each situation where we listed a fear, we ask ourselves what a person of integrity and dignity would do if they found the courage to act despite their fear. The AA "Big Book" directs us to apply the fear prayer: "We ask Him to remove our fear and direct our attention to what He would have us be."[40] In each case, we make a conscious decision whether to set aside our fear or make use of it in some way to initiate needed changes. We list what we now think we should do in response to each provocation in the Resolution column.

In a similar fashion, we go back through our lives, covering (at minimum) the top ten trouble spots in all categories.

When we get to "guilt or harms done," we review our brainstorming list with someone who has more experience with the Twelve Steps to ensure our perspective and our resolutions are honest and appropriate.

Exploring Sexual Conduct

Specifically in the area of harms done, we consider whether we have adequately addressed our sexual conduct. Have we used sex to manipulate someone into paying for a meal or for our room and board? Have we sought to obtain validation for ourselves through sex or allowed people to think we loved them when we did not? If so, we now add the people affected to the "harms done" table. In the fourth column, My Error/My Part, we list selfishness, dishonesty, and inconsiderate attitudes and behavior. We list where we created jealousy, suspicion, and bitterness. In the fifth col-

---

[40] *Alcoholics Anonymous.* (2001) New York, NY: AA World Services, Inc., 68.

umn, Resolution, we list what we now think we ought to have done instead of what we did, and what we will want to do in the future. As the AA "Big Book" notes, "...we tried to shape a sane and sound ideal for our future sex life."[41] We keep in mind that our aim is to use our sexual power in an authentic and meaningful way. Again, as with resentments, we are not yet planning for or making amends. We are simply using our new frame of reference to define an approach that we can live with in peace and dignity. In full recovery, we find we can share a finer intimacy than ever.[42]

Example Resolutions

- *For a resentment:* Use my Higher Power to help me find the courage to do the right thing (be specific), instead of letting fear and anger stop me from doing what I know is right.

- *For a fear:* Understand that my fear of gaining weight is normal for someone recovering from an eating disorder. Trust that my body will be restored to health and balance if I take care of basics (eat when hungry and stop when moderately full) and resolutely turn my thoughts to how I can be of service to God or the greater good.

- *For a shame:* Work on using my voice and realize that I am not here to make everyone happy. I am here to become the authentic person I believe I was meant to be, with grace and dignity.

[41] Ibid., 69.
[42] Ibid., 134.

- *For a guilt:* Quit setting expectations for other people and be grateful for what I myself can do. Search for, recognize, and appreciate the good in everyone. Seek ways to be of service, either to the person I hurt or to people similarly situated.

- *For a despair:* Continue doing the work required by the Steps and rely more on God or my Higher Power/higher purpose to provide perspective, so I do not fall back into old behaviors that used to make me untrustworthy.

Feelings Serve a Purpose

Once done with all eight topics, we look over the completed pages. We carefully consider how our reactions to life situations have put us in positions where we felt resentment, fear, self-pity, shame, guilt, confusion, frustration, and despair. Writing about these has not made us immune to these emotions, but by now we have a starting point to develop some confidence that we need not actively seek escape from our emotions in the future. Our efforts so far have shown us that avoiding our feelings holds no true relief, no real joy, and serves no good purpose. *We begin to build trust in our capacity to handle our feelings by relying on our God, our Higher Power, or our higher purpose instead of our eating disorders to see us through situations of emotional disturbance.*

We remember that recovery takes time: it is a process, not an event. Until we have built up a solid and durable habit of reliance on a Power or purpose greater than ourselves to provide peace and perspective, we are quite likely to resort to using our eating disorders when upset. Yet, we have already begun to see that a different perspective—one that requires us to take care of our basic needs so we can turn our attention to what really matters—has started to provide the relief we were seeking all along.

Upon completing our 4th Step inventory, others assure us we will still experience many of the same unpleasant emotional responses as before. Yet, there is a real difference: our work so far has shown us a coherent set of resolutions to situations that cause us pain. When we apply these solutions consistently, relying on our God, Higher Power, or higher purpose to provide the peace, perspective, and power that was formerly missing from our daily lives, *we find we can now turn even heavy emotions to good purpose—regardless of the circumstances*. We soon see that our emotional responses to life are not as extreme and overwhelming as before. The key lies in resolutely putting first things first, taking care of basics, and then turning our thoughts to how we can be useful.

By putting service into a position of central importance, we not only find relief from our neediness and suffering, we discover we can use our emotions to a good end. Rather than running from our feelings, we see that they exist to ensure we take care of basics and help us empathize with the plight of others. Our emotions now provide the fuel we need to make meaningful changes in our lives. If hungry, angry, lonely, or tired, we deal with these first, so we can turn our attention back to service.

As we do so, we see how our emotions actually motivate us to be better people. When we feel sad, we can focus on what would bring joy to others. When we feel pain, we can now address personal and societal issues directly. We can reflect and be grateful that we are now able to experience depth of feeling and attachment without having to numb ourselves. Our ability to experience pain without running from it becomes a strength that can bring hope to others who struggle as we once did. We can share our experience, strength, and joy with others. Sometimes we find it amazing that we can now just be present with others, rather than trying to solve everyone's problems. When we feel guilt, we find we can now admit and correct our mistakes. When we feel overwhelmed, we find we can now stop whatever we are doing and prioritize according to what matters in the larger context provided by our Higher Power or higher purpose.

If you have made it this far and completed a personal inventory of the sort we describe, you are well on your way to a solid and sustainable recovery! Please do not stop now. Steps Five through Nine provide direction on just how we go about getting out of our own way, so we can have a life we truly love and enjoy in peace and freedom.

Chapter 6

INTO ACTION (STEPS 5—11)

*W*hile Steps One through Four challenged our think-ing and orientation to life, Steps Five through Nine challenge our discipline and willingness to live as we agreed we would in Step Three. Steps Ten and Eleven then pro-vide us with practices through which we continue to grow stronger and more resilient in our recovery.

Step Five: *Admitted to God, to ourselves, and to another hu-man being the exact nature of our wrongs.*

In the first four Steps, we engaged in reflection and did our best to align our thinking with ideas that hold the promise of a new purpose, freedom, and happiness. With Step Five, we embark on the second phase of our journey: we begin to demonstrate whether those reflections have truly signaled the start of what Dr. Carl Jung described as the "huge emotional displacements and rearrangements" necessary for full recovery. Step Five is the first true "ac-tion" step.

As we put into practice our new insights and resolu-tions, we create and solidify new patterns of thought and behavior. Our old habit was to turn to our eating disorders for comfort and release. Our new habit is to turn to the comfort and security of a new perspective, which we achieve through continuous practice. *Relying on the idea of our God, Higher Power, or higher purpose regularly in our day-to-day lives builds resilience.* Eventually, even in times of crisis when we would normally have turned to our eating disorders, we will be able to rely on something else—something more meaningful—to carry us through.

Step Five asks us to be accountable. We need to admit the truth of our dysfunctional thinking and behaviors not only to ourselves, but also to others who can be objective and help us understand anything we might have missed in our Step Four inventory.

Rarely do we find it helpful to focus on what the people we identified in our 4th Step list did, or are still doing. Even in the most extreme situations, including physical and emotional abandonment and/or abuse, there is nothing we can do that will change what happened in the past. We need to learn from our experiences, but ruminating on what we may feel was a raw deal does no good; little recovery can be found in reflecting on the errors of others. Nor will we have much success working the Twelve Steps unless we are physically safe, whether the current threat is from others or ourselves. The first order of business may be to take advantage of professional help or personal support, so we can find enough safety and stability to work the Steps. We think a note of caution is warranted here, for there will always be some source of turmoil in our lives. Once we are physically safe and stable enough to work on our recovery, we should not delay in picking up and moving forward with the Steps.

Our job in Step Five is to focus on what we thought, said, and did that put us in situations where we were vulnerable, threatened, and hurt. Did we lie to ourselves or others? Did we cheat people of our time and attention? Did we complain (if only to ourselves perhaps) about how unfairly we were treated without taking action to resolve the problems? Did we nurse grudges against people who were also struggling to make sense of life? Did we feel victimized by our social "standing," family situations, or prior actions? Did we blame society for our reactions to what happened to us? Did we hold institutions liable for our attitudes and outlook on life?

In general, we found we relied quite heavily on other people—sometimes parents, but also siblings, other relatives, life partners, friends, and occasionally our own children—to take care of our most basic physical and/or emotional needs, when we should have been able to do that ourselves. One goal of Step Five is to expose the thinking that lay behind our unhealthy dependence on others, as well as any thinking and behavior that was objectively wrong.

Admitting Errors and Accepting Feedback:

- **Builds objectivity:** *Step Five asks us to express what we were thinking and doing in an objective way,* reinforcing the habit of working on solutions instead of getting caught up in the problem. The more we practice taking an objective view of ourselves, the easier it will become, and the better we will be at this vital activity.

- **Holds us accountable:** *Step Five asks us to expose and admit the errors in our thinking and behavior.* Although we were surely hurt by other people's neglect, attitudes, and actions over the course of our lives, Step Five focuses only on what was wrong with how *we* responded to life situations and how *we* could have responded differently. Thinking of ourselves as victims is not helpful, even if we have been victimized in the past. The power of our recovery lies not in our "victimhood," but in our ability to think and act as people of conscience and courage—regardless of circumstances. As adults, we are responsible and accountable only for our own thoughts and actions. As long as we refuse to admit the whole truth about what we thought and did, we run the risk of "staying as sick as our secrets." Accountability with a safe person exposes our errors and gives us a much better chance of addressing them consciously and deliberately.

- **Provides outside perspective:** *Step Five asks us not only to admit our wrongs, but also requires us to own up to them with one or more people who can challenge our current thinking.* Most likely, we are unable to be completely objective about what exactly is going on in our lives. Talking openly with at least one other person gives them the opportunity to point out things that we might have overlooked, either consciously or unconsciously. Many of us found our sponsors and confidants completely "nailed" things we had not recognized at all that later turned out to be our biggest impediments. Opening ourselves up to feedback gives us a better chance of fully identifying—and steering clear of—the black holes in our thinking that led us into trouble in the past.

- **Demonstrates willingness:** *Step Five asks us to open ourselves up to feedback from others* in order to demonstrate—to ourselves and to others—that:

- We are no longer willing to stay as sick as our secrets

- We are willing to let go of the idea that we, and our experiences, are so unique that others cannot appreciate or empathize with them

- We are willing to trust at least one other person with the truth about ourselves

- We are willing to be objective

- We are willing to take responsibility for our recovery

- We are willing to change

In our experience, taking Step Five is essential for recovery.

Preparation for Step Five

Finding the right person, audience, or "recipient" with whom to share our 5th Step is important. Parents, spouses, and children might be unsuitable, because they are emotionally engaged with us and may lack the needed objectivity. They might also be hurt by what we have to say. Good candidates include other members of EDA who have worked the Steps, members of other Twelve-Step programs who have worked the Steps, therapists, pastors, or friends who have sufficient strength and wisdom to be placed into such a position of trust. It is also important that the person we ask be someone who will keep our sharing confidential.

Before asking someone to hear our 5th Step, we first recognize that we are asking a rather big favor as the time and attention required for such a conversation is substantial. The person we plan to ask might be busy and need to make room for us on their calendar. We should be prepared to wait a bit (though preferably not more than a week or two, because we need to keep up our momentum with the next Steps). Also, not everyone is likely to be willing or able to meet with us for this type of conversation, so we make a short list of people who meet the qualifications. Then, if we are turned down, we are prepared to take this news as calmly as possible and ask someone else on our list.

When ready to share, we carefully review the first three Steps. Perhaps we feel less sure now than we did when we took them! If so, we acknowledge that we are probably a bit frightened, and we resolve to mention this to our 5th Step recipient. *We want to hold nothing back*, even though our pride is sure to be hurt by our admissions. We ask ourselves if we are now willing to take action that will bring more lasting relief from the troublesome thoughts and behaviors we experienced in our eating disorders. We bring our written 4th Step with us, along with additional paper for taking notes. Our recipient will probably take notes as well. We sit down together in a place where we are not likely to experience distractions, putting aside anything that might prevent us from focusing on the task at hand. We usually say something like the following:

To your 5th Step recipient:

I want to thank you for meeting with me today. I recognize that you are sacrificing time and energy that might otherwise have been spent with your family, on your vocation, or on something you deeply enjoy in order to help me. I am very grateful for your support.

As we have discussed, I am working on a program

through which I hope to recover from an eating disorder. Rather than using it to distance myself from unwelcome thoughts and feelings, I must now face them and deal with them directly.

In the past, feelings of fear, resentment, self-pity, shame, guilt, confusion, frustration, and despair regularly over-whelmed me and rendered me unable to work or focus ef-fectively without resorting to my eating disorder. So, to fully recover, I have to change the way I think and respond. By talking with you today, I hope to expose the errors in my thinking and behavior and get your objective feedback, not only on what my issues were and are, but also on how I plan to act when the same thoughts and feelings crop up again.

I need to make clear to you that my job today is to focus entirely on what I myself thought and did, rather than on what others said or did to me. If I stray from that goal, I ask you to please hold me accountable and pull me back.

I have with me a set of written pages that represent my best effort at a searching and fearless moral inventory of myself. My goal today is to thoroughly review this material with you. I ask that you point out any patterns or ideas that I may have missed, either as we go along or at the end—whichever feels more comfortable to you. I hope you do not mind if I take notes?

I am ready to begin when you are.

Taking Step Five

We wait for our audience to signal they are ready. Then, we "pocket our pride and go to it,"[1] sharing our written 4th Step notes in detail. Though it is sure to be embarrassing at times, we do not skip or avoid discussing anything we

---

[1] *Alcoholics Anonymous.* (2001) New York, NY: AA World Services, Inc., 75.

have written or anything new that comes up in the course of our review. If we are completely honest and transparent with our audience, there will be moments of connection and recognition, even if our 5th Step recipient has no experience whatsoever with eating disorders. We trust that human beings have similar thoughts and feelings regardless of the specifics of their life circumstances. No matter how alone we may have felt, those in whom we place our trust and confidence are sure to have thought and felt the same way at various points in their lives.

When done, we explicitly ask our 5th Step recipient if we have missed anything, or if anything is weighing on them that they would like to say. If they have comments, we take notes, because we are likely to be somewhat exhausted and want to be sure to remember everything! Finally, we heartily thank our 5th Step recipient for their invaluable help and support.

Upon returning home, we take a quiet hour to reflect upon our experiences.[2] During this reflection, we review our work on Steps One through Four. Have we left anything out? Do we feel like we have made a solid beginning? Many of us experience strong emotions during and immediately after taking this Step. We allow ourselves to feel whatever comes up for us at this time. Perhaps we are still scared because we want to act out, or we want to act out because we are scared of the work ahead. Maybe we had expectations of our 5th Step that were not satisfied. Sometimes we are overwhelmed or disappointed by what we experienced. *At this crucial juncture, it is important that we honor the truth of what we are feeling and do not fall back into old eating-disordered behaviors.*

---

[2] Ibid., 75.

While we cannot expect that our lives will now be magically different (for there is much work left to do), we can certainly be happy that we have been able to complete such a big chunk of this challenging process. We have demonstrated our sincerity and willingness to make enormous changes in our thinking and behavior in order to turn our former misery to some good purpose. We give ourselves credit for this and allow the feeling of accomplishment to sink in.

After an hour's reflection, we take pen to paper again for just a few minutes to write down everything for which we are grateful. If we have developed a relationship with God, we give thanks from the bottom of our hearts that we know Him better.[3] If we have connected with a Higher Power or higher purpose, we express our deep appreciation for the perspective and power these can bring into our lives. We might express gratitude for the patience of the person who heard our 5th Step, for new hope and new opportunities, or we might simply give thanks for being alive. Writing this list is crucial whether we feel grateful or not; we have certainly gone through an emotionally draining experience. At moments like this, putting key tools of recovery into practice is essential. We are at our most vulnerable when overwhelmed by emotions we haven't fully processed. Writing even a short gratitude list demonstrates that no matter what we are feeling, we can start to trust our growing internal strength and commitment to recovery.

If you got through your 5th Step—including the hour of reflection and the gratitude list—congratulations are in order: you are ready to move on to Step Six!

---

[3] Ibid.

Step Six: *Were entirely ready to have God remove all these defects of character.*

After taking Step Five, we are bound to experience shifts in our thoughts, feelings, and perceptions of the world. This could manifest as a new sense of connectedness to humanity, or increased confidence in our ability to be objective about our old ways of thinking and behaving. We may feel delighted, happy with our place in a world where we can engage in ways that feel exciting and new. On the other hand, we might think our changes have not been deep enough, forcing us to question ourselves and our ability to continue. Perhaps we are disappointed, because we secretly hoped that after our 5th Step we could go about in perfect peace and ease without having negative emotions ever again. *Whatever we are feeling, we honor it,* trusting that we are not alone in our experience.

Many of us were horrified at the idea that we must go back and repeat something like a 4th Step with every new negative thought and feeling we encounter. But challenges like these are to be expected as we make our way towards a full recovery. Our experience has been that by the time we get to Step Ten, where we deliberately address how we think and feel on a daily basis, *the process will be far easier and so beneficial that we look forward to it.* For now, we can be content to have our feelings and trust that we will recover if we act based on reliance on our God, Higher Power, or higher purpose, rather than reacting to our emotional states as if they were of central importance. We take care of basics and continue to turn our attention to how we can be useful in the here and now.

In Step Six, we again consider what happened every time we put ourselves, and our emotional states, in a position of central importance in our lives. Somewhat ironically, we were actually weakened and diminished, since putting ourselves at the center meant we lost sight of the broader context in which our lives made sense. It also meant we were vulnerable to crippling levels of resentment, fear, self-pity, shame, guilt, confusion, frustration, and despair. These defects of character—all stemming from self-centeredness—were truly paralyzing, keeping us in a state of constant pain and misery. Focused solely on our own suffering, we were unable to be of much service to others.

When we took Step Three, we agreed to turn our will and our lives—our thoughts and actions—over to our God, a Higher Power, or service to the greater good. But our self-centered pain and fear held us back; many of our defects were still with us. This felt unsettling—even depressing—for most of us. What were we to do about these issues? That is what Steps Six and Seven are all about. In Step Six, we consider *whether we are entirely willing to face and be rid of everything that has been holding us back.*

At this point, although still afraid of change, we were pretty thoroughly fed up with our old patterns of thinking that kept us in a state of emotional turmoil. We could see how they hurt us, hurt those who loved us, prevented us from doing the right things, and kept us stuck doing the wrong things. We recalled how desperately miserable we were when we defied our natural instinct for self-preservation by acting out, over and over again, through our eating disorders. We knew we had to be rid of the defects of character that fueled these behaviors, but we were not yet sure how to go about it.

The first thing we needed to do was to recognize that our natural desire for safety, security, validation, and connection to others sometimes led us to take actions that, in retrospect, completely undermined the very objectives we sought. To find validation, we may have been boastful or manipulative, yet we can think of no example where self-aggrandizement or manipulation obtained the desired result without an *even more* undesirable effect on our character. To find security, we may have greedily taken credit for things not our due, stolen actual money or property, or lustfully engaged in sordid affairs—heedless of the truth that doing so left us far more insecure and untrustworthy than ever. To establish what felt like safety, we may have angrily demanded that everyone honor "boundaries" that had little to do with the basic respect with which all should be treated, only to find little lasting peace or freedom through distancing—even alienating—friends and family. Angry with ourselves as well as others, we steadfastly refused to allow ourselves to consider changes that would have enabled us to recover far sooner.

As we struggled to form ideals we hoped to attain, we may have found ourselves enviously comparing our qualities, attainments, and possessions unfavorably with those of others, dimly aware that such thinking leads nowhere healthy. Most of us spent years paralyzed by fear of change, somewhat lazily repeating old patterns because they were easier than seriously contemplating alternatives and making changes. We may have dismissed ideas about what we could do to effect real changes in our lives because they just seemed too hard. Sometimes we didn't take action because we felt deeply inferior to those around us, as if the processes that worked for others would somehow not work for us; we felt as if we were broken in a completely novel and unfixable way. Conversely, we may have looked askance at the recovery of others, dismissive of helpful ideas because we felt ourselves a little—or perhaps a lot—superior to those who would have offered us a hand or a shoulder.

We need to carefully consider the criteria by which we determined that we were "fine" in the past. By the time we reach Step Six, we realize that quite a lot of what we thought and did before embarking on recovery was actually problematic, yet many of us still clung to old ideas because we deemed them "safe," or less than serious. Some *troublesome character traits* may need to be re-considered, because they are not "safe" at all:

- *Pride,* because it creates barriers to authenticity and connection with others.

- *Procrastination and other forms of laziness* (including our sometimes life-long excuses for failing to take action we know is good and right), because inaction is the fastest way back to old patterns.

- *Self-righteous indignation,* because it leads to resentment and self-pity.

- *All-or-nothing thinking,* because it limits our options and forces us to cram our messy realities into rigid compartments that have little to do with life as we need to understand it to be effective.

- *Lust,* because fantasizing about and desiring attention for ourselves leads away from true love that is focused on care for other human beings. Instead, it leads to feelings of unrequited longing, to situations where we are likely to break the trust others have in us, to actions that hurt our integrity, or to some combination of the above.

- *Focusing on our own "needs" that are not universal, basic human needs*, because these only hinder our recovery. Examples include: requiring special foods when not medically necessary, demanding specific attitudes and behaviors from other people as a prerequisite for our recovery, and privileging our ambition for recognition and reward over other goals.

- *Gossip*, because it violates relationships of trust, hurts others, and lengthens the list of things for which we will later need to make amends.

Though this is not a comprehensive list, it may indeed feel overwhelming. Please understand that the purpose of Step Six is not to provide ourselves with excuses for beating ourselves up, but to ensure that we do not fall prey to the same kind of thinking that caused our troubles in the first place.

We all had difficulty giving up some of our old ideas, even when we understood how problematic they were. But resistance to change need not be a long-term impediment to recovery, so long as we abandon ourselves completely to the idea that we will do everything in our power to recover from the crippling self-centeredness that fueled our defects, understanding that these will not be removed from us without our own action.

This is the point where we move on to Step Seven.

Step Seven: *Humbly asked God to remove our shortcomings.*

In Step Six, we realized that many of the character defects that gave rise to our eating disorders can persist long after we become willing to let them go. It is humbling to recognize that we can no more *will ourselves* to be free of self-centeredness—or of the vulnerability to pain and misery that it causes—than we can *will ourselves* to be free of our eating disorders. Once we can honestly admit that we cannot fix our fundamental issues by focusing on ourselves, we are ready to work Step Seven.

Before taking this Step, we will want to consider what humility really means. When we first worked the Steps, many of us mistakenly thought of humility as something more closely aligned with humiliation than with dignity, peace, and power. We may have found the idea distasteful, even distressing. Our lives up to this point had been all about striving: achieving something for ourselves; vying for validation, attention, and love; earning respect and reward.

Most of us believed that the purpose of life was tied up with personal achievement. If we managed well and worked hard, we thought we could or would end up with the man or woman of our dreams, an excellent education, a great career, a solid marriage, properly-reared children, a performing financial portfolio, an attractive home, a reputation for wisdom and humor—the list of attainments we sought was boundless! Some of us craved Olympic Gold, a Nobel Prize, a Pulitzer, or an Oscar. Still others were content to embody the ideal of the starving artist, our unappreciated genius to be recognized only after we shuffled off this mortal coil. We thought altruistic service, generosity, and charity were surely important and quite necessary if we were to be seen as a worthy sort of person. But our generosity was limited by competing selfish desires: we could either be stingy with our time and resources because we thought we needed these for ourselves, or we could satisfy our desire for recognition by working for something mainly because we thought that it would make us look good. Before embarking on our journey in recovery, very few among us thought anonymous and selfless service would ever be an important and meaningful use of our time. Yet, while our accomplishments made us proud, they did not bring us lasting peace or joy.

In recovery, we begin to realize we had missed an extremely important point: *one cannot build a meaningful life on the basis of self-satisfaction alone.* Without depreciating material, physical, creative, or scientific achievement in any way, we know we made a mistake when we set goals in these areas for the sole reason that we wanted to accrue things for ourselves. This error, we think, is at the heart of our issues. So long as we believed self-serving goals and ideals to be worthwhile, we remained lost in the misery of our eating disorders, easily victimized and prone to resentment, frustration, and fear. We fled from ideas and activities that might have developed our character and enabled us to be more resilient. We could not form the critical relationships of trust and reliance that are necessary for recovery. We were unable to sustain anything like a reasonable perspective regarding ourselves, or the events in our lives. Ironically, we think of this as one of the positive outcomes of our eating disorders: they brought us to the humbling realization that many of our ideas and ideals—our core values—just did not work.

We think our problem was that we did not fully appreciate that all the accolades and rewards in the world would be empty and pointless without being linked to something more important and more durable than we are—a higher purpose or a Higher Power of our understanding. *The perspective that we exist (either because we were made that way, or because we have taken Step Three) to serve something outside ourselves now provides the foundation we need to respond consciously and deliberately to all that happens in our lives.*

It turns out that humility—having a modest view of our own importance relative to things that matter in the long run—freed us to experience life on an altogether different plane. With humility, we are not called upon to defend our ideas or positions. We are much less likely to offend or take offense. We can make useful contributions without drawing attention to ourselves. We can get our feelings hurt without needing to launch a counterattack. We need not rush about; there is plenty of time. We can be thoughtful and well-considered in our responses to life's provocations and opportunities, and thus we can be far more effective and influential than ever before. We now realize that our character, integrity, and purpose matter far more to our day-to-day happiness—and our relationships with others—than any achievement we could have imagined. We begin to appreciate humility as a necessary and vital frame of reference rather than some unpleasant condition to which we must be regularly reduced.

Those of us who were still in the habit of extreme thinking were troubled by these ideas. When we considered the humble service of Mother Teresa, we recoiled. How could we, as selfish and pre-occupied with our own issues as we have proven ourselves to be, now emulate her kind of selflessness? Surely we were to continue with those aspects of our lives that had been successful, weren't we? Let us reassure you: every experience, talent, capability, attitude, and action can be put to good purpose. We are not casting aside anything of value. We are never less than before, though we can hope we may become less arrogant, presumptuous, abrasive, and impulsive. The point is that we are able to leverage all that we are and all that we do to serve something bigger and better than ourselves. This all sounds grand and exciting—and it can be—but the process entails careful, deliberate, and humble work.

By this point, most of us had caught on to the idea that our eating disorders were actually symptoms of fundamental, underlying issues. But while we understood that our approach to life needed an overhaul, we were still unsure how we were to go about making changes that would last. We remembered that in Step Three we made a decision to turn our will and our lives over to the care of God as we understood God. We then recalled the difficulty and pain of facing our issues all at once when we took Steps Four and Five. When we imagined a life in which we miserably faced and eliminated all our outdated ideas, many of us rebelled. We wanted to find an easier, softer way.[4]

But there is good news. We don't need to "fix" ourselves; it doesn't work anyway! Apart from a few minutes each day spent on Step Ten, we don't waste time dwelling on issues that result from our self-centeredness, unless we are focused on how we can use them to some good purpose. Reflection is a useful tool, but rumination can lead us to lose sight of the bigger picture. We recall that self-centered fear—loss of what we already have or hope to have—seems to be at the root of our defects. So, rather than continuing to focus on ourselves, our main concern now should be how we can get out of our own way, so we can turn our attention to what matters in the long run: service to the greater good, our God, Higher Power, or higher purpose.

This is exactly where our sponsors step in to help us identify *character-building activities* that open us up to new experiences. We find we can leverage the pain of our

---

[4] *Alcoholics Anonymous.* (2001) New York, NY: AA World Services, Inc., 58.

defects to good purpose, *replacing old patterns of thought and behavior with meaningful action.* If we were prideful, we can work to create capabilities in others. We can mentor young people, share our honest stories with other EDA members, and steadfastly avoid taking credit for good deeds. We find we can always credit someone else for our successes. If we were manipulative, we can have empathy for those who demand that others conform to their will, and we work to expose manipulation and dishonesty wherever we find it. If we were silent "victims," we work to find our voice, write gratitude lists, and find reasons to compliment those around us for work well done. If we were greedy for attention, fame, or fortune, we can share our time and resources with those less fortunate. If we were jealous spouses, we can encourage our partners to enjoy hobbies and pursuits that would have frustrated and frightened us before recovery. If we were lazy in our efforts to care for others, we carefully set new, reasonable goals at regular intervals to stretch our capacity little by little. These are but a few examples of how we may, through reliance on our Higher Power or higher purpose and on the guidance of others, develop strength where once there was weakness. We stress that these new character-building activities should not be taken on all at one time. We must work diligently and patiently, not obsessively. Counsel with a sponsor is advised, so that we neither do so much that we become overwhelmed nor do so little that we remain weak.

As we work on our Step Seven exercises, selfishness will start to diminish. We take care of ourselves so that we can better serve God and/or the greater good, and we discover that what we thought were our shortcomings either turn out to be our greatest assets, or they slowly weaken like a muscle that isn't exercised. We do not need to worry about our defects! We can let them go, and rely on our Higher Power or higher purpose to do the work of removing them while we work on strengthening our character.

Those among us who are spiritually inclined are encouraged to offer what has become known as the 7th Step Prayer:

The 7th Step Prayer

My Creator, I am now willing that you should have all of me, good and bad. I pray that you now remove from me every single defect of character that stands in the way of my usefulness to you and my fellows. Grant me strength, as I go out from here, to do your bidding. Amen.[5]

Others may use an **alternative statement** such as the following:

I recognize and accept that I have been living with many self-oriented concerns and issues that have held me back from cheerful service to the greater good. I now let go of worry about my shortcomings and I choose to focus instead on serving effectively and well. I trust that as I focus more on my service than on my issues, the shortcomings that stand in the way of my usefulness will diminish, and the authenticity, integrity, dedication, and skills that my service requires will grow stronger. My daily follow-through on my commitment to serve will become my strength.

We recommend you write down any form of this prayer or statement that feels right to you, so you can read it aloud daily and apply it throughout the day. This may feel awkward at first, but if your intention is true and authentic, it will inspire huge changes. You are now on a new

---

[5] Ibid., 76.

and stable footing, *solidifying your recovery by putting intentions into practice.*

We encourage you to move on to Step Eight as soon as possible. We have no doubt you will start to find a new delight in life (and some of the peace and freedom you long for) through the character-building actions that are part of your 7th Step. But you are still at high risk of returning to old patterns of thinking until you have worked *all* the Steps. Having gotten this far, you have already put a lot of thought and effort into your recovery. Now is the time to see things through to completion. We are confident you will never regret the time and effort.

Step Eight: *Made a list of all persons we had harmed and became willing to make amends to them all.*

As the AA text notes, "we already have a list of persons we have harmed and to whom we are willing to make amends. We made it when we took inventory."[6]

You may be a little apprehensive about starting this Step because you may still feel distressing emotions about the people you listed on your 4th Step. Please understand that such misgivings are quite normal. It is unlikely that your mind will become so trained to the new way of thinking that you will not harbor troublesome feelings ever again. But when they do come up, we put ourselves somewhere safe and consider the following question: "Do I want to continue to stay stuck in self-pity, resentment, and fear, or do I want to walk free of these encumbrances?" Hopefully, we have developed enough perspective to see that we actually have a choice!

[6] Ibid.

In Step Four we saw how our errors created and per-petuated hurtful situations. Now we need to find the cour-age to change what we think, possibly more extensively than we outlined in the Resolutions column on our Step Four inventory. In Steps Six and Seven we have been prac-ticing moving past our crippling emotions so we can take a new attitude when things come up in our daily life. Now we are being asked to consider *taking restorative action that addresses our errors of the past.*

We review our 4th Step inventory list one more time. It may not be perfect, but we leave it alone rather than trying to correct it. We have reviewed and gotten feedback when we gave our 5th Step, and now we need to move forward rather than belaboring work already completed. We will have additional opportunities to work on inventory items in Step Ten. Each day is a new beginning with a fresh set of opportunities to apply these principles.

The long form of EDA's Step Eight[7] says, "*We made a list of people we had treated badly, no matter how they treated us. We accepted responsibility for our part and made an effort to forgive them for their part.*"

Forgiveness brought us peace, yet perhaps we cannot forgive everything. Sometimes people have treated us (and others) in ways that are simply unconscionable. In such cases, we remember that we ourselves seemed helpless in the grip of our eating disorders. At times, we felt that we had no effective choice in what we thought and did. We were powerless in the grip of emotions and unable to man-age our thoughts and behavior. Now that we are asked to forgive people who hurt us, we consider that perhaps they,

---

[7] Reference Appendix A: "The Twelve Steps and Twelve Traditions of EDA" in this volume.

too, were swept away by tides of emotion and patterns of thought and behavior that they could not seem to control. We now know that we had to find a different context to get any kind of durable objectivity. This has not been an easy matter for many of us who were unsure if we could make this new perspective work for us in the long run. How difficult must it then be for others to change, when we find it so difficult ourselves? We remember that those who hurt us are as vulnerable as we are, though it may not always seem that way.

While forgiveness is critical to our own recovery, we feel it is important to point out that in cases where we were the object of, rather than the perpetrator of, serious injuries such as rape or battery, we are personally accountable for ensuring the situation is safe for everyone. In other words, if there is a present danger to others, we think it advisable to contact the proper authorities to ensure that the perpetrator is in custody or otherwise publicly tracked (if at all possible).

Making amends to people we have not forgiven may feel insincere, but doing so opens a door through which empathy and forgiveness can enter. All that is required is the recognition that other people suffer from thoughts that create pain and misery just like we do. When we feel empathy for the people on our list, even if we do not like their behavior, we may be ready to move on to Step Nine.

If willingness to make amends does not come easily, we suggest prayer. We pray for the health, success, and happiness of those to whom we need to make amends, even if it feels disingenuous at first. If we keep up this daily practice for a while, we may find we come to mean what we say.

Step Nine: *Made direct amends to such people wherever possible, except when to do so would injure them or others.*

The long form of EDA's Step Nine[8] suggests, *"After counsel with a sponsor, or an EDA (or other Twelve-Step group) member who has worked the Twelve Steps, we went to the people we had injured and admitted our fault and regret. Our statements were simple, sincere, and without blame. We set right the wrongs as best we could and expected nothing in return. Accountability set us free."*

Step Nine in the AA text[9] covers most types of situations in significant detail. As we go about making amends, we keep in mind the following points:

Keys to Step Nine

- We must be willing to go to any length to set right the wrongs we ourselves committed in thought, word (written or spoken), and deed.

- We should review our plan with someone who has perspective. It is altogether too easy to overlook needed action or blow things out of proportion. In cases where we behaved badly toward someone who criminally abused us, we advise talking with a trusted counselor about whether to inform proper authorities of the crimes, and then turning our attention to helping others who have been hurt as we were, rather than by making amends directly to the perpetrator. Our

---

[8] Reference Appendix A: "The Twelve Steps and Twelve Traditions of EDA" in this volume.
[9] *Alcoholics Anonymous.* (2001) New York, NY: AA World Services, Inc., 76-84.

goal is restitution for our own errors, but making amends to people who treated us criminally could be seen as justifying or condoning the crime. To repeat: we prioritize the safety of others (those who might be in danger from the same individual) over our personal need to set right our wrongs directly with the perpetrator. In such cases, we help others instead.

- We should also review our plans for restitution to those who might be unduly affected, especially where financial amends are indicated. We have no right to deprive our families of our time and money without their consent. We must make it clear, however, that setting right our wrongs is essential to our recovery. We must put a plan into action that enables us to make full restitution, however slowly.

- We must not take any kind of arrogant attitude when we approach people we have hurt. We do not discuss our new perspective, our success so far, or anything that might unduly irk—or further injure—anyone else. We briefly explain what we are trying to do and why, no matter how vulnerable this may make us feel. We state what we did and we apologize. *We make no mention whatsoever of anything the other person said or did.* We state what we would like to do to repair damages we caused. Although we cannot expect to get it, we ask forgiveness from the person we harmed. We ask if there is anything else that we can do to make amends and listen carefully to the response. We try to agree with any terms suggested, unless others must first be consulted. We thank the person for taking time to talk with us and we take our leave.

- We can have no expectations of the other people involved. Although usually the results are heartwarming and restorative of our trust in others, this may not always be the case. Our family members and spouses may not want us to approach other people with ideas about financial restitution until we have first made restitution to those at home. Some people to whom we wish to apologize may not accept our apologies or our amends. Others may not forgive us. It does not matter, so long as we have made every effort to do our part.

- We can have no expectations about how we ourselves will respond to the act of making amends. We are likely to feel vulnerable and exposed and can expect to experience rejection, remorse, and pain. We must not, however, shirk from our job now. We need to demonstrate to ourselves and to the world the sincerity of our stance. With Step Nine, we reestablish integrity and build a foundation for trust. Nothing does this so well as the humble admission of errors and follow-through on commitments to right the wrongs.

Once we have apologized and started making amends to those who are within our reach, we will indeed begin to experience the 9th Step Promises:

The 9ᵗʰ Step Promises

If we are painstaking about this phase of our development, we will know a new freedom and a new happiness.
We will not regret the past nor wish to shut the door on it.
We will comprehend the word serenity and we will know
peace. No matter how far down we have fallen, we will see
how our experience can benefit others. That feeling of uselessness and self-pity will disappear. We will lose interest in
selfish things and gain interest in our fellows. Self-seeking
will slip away. Our whole attitude and outlook upon life
will change. Fear of people and of economic insecurity will
leave us. We will intuitively know how to handle situations
which used to baffle us. We will see that our service to
God, our Higher Power, or the greater good has done for
us what seemed humanly impossible. Are these extravagant
promises? We think not. They are being fulfilled among
us—sometimes quickly, sometimes slowly. They will always materialize if we work for them.[10]

It may be important to point out that the 9ᵗʰ Step
Promises usually start to come to pass after we are halfway
through our 9ᵗʰ Step amends. Due to the toll of guilt and
shame, some people may not experience significant relief
until they have completed all possible amends.

The good news is that the hard work of establishing
our new foundation is mostly complete. Now we must
build upon it, for if we don't, we will be wasting both an
opportunity and the effort we have put in so far. The benefits, and all of the promises, come from *continuous reliance
on the foundation we have put in place*.

[10] *Alcoholics Anonymous.* (2001) New York, NY: AA World Services, Inc.,
83-84. Substituting "we have fallen" for a phrase that is inappropriate for the
current context, and substituting "service to God, our Higher Power, or the
greater good" in place of language that is less inclusive.

Steps One through Nine helped us deconstruct our old ideas that did not work, outline new ones that do, and establish a foundation of trust and integrity. Steps Ten through Twelve enable us to build the sort of life we really wanted and needed all along.

Step Ten: *Continued to take personal inventory and when we were wrong promptly admitted it.*

Nothing keeps us out of trouble and happily engaged as well as Steps Ten through Twelve. Step Ten involves an honest daily appraisal of our situation, including a firm resolve to address outstanding issues. Step Eleven includes a daily commitment to connect with and serve God, our Higher Power, or the greater good to the best of our ability. Step Twelve provides us with steady opportunities to apply, and thus reinforce, what we learned as we gained recovery through vigorous work with eating-disordered people in our communities.

The long form of EDA's Step Ten[11] suggests:

> We continued (and continue) to listen to our conscience. When troubled, we get honest, make amends, and change our thinking or behavior. We continue to notice what we do right, and we are grateful when engaged in right thinking and positive action.

When we are able to be deliberate and calm in our interactions with others despite our own troubles, we are demonstrating reliance on our new perspective that places

[11] Reference Appendix A: "The Twelve Steps and Twelve Traditions of EDA" in this volume.

a higher value on service than on our own personal challenges and rewards. The results of taking this approach are usually excellent. Sometimes, despite the best of intentions, we get caught up in self-will. When that happens, we remember that we are all still works-in-progress. We take our limitations as they come, knowing our experiences help us empathize with others. We are grateful to be human and we do our best to find and share the humor in our problems. We take care of the basics and try to restore ourselves to balance[12] quickly, so we can return to a focus on service.

If we lose perspective, we also lose our peace and the power to stay free of our eating disorders. To maintain what we have worked so hard to develop, we suggest *setting aside some time each day to complete a written inventory*. In it, we review the events of the last twenty-four hours and we consider the day ahead. We think about where we have been troubled, felt ill at ease, or thought and did things we might want to do differently in the future. We identify scenarios that we are concerned about and earnestly think about how we want to act, instead of reacting and possibly causing more turmoil. We think about things we thought, said, or did for which we might need to apologize or make amends. We do not hesitate to admit our errors. We endeavor to set right new wrongs every day.

We are not granted freedom from making mistakes. We are granted freedom from our eating disorders, contingent on being willing to admit and correct our mistakes as we go along.

Throughout each day, we are bound to run into situations that cause us concern. Most of us are not situated such that we can readily complete a written inventory to

---

[12] Reference Appendix B: "A Perspective on Balance" in this volume.

sort things out as they occur. At work or home, we may not be able to go off somewhere and gather our wits. When troubled, therefore, we make a mental commitment to notice what is going on inside us so we can write about it later. If we took corrective action at the time of the disturbance, we might not need to write about the situation. Nevertheless, it can be helpful to reflect on whether and how our solutions work. Then we turn our thoughts back to the tasks at hand.

It is important to acknowledge and pay attention to our feelings, as they alert us when something needs to be addressed. Perhaps we have just made a mistake, and our best course of action is to face the issue directly. Perhaps another person has made a mistake, and we are having feelings about it. We try to avoid rash action, because in the midst of emotional upheaval, we might make a poor choice. We wait until we are able to regain perspective before responding to the situation. In the meantime, we do our best to keep calm and carry on with what really matters.

Sometimes, all that is required to regain perspective is to ask ourselves if we are taking care of basics: *Am I hungry, angry, lonely, tired, or ashamed?* We are sure to be more reactive and self-focused when we neglect to take care of our basic needs, such as adequate nutrition, safe outlets for expression, connection with others, and sufficient sleep. When we take care of basics, it is much easier to find a sane and reasonable perspective no matter what else is happening around us. Here is how some of us think about this: when we do not take care of ourselves properly, our most primal self is neglected, which causes it to emerge and selfishly demand attention. If we do not address the needs, we are gradually overwhelmed with feelings of aching neediness, resentment, and self-pity, and *our behavior becomes unpredictable.* Worse yet, we might return to old behaviors that used to serve us (and us alone). When we take good care of ourselves, the "tiger within" settles down, and we can then utilize its strength and power to serve others (and a Power or purpose greater than ourselves) more reliably.

Some key ideas that help maintain perspective and restore balance include:

- Do *first things first:* take care of basics and then prioritize by what really matters in the long run.

- Do *one thing at a time:* this creates sanity out of chaos. The AA slogan, "One Day at a Time" encourages us to take it easy. We need not solve all our problems at once! Yet, when we become overwhelmed, even one day at a time can feel like too much for us. Doing the next right thing keeps us focused and moving forward.

- *Find the positive:* no matter how difficult our situation, there will always be reasons for respect and gratitude. It helps a great deal to remind ourselves about what is going right in ourselves, our loved ones, our colleagues, society, and the world.

- *Find the humor:* life is short and lives are precious, but our responses to life's challenges are often hilarious. Holding a perspective that allows for humor can reduce shame, allowing us to talk about our experiences in a way that neither minimizes nor dramatizes.

- *Be an adult:* Ask others for input and make your own decisions. Then be accountable for your decisions and keep your word.

- *Deal with problems directly:* when anxious, get outside, do something that focuses attention on your physical senses, pray, or meditate.[13] Then deal with the problem head-on.

- *Get open with others:* honesty restores integrity. We build trust with ourselves by being authentic with others. And, as the saying goes, we are only as sick as our secrets.

- *Be kind:* Make an effort each day to be kind to someone who may not expect it, express appreciation, or follow up with a friend who may be struggling. It is easier to maintain perspective when we remind ourselves that others, like ourselves, need support. Small things can mean a lot!

- *Be flexible:* Develop willingness to look at things differently. Recovery is not rigid.

- *Do the work:* Thinking about perspective and balance can be helpful, but we have to do the work of taking care of ourselves. Then we can focus on how we can be of service. The Steps do not work through osmosis!

In our daily inventory, we reflect on what we felt throughout the day. We honor these feelings and allow them full expression. We think about situations where we

[13] Activities that focus attention on our physical senses can mean anything that feels good to you: walking in the sunshine or the rain, petting a dog, mowing the yard, gardening, building something, repairing or cleaning a car, housework, hugging and physical intimacy, hitting a ball with a bat or a tennis racquet, martial arts, singing, drumming, playing other musical instruments. It all helps!

might have let our emotional states or self-centered thinking prevent us from doing the right thing, and we think about what we would want to do differently in the future.

While our daily inventory should include a review of situations and ideas that evoked strong, negative responses (e.g., resentment, fear, self-pity, guilt, shame, confusion, frustration, despair), as well as consideration of what we could have thought or done instead, we think that wrapping up each session with a respectful and appreciative reflection on what is going right is absolutely essential. Especially in early recovery, it can be easy to slip back into negative thinking. If this happens, we are unlikely to keep up the practice of Step Ten unless we change: an unbalanced inventory usually feels terrible! Therefore, we encourage spending roughly equal time reflecting on what we have done well and what makes us happy. Along these lines, we recommend a *brief daily gratitude list*. Realizing how much we sincerely appreciate and love those around us can be surprising; it quickly becomes a delight to express every day how much we care about the things that matter. Thinking about what gives us joy helps us to increase it, not just in ourselves, but also in others. After writing about gratitude for a few minutes, we turn our attention to actions we can take—small goals we can set for ourselves—that help us grow as human beings, such as character-building exercises or anonymous acts of kindness. This helps to prepare us for our daily practice of Step Eleven.

Once we have begun incorporating Step Ten into our daily life, we gradually begin to realize we have ceased fighting anything or anyone—even our eating disorders. We are seldom interested in behaviors that had formerly seemed inescapable. We no longer want to waste our time so selfishly! If tempted, we generally recoil as if from a hot flame.

With time and practice at this Step, we react sanely and normally to life's provocations, and this is usually effortless. A new attitude toward food and body image materializes without any focused thought or effort on our part. It just comes! That is an amazing thing for most of us. In full recovery, we are not fighting ourselves, neither are we avoiding temptation. We feel as though we had been placed in a position of neutrality—safe and protected. We have not even "sworn off." Instead, the problem no longer exists for us. That is our experience so long as we consistently rely on God, our Higher Power, or higher purpose to direct our vision, thoughts, and actions—and continue to take our personal inventory.[14]

Step Eleven: *Sought through prayer and meditation to improve our conscious contact with God as we understood God, praying only for knowledge of God's will for us and the power to carry that out.*

Step Eleven challenges all of us—religious, spiritual, agnostic, and atheist—to push past our limitations and get into action. It prepares us to face the day with renewed commitment and resolve to do our best, as we strive to be of cheerful service to those around us and to God, our Higher Power, or the greater good—whatever that may be for us. While there is no one right way to do this, we find that a daily discipline is well worth the effort. Each day, when thinking about the twenty-four hours ahead, we consider out goals from the 10th Step inventory. We think

---

[14] *Alcoholics Anonymous*. (2001) New York, NY: AA World Services, Inc., 84-85. Entire paragraph paraphrases text.

about how our activities can positively affect those around us and what we can do that matters in the long run.

Those of us who practice a particular faith or religion often find ourselves able to connect more strongly than ever to the ideas that we knew and trusted all along. As a result of working the Steps (which allow us to sweep away the debris that had been blocking us), we are finally able to live according to the faith we always knew was right for us.

Those of us who do not come from a tradition or practice of faith need not find Step Eleven especially problematic. We remind ourselves that "God" in EDA literature can mean the Deity, a deity, a spiritual entity of one's own understanding (a Higher Power), or a non-spiritual conception (a higher purpose), and we remember that *reliance on any one of these ideas can provide the perspective we need to find balance, peace, and freedom.*

No matter what ideas we start with, Step Eleven reminds us that we derive the power of perspective from focusing on something, or some One, greater than ourselves. Some of us simply care for ourselves so we can be free to turn our attention to causes that matter to us. Some of us understand God as the power of love. Some of us find joy and peace through recognizing and dedicating our lives to God as we understand Him from the Bible, Torah, or Qur'an. Others of us leverage Eastern meditation practices, building on every effort to love, honor, and respect ourselves, because we believe that God lives within us—as *us.* Perceiving of ourselves as beings of love, we find meaning and joy in bringing that sacred gift to everyone we meet, and into everything we do. Taking this position frees us to care for ourselves, and others, with great kindness, compassion, and dignity.

Whether we practice formal prayer and meditation, or practice conscious reliance on a higher purpose, our understanding will likely evolve over time. Step Eleven encourages us to start with whatever conceptions we trust, and work mindfully and deliberately to explore how we can use the power of these ideas in our day-to-day lives. Step Ten helps us establish integrity: we learn to be true to ourselves through our daily inventory. Step Eleven then helps us establish and grow our relationships of trust, whether we start with trust in God, in the power of love, or in the idea that we can organize our time and energy to serve a purpose about which we care deeply.

Step Eleven ask us to seek conscious connection with a source of power so we may turn our attention to carrying out whatever is required of us each day. Regardless of our position on matters of faith, all of us have come to understand that we are here to serve others. We think it helpful to consider what service really means. A good example is the following prayer from St. Francis of Assisi (also known as the 11th Step Prayer):

The Prayer of St. Francis of Assisi[15]

Lord, make me a channel of thy peace;
that where there is hatred, I may bring love;
that where there is wrong, I may bring the spirit of
    forgiveness;
that where there is discord, I may bring harmony;
that where there is error, I may bring truth;
that where there is doubt, I may bring faith;
that where there is despair, I may bring hope;

---

[15] There are many versions of this prayer. To the best of our understanding, the AA *Twelve Steps and Twelve Traditions* could be the original print version of the prayer that includes the line "For it is by self-forgetting that one finds." We have added "self-fulfillment," because "finds" suggests an object. We could have substituted "meaning," "hope," "joy," or "peace," but "self-fulfillment" seemed to fit best.

that where there are shadows, I may bring light;
that where there is sadness, I may bring joy.

Lord, grant that I may seek rather to comfort than to be
    comforted;
to understand, than to be understood;
to love, than to be loved.

For it is by self-forgetting that one finds self-fulfillment.
It is by forgiving that one is forgiven.
It is by dying that one awakens to eternal life.

The format of the prayer or affirmation does not matter, provided we are willing to reflect on it—or something
like it that works for us—on a daily basis. Atheists and agnostics might use an **alternative statement**:

As I practice reliance on a way of thinking that enables
    me to find peace and perspective, I now seek to make
    use of my emotions and my circumstances to serve the
    greater good:
that where there is hatred, I may bring love;
that where there is wrong, I may bring the power of for-
    giveness;
that where there is discord, I may bring harmony;
that where there is error, I may bring truth;
that where there is doubt, I may bring reason;
that where there is despair, I may bring hope;
that where there are shadows, I may bring light;
that where there is sadness, I may bring joy.

I will find more strength and peace by seeking
to comfort rather than to be comforted;
to understand, than to be understood;
to love, than to be loved;

For it is by taking care of basics, and then turning our attention to what we can do for others, that we find meaning and purpose;

it is by forgiving that we find freedom from victimhood;

it is by letting go of attachment to our emotions that we find perspective;

it is through surrender to serving the greater good that we find peace.

When some of us first read the Prayer of St. Francis, we had difficulty believing in its veracity, for we had not yet experienced the promised outcomes first-hand. Perhaps you think the ideas sound noble, but remote. It may help to remember that one purpose of Step Eleven is to connect lofty ideas to our daily realities. When we take care of our own basic needs, and then make a concerted effort to put into practice the unselfish ideas expressed above, we soon see for ourselves that *the process does work*. It doesn't have to be remote! Step Eleven means committing oneself to action: we take care of basics so we can do the next right thing that helps others. As we keep this up, we find that love—our passion for what is good and right, or our love of God—is the driving force in life, and in recovery. Our willingness to put the power of our love into serving something greater than ourselves makes life worth living.

On awakening each day, we think about our opportunities to bring God's vision or the vision of the greater good into all of our activities. If we practice Steps Ten and Eleven on a daily basis, we will go out into the world at peace with ourselves, ready to be of service. We find ourselves thinking about others in a caring way we had not fully appreciated before. Our capacity to be genuinely helpful expands as we look for ways to bring peace and joy to others. Just as working the prior steps clears away the obstacles to a relationship with God, our Higher Power, or our higher purpose, working *Step Eleven enables us to form deeper and more authentic connections with everyone.* We are able to love people exactly as they are—without unreasonable expectations—when our peace and power comes from something greater than ourselves.

Working Step Eleven can consistently resolve even the most complicated relationships and enhance our most intimate ones. By relying on a power or purpose greater than ourselves to frame up our experiences, we can embrace the physicality of our bodies, the power and intensity of our emotions, and connections of trust—free of fear—with deep love, joy, and delight that had never seemed possible for us before. We can be free at last.

Our daily practice of Steps Ten and Eleven help ensure that we do not overlook any serious matters. We have not come this far to be blindsided by unanticipated situations we had not anticipated. We can get through anything, one thing at a time, if we keep in mind that weathering today's experiences without resorting to old patterns will put us in a position to be helpful to others who may face the same issues later on. Throughout the day, as we feel agitation or doubt, we pause and search or ask God for the right thought or action. We remember we are not running the show; we are here to serve. We may repeat "Thy will be done," reflect on the idea that peace comes from humble service, or commit ourselves anew to experiencing life on life's terms—many times a day. We are then in much less danger of excitement, fear, anger, worry, self-pity, or foolish decisions. We become much more efficient. We do not tire so easily, for we are not burning up energy as we did when we were trying to arrange life to suit ourselves.[16]

Making immediate use of these newfound insights is important, for it is through sharing our new strength with others that we develop an appreciation for just how amazing a transformation we have had. We need to further cultivate our newfound integrity to ensure that we do not revert to old patterns of thinking and behavior. In the context of our entire lives, we have been practicing our new reliance on a Higher Power or higher purpose for a relatively short span, so we need as much practice as we can get! The next chapter, "Working with Others," describes exactly how we can best insure ourselves against a return to eating-disordered ways as we continue building a strong and vibrant life of purpose and joy.

---

[16] Adapted from *Alcoholics Anonymous*. (2001) New York, NY: AA World Services, Inc., 88.

Chapter 7

WORKING WITH OTHERS (STEP 12)

S **tep Twelve:** *Having had a spiritual awakening[1] as the result of these Steps, we tried to carry this message to others with eating disorders and to practice these principles in all our affairs.*

In the course of working the first eleven Steps, we will certainly have undergone a fundamental transformation, an experience most of us describe as a spiritual awakening. Although we are the same people as before, we are now on new footing with life. We have faced our issues, made a good start at correcting the mistakes in our thinking, and are engaged in making restitution for the damage we caused. We have commenced a daily practice that builds inner trust, as well as trust with other people. We take care of ourselves so we can be free to serve our God, our Higher Power, or our higher purpose. We need not hold ourselves back from life.

Instead of being sidelined by our issues, we now *make use of them to help others.* Practical experience has shown us that nothing ensures continued freedom from an eating disorder as much as working with people who still have one. Chapter 7 of the AA text, which is also titled "Working with Others," describes what it's like to share our experience, strength, and hope with others who

---

[1] The term "spiritual awakening" can refer to an event—a vital spiritual experience—or to a gradual change. We who are atheists also experience a transformation, enabling us to place service before selfishness.

are afflicted as we once were, and our results have been exactly the same:

> Life will take on new meaning. To watch people recover, to see them help others, to watch loneliness vanish, to see a fellowship grow up about you, to have a host of friends— this is an experience you must not miss. We know you will not want to miss it. Frequent contact with newcomers and with each other is the bright spot of our lives.[2]

Helping others is the foundation of our recovery. A kindly act once in a while is not enough.[3]

General Principles for Working with Others

Remember that our only aim is to be helpful. We may question, but never criticize, any of the information or responses we may get from those we wish to help. Every conception of God, a Higher Power, or a higher purpose can work effectively if resolutely relied upon to provide the needed perspective and peace.

We are honest about our own stories and we empathize with the stories of others. When we do this, we find that our present as well as past experiences provide insights that help us connect with others. There is common ground not only in our former eating-disordered patterns, but also in our emotional responses to life.

We emphatically assure everyone suffering with an eating disorder that they can get well *regardless of anyone or anything*. The only condition is that they practice reliance on their own conception of God, a Higher Power, or

[2] *Alcoholics Anonymous.* (2001) New York, NY: AA World Services, Inc., 89.
[3] Ibid., 97.

a higher purpose, and "clean house"[4]—by which we mean owning up to errors, making amends, and behaving with integrity and dignity in current situations.

We listen patiently when our sponsees blame anyone else (e.g. family members, employers, creditors, institutions, or society as a whole) for their emotional states or for their eating behaviors, even if there is plenty wrong with what these others may have done or may still be doing. We do not criticize. We empathize. While bullying, teasing, abuse, and societal pressures are certainly factors in the development of our eating disorders, *focusing on the errors of other people never helps anyone recover*. We remind sponsees that blaming others for our attitudes and actions undermines our accountability and responsibility as adults. We encourage them to focus on what they think a person with integrity and dignity would do instead, and we guide them to accept their part in any conflict.

We find it best to encourage sponsees to work directly with life situations as they are, rather than trying to "fix things" for them; doing so would deprive them of the opportunity to grow and mature in recovery. One exception is when a sponsee's situation is not physically safe. In that case, our first objective is to do everything we can to help them get out of harm's way. We will make little headway with people whose safety is truly an issue.

If we have thoroughly worked the Steps ourselves, we will not be "triggered" by what other people say or do; if we are, we will have material for our own daily 10th Step and an opportunity for our own growth. People in recovery are resilient: we take what we find and we put it to good use!

[4] Ibid., 98.

Meeting with Newcomers

Arrange to meet a newcomer for the first time through their therapist, treatment center, or a mutual friend rather than through family members who may have expectations or preconceptions. One-on-one is often best, although going with an EDA friend is advisable if the person seems dangerously unstable or under the age of eighteen. *Let the newcomer share their experience with you.* This is valuable, because not only does it validate their thoughts and feelings, but it also shows you how best to approach them when introducing ideas that might be unfamiliar or might conflict with theirs.

Share some of your own experiences of an eating disorder. Give an account of the struggles you had in trying to stop. Find out if the newcomer has had similar experiences. If you are satisfied that he or she both has an eating disorder and wants to recover, you can start to discuss the tenaciousness and progressive nature of the condition—because you have a solution. It may be helpful to cite research that shows that eating disorders are the most fatal of psychiatric disorders. Explain the strange mental state that precedes acting out and prevents normal functioning of willpower.[5] Make sure you communicate that many people are able to recover on their own or with professional help. But if the person admits they have exhausted all other resources and is without hope of ever finding durable recovery, you may have found someone who can be sincere and open-minded about applying the principles of Twelve-Step recovery.

At this point, find out if the person wants to know how you got better. If so, *share your story of recovery.* If

[5] Ibid., 92.

applicable, stress the spiritual feature freely. Explain that a radical transformation in thinking was required for you to find peace and freedom. The key idea is to help the newcomer understand that they will have to establish a different basis for living—not a trivial undertaking! They do not have to accept your ideas about God, a Higher Power, or higher purpose: they are free to choose whatever conception they like. However, they need to understand that they must be willing to believe in *something* greater than themselves and live according to the principles of honesty, equality (respect), accountability, love, trust, and humility.[6]

Your prospect's religious conviction, training, and education may be far superior to yours. If so, they may wonder how you were able to recover when they are still struggling. Explain that in the experience of AA and EDA members everywhere, faith alone is usually insufficient. To be vital, *faith must be accompanied by self-sacrifice and unselfish, constructive action.*[7] Outline the program of action you followed, explaining how you made a self-appraisal, how you straightened out your past as best you could, and why you are reaching out to others. Let the newcomer understand that helping other people is part of your program of recovery. Your hope is that they will try to help others when they recover, as you are doing now. Convey the idea that putting others' welfare ahead of their own is critically important.[8]

Also during this first visit, tell the newcomer about the Fellowship of EDA and provide a brief overview of the

---

[6] Ibid., 93. EDA Motto: H.E.A.L.T.H (honesty, equality, accountability, love, trust, humility).
[7] Ibid.
[8] Ibid., 94.

Twelve Steps. If they show interest, direct them to the web page for this book, *www.4EDA.org/EDAbigbook.html*. Be prepared for them to give reasons why they do not need to engage with *all* aspects of the program. Perhaps they are convinced that they have done no harm to anyone and do not need to take any type of moral inventory. Do not contradict such views. Tell them that you once felt as they do, but that you doubt you would have made much progress if you had not changed your mind and taken action. Reassure them that they are under no pressure to continue and need not see you again. They may have helped you far more than you have helped them. If your talk has been sincere and calm, full of empathy and mutual understanding, you may have made a friend.[9] In any case, you may have conveyed the idea that "staying the course" with an active eating disorder leads to no good end. Hopefully you sparked hope that recovery is possible.

We think it best to wait a bit before starting a newcomer on the Steps. If they are eager to begin, make it clear that you in no way want to rush or push them into any kind of commitment. To be successful in any program, the desire for recovery must come from within. If the individual thinks they can get better through other means, by all means encourage them to pursue the approach they think is best. We have no monopoly on recovery; we merely know what worked for us.[10]

Do not be discouraged if a prospect does not respond at once. Move on and be open to another person who may need to hear your message. Also, if after working together for a while your newcomer seems interested only in having

[9] Ibid., 94-95.
[10] Ibid., 95.

a shoulder to cry on and is not making much of an effort to pick up the tools, it may be necessary to back off until they are ready to work in earnest. There is not much point in spending your time with someone who is reluctant to get better, when others who are ready to make the necessary changes are looking for guidance. We are not on a quest to save people from their eating disorders. We simply open the toolkit of the program and present our experience with the tools. Offer friendship and fellowship, letting the person know that if they want to get well, you will do whatever you can to help.[11]

If you have found someone ready and willing to work on their recovery, you may be called upon to provide more than just inspiration and emotional support. They might be in desperate circumstances, broke, or homeless. They might need shelter, a meal, or a little money. But discretion is warranted, keeping in mind that most people will do better in recovery if they have to support themselves financially. Newcomers must learn to rely *not on other people*—or you—to carry them through the process of putting their lives back in order, *but on their conceptions of God, a Higher Power, or a higher purpose*. We are here only to point the way and to continue to share our experience, strength, and hope as others begin the program.[12]

Burn into the consciousness of every newcomer that *he or she can recover regardless of any relationship or life circumstance*. The only condition for recovery is that they rely on God, a Higher Power, or a higher purpose to guide them, and that they hold themselves accountable for their own thoughts and actions—past and present.[13]

[11] Ibid., 94-95.
[12] Ibid., 96.
[13] Ibid., 98. The AA text calls this "cleaning house."

You may have to work with a newcomer's family to help them understand this approach. Make yourself available to answer questions and help them understand some of what their loved one is experiencing. You may have to remind both your prospect and their family that recovery is not an overnight matter. There is much that requires patience and forbearance on everyone's part. At no point should you ever take sides in any family dispute; sometimes family relationships can be mended and sometimes they cannot. But recovery is not dependent on anyone's relationship with another human being. Rather it *is* dependent on each person's reliance on God, a Higher Power, or a higher purpose to provide peace and perspective.[14]

Living in Recovery

Once we have formed a solid foundation for recovery, are actively applying the principles of the program, and relying on God, a Higher Power, or a higher purpose to guide our thoughts and actions, we are able to do all sorts of things that used to "trigger" us. We can go anywhere and do anything that normal folks do, without reengaging our eating disorders.

Our lives in recovery are full: we are a busy lot. We work, we play, and we help others. We enjoy our lives. When we go places, we see what we can bring to the occasion rather than what we can get out of it. We need not worry about how others perceive of us nor ruminate over how well we performed in any social situation. Our calm, strength, sense of humor, and resilience come not from our peers, but from

---

[14] *Alcoholics Anonymous.* (2001) New York, NY: AA World Services, Inc., 98-100.

God, a Higher Power, or from our commitment to serve the purpose most dear to us. As the AA text notes, our job now is to be at the place where we may be of maximum usefulness to others, so we never hesitate to go anywhere if we may be helpful.[15] We go to halfway houses and jails, support victims of domestic violence, cook for friends who are ill, and volunteer to tutor disadvantaged children. We help wherever we can, grateful to be of cheerful service.

Through this work, we are regularly reminded how fortunate we are to live in freedom. As we seek to understand each sponsee's challenges, brainstorming new ways for them to look at their attitudes and actions in the face of life's provocations, we find ourselves formulating answers that we can apply should we find ourselves in similar circumstances. Of course, a sponsor need not have all the answers. We offer our experience, strength, and hope where we have it, and demonstrate humility where we do not. In the latter case, finding someone with more relevant experience to serve as a resource may be the best option.

We share our experiences in working the first nine Steps, and we also freely share parts of our own personal daily inventory, modeling how to use Step Ten to gain perspective and deal with issues effectively. Again, this practice not only helps our sponsees, but it also keeps us honest and grounded in our own recovery. Even when those we try to help falter, our efforts to carry the message of recovery make us stronger and more appreciative of our own lives. It is an amazing, joyous, and wonderful experience to share the Steps with others who begin to experience the freedom of recovery, and then watch as they reach out to help still

---

[15] Ibid., 102.

others.[16] Being authentic, showing sponsees what works for us, and then seeing them emerge into health and happiness is so rewarding that we gladly continue to do so long after we have recovered ourselves.

If you are ready to start working with others, you need not look far to find people who want to recover from an eating disorder. We encourage you to join an EDA online or phone meeting, or write to *sponsors@eatingdisordersanonymous.org* and offer to sponsor someone. Below, we describe an approach for taking people through the Twelve Steps of EDA, which we offer as a program of recovery from an eating disorder.

Suggestions for Taking a Sponsee Through the Twelve Steps of EDA[17]

Note: when taking someone through the Twelve Steps of EDA, we refer to the current version of this volume, *Eating Disorders Anonymous.* Some sponsors also use the AA text, *Alcoholics Anonymous.* Both are available online.

Step One: *We admitted we were powerless over our eating disorders—that our lives had become unmanageable.*

Preparation for Step One: Before your first "official" meeting, provide your sponsee with your phone number

---

[16] Ibid., Page 89.

[17] Early members of EDA found a spiritual awakening by working straight from the original text, *Alcoholics Anonymous,* substituting the words "acting out" for "drinking" and "eating disordered" for "alcoholics." Some sponsors continue to use this approach. While this volume is not intended to be used merely as a supplement to *Alcoholics Anonymous,* we highly recommend that the reader become familiar with the original text. The chapters in this book are organized in concordance with the chapters in the AA text so that the reader may readily refer back to the original material.

and ask them to call you to set up a get-together. Acquaint them with the idea that you will be reading material from the above-listed source(s) *together* in order to develop a balanced awareness of how to work the Steps. Ensure they have access to the literature. Remind them that if they are to recover they must first and foremost remain true to their own hearts and values by being honest with you, with other people, and with themselves.

Homework: Ask your sponsee to read the Preface, Doctors' Opinions, and Letters of Support. Also have them make an *Eating Disorder Log,* which is a history of their eating disorder: when the thoughts and behaviors started, the different manifestations and progression, and anything that seems to tie into their eating disorders, such as what led them to "pause" or get worse. This Log will help you, their sponsor, have a better understanding of how to connect suggested readings to your sponsee's different symptoms: obsession with food, weight, or body image; use of diet pills and/or laxatives; over exercising; bingeing; restricting; misuse of insulin; and/or purging.

Meeting: If your sponsee does not already know your story, this first meeting is the time to share it with them. Review your own Eating Disorder Log or recount your own experiences, focusing on the progression of your eating disorder and on the mental state that preceded your acting out. Then, have them share their Eating Disorder Log with you. Together, read the front matter of this text that was given as homework. Emphasize that the obsession and the cycle cannot be broken unless a *fundamental change* occurs. Help them understand that the purpose of working the Twelve Steps is to create such a change.

Homework: Ask your sponsee to read the introduction of Chapter 5, "How It Works," stopping *before* Step One. Have them write down examples of how they are powerless over their eating disorder, including any unsuccessful attempts to control or moderate their thoughts and behaviors. Make sure it is clear that we are not yet discussing unmanageability or detailing the negative consequences of their eating disorders (although these certainly contributed to feelings of powerlessness when even *consequences* did not stop us). Then, ask them to read Chapter 1, "Gisele's Story of Hope," and the stories "Free at Last" and "A Life Solution." Remind them to keep in mind that we are each responsible for our own recovery and for developing our own ideas about balance.

Meeting: During the next meeting, review your sponsee's examples of powerlessness to make sure they have a clear understanding of how they are powerless over their eating disorder. Read some of the previous assigned passages together, focusing on the ideas that have been most helpful to you in your recovery and acknowledging that these ideas developed over time. Respect that your sponsee's ideas about God and balance may not be the same as your own. Focus on the progression and durability of the eating disorder and on different areas of unmanageability in their lives, with or without the behaviors. Have your sponsee consider the effects of their attitude and behavior on other people, educational goals and achievement, work ethics and work quality, relationships, health, and their living situations.

Homework: Have your sponsee read Step One from Chapter 5, "How It Works," and answer the questions on page 116 about how they used their eating disorder to make their life feel more manageable. Have they been able to trust themselves to do what needs to be done every day without resorting to any harmful behaviors? Ask them to write about the different areas of unmanageability in their lives including what they lost, missed, or are missing as a result of having an eating disorder. Then ask them to read Chapter 2, "There Is a Solution," and Chapter 3, "More about Eating Disorders."

Meeting: At the next meeting, review your sponsee's powerlessness and unmanageability lists. Together, read Chapters 2 and 3. Again focus on the concepts of powerlessness and unmanageability presented throughout the readings. Discuss how the problem centers in the mind rather than in the body (this later ties into Step Two and being restored to sanity). In Chapter 2, discuss the things that, *in and of themselves,* are NOT the solution, such as self-knowledge; willingness; consequences; and faith without reliance on God, a Higher Power, or a higher purpose. We have to *rely on something greater than ourselves* before other components of a solution fall into place.

Homework: Ask your sponsee to add to their powerlessness and unmanageability lists if they feel they left anything out. In preparation for the next meeting, ask your sponsee to read Step Two in Chapter 5. Have them define their own conception of a Higher Power. Ask them to write out two lists: one of the things they *can* believe in that are a power or purpose greater than themselves, and the other of things they *can't* believe in that are actually obstacles to forming a connection with their Higher Power or higher purpose. Finally, ask them to read Chapter 4, "We Agnostics, Atheists, and Believers."

Step Two: *Came to believe that a Power greater than ourselves could restore us to sanity.*

Meeting: At the next meeting, start reading Chapter 4 together. Remind sponsees again that different perspectives give us a deeper understanding of the steps, and how to apply them. When it mentions that any concept of God, Higher Power, or higher purpose will work as long as it is greater than ourselves, ask your sponsee to read their concept. It is NEVER wrong. Let them know they are making great progress, since they believe—or are *willing* to believe—in something profoundly meaningful to them.

Discuss how in the 2nd Step we have come to believe that *reliance* on this power or purpose greater than ourselves—something solid and trustworthy—can restore us to sanity by removing the need to rely on eating-disordered thoughts and obsessions. Affirm your own experience of finding peace, perspective, and power this way. Invite your sponsee to express what being restored to sanity looks like from their perspective. Discuss how you started to open yourself up to—and began depending on—your Higher Power or higher purpose in daily life. We need to see the truth of the matter: that we are powerless to recover when we are relying on ourselves alone to provide perspective. With the help of God, a Higher Power, or a higher purpose, we can find a new perspective—and freedom from our eating disorders.

Homework: Ask your sponsee to read Appendix B: "A Perspective on Balance." Have them reflect on how their concept of a God, a Higher Power, or a higher purpose can help them develop their own ideas about balance. Have them define what balance means to them now and what being restored to sanity would look like in their lives. Ask them to also read Step Three in Chapter 5, including the 3rd Step prayer or 3rd Step commitment. Then have them rewrite a prayer or commitment in their own words.

Step Three: *Made a decision to turn our will and our lives over to the care of God* as we understood God.[18]

Meeting: At the next meeting, have your sponsee read you their definition of balance and explain what sanity looks like to them. Unless there is something destructive or harmful involved, you should accept their ideas with as much enthusiasm as possible, emphasizing that our ideas about balance—like our ideas about other things—will naturally evolve with time and practice.

Read the Step Three homework together. If you are both comfortable with the idea, let your sponsee pray aloud either the 3rd Step prayer or 3rd Step commitment in their own words, and then the two of you can recite them together. If less comfortable with prayer yourself, read your 3rd Step commitment to them, and have them read their 3rd Step commitment to you. If not using the EDA 3rd Step prayer at all, make sure their commitment includes the idea of turning their will and their life over to serve a greater purpose, whether it be God's will for them, their Higher Power's inspiration, or simple service to the greater good. They do this *so they can recover*.

---

[18] "God" in EDA literature can mean the Deity, a deity, a spiritual entity of one's own understanding (a Higher Power), or a non-spiritual conception (a higher purpose). Reliance on any of these conceptions confers a perspective that transcends our immediate physical, social, and emotional circumstances and allows us to "keep calm and carry on" with what really matters.

This can sound like a lot to a newcomer. Remind him or her that the main point of Step Three is our willingness to set aside our daily drama, so we can be of use in the world. While the rest of the Steps enable us to do this with increasing agility and grace, the purpose of Step Three is to set the intention firmly in place and start working toward it. Talk with your sponsee about how they can use their 3rd Step commitment to help them establish and maintain balance.

Homework: Congratulations! Your sponsee has just made the decision to go forward with the rest of the work. Ask them to use their 3rd Step commitment or prayer in the morning and throughout their day. Remind them to use it when working on Step Four, which they should begin to read, stopping at the 4th Step Inventory.

Step Four: *Made a searching and fearless moral inventory of ourselves.*

We think it is important to take our time with Step Four, because it includes an exercise that requires careful thought from a new, more objective perspective. Sponsees need to feel supported throughout the process. We break things down for them so they do not get confused or overwhelmed, and offer our support if needed. The meetings in which we review their lists and describe how to set up a 4th Step inventory are quick.

4th Step Inventory: Exploring Resentment

Homework: Using resentment as a topic of exploration, ask your sponsee to make a list of people, institutions, or principles—the Sources—with whom they are angry, or against whom they have resentments. Explain the definition of resentments and clarify what we mean by institutions and principles:

- A resentment is usually an unresolved anger or bitterness that lurks in the background of our minds, ready to jump out whenever an opportunity presents itself.

- Institutions can be groups of people; organizations; or places such as banks, credit card companies, magazines, police departments, states, cities, countries, restaurants, colleges, and universities.

- Principles include ideas such as "love at first sight," "honesty is the best policy," "you live under my roof, you follow my rules," racism and other forms of prejudice, and sayings such as "fake it 'til you make it."

Give your sponsee a few days to brainstorm the sources of their resentments. Caution him or her to try to stay objective. This is a great opportunity for them to begin to rely on their Higher Power or purpose! If they do not, it will be hard for them to focus on solutions. Ask your sponsee to consider family members, former relationships, past and current friendships, jobs, cell phone contacts, email addresses, and social media. Remind him or her not to worry about the details at first. Your sponsee should go back through their life, listing those people, institutions, and principles that bring up feelings of resentment. Then schedule a meeting in a few days to continue in person.

Ask your sponsee to read the introduction to Step Four in Chapter 5, pages 132-37, as well as Appendix D: "Example Step Four Inventory."

Meeting: Have your sponsee put an asterisk by the top ten entries on their resentments list—the people, places, or things about which they feel the most intense emotion. When they fill out the Inventory, have them start with those.

Show your sponsee how to set up a two-page, five-column Step Four Inventory in a notebook, with columns labeled: Sources (person/institution/principle), Reasons/Why, At Risk/Affects My, My Error/My Part, and Resolution. Have them enter the Sources of their resentments in the first column. Then, show them how to list each reason why they are angry or resentful in the second column, doing so on separate lines. Encourage them to make their reasons specific. For example, instead of saying that someone upset you, give an example of what they did or didn't *do* that upset you. Ask them not to attempt to complete the last three columns until you guide them to do so at the next meeting.

Homework: Ask your sponsee to complete the first two columns—Sources and Reasons/Why—of their resentment inventory.

Meeting: At the next meeting, read the first part of the Step Four Inventory on resentment in Chapter 5, to the end of the "At Risk/Affects My" section. For each reason (not for each source), ask your sponsee to consider how it affects their: pride; self-esteem; ambition for reward, recognition, or validation; finances; sexual or intimacy needs; and/or family or social relationships. Delve into each one specifically. Self-esteem is the way we feel about/value ourselves, or how we think people feel about/value us. Ambitions can be long term, such as dreams and goals for our future (jobs, finances, relationships), but they can also be short term desires or wishes, such as wanting to be respected, or wanting to be included. Have your sponsee consider whether any key relationships—especially at home, at work, in the community—are threatened by the cause of their resentment. Make it clear to your sponsee that, in most cases, impact to any one part of our lives is likely to affect many other aspects. Getting it all down on paper is important, but it is not necessary to document every possible connection for every perceived threat: if we did, the 4th Step Inventory could take years!

Homework: Ask your sponsee to complete the At Risk/Affects My column of their resentment inventory.

Meeting: At the next meeting, read the rest of the resentment portion of the Chapter 5 section on Step 4, focusing on My Error/My Part. As you are reading, point out that we use the resentment prayer for each individual *before* looking at our part. Explain that most At Risk/Affects My entries can be connected to selfishness, self-seeking, dishonesty, and/or fear, whether before the instance (anticipation), during, or even after it happened (as it pertains to how we reacted and how we treated others later on). For clarification, see page 145 in Chapter 5.

Homework: Ask your sponsee to consider each person on their resentments inventory with empathy and compassion, perhaps using the resentment prayer[19] before completing the My Error/My Part column.

Meeting: Once the first four columns of the resentments inventory are complete, meet with your sponsee in person. Remind them that our purpose is to honestly admit our wrongs and become willing to set these matters straight. You have already asked your sponsee to read through the resentment prayer for each person. Perhaps sit down with them and go back through their resentment list, making sure they have understood their part.

Your sponsee should now be ready to fill out the last column, Resolution. Picking out a few situations from their list, ask your sponsee what helpful attitude they can now take, what "kindly and tolerant view" of the other people involved they now want to have, as they prepare to leave their resentments behind. Remind your sponsee that we leave resentments behind so that we can recover—not for any other reason. Mention that they do not need to make amends yet: you are only checking to see if they are starting to experience the new perspective that a reliance on God, their Higher Power, or higher purpose is giving them.

Point out that when they encounter additional provocations from the people on their resentments list in the future, they have some recourse of thought and action to take—ones they have reviewed with you. Make sure your sponsee's Resolutions column reflects attitudes and positions that a person of integrity and dignity might take. Review Appendix D together, with a reminder that they need

[19] *Alcoholics Anonymous.* (2001) New York, NY: AA World Services, Inc., 67. "When a person offended, we said to ourselves, 'This is a sick man. How can I be helpful to him? God save me from being angry. Thy will be done.'"

to *define their own resolutions*, seeking guidance and perspective from their God, Higher Power, or higher purpose.

Homework: Have your sponsee complete the Resolutions column.

Congratulate your sponsee for all they have accomplished so far! Remind them that none of us are able to maintain anything like perfect adherence to our ideals; the point is that we are willing to practice living up to them—starting immediately.

4th Step Inventory: Exploring Fear

Your sponsee is now ready to move on to a fears inventory. Together, read the section "Exploring Fear" in Chapter 5. With your sponsee, set up another two-page, five-column inventory for inventorying fears in the same way we did for resentments.

Homework: Ask your sponsee to take a few days to identify the Sources of their fear: what makes them feel afraid. Use a separate brainstorming page for this, as we did with resentments. Show him or her how to pull fears from the fourth column (My Error/My Part) of the resentments inventory. Then pinpoint specific ones, such as fear of dying, fear of being alone, or fear of not being good enough. Ask your sponsee to list any other fears that are not connected directly to resentments, such as fear of heights, fear of bugs, fear of the unknown, fear of food, fear of weight gain or loss, fear of losing what they have, fear of not getting what they want, fear of success, or fear of failure. Remind them to consider fear of loss—for instance, loss of love, intimacy, respect, and control—as well as fear of their own powerful emotions.

Meeting: Ask your sponsee to start completing the inventory columns for fear:

- For the **Sources** column, ask them to draw from their homework. Have them focus first on their most intense fears. Go through the list with them to help identify fears you see playing out in their day-to-day behavior. Sometimes sponsees are so anxious they seem unable to fully understand the fears that are most closely tied to their eating disorders. It is important to be gentle with this topic in particular. Nevertheless your insight may prove invaluable, so do not hesitate to ask about or question anything your sponsee may have omitted.

- For the **Reason/Cause** column, ask them to ransack their memory to see *why* they have fears. What reasons are there for fear? Some have more than one cause. "Fear of dying" might include: "My grandmother died and I didn't get to say goodbye," "My best friend died at a very young age," "I see people dying when they relapse," or "I regularly hear about people dying on the news."

- For the **At Risk/Affects My** column, have your sponsee list the same categories as on the resentments inventory: pride; self-esteem; ambition for reward, recognition, or validation; finances; sexual or intimacy needs; or family or social relationships. Ask your sponsee to list everything and everyone that is threatened or affected by the attitudes and actions they take—or don't take—because of their fears.

- For the **My Error/My Part** column, ask yourself and your sponsee if there might be a fundamental issue underlying all their fears. The AA "Big Book" suggests that we are consumed by fear because self-reliance has failed us; we couldn't rely on our own abilities to make things happen or to stop things from happening. We have fears because we are not in control. Permitting ourselves to continue in our eating-disordered behavior after realizing it was dangerous meant we lost confidence in our ability to do the right things: self-reliance failed us absolutely in that regard! Realizing we were unable to fully trust ourselves, we often became overwhelmed by fear. Most of us responded by becoming rigid and controlling in an effort to make life feel safe. Yet, we cannot control whether we get old or sick, even though we can influence things a bit. We cannot control whether people like us or leave us, even though our attitudes and actions can influence these outcomes, as well. Now, in the My Error/My Part column, ask your sponsee to list how they tried to control outcomes that were not in their control.

- For the **Resolutions** column, ask your sponsee to reflect on the new perspective provided by reliance on their Higher Power or higher purpose. Remind them that our fears exist for good reason: to help us focus our attention on what really matters. Ask your sponsee to write down a sane ideal for their fears. What would a person of integrity and dignity do if they found the courage to act despite their fear? Would such a person decide to set aside their fear, or make use of it in some way to initiate needed changes? What can we do, and what must be left up to our Higher Power or to the natural order of the universe? Those of us who are atheist or agnostic may not be able to trust that there is any design or conscious presence in control of the universe, but this should not matter; our own thoughts and actions are all we can ever control—regardless of our position on faith. The main thing is that we learn to think and act with conscious intention despite our fears. We ask our sponsee to get all their thoughts down on paper.

Example Resolutions:

– Continue doing the work required by the Steps, and rely more on God/a Higher Power/higher purpose to provide perspective, so I do not fall back into old behaviors

– Work on using my voice and realize that I am not here to make everyone happy: I am here to become the person I think God intended me to be, and/or put my talents, training, and energy toward serving the greater good to the best of my ability

– Recognize that my fear of financial instability could stem in part from my repeatedly overdrafting my bank account, because I was helpless in my eating disorder and could not stop bingeing. I can now use this fear to motivate me to build a stronger reliance on my Higher Power/

> higher purpose, so I need never return to my old
> helplessness and insanity

Describe how turning our thoughts to ways we can best be of service helps us outgrow fear. Direct sponsees who are comfortable with it to:

The Fear Prayer

> We ask Him to remove our fear and direct our attention to what He would have us be.[20]

We advise our sponsees to use this prayer—or idea— as fears crop up, in the same way we use the Resentment prayer that reads, "This is a sick person. How can I be helpful to him?" For those who are not comfortable with prayer, we explain how directing our attention to how we can best serve the greater good in each situation can help us to overcome both resentment *and* fear.

Homework: Ask your sponsee to complete the fears inventory.

4th Step Inventory: Exploring Sexual Conduct

At this point, sponsors in EDA usually address the topic of sex by taking one of two approaches. In the traditional AA approach, sponsees complete what is known as a "sex inventory." Some sponsors prefer this when working with newcomers, because it can be shorter and therefore easier to keep up the enthusiasm and momentum. Other sponsors (especially those working with sponsees who have already completed the Twelve Steps in another program) prefer the

---

[20] *Alcoholics Anonymous.* (2001) New York, NY: AA World Services, Inc., 68.

approach described in Chapter 5 of this text, in which sex is a topic to explore within the more general inventory categories of self-pity, shame, guilt or harms done, confusion, frustration, and despair.

For those following the traditional AA approach:

Meeting: *Completing the Sex Inventory.* Together with your sponsee, read the following excerpt from the AA "Big Book":

> Now about sex. Many of us needed an overhauling there. But above all, we tried to be sensible on this question. It's so easy to get way off the track. Here we find human opinions running to extremes—absurd extremes, perhaps. One set of voices cry that sex is a lust of our lower nature, a base necessity of procreation. Then we have the voices who cry for sex and more sex; who bewail the institution of marriage; who think that most of the troubles of the race are traceable to sex causes. They think we do not have enough of it, or that it isn't the right kind. They see its significance everywhere. One school would allow man no flavor for his fare and the other would have us all on a straight pepper diet. We want to stay out of this controversy. We do not want to be the arbiter of anyone's sex conduct. We all have sex problems. We'd hardly be human if we didn't. What can we do about them?
>
> We reviewed our own conduct over the years past. Where had we been selfish, dishonest, or inconsiderate? Whom had we hurt? Did we unjustifiably arouse jealousy, suspicion, or bitterness? Where were we at fault, what should we have done instead? We got this all down on paper and looked at it.[21]

---

[21] Ibid., 68-69.

Instruct your sponsee to identify anyone with whom they had a sexual relationship. As with brainstorming resentment and fears, it is helpful to reach as far back as memory serves to identify where we may have used our bodies and sexual attraction—perhaps even before losing virginity—to manipulate, reward, or punish others. Have sponsees list names on a separate page first, as they did for resentments and fears. Then ask them to set up an inventory worksheet. Again, have them focus first on the relationships that spark the most intense emotions.

- On the far left column, Source, have them list the *name* of the other person(s) involved.

- In the second column, Reason, have them list each *situation* in which they have been selfish, dishonest, or inconsiderate. Examples include: using sex to manipulate someone into paying for a meal; seeking to obtain validation for ourselves as human beings through flirting or sex; allowing people to think we loved them when we did not, because we thought we needed them in our lives.

- In the third column, At Risk, have them list *who had been affected or hurt* by their actions. Be sure to consider the individual person, significant others (if applicable), family members, other individuals (such as friends), and even themselves.

- In the fourth column, My Error/My Part, have them list selfishness, dishonesty, and other *inconsiderate attitudes and behavior*. Ask them to identify where they may have created jealousy, suspicion, and bitterness. Ask them to present in black-and-white where they themselves were at fault.

- In the fifth column, Resolution, ask your sponsee to list what they now think *they ought to have done instead*, and what they would want to do in the future under similar conditions.

The next paragraph on page 69 of the AA "Big Book" says,

> In this way we tried to shape a sane and sound ideal for our future sex life. We subjected each relation to this test— was it selfish or not? We asked God to mold our ideals and help us to live up to them. We remembered always that our sex powers were God-given and therefore good, neither to be used lightly or selfishly nor to be despised and loathed.[22]

Homework: Ask your sponsee to complete their sex conduct inventory, and also to write out their ideal for future sexual attitudes and behavior *for themselves*—not for their partner—as a person in a relationship who uses the power of sexual intimacy in an authentic and meaningful way. Together with your sponsee, read the following excerpt from the AA "Big Book":

> Whatever our ideal turns out to be, *we must be willing to grow toward it*. We must be willing to make amends where we have done harm, provided that we do not bring about still more harm in so doing. In other words, we treat sex as we would any other problem. In meditation, we ask God what we should do about each specific matter. The right answer will come, if we want it. God alone can judge our

[22] Ibid., 69.

sex situation. Counsel with (other) persons is often desirable, but we let God be the final judge. We realize that some people are as fanatical about sex as others are loose. We avoid hysterical thinking or advice.

To sum up about sex: We earnestly pray for the right ideal, for guidance in each questionable situation, for sanity, and for the strength to do the right thing. If sex is very troublesome, we throw ourselves the harder into helping others. We think of their needs and work for them. This takes us out of ourselves. It quiets the imperious urge, when to yield would mean heartache.[23]

Continue reading Chapter 5, up to the examples of resolutions on page 155.

For those following the EDA approach:

Meeting: When you next meet with your sponsee, read the section titled "Exploring Sexual Conduct" in Chapter 5 and review Appendix D. As you go through the examples, share some of your own experiences in each category, making clear the attitude you now take (your resolution) in each one. Ask your sponsee if they have any questions about the categories, examples, or resolutions. Remind them that they need not make any amends just yet: rather, they should be trying for a new perspective that will keep them from getting caught up in old patterns of thought and behavior.

Homework: Regarding sex, ask your sponsee to create an ideal for themselves—not for their partner—as a person in a relationship who uses the power of sexual intimacy in an authentic and meaningful way. Remind him or her to reflect

---

[23] Ibid., 69-70. Emphasis and reference to "other" added.

on the perspective provided by their reliance on God, their Higher Power, or higher purpose with respect to this topic of sex and physical intimacy. In full recovery, most of us discover a new joy and tender appreciation at every level of connection with our partners.[24] This is possible when we do our 4th Step work carefully! Ask your sponsee to complete the remaining inventory categories: self-pity, shame, guilt/harms done, confusion, frustration, and despair. Encourage them to call if they get bogged down or confused, and tell them that—barring extenuating circumstances—they should plan to complete this assignment in two weeks or less. Also, ask them to read the remainder of Chapter 5. They should now be ready to launch into Step Five.

Preparation for Step Five: After your sponsee calls to tell you they completed their inventory, but before they meet with anyone for their 5th Step (and remember, you may be the one they select to hear it), we suggest the following:

Ask your sponsee to read Chapter 6 up to the section "Taking Step Five." Ask them to list anything they are ashamed or embarrassed about that didn't seem to fit into any category on their inventory, as well as anything else they need to share in order to stay free from their eating disorder. Also, ask them not to make any plans for the day of their 5th Step, in case it takes longer than expected. Let them know that they should also arrange to take an hour to themselves after the completion of their 5th Step.

Step Five: *Admitted to God, to ourselves, and to another human being the exact nature of our wrongs.*

---

[24] *Alcoholics Anonymous.* (2001) New York, NY: AA World Services, Inc., 134.

Discussion: At the next meeting, read the last section of Chapter 5 together. Then, *if* they have chosen you as their 5th Step recipient, *hear out your sponsee's 5th Step*. Have them start by reading across their 4th Step inventory rows, one by one. Let them know you are taking notes of their "defects of character" and anything else that may need to be addressed at a later time. If something is disclosed that is disturbing, do your best not to react: strive to remain objective—the better to help your sponsee see their part. Remember: *it is their part that will set them free.* After they have completed reading their 5th Step, read the section in Chapter 6 on "Taking Step Five" together.

Homework: Once your sponsee has given their 5th Step, ask them to turn their phone off and go to a quiet place for an hour to review their 1st through 4th Steps and reflect on the last paragraphs you read together. Ask your sponsee to call you after the hour is up to let you know if they have left anything out, and remind them to write a short gratitude list as part of their period of reflection. Gratitude can help restore balance at the end of what may be an emotionally challenging effort. Then, tell them to give you a call the following day for the next assignment and wish them peace, quiet, and serenity.

Preparation for Step Six: When you speak next, ask your sponsee to read the section in Chapter 6 on Step Six. They may be interested in looking up additional information about defects of character, but their approach does not matter so long as they are honest and do not wallow. Remind your sponsee that they can refer back to their 4th Step should they need to refresh their memory, and remind them that they can ask you if they have any questions.

Step Six: *Were entirely ready to have God remove all these defects of character.*

  Meeting: At the next meeting, complete the 6ᵗʰ Step with your sponsee. Read the assigned Chapter 6 section together, and then have him or her read their list of shortcomings. This is where you might delicately point out any missing items noted when hearing their 5ᵗʰ Step. Ask your sponsee to pinpoint four or five major issues that could interfere with their freedom from their eating disorder and stop them from being of service. Remind them that unwillingness to take care of our basic needs, as well as selfishness, ought to be considered.

  Homework: This is where you can get creative in providing suggestions to start building character as a means to move past personal challenges and limitations. Ask your sponsee to start doing random acts of kindness every day anonymously, meaning that no one should know about or see them except you, their sponsor, to make sure that they are on the right track. In the meantime, tell them to think of a hobby, service commitment, or creative work to replace one bad habit. It is important to remind sponsees that we don't focus on the habit we want to replace; we put our energy and attention on the new activity instead.

  Preparation for Step Seven: Ask your sponsee to read the section on Step Seven in Chapter 6 and then rewrite the 7ᵗʰ Step prayer or statement in their own words. Once they have done this, ask them to write an asset list, one for every defect, until both lists are equally long. The purpose of this exercise is to remind sponsees that even our worst defects contain something of value that can be used to good purpose. Consultation with friends and family is fine if they need help. Ask your sponsee to start using the 7th Step prayer or statement as they embark on this new journey to become a more resilient and reliable person. As EDA members go out from Step Seven, we rely increasingly on God, a Higher Power, or a higher purpose to build our character, so we no longer need to turn to our old ways of coping. *The stronger our reliance on something greater than ourselves, the stronger our ability to live free of anything that gets in the way of our service.*

This is an important point: *we don't work on defects, we work on building character*, which is the complete opposite. For instance, we overcome dishonesty by using our voice and speaking our truth in ways that serve the greater good. We overcome selfishness by thinking of others and quietly working to make life better for them. We begin to master fear by taking small risks that demonstrate our willingness to change: allowing ourselves to express anger in a safe way; eating a "fear food" with the support of friends or family; speaking up, accepting the risk that we may be criticized, and allowing ourselves to change our minds if we are wrong. Sponsors need not provide such character-building exercises for every defect, and sponsees need only work on one or two at a time depending on what they consider to be the key issues to be addressed. You may want to run ideas by your own sponsor, and let your sponsee know later what you think would be most effective.

Step Seven: *Humbly asked God to remove our shortcomings.*

Meeting: At the next meeting, wrap up the discussion outlining character-building activities. Ask your sponsee to read the section on Step Seven, stopping before the 7th

Step prayer. Then ask him or her to read their list of assets. Next, read the 7th Step prayer together, or hear their 7th Step statement. Just like the 3rd Step, have them say their own version of the 7th Step prayer or statement first. Then, if you are comfortable with it, together read/recite the 7th Step prayer. Remind your sponsee that it is their responsibility to use the 3rd, 4th, and 7th Step prayers/statements, along with character-building exercises, to grow into the men and women they need to be if they are to be of useful service to their God, Higher Power, or higher purpose. Consistent follow-through on our intention—to rely on something that requires us to act with courage and dignity—grants us the power to fully recover. Our only job as sponsors is to help sponsees figure out what they need to do, and encourage them to do it.

Preparation for Step Eight: Ask your sponsee to read the end of Step Seven and all of Step Eight in Chapter 6. Remind sponsees that we often do not have much perspective on whom we have harmed and in what ways, so they should reflect carefully. Without worrying about making amends at this time, we ask them just to make a list of persons they have harmed and how.

Step Eight: *Made a list of all persons we had harmed and became willing to make amends to them all.*

Meeting: At the next meeting, read the Step Eight homework together. We do not discuss their entire 8th Step list at this point, *only the amends they can do now*—at this point in time. We discuss the format of amends and make sure there are grounds for specific action. (Sponsees sometimes think they owe amends in cases where non-action would serve the best interests of all concerned.)

Preparation for Step Nine: Ask your sponsee to read Step Nine in Chapter 6. Have them write out amends they can make at the current time to people they can easily find and make arrangements to see.

Step Nine: _Made direct amends to such people wherever possible, except when to do so would injure them or others._

Meeting: At the next meeting, review your sponsee's pre-written amends, making sure they are appropriate, sincere, and don't describe what the other person did—no matter what that may have been. Read up through Step Nine in Chapter 6 together, emphasizing how to schedule the amends "appointments" at times that are convenient for the other people involved. Remind sponsees that amends to those closest to us—spouses, partners, children, and parents—involve much more than a simple apology and a commitment to right the wrongs. We need to be accountable to people who have seen us at our worst, ensuring we do everything in our (newfound) power to protect them from further harm from our selfishness and unreasonable expectations. We are sure to make mistakes as we go along; we are only human. Our perspective will no doubt become clouded whenever we are angry and afraid. Therefore, we firmly resolve to make living amends, which means taking a kindly and helpful attitude toward those around us—no matter what they do. We commit to continue taking personal inventory, setting right new wrongs as they occur (Step Ten), and we commit to rely on God, a Higher Power, or a higher purpose for our strength, rather than leaning too heavily on those around us (Step Eleven).

Homework: Give your sponsee two weeks *at most* to begin to make amends, or at least to have them scheduled.

Step Ten: *Continued to take personal inventory and when we were wrong promptly admitted it* (and)

Step Eleven: *Sought through prayer and meditation to improve our conscious contact with God as we understood God, praying only for knowledge of God's will for us and the power to carry that out.*

Although Steps Ten and Eleven are sometimes described as "the maintenance Steps," they are essential to the growth of integrity and perspective. We think it important to get sponsees started on the practices associated with these Steps as soon as they have been able to develop a frame of reference through which they can begin to see themselves objectively. For some, a good starting point is right after Step Three! Our experience is that sponsees who are actively engaged in a daily practice that focuses on solutions and service have a much easier time with Steps Four through Nine.

Step Ten is such a vital practice that we think every effort needs to be made to ensure sponsees get off to a good start. We share examples of our own daily Step Ten work, remembering this can be inspirational: it models the practices that help us, so our sponsees can see how they work in real life. At this point, you may share your own experiences with Step Eleven freely. As with Step Ten, we model how to "do recovery" by being transparent and authentic. We continue to impart what works for us day in and day out. Once sponsees get the hang of this, they will be more likely to share what works with others in the same authentic and grounded way.

Meeting: When your sponsee has made some amends and has others scheduled (no more than two weeks later), meet with them to discuss their experiences and the next set of amends. This is a good time to review the 10th and 11th Steps together in Chapter 6. Make sure to go over: the spot check inventory, the end of day review, what to do in the mornings upon awakening, and what to do throughout the day. Have your sponsee provide some examples of how they are applying the tools in the context of issues that typically come up at home and in the workplace. Have your sponsee read the Step Eleven prayer or statement with you.

Homework: Ask your sponsee to do everything suggested in the Chapter 6 sections on Steps Ten and Eleven. It is strongly suggested that you ask your sponsees to email you their written 10th Step inventory so you can monitor whether they are doing it correctly. If appropriate, continue to share your inventory with them and check in with them about their Step Eleven practice regularly. In the meantime, ask them to read Chapter 7, "Working with Others," stopping at the section "Taking a Sponsee Through the Twelve Steps of EDA."

Step Twelve: *Having had a spiritual awakening[25] as the result of these Steps, we tried to carry this message to others with eating disorders and to practice these principles in all our affairs.*

After your sponsee has consistently emailed you their 10th Step inventory *for one week* and has made significant progress on their amends (including living amends to those closest to them, such as children and spouses), meet with them to read the Chapter Twelve homework together.

Meeting: Ask your sponsee to look for opportunities to start sponsoring at EDA meetings, including phone and online meetings. Suggest they continue working Steps Ten and Eleven, continue making amends and character-building assignments, and start attending the EDA meetings that focus on Steps Ten, Eleven, and Twelve (if available). Suggest they contact the EDA General Service Board and ask to be placed on the Sponsors list. Working with others should now be a key focus, as it will help your sponsee solidify the positive habits of thought and action they have acquired through working the Steps.

Congratulations! Your sponsee has just completed something amazing and transformative, and you have been there literally every Step of the way! We know that sharing your journey with others will be for you what it has turned out to be for us: a wonderful opportunity to turn a life of pain and misery into one that inspires others through honesty, integrity, compassion, and hope.

---

[25] The term "spiritual awakening" can refer to an event—a vital spiritual experience—or to a gradual change. We who are atheists also experience a transformation, enabling us to place service before selfishness.

The benefits we experience as a result of working the Twelve Steps go much further than relieving the pain and suffering of an eating disorder. The joy we feel at being able to turn bad experiences to good, the delight we know as we become happily useful, and the exhilaration and connection we feel as we appreciate the deep bonds we establish with others all serve to remind us how much we have to offer.

We wish you success and joy as you go out from here to continue to develop your relationship with—and serve—your God, Higher Power, or higher purpose, for therein lies true peace, freedom, happiness, and meaning. We hope we cross paths with you as we journey through life in recovery together. As the AA chapter "A Vision for You" concludes:

> Our book is meant to be suggestive only. We realize we know only a little. God will constantly disclose more to you and to us. Ask Him in your morning meditation what you can do each day for the man who is still sick. The answers will come, if your own house is in order. But obviously you cannot transmit something you haven't got. See to it that your relationship with Him is right, and great events will come to pass for you and countless others. This is the Great Fact for us.
>
> Abandon yourself to God as you understand God. Admit your faults to Him and to your fellows. Clear away the wreckage of your past. Give freely of what you find and join us. We shall be with you in the Fellowship of the Spirit, and you will surely meet some of us as you trudge the Road of Happy Destiny.
>
> May God bless you and keep you—until then.[26]

---

[26] *Alcoholics Anonymous.* (2001) New York, NY: AA World Services, Inc., 164.

PERSONAL STORIES

PART I
PIONEERS OF EDA

PART II
THEY STOPPED IN TIME

PART III
THEY LOST NEARLY ALL

PART I

PIONEERS OF EDA

(1)

FREE AT LAST

When this third member of EDA recognized that full recovery would remain out of reach until she rebuilt self-trust, she consciously accepted responsibility for addressing her own basic needs and began taking small risks to express emotions safely. As trust grew, so did love, joy, peace, and freedom.

$\mathcal{P}$lease allow me to start with a warm welcome to anyone new to the fellowship of Eating Disorders Anonymous. We are a group of men and women who have found a path to recovery and we are sharing our stories—and our process—so that others might find support, peace, and freedom from their eating disorders. If you have just discovered you have an eating disorder, or have been engaged in a lifelong struggle with one, do not despair. You are not alone. It took most of us a long time and a great deal of patience and persistence to find lasting relief, but we have! Whether you are new to recovery or strengthening and building on an existing recovery, we hope that you will find a sense of connection with us and feel the hope and joy in our stories.

Mine is not particularly remarkable. I had a normal, middle-class childhood in a small Midwestern town, loving parents, and an older sister who doted on me. I was never molested or mistreated. I was not especially overweight, nor was I very thin. I was not particularly attractive or ugly. Although I certainly had adversarial relationships with some children, I was not bullied, and I did not feel singled out in any specific way. As a child and teenager, prior to developing an eating disorder, I do not think I was more anxious or depressed than my peers. I can find no primary "cause" that explains why I should have developed one, other than my own "childish" reactions to life as it unfolded for me. Yet I became severely bulimic.

I was almost sixteen when I first read about bulimia in a "Dear Abby" column. I was repulsed by the idea, but then realized that throwing up meals was a solution to other problems I was facing. I had just started a very restrictive diet (my first), because I had gained weight lying around for a few weeks after an exciting and active trip to Europe. My mother, startled to see me eat so little, put great pressure on me to eat "normally." I felt typical adolescent rage at these attempts at control. I did not want her to worry, but I could not satisfy both my mother and my desire to return to what I deemed a healthy weight. More importantly, I was upset with myself because I could not stop eating more than I thought I "should," even though I was losing weight. My diet was so restrictive that I binged when my body had "had enough" of holding back, and I was terrified of those binges—they made me feel absolutely helpless. I had never been so afraid of myself. Throwing up took care of all these problems. Then I discovered something really amazing: throwing up relieved my rage. It also relieved my fear, resentment, frustration, self-pity, and despair; in fact bulimia addressed all my disagreeable, unmanageable, over-the-top, adolescent emotions. With bulimia, I no longer felt out of control. Bulimia worked so well that it soon became my main method of coping.

I thought that putting my emotions "on hold" would let me behave like a sensible adult instead of the overly emotional, wretchedly awkward teenager I was. For a short while, this seemed to work; and, from the outside, things looked great. I received a coveted appointment to the United States Naval Academy. I also earned a full scholarship to a State university. However, putting my emotions "on hold" meant I would remain emotionally stuck, awkward, and exposed during what should have been my development into a mature young adult. I do not fault myself for the escapist path I chose at sixteen, but the repercussions of that decision stretched well into my later years. Although I have regrets, I am grateful today to have a story of recovery to share.

While I lived at home with my parents, my eating disorder was active, but not yet completely out of control. I was a tough kid, and for the first two years, I did not see much impact from the destructive course I had chosen. There were *plenty* of repercussions, of course, but I refused to see them. I functioned well enough at school and work, and made plans for the future. I left for college with high hopes and big dreams. My life seemed full of promise.

Once I was finally in college, I had the whole complement of new and exciting experiences: freedoms and relationships and opportunities for learning I had only ever dreamed about. This should have been a delightful time of exploration and growth, and at many levels it was. But thanks to my eating disorder, I was *emotionally unprepared* for most of these experiences. I had become childlike: held hostage by my eating disorder and unable to trust myself to do the next right thing in any given situation.

When I first got to college, I had a meal card and could eat whatever and whenever I wanted. It soon became clear that people were suspicious that I was bingeing and purging, and they were willing to confront me. Embarrassed, I stopped using the meal card and learned how to steal from vending machines. What a great solution—now

I was a thief! Bulimia and lack of sleep meant I could barely stay awake in class. My grades slipped, but I was unable to stop behaviors that guaranteed they would only get worse. I lived in constant fear of discovery. The more horrible I felt, the more I binged and purged.

Before long, things began to get dangerous. I had started taking laxatives and one time nearly died of dehydration. I was afraid they would find me dead in a bathtub, too weak to lift my head to drink any liquids. I somehow survived, but only a few months later had a grand mal seizure and was hospitalized. You would think that these terrifying experiences might have woken me up! I did stop using laxatives, but was absolutely unable to stop bingeing and purging even though the damage was now horrifying and obvious. Bulimia made me oblivious not only to my own pain, but also to the pain and endangerment I created for others. I was too scared of my emotions to stop or change my eating-disordered behaviors, even for a day; I felt overwhelming shame, self-pity, frustration, and resentment. Ironically, despite the mortal peril, bingeing and purging made life seem almost manageable. With its help, I felt I could at least get up and do things that seemed purposeful. But in reality, I was a constant threat to myself and others. I could not be trusted. I lied, I stole, I cheated.

Bulimia is expensive. I pretended to deposit checks into ATM machines so I could pay for food that I would binge and purge. I lied when called into the bank on charges of fraud. Work and school served as a partial distraction from my ED, but I was constantly agitated and couldn't concentrate on anything for very long. I lost my scholarships. I started donating plasma, but still couldn't pay my bills. I moved in with my boyfriend. With each new defeat I became progressively more helpless, dependent, and shame-filled.

I discovered alcohol was much cheaper than binge-ing and purging. Eventually, I began to prefer drinking to bulimia. After enough blackout drinking-and-driving epi-sodes, I tried "controlled drinking." I bought *just enough* alcohol every day to get numb, but not so much that I could not get up the next day. As with food, once started I could not stop until everything was gone. With controlled drinking I managed to graduate college and held a decent job for almost a year. But bulimia and alcohol left my mind and body so damaged that I could not walk down a hallway without hanging onto the walls for support. This was insan-ity—and I knew it. Finally, I sought the medical treatment I had so long resisted and was told I had liver damage at the age of twenty-three.

I thought I just needed to stop the behaviors and that everything would be perfect if I could simply dry out. But much to my surprise and chagrin, I was not accepted into any kind of treatment program. Clearly, I was not a good candidate anyway, but I was very angry when my counselor suggested I try Alcoholics Anonymous (AA). I adamantly refused. After a few more weeks with my drinking no long-er arrested by work responsibilities, I had to admit I was beaten. I could not even drink much before getting the dry heaves, so that was no longer an option. I had no money or energy to deal with food at all. So I became willing to try AA, even though I was convinced it would not work for someone like me.

In the halls and basements where AA meetings are held, I found people who, despite sad sack stories like mine, were clearly happy, joyous, and free. These people— doctors, bus drivers, lawyers, and housewives—told stories shockingly similar to mine. But unlike me, these folks were sober and they were having a blast. Their lives were filled with a meaning and purpose that mine had never known. This was darned attractive stuff. I began to believe that this dreadful program could work for me, too. I was willing to be honest and open-minded, and do what was suggested— at least a little.

A life-long atheist, I struggled with the spiritual aspects of the Twelve-Step program. People in meetings eagerly pointed out that the Twelve Steps required only that I find *my own conception* of God. I thought this suggestion silly; if I earnestly could not bring myself to believe in any God, how on earth could I invent one? But I knew my life depended upon willingness to find some Higher Power that could restore me to sanity. One fellow said he believed in G.O.D.: "Good, Orderly Direction." I struggled even with that. Whose "good, orderly direction" was I to take? This sounded suspiciously like the "self-will run riot" I had come to understand as my fundamental issue. But I had to admit something was working for my atheist friend; he was sober and happy in AA. So I decided that my Higher Power would be "the life-engendering force in the universe." I believed the forces of physics and nature would restore me to sanity if I let them. This worked surprisingly well, and the program's spiritual angle was no longer a struggle for me.

Thanks to the grace of the Twelve Steps, the patience of hundreds of people, and a capacity to be honest with myself, I got and stayed sober. I worked hard in AA and it paid off. I have never found any reason to take a drink since. As of this writing I am delighted and grateful to have several decades of continuous sobriety.

As awesome as early recovery was for me, I knew right away that maintaining recovery would require sustained daily effort. Before the Twelve Steps, I thought I just had to deal with my drinking and eating problems, but soon learned I had to deal with the thinking problems that *caused* these behavioral issues. For me, the emotional and psychological underpinnings of my eating disorder are *absolutely identical* to those of my alcoholism. When all my energy went into setting my relationships right with others and recovering through the Twelve Steps, I found a sudden and total peace with food. I ate when hungry and stopped when moderately full. I didn't eat when I wasn't hungry. Amazingly, this worked! *I found I could eat anything safely, if I was paying attention and working my Twelve-Step program.*

For the first four years, I had no issues whatsoever with food. I had recovered from my eating disorder thanks to working the Twelve Steps. At the core, I was humbly grateful to be alive, sober, and free. I was happy, joyous, and extremely grateful.

I would be thrilled to tell you my life just kept getting better, but that was not the case. You may have noticed that there is not yet one word about EDA in this story. That is because there was no EDA at all until the year 2000, and we are now talking about the year 1990. Here is the rest of the story, leading up to the formation of our Fellowship and the years since.

At about four years sober, I developed a serious resentment against a co-worker who was getting credit for something I thought should have gone to me. My eating became erratic; food helped me stuff my feelings. I knew what was happening, and it scared me. I did not want to return to bulimia, so I attempted to retake the Steps (especially focusing on Steps Four through Seven) to change how I felt. But I was powerless when it came to my emotions. Despite my best efforts, I had not worked hard enough to enlarge and expand my relationship with my Higher Power. The laws of physics had not changed, and "the life-engendering force in the universe" had not changed, but *my ideas about my purpose in life still needed to change*. Without a personal and direct relationship to a Higher Power or a higher purpose, I was unprepared to cope with the anger and fear that overwhelmed every attempt I made to change my thinking. I felt as helpless as I had at sixteen. Everything intensified my resentment. Self-pity became a regular indulgence. I was as far from recovery as I had ever been in my life. I began to binge and purge with a ferocity I had never before experienced. My recovery quite literally went down the toilet. I was angry at myself, my life, and with the Twelve Steps.

I soon began to try to "control" my bulimia as I had formerly "controlled" my drinking. I would binge and purge at most meals, and tried to maintain a semblance of normalcy in between. But this was not working. I spent many days at home suffering from various "illnesses," during which time I was up to no good at all. I again sought treatment, and this time I got it *because I was willing to go to any length* to regain the sanity I had lost. I started with an inpatient treatment program, ostensibly for depression and anxiety, though my therapist and I both knew we were focusing on recovery from an eating disorder. I hoped to emerge from treatment better, stronger, and fundamentally different. I tried to change my thinking entirely, doing everything that was asked to the full extent of my ability. I was rigorously honest. I did not try to hide from, or suppress, my emotions. I did not do any "behaviors" in treatment. I had hoped that a miracle of recovery would come to me upon surrender to the discipline of the center—but this was not to be. Unexpectedly, my failure did have one solid and positive result: it gave me near certainty that I could, and would, somehow find recovery through the Twelve

Steps. They had worked before, and somehow I sensed that they would help me regain the sanity, peace, and freedom I had lost. I resolved to try harder.

I began to talk about my eating disorder with my AA sponsor. I continued to attend AA meetings and brought up the issue there. Several thoughtful people suggested another Twelve-Step program that focused on eating be-haviors. I dutifully started attending meetings. At first it was exciting to discover that others were finding recovery through abstinence from specific foods and by following a disciplined pattern of eating, but I found no relief at all that way. As I had in the treatment center, I followed sugges-tions, eliminated specific food components, and weighed and measured. I found a sponsor, and then found another. I worked the Steps. I went to meetings every day. I went to Twelve-Step retreats. But nothing changed inside me, and I stopped going to those meetings after a year of earnest ef-fort. I was miserable and exhausted.

For another year I continued to attend my AA meet-ings, where I was rigorously honest about my eating disor-der. Although people were often horrified, my resentments and self-pity began to ease up. Gradually, my bingeing and purging also faded away, and I stopped having to talk about it. I was anxious about this newly regained recovery and afraid that the bulimia would resurface. But my life had improved tremendously, and I was deeply grateful.

My husband and I decided to have a child. Mostly free of my eating-disordered thoughts and behaviors, I rejoiced when we had a healthy baby boy. I was incred-ibly humbled to have been granted the delight and solemn responsibility of motherhood with first one son and then another. I opted to stay home with the children, while my husband agreed to shoulder the entire financial burden for the family. I was happy. Occasionally, though, my husband would suggest new business ventures and activities, which I thought threatened our financial stability or my ideas about how things should be. Rather than hear him out, I usually resisted changes that might have better accommodated his needs: I was selfishly risk-adverse. He began to lose patience with me, and I began to feel ever more angry and helpless. Didn't he realize how hard I was working to raise the kids properly? I began to feel victimized, then resentful, and finally, self-pitying. The insanity returned. Sure enough, bingeing and purging followed quickly on the heels of resentment, self-pity, and fear.

At this point, thanks to sponsors and friends in Twelve-Step programs, I could better articulate what I was feeling. So I went back to the abstinence-based Twelve-Step program determined to do things "properly." I had learned a great deal in the intervening years and thought that surely there was something amiss with my application of that program's Twelve Steps. I worked with a series of sponsors, completing multiple 4th and 5th Steps. I became convinced that my conception of a Higher Power was inadequate. I became willing to surrender to the tenets of an organized religion if that was what it took. I spoke with pastors and with family. I attended Bible studies. I read the New Testament. Unmoved, I tried other approaches. I read books on Buddhism and began a yoga and meditation practice. I attended sweat lodge ceremonies and started a drumming group at my church. I tried my best to adopt and adapt other people's conceptions of God. At times, one idea or another seemed to hold promise, but the bingeing and purging did not fully abate. At other times, it grew worse. I discovered that I could even binge on the healthy food that I normally found completely unappealing. This would have been a laughable insanity, except that my family's well-being depended on my solving this problem. I desperately needed a solution.

I grew weary of avoiding the foods my sponsor told me were my problem; I knew that when my emotional state was clear, I could eat anything with impunity. I urgently wanted that peace and freedom. So I stopped going to the abstinence-based Twelve-Step program and started to attend a therapy group for people with eating disorders. It was there that I met Gisele, who was struggling with alcohol as well as an eating disorder. Happy to be helpful, I encouraged Gisele to go to AA meetings—and she did. Soon after, she became determined to start something like AA for people with eating disorders.

Here is where the real story of Eating Disorders Anonymous began: Gisele started something altogether new. In her new meeting, there were no food plans and no commitments or references to "abstinence." This was a Twelve-Step program with a difference. After about a month, Gisele managed to convince me to attend.

The early gatherings of what we began to call "Eating Disorders Anonymous" were small, generally including only three people: Gisele, Joanie, and myself. Each of us was trying to find a better way to live. We desperately wanted to make the changes in ourselves that would make the world a better and safer place for our children. At this point, every one of us was still engaged in maintenance-level, eating-disordered behaviors, so there was no pretense about having found "a solution." For quite a while, we were not sure the "abstinence-free" approach would even work. Yet, within our tiny group, compassion and trust were growing deeper and broader. I knew that Gisele, a strong person with a huge heart and a great sense of humor, loved her daughter as much as I loved my sons, and yet there we all were, stuck in behaviors we hated. We all felt silly and stupid. We all "knew better."

As we examined what we knew to be true, we found our common experiences had remarkable alignment around a few key ideas. We were all in agreement that *food was totally beside the point*. We knew that *the emotions we were unable to accept and address* were thwarting our efforts to act sanely, despite our love for our children and all that is good and right in the world. We also began to see that *the mutual trust and respect* we built within our small fellowship were helping: as we became honest with each other, we learned to trust one another. And we began to get better.

Although none of us were completely well, we were relying less and less on our eating disorders to get us through each day. It was a hopeful time, but despite several months of improvement after joining our little EDA fellowship, I had to admit I was disappointed in my own slow progress as well as that of our group. I had good weeks when I was happy and never thought about food; I had terrible weeks when I could not stand living with my emotional baggage and binged and purged a great deal. I wanted more and better for my husband and my kids. The peace and freedom I had once enjoyed in recovery was elusive. The others in our small circle were engaged in individual therapy, so I decided to give counseling another try. A friend gave me the name of someone who was both in AA and recovering from an eating disorder.

Unlike my previous experiences, I quickly grew to trust this new counselor. I knew her experiences were similar to my own, and I had confidence in her recovery. This time I was not only willing to change, *I was willing to trust someone to lead me through the process of change.* She encouraged me to take a less harsh and rigid view of recovery, and I discovered something important: in all my previous efforts to work the Twelve Steps—and finding recovery in AA—I had failed to grasp that it was *my responsibility* to understand and meet my own needs, no matter what. I know that sounds obvious and simplistic, but somehow I had missed this vital piece of information. *Our commitment to take care of our own basic needs is the basis of self-trust.* It became clear that I had never fully understood the idea behind "First Things First."

I learned I could be safe, even when letting myself think terrifying thoughts and feeling my most awful emotions. I learned to have compassion for myself. Outside of therapy, I began the Twelve Steps again, but rather than working them more rigorously, I worked them more gently, more patiently, with less judgment. I am intensely grateful for my experiences in counseling. It was there that I really began to see that only having trust in others or a Higher Power—without taking the action to build self-trust—simply could not work.

Trust turned out to be the key for me. Without trust I could not recover; with trust I could. Faith in my Higher Power alone had proved insufficient to overcome my eating disorder, but consistent and deliberate action motivated by the idea of serving a higher purpose—building a recovery so I could better serve my family, my community, and my fellow members of EDA—began to provide relief. I was never able to build a personal relationship with a spiritual entity, but I was able to build what was needed through my daily commitment to serve the greater good to the best of my ability. Before a year went by, I regained perspective and balance and felt more solid in my recovery than I had felt since I first broke self-trust. *It became clear to me that achieving balance and perspective was more supportive of lasting peace and freedom than achieving "abstinence."* (A brief discussion of the concept of balance can be found in Appendix B.) So in essence, my recovery from my eating disorder started in EDA, grew stronger through my work in therapy, then broadened and solidified through my work with the EDA program.

Slowly, our little group grew and got stronger. Together, we continued to get better. At one point, we early members contacted the AA General Service Office in New York and obtained permission to use limited excerpts (with citations and caveats) from the first 164 pages of AA's text, *Alcoholics Anonymous,* in our EDA literature.[1] Applying what we had learned from our direct experiences, we developed some of the foundational documents for EDA, including the "Keep it Simple" version of EDA's Twelve Steps. We built a website and left flyers at local therapists' offices. We took our meeting on the road to local treatment centers. We started holding meetings throughout the Phoenix metropolitan area. More members began to find and sustain recovery. We formed a General Service Board to help EDA groups carry the message. We created brochures on each of the eating disorders, an EDA Meeting Guide, and a Starter Kit to help people get new EDA meetings going. The Promises of the program slowly came true for us as we carried the message of recovery to others.

We went through good times and bad. We experi-

---

[1] EDA's program of recovery is adapted from the first 164 pages of *Alcoholics Anonymous,* the "Big Book," with permission from Alcoholics Anonymous World Services, Inc. Permission to reprint and adapt this material does not mean that AA has reviewed or approved this or any other EDA material. AA is a program for recovery from alcoholism only. Use of AA material in the program of EDA, which is patterned after that of AA but which addresses other issues, does not constitute endorsement by or affiliation with AA.

enced incredible delight and excitement as we banded together and bonded in the grand adventure of recovery, and
also periods of doubt and struggle. Some people took issue
with our less rigid approach. EDA's endorsement of balance
(not abstinence) proved confusing to both newcomers and
Twelve-Step old-timers. We had to remind ourselves—and
each other—that recovery is a process, not an event. Some
EDA members are granted an immediate reprieve from
their eating-disordered behaviors, but far more find their
recovery is gradual. As we practice new ways of being in the
world that permit us to let go of old behaviors, they begin
to lose their power, and we are gradually restored to sanity.

Thankfully, the simple truth of these ideas carried the
day. EDA's position is that living in recovery is so much
better than living with an active eating disorder that no one
who has experienced both will go back to old patterns for
long. However, they need to understand the key: *building
self-trust and integrity for the purpose of serving the greater
good*.

Some among us thought this approach too complicated for the newcomer. How could they know whom to
trust if we did not have some universal measuring stick, like
length of abstinence or sobriety? Some EDA members were
adherents of a specific religion, finding other concepts of
God troublesome and offensive. Some of our newer members cast aside anonymity in an attempt to carry a "more
authentic" message of recovery. Leaders occasionally signed
up for more than they could deliver and failed to show up
for meetings to unlock the doors. One EDA sponsor took
on hundreds of sponsees at once, starting something that
resembled a cult more than a humble service. Our online
bulletin board—a forum for sharing recovery—was over-
run by disturbingly inappropriate spam. Lacking resources

to provide proper monitoring, we sadly shut it down. Not everyone kept coming back, and not everyone got better.

But more and more of us did get better, and we stayed better, too. As we learned what we needed to do to stay in balance, many of us began to experience full recovery—free of eating disordered thoughts as well as behaviors, no matter the situation or provocation. EDA meetings began to spring up around the country, and then overseas. Today, EDA has a foothold in forty states and ten countries. It is an amazing and wonderful thing to watch our Fellowship grow!

Like other members and EDA itself, I have grown and changed with time. I gradually learned to build gratitude and patience in much the same way as I learned to build trust: through conscious and deliberate action. In early recovery, gratitude seemed to come automatically when working the Steps. At other points, gratitude came haltingly, in a miserly trickle. Sometimes I could not seem to find gratitude or patience when I needed them most desperately. I went through periods when I struggled in my relationships, but I found great relief in a daily journaling practice that I still maintain. I find it well worth the time to write out my Step Ten, reflect on my many reasons for gratitude, and think about the day's goals. Despite years of consistent effort, I am still not a patient or deliberate person. But thanks to daily journaling, I now get to start the day in peace and with perspective—a positive way that feels so right to me. I also still find it absolutely critical to take some meaningful Twelve-Step action every day, for then I am happier, more purposeful and patient, more gracious, and less likely to suffer from fear, self-pity, or resentment.

My experiences working the steps are outlined in Appendix C: "An EDA Member Works the Steps." These days,

I have a regular practice. I take inventory throughout the day, and when wrong, I try to admit my mistakes promptly and without regret. I seek to understand and to do what is right in each situation. I still often fall far short of the mark, but I now trust that my best effort is good enough. I have gotten through some very difficult times without losing my sanity or obsessing on food, weight, exercise, or anything else. My daily Step Ten helps me deal with these difficult times effectively. It is amazing how a sincere effort to right a wrong can restore peace and balance!

I have had many years of solid recovery from my eating disorder, although I cannot claim a "perfect" recovery. I have engaged in old behaviors on rare occasions where I felt guilty of some wrong and helpless to address it. That is, without question, an irrational, irresponsible choice. Invariably, when I completely lose perspective like that, I find I have fallen down on some aspect of my program. At times, I have not kept up relationships with friends with whom I can be completely honest. At times, I have not been completely honest with myself about what I am thinking and feeling. I *always* find I have not troubled myself to think about how I can turn even the worst situation to some useful purpose. I *always* find I have not been focusing enough on how to best maintain balance and serve others. At least, I now fully trust the solution. I have had to forgive myself, try to understand what happened, and figure out what I will do differently should a similar situation occur. My friends remind me that I am still learning, still a work in progress. Losing perspective is frustrating, but each event reminds me of how much I have to lose and how much I still need to work my Steps.

I worried for years that my "imperfect" story would not serve as a bright-enough beacon of hope. Over the years, I have seen and heard from many people who have never looked back, never repeated old behaviors, and never had any reminders—save their own stories and their work with others in EDA—of what it was like to be back in the dark days. I am grateful for and humbled by these wonderful people. Some of their stories are in the latter part of this book. I hope you find them as delightful and inspiring as I do. My good news is that I have never found myself mired as I once was. My "reminders" have been few, mercifully short-lived, and years apart. The work required for recovery is ridiculously easy compared to having an active eating disorder and living with self-pity, resentment, shame, and fear. I know the EDA program works; I live in freedom, not fear.

Full recovery is a blast. I've been delighted to be involved in the growth of the Fellowship of EDA. I am humbled and grateful to work with some amazing people. I am absolutely thrilled to be working with EDA members on our joint effort to share our experience, strength, and hope with others. I have been privileged to attend graduate school in a field I love, start businesses and work hard to see them succeed, teach archaeology and mountaineering to a lot of wonderful kids, backpack through the Grand Canyon, climb mountains in several states, and watch my children emerge into adulthood. I am still happily married to the same great guy, thankful for his patience, forgiveness, and love. I am grateful I was able to make amends before my father passed, and I am happy to have a wonderful relationship with my mother. I love my life and I adore my family. I have hope for the future. I am grateful every day for my recovery, and for the joy of others' recoveries.

There are many paths to peace and freedom from an eating disorder, but the Twelve-Step program of EDA

works for me. If someone as stubborn, impulsive, frightened, untrusting, and rigid as I was can recover, there is
hope for everyone! Please keep coming back. Take what you
can use and leave the rest. Enjoy recovery, and share your
story with others who may need to hear it. If you do, you
will find that the old saying, "To thine own self be true,"
will bring you lasting peace and freedom.

A LIFE SOLUTION

Accepting powerlessness over her eating disorder and responsibility for her actions helped her find an answer that works in all aspects of life.

As far back as I can remember I struggled with food and body image. It seemed as though people close to me used food as a way to control my behavior, whether it was by forcing me to finish everything on my plate or sending me to my room without eating as punishment. I am one of four siblings, yet I am the only one who has an eating disorder. As I look back, instead of feeling the feelings and healing from them, I internalized the pain and used self-sabotaging behaviors to numb myself.

Growing up, we moved a lot; I have lived in three countries and five states. There was sexual, physical, and emotional abuse early on as a child, and later rape. I believe that the abuse was one of the main reasons I did not feel okay in my own skin. I was always trying to run away and numb myself any way I could. The first of countless times I ran away was when I was three and a half, and this continued through the years until I turned eighteen and was able to legally move out on my own.

I felt ashamed of my body and of developing into a woman. I was always trying to cover up my body by wearing tights over my legs or long sleeves, even during the summer. I internalized comments made by others, such as, "You're so flat you make the walls jealous" or "thunder thighs." Instead of ignoring these remarks, I internalized them as truth and felt ashamed. These shameful feelings were relieved with sports and, more importantly, with alcohol; so began my journey as an alcoholic with an eating disorder. No matter how much food I ate, or how much weight I lost, or how well I did in sports, it never seemed to numb the pain permanently. Drinking and eating-disordered behaviors provided temporary release, but never the long-lasting kind I was truly seeking. In high school, I experimented with diet pills that caused me to pass out during heavy exercise. Although playing basketball and running track definitely helped me feel semi-normal, I found myself needing more and more to feel happy. I had heard of bingeing, purging, and restricting, but thought that I would never do such things. I was in total denial about the struggles I had with food and my body. I deemed bingeing acceptable during sports seasons, because I knew I would "run it off." However, that fleeting comfort would come to a halt sooner rather than later.

During my sophomore year in high school, one of my best friends introduced me to purging. We were talking during a binge episode, and for the first time ever I brought up the sexual abuse I experienced as a child. I began to feel sick to my stomach from all the food I had just eaten, and my friend showed me how to make myself feel better instantly by "getting rid of it." I felt like I had found a solution to numb both the pain and the never-ending internal disgust I felt for myself. A combination of drugs, alcohol, and eating-disorder behaviors off-season, along with a mixture of intense exercise, bingeing, and purging during athletic season got me halfway through my senior year. As soon as I turned eighteen, midway through my senior year, I moved out of my parents' house. I had always blamed them for all of my problems and figured this would make me get better.

Unfortunately, with no constraints everything got worse: my eating disorder, my drinking, and my drug abuse. I nearly didn't graduate from high school. I had a college basketball scholarship opportunity that I completely avoided in order to remain in my vicious cycle. I stayed at a local college with roommates who had their own struggles, and this took the focus off of me. Near the end of my first semester, I was fully in my eating disorder, swinging between diet pills (and other drugs that took away my appetite) and drugs that would heighten my bingeing or facilitate my purging.

During this time, I was out drinking one night and went into the back alley of a local bar to induce vomiting. I became physically weak and unable to move when someone attempted to pick me up. He said he was going to "take care of me" and make sure I didn't get hurt. But this was not the case. After that night, nothing could soothe the pain and agony I felt. A few weeks later, I finally told my mother about the rape. We decided that it would be a good idea to get away from the people and the places that were causing harm in hopes of a fresh start. But even moving did not help, because once again I found the "partiers" and other people with eating disorders. It was all the same, just a different town.

Even though the other people I was around were engaging in the same behaviors, they became concerned. In fact the basketball coach, who had previously attempted to recruit me, didn't want me to have anything to do with the team, because I was in such bad shape and had lost so much weight. Since the season was almost over, she told me I'd better get my act together before the next one, or I would not have another chance. This threat didn't slow me down one bit; in fact it fed into my eating disorder even more.

One evening, I started purging and found myself vomiting uncontrollably; I couldn't stop. I was choking on my own vomit and someone had to give me the Heimlich. You would think this would have scared me into recovery, but it didn't. I just figured I had eaten the wrong type of food. A short time later, when others saw that this near-death experience didn't change my behavior, someone contacted administration and a mini-intervention took place. I was sent to a facility that treated eating disorders for about three months (between inpatient, day patient, and outpatient services).

Back then, there was a lot of emphasis on daily weigh-ins and calorie counting to ensure each patient was eating enough. If not, the remainder would be made up at the end of the day with a liquid, nutritional supplement. Up to that point, I had not really obsessed over numbers on the scale or calories in my food, but since I was unable to act out in my usual way, this became my new obsession. For a few months, it worked. I did not restrict, binge and purge, over-exercise, or use diet pills. However, my great obsession with numbers soon gave way to my old methods. Why? Because when I was not using behaviors, I felt disgusting in my own skin and almost failed out of college. But once I gave in to the cycle again, I started getting good grades and even graduated. It became evident to me that I needed my eating disorder to survive: I didn't know how to live without it.

After college, I landed an opportunity to become a high school guidance counselor while the county paid for me to earn my master's degree. After two years of complete hypocrisy trying to get teenagers to give up their eating disorders, drinking, drug usage, and promiscuous behavior, I couldn't live with such lies anymore and "no-showed" for the following year.

In the meantime, one of the many part-time jobs I worked while counseling became a full-time job at a restaurant/bar. This allowed me to drink and "use" the way I thought I needed to in order to survive. I lost my first home in foreclosure and had credit card debt "up the wazoo" due to all of my spending on food, clothes, and bars. My car was almost repossessed a few times, which I only avoided by hiding it down the street from where I lived. Eventually, I even filed bankruptcy due to the amount of debt I had incurred. I wanted to die. My family could no longer deal with me, because they could not stand to see me slowly killing myself any more. I would pray for God to just let me sleep and not wake up—and felt damned every morning when I would. Nothing could make me feel better, no matter how hard I tried. "Fortunately," I had discovered a certain substance that allowed me to feel a new type of numbness, and this became a daily habit as well. I was able to admit that I had a problem with this substance, along with any type of diet and mood/mind altering pill. I tried to stop drinking and drugging (while holding on to my eating disorder for dear life), but I always ended up back where I started. I simply could not stop. I could not get rid of the thoughts! I could not live! I would try to stop my eating disorder behavior, but then I would pick up a drink or a drug. They were so enmeshed.

Somehow, through a series of events—people trying to help others through their struggles with eating disorders, drugs, and alcohol—I found my way to the Steps.

I discovered a sponsor who took me through AA's "Big Book," chapter by chapter, paragraph by paragraph, sentence by sentence. We used it as it pertained to each of my "-isms," not only individually, but also as a group. Medical professionals had told me years before that I would never recover from my eating disorder, so I was doubtful about the effectiveness of the Step process. I had attempted the Steps previously for my drinking and drugging, but never for all three problems, which explains why I was unsuccessful. The purging stopped and I situated myself with roommates, family members, co-workers, and friends, so for the most part meals were with others. I would work all day, go to an evening Step meeting, eat dinner, and do Step work along with prayers.

On the weekends, I would stay busy with the Step fellowship trying to learn how to live life in recovery while having fun. I attempted to be of service by carpooling people to meetings, calling those who were struggling, or taking on service positions such as setting up for meetings or greeting people. I was told that although I could not sponsor until I had gone through all Steps, there were other ways to be of service while trying my best to stay out of my self-centered thoughts. Although I wasn't bingeing or purging, I still found ways to over exercise while going to the gym, until it was pointed out that this was also part of my eating disorder.

It was suggested that I leave that up to God for now. I had to let my body heal from all of the damage I had done. There were many views, ideas, opinions, and perspectives I had to put aside. Through the Steps, I developed my own conception of God, setting aside the former God that I thought was punishing me from my childhood. I had to believe that He did not "give me" my eating disorder. One way I looked at it was I believed—and still do—that we are all given free will and we are not puppets in this world. I chose to seek comfort and distraction through my different eating-disordered actions, instead of seeking professional help. I had to let go of resentments that were holding me hostage and keeping me sick. I saw my reactions to my life and past were my responsibility and I had to move on.

Today, my past no longer haunts me or holds me back from living life and interacting with people. Due to the spiritual awakening I found as a result of working the Steps, I neither act out in my eating disorder in any way, nor do I obsess about the symptoms, food, weight, or body image.

Now, I say I am recovered from my eating disorder and hopeless state of life. This is a result of remaining connected to a God of my personal understanding through working the Steps and helping others. My personal belief is once eating-disordered, always eating-disordered. This means if I act out in any way, I will not be successful. However, as long as I continue living Steps Ten, Eleven, and Twelve, and going to EDA meetings, I do not live in fear of going back to my old habits.

At times, I would have a gut-wrenching feeling I did not want to acknowledge and would consider acting out. But this fleeting thought was replaced with the truth: it would not be just one time. God has restored my sanity, meaning I am now able to see the truth about my condition—one I do not fear as long as I continue doing His work. There have been challenging situations in which I found it difficult to eat because of feeling so terrible, but since I know and accept I am powerless over my eating disorder, I do not want to ever go down that path again. There have been times I felt like eating everything in sight, but I know and accept that one incorrect choice may lead to another. In times like these I pray, meditate, or call a friend to join me for a meal, so I can eat despite the feelings.

I use food for its intended purpose, like air; I no longer use it to self-medicate or soothe/numb any pain or discomfort. I have lost relationships, family members, and friends through death and changing jobs, but I have never gone back to my eating disorder.

I did not know I could have a long-lasting, healthy and intimate relationship, but I found one. For my wedding, I knew I could not go on the typical diet of many brides-to-be. And after five years of recovery, I instantly got pregnant! I thought I had permanently damaged my body, but happily this was not the case.

During my first pregnancy, I was completely immobilized on bed rest for the last two-and-a-half months and gained a lot of weight. I did what I had to in order to take care of the baby growing inside of me, and left my body and its weight up to God. I also could not diet like some new mothers do to have their weight fall off quickly, because that could lead me back to the dark days. Once again, I had to trust God that if I continued trying to live His will, I would be taken care of spiritually, emotionally, and even physically.

I got pregnant again ten months later! And even though my body has not been restored fully to its original shape and size, I have accepted that it is a beautiful God-given gift for a thirty-seven-year-old woman with two kids. In fact, I have accepted my curves and consider myself sexier than ever. I'm even back into a bikini, which I never thought possible, and feel great in it! I also feel great in my own skin.

I no longer feel a victim to my past. I have healthy relationships with my family members, and have forgiven them as they have forgiven me. I have a loving relationship with a God I take everything to, and I desire that connection continuously. When difficult things happen, I acknowledge and work through them, but do not make them bigger than they are. I no longer obsess about me, me, me—now I constantly look for ways to help others. I meet with others who have eating disorders to take them through the Steps as they are laid out in the "Big Book," while still going to EDA meetings. I try to apply the principles from the Twelve Steps to all aspects of my life, not only in meetings. I am free to eat anything, go anywhere, and do anything without the fear of going back. This is all due to the connection I have with the God of my understanding, who is my defense against my eating disorder so long as I continue to do this work. EDA has provided me with a solution to life. Thank God!

A PROGRAM FOR PEOPLE WHO WORK IT

Going to any length for recovery is just the beginning of her story.

Standing in the kitchen of my tiny studio apartment, I stared at the food in the cupboard. I was starving. I had stuck to my rigid allotment of calories for the day, repeatedly using drugs to alleviate the hunger pangs, but my stomach still growled in agony. *Feed me*, my body begged. I shut the cupboard and went to bed.

I couldn't sleep. I was starving and wired from the drugs. I rolled out of bed and stumbled into the kitchen. I started eating. Just one at first, then two, then a handful, and then… the box was empty. What happened? I panicked, throwing the tainted box into the trash. *Well, I've already ruined my diet for the day, so I might as well go all out, right? I can exercise it off tomorrow anyway.* I proceeded to eat more.

I always wished I could purge. I would lean over the toilet, doing all the tricks I had heard of or read about on the internet, crying and pleading with my body to get out the poisonous binge, but I could never do it. Exercise and drugs would have to get rid of the excess calories.

I was fourteen when I went on my first diet. I was barely overweight and a very active kid. I played outside every day and took as many dance classes as my parents' budget would allow. I loved to dance. I dreamed of becoming a famous ballerina, performing in front of hundreds of people in grand venues. *If I could only lose weight, then my dream could come true.* This was my mantra for many years. I dieted on and off throughout high school. I would gain weight, lose it, then gain it back, then lose it again. I wanted to be skinny like my dance friends, but an overwhelming depression often got in the way of my diet plans.

I took my first drink when I was seventeen. That same night I lost my virginity to a cute stranger. I had been desperate to lose my virginity—to be one of the cool kids—but I was terrified. Growing up in a strictly religious family, I feared I would be sent to hell if I had sex before I was married. The alcohol quieted those fears, and what could have been a special experience with someone I loved was instead a drunken plea to be part of the "cool club."

By the time I got to college, I was drinking daily, or as often as I could get alcohol. I was lonely and didn't know how to live on my own. Because my dorm meal plan allowed me to eat to my heart's content, I started using food as a coping tool for my depression and loneliness. I blamed it on the "munchies" from the alcohol. The drinking and bingeing continued, with brief periods of desperate dieting to lose the weight I was rapidly gaining. When I was twenty years old, at the beginning of my senior year, a girlfriend introduced me to the drug that would quickly become my best friend. I always thought that people who used this drug were skinny, so I was curious about trying it. I was willing to go to any length to lose weight. So I took the drug and quickly felt a sense of relief. *This is it*, I thought. *This is how I can finally be thin.*

It worked for a while. I was able to work hard in school, exercise for long periods each day, hold down a job, and stick to my restrictive diet. As long as the number on the scale was going down, I felt like everything would be okay.

Perfectionist that I am, I graduated college with two bachelor's degrees in three years. I immediately started graduate school, certain that someday I would go on to accomplish great things in the world.

The only thing standing in my way, or so I thought, was the bingeing. I was very successful at restricting and forcing myself to exercise each day, but when night fell and everyone else went to bed, I ate. It was my secret time: I could eat all of my forbidden foods and no one had to know about it. They would applaud me for my willpower to eat "healthy" during the day, boosting my ego and confidence. They didn't know what happened at night.

I grew concerned about my drug use. My extremely limited income during graduate school posed a problem for such an expensive habit. I decided to see a psychiatrist. The doctor prescribed a legal drug, which I used to replace the illegal one. I was relieved I could continue my restrictive diet and grueling exercise, and now my insurance would cover my diet drugs! But the psychiatrist also referred me to a therapist, with whom I agreed to work. I owe my life to that woman; I still see her regularly.

I told the therapist I had a problem with binge eating. "The problem is I eat so much at night that I can't seem to lose any weight. I follow a strict diet and exercise plan, but I can't stop eating at night!" I lamented. The therapist told me that in addition to a serious drug habit, I suffered from an eating disorder and needed treatment. She also told me she had been recovered from anorexia for many years, and that recovery was possible for me, too. I agreed to see a dietitian, who confirmed I had an eating disorder and helped me develop a meal plan to get started on the road to recovery.

I was overwhelmed. *I'm not skinny enough to have an eating disorder,* I thought. *I don't throw up my food. I just want to lose weight. There's nothing wrong with that.* I continued to see my treatment team, refraining from illegal drugs but still drinking heavily and abusing my prescription medication. I dropped out of graduate school, having failed several classes. I lost my job at the coffee shop where I had worked for two years, because I had failed to show up to work too many times. Nothing was important anymore except losing weight. My reason for living was to become as thin as possible.

A short time later, I entered my first inpatient treatment center, because I was out of options. Unemployed and unable to pay my rent, I thought at least treatment would give me a place to stay for a while. I completed inpatient, residential, day treatment, and intensive outpatient. I also went to AA meetings and stayed sober for a few months at a time, but never worked the Steps. I used the meetings as a place to find friends and hook up with guys. I wanted recovery, but I wanted to be thin more.

I went in and out of treatment centers for a couple of years. I would stay sober for longer periods of time (the longest being twenty months) and I took pride in my recovery, becoming an activist for eating disorder awareness and recovery. *I did it and so can you!* I would cheer. But I refused to let my weight go above a certain number and I continued to restrict and binge regularly. I was a fraud.

I ended up unemployed once again, living on a friend's couch, using whatever drugs we could get our hands on. I would watch my friends use certain drugs and then start eating, which terrified me. I refused to use those, sticking exclusively to ones that would suppress my appetite. The problem was that none of them worked anymore; there was not a single drug out there that would quiet my mind.

My friend would get food from a charity program, which I refused to eat. *I will not be a victim. I don't need a f---ing handout*, I thought. But when the dizziness and physical pain became unbearable, I would give in and eat something. I felt guilty, knowing that the food was intended for needy families, not anorexic drug addicts like me. I disgusted myself.

I became so underweight that I could hardly move. I would get up only to go outside and chain-smoke cigarettes or drive to my drug dealer's house. I knew I was dying, but I wanted to die at the lowest possible weight. Although I was suicidal, I lacked the mental capacity to formulate a plan to kill myself. My brain and body were shutting down.

I had been to treatment. I knew what I needed to do. But the compulsion to restrict and lose weight was more powerful than my desire to live. Each night, I prayed for God to let me die in my sleep.

My Higher Power had a different plan for me. One day, I reached out to a woman I had known from AA. She worked for an eating disorder treatment facility. She listened to my problems and gave me the number to call for an intake assessment. I went to treatment for the last time, broken and desperate enough to go to any lengths for my recovery. Every day I thank God for that desperation.

Having grown up in a family where I felt religion had been shoved down my throat (no pun intended!), I was reluctant to seek a Higher Power. I didn't understand what God had to do with recovery. My sponsor suggested I think about the morning sun. "The sun comes up every morning and gives us life. We wouldn't be able to live without the sun. Why don't you start by thanking the sun for rising each morning?" I thought she was being ridiculous, but I was willing to try anything. So I did. The beautiful thing about the Twelve-Step philosophy is that I have the freedom to meet God however I understand God. My Higher Power is whatever I make of it. And for me, nature's beauty is God as I understand God.

Not everyone reaches the low point I did. The truth is, I could have recovered sooner, but lacked the willingness to let go of controlling my weight. I insisted on associating my worth with the number on the scale. So the most important and freeing thing I have done for my recovery has been to hand my weight over to my Higher Power. At first, that power came in the form of a dietitian. I trusted her to monitor my weight. I gave over my most prized possession, my body, to something greater than myself.

My sponsor took me through the "Big Book" of Alcoholics Anonymous. We read it line by line, and when we reached a Step, she taught me how to work it. I had known for years I had an eating disorder, but now I admitted I was powerless over it. I looked closely at my resentments and character defects. I made amends to the people in my life whom I had hurt. I wrote a letter to my former boss, who had been a wonderful mentor to me, and whom I had failed incredibly, leading to the end of our relationship. She never responded to my letters, which was extremely disappointing, but I am entirely willing to make amends with her if I see her someday.

I restricted and binged for several months into my recovery. Unlike drugs and alcohol, I couldn't simply cut food out of my life; after all, that had been the problem in the first place! But I started to use my behaviors as learning experiences. After each slip, I asked myself, *What happened that made me feel like food was the only way to cope? What can*

I do differently next time? It has now been a couple of years since I've used eating-disordered behaviors. I've made peace with food and I have never felt so free.

I started an EDA meeting where I live. We have grown and blossomed into a beautiful fellowship of love and support for each other. I wish there were more EDA meetings in the area, and we often talk about starting them.

I went back to school to earn my master's degree in psychology. Today, I work as a counselor for the same company where I went to treatment for the last time. It has been made abundantly clear that I can only keep my recovery by giving it away.

Many women come to me for help working the Twelve Steps. I take them through the "Big Book" of Alcoholics Anonymous, just as my sponsor did with me. When we finish Step Twelve we start over at Step One. What a blessing it has been to watch other women recover and be a part of their journeys. Working with others has been one of the most rewarding experiences I have ever known.

Many of us come and go. Some aren't ready and others aren't willing. I pray they realize there is no need to become as completely hopeless and desperate as I was before seeking recovery. The old-timers in AA used to tell me, "This isn't a program for people who want it. It's not even a program for people who need it. *It's a program for people who do it.*" And so I do it, day after day, whether I want to or not.

And this is just the beginning of my story.

ONE DAY AT A TIME

True honesty has her showing up for life—one day at a time.

 am a recovering anorexic, bulimic, compulsive eater, emotional eater…well, you get the point. I've been all over the board with abusing food. I began my battle around the age of eleven and am now almost twenty-two. I have wasted about half of my precious life on this awful disease, and I am not willing to let it have another minute. I have been actively seeking recovery for about a year.

So many things contributed to my eating disorder that I don't know exactly where to begin. There wasn't one magical moment when I decided that I was a piece of crap, fat and useless, and therefore I was going to starve myself. I was never a thin child. I was always a little chubby, though very strong in mind, body, and spirit. I was tall for my age, towering over everyone in school. I developed early, when I was about 10. I got my period and breasts that were all of a sudden a very large cup size. I wasn't uncomfortable with my body at that point, but I did become uncomfortable when people close to me began pointing things out. My stepfather remarked that I was "busting out at the seams" of my jeans, which had been handed down twice. For reasons unknown, my "best friend" put a picture of me in a bathing suit on an envelope that contained an "I hate you" letter, and wrote that I didn't just need a ThighMaster, but a tummy master too.

Around this time, my stepfather left, leaving my mom with three kids to support. We moved in with various relatives until we got government assistance to have a place of our own. For privacy, I turned the walk-in closet in the master bedroom into my room. Bed, nightstand, and dresser—it was huge! My mom worked nights at a local bar and I watched the kids. I felt guilty about eating at this time, because I knew my mom was skipping meals so there would be enough food for us kids. I started skipping meals too. I also stole food for us from my friends' and family members' homes. I thought it was the least I could do. Besides, I was fat enough; I didn't need to eat with all the reserves I had built up. My uncle, who was helping to provide for us, was also molesting me. Through all of this, we moved and moved and moved. There was not much stability in my life.

I continued to starve, skip meals, and exercise excessively. I went to the library to research eating disorders so I could be better at it. I didn't start purging until about age fourteen, when I caught a friend doing it and thought, *Aha! Now, I don't have to be hungry and I can get even thinner— like her!* It didn't register that we were already wearing the same size clothes, and she was many inches shorter.

When I was sixteen, I had a weird condition with my spleen that caused my stomach to shrink. I lost a lot of weight before and after surgery. I went several years without being acutely active in my disease. Then, when I was about nineteen, I went to a psychiatrist for help. He told me that it was obviously a control issue and that I didn't have an eating disorder because I hadn't lost "enough" weight.

I was in an abusive relationship when I started purging again. This was my first experience with overeating; our whole relationship was based on food. He was so controlling. Sometimes, the only way to get away from him was to make myself throw up, because he couldn't stand the sound or smell. I lost a lot of weight when we broke up: food wasn't my only outlet anymore. When our relationship ended, I was free. It felt fantastic.

I went another year before the obsession crept back in yet again. I began restricting and purging everything I ate. I would spit out food. I lost a great deal of weight very quickly. I confessed the situation to a guy at work with whom I had a really great friendship. As a result of this admission of truth, I went to a treatment center. Unfortunately, I left after just a few days—I hadn't seen a nutritionist, a therapist, or an internist. I knew it was a mistake to leave, but I was frustrated because I did not feel like I was getting any help at all.

And now for the real recovery story: I've always known that God has me here for a reason, so in times of desperation, when I wanted to give up, throw in my towel, and even end my life, I have never given in and instead always plunged forward. My brothers and sister were also a great source of strength for me. A laugh, a thank you, even to see them sleeping, these little things really kept me going in hard times. The guy at work I mentioned is now my husband. He's a member of another Twelve-Step fellowship. He suggested I look for an Anonymous group and I found EDA. Now, I attend face-to-face meetings, online meetings, and do service work.

Honesty has been the biggest difference for me. I used to lie and manipulate; now I show up, shut up, and do the next right thing. I am honest with myself and honest with others. I pray daily, journal, and eat real food. Sometimes not enough, sometimes too much, but that's okay, because the difference is that now I notice—and I am able to deal with it honestly.

I work a program of progress, not perfection...every day. One day at a time. Perfection is what got me into this mess. Only God is perfect. I am not God. He brought me to it; He'll bring me through it. Reach out! Help is up there, out there, and in there.

ONE STEP AT A TIME

By taking and working one Step at a time, she found a power greater than herself and said goodbye to her eating disorder.

$\mathcal{I}$ grew up in a suburb of Philadelphia in an Italian-Irish household. My father liked to drink and my mother was always on a diet. As a result, I grew up with a lot of rigidity around food. There were certain foods I wasn't allowed to eat and certain foods my mother made me eat. I couldn't leave the table without being scolded to finish my plate. I had no idea what a balanced diet or what freedom around food looked like. Whatever diet my mother was on, so was the family. My parents were strict and wanted us to achieve in school and sports. They were also very protective about the friends we hung out with and what we were wearing.

I am the middle child with two sisters. My older sister has cerebral palsy and is physically handicapped, while being extremely smart. My little sister was very beautiful and also smart. I was the middle child and felt kind of disregarded, but not because my parents disregarded me. They were actually very loving. I believe it was just that my parents had a life as well as two other children to take care of. I was troubled and needed more attention. My sisters were blonde-haired, blue-eyed, and frail; I had curves and was definitely not fragile at 5'10". My older sister couldn't walk well because of her cerebral palsy and was falling all the time, while my younger sister was the baby who could do no wrong. So I was mommy's little helper, and there wasn't a lot of extra time for my parents to spend with me. We went to church and got a lot of religion, but I couldn't connect with spirituality. My father's nickname for me was Chubs. He used it in an endearing way, and it never bothered me until puberty.

At the beginning of high school, I had beautiful friends. They would put on their bikinis and get all the attention when we would all walk down in front of the lifeguards. I was in a one-piece and didn't look like them. I was taller, and while it's not an issue now, it was then. I was big, brown-haired, brown-eyed, and insecure about all of it.

So I went on my first diet and lost weight. I'll never forget when I went on a vacation with my parents and family friends. My father's friend was telling me how good I looked. I was wearing bikinis on the beach and that was when I realized there was something to having a flat stomach. However, because of my body type, maintaining it was a struggle. I wasn't naturally that way. So that's where my eating disorder started. I was fighting to be something I wasn't. It didn't seem like a big deal in the beginning, but it turned into an obsession, affecting every day of my life.

I graduated high school and moved to Florida to go to college. That first year I made a friend, and after freshman year we moved into an apartment together. She had an eating disorder and over-exercised, restricted, and abused laxatives. Slowly, I started exercising more and more and eating less and less. Then, when I did eat, she would say, "Here, have this," and give me a laxative. I started taking them. I would barely eat and when I did, I would purge with laxatives. I was in bad shape.

I went back home for the holidays, and, by this time, my older sister had been diagnosed with anorexia. My mother took one look at my thin body and stated that I was not going to go back to Florida; she was afraid I was also anorexic like my older sister. This was too much on my mother. Despite her best efforts, she was powerless to help us and powerless over our addictions. She wanted me to get help and I said, "No, I'm just going to stop." So I put on a little weight and went back to Florida. But my eating disorder continued.

In my late twenties, I discovered drugs. I had graduated from the University on the Dean's list and was excelling in my career. I was in a serious relationship, hoping to get married, and had bought a house with my longtime boyfriend. Actually, I wasn't really "in" the relationship; I was "around" the relationship. I wasn't eating. I was restricting and drinking at night. I was weighing myself *at least* once a day. I was sick physically, spiritually, and mentally. For all those years, I had body dysmorphic disorder: I would see something different than what was actually there.

Then I found drugs, and in less than three years I had lost my family, friends, car, job, and apartment. I wasn't eating, so my disorder was happy. I decided to get clean from drugs and alcohol. I remember as soon as I did, I went on a diet and started exercising. I started by walking, then running, then running further, then running many miles, then running many miles many times a week. This was how I was living in my sobriety. (Despite my eating disorder, this year I have earned a fifteen-year medallion through Alcoholics Anonymous.)

Through my sobriety, I continued to restrict, overexercise, and abuse laxatives. I was in several relationships I wasn't present for...always having to keep my eating disorder a secret. Anxiety was a constant factor in my life. I was continually questioning myself as to why I was so abrasive and unsettled in my own skin. At this point I had become extremely thin. People would ask me, "How do you stay so thin?" I fed off that—just loved it. It was my deep, dark secret. The very fact that I am writing these words is a miracle in itself. I've been living with an eating disorder since I was eighteen. I'm forty-eight now, and until I got into Eating Disorders Anonymous I believed the lies that are fed to us through television, society, and social media: that having the perfect body and material possessions equal happiness.

I actually thought I was the only person doing what I was doing with no idea other people behaved this same way. I thought it was the way of the world: society tells women to be skinny and beautiful, no matter what it takes. My father was telling my mother to lose weight. My father was calling me Chubs. The lifeguards paid attention to me when I wore that bikini. My first love broke up with me for a thin girl. My perception was that I wasn't a "pretty little thing," and men wouldn't want me for who I was. Everything was confirming I was alone; it was only me, going through life this way.

When I got pregnant with the man I was dating, I had the courage to stop restricting and abusing laxatives. I was not going to hurt the child inside me. That was seven years ago, and I was eight years sober. I don't know where that willpower came from; I just decided I was not going to do it anymore. This baby was precious and a miracle to me. I had always wanted a child.

I made it through my pregnancy, had my son, and then told myself that I was going to get myself "together." What happened was that I had so much time away from the ritual of exercising and laxatives that I didn't go back to them. But as the days went on, I was acting out in other ways: restricting all day, bingeing all night. I would restrict for a day and eat too much the next. I was told I had post-partum depression and was put on medication. It didn't help. The antidepressants hurt my stomach, but they did somewhat numb me out. This continued for two years.

Then, an AA mommy/baby meeting started that was open to women who had kids—childcare provided. This was great, because I had been struggling to attend meetings. I was very active in AA before my pregnancy, but now I was at home all the time with my son, depressed and crying, suffering with an eating disorder (not knowing I had one), and telling myself I was weak because I couldn't control my bingeing.

I met a great woman at this meeting. She would ask me if I was okay and I would say, "No, I'm not. I'm in pain. My body is in pain." She probably thought, *This girl has a lot of clean time; she should be happier.* When she would ask me, "Do you have an eating disorder?" I would reply, "No, my sister has an eating disorder, why do you ask?"

She was very gentle and would wait a couple more months before asking me the same question again. She suggested I go to an Eating Disorders Anonymous meeting to get help. I would tell her I didn't have an eating disorder. She would ask me questions like, "Do you weigh yourself?" I told her, "Every single day." She would ask, "Are you happy with what you look like?" I would say, "Not at all." She would ask, "Do you binge and purge?" And I would reply, "No, my sister does that." When in reality, I was over-exercising and abusing laxatives, which is the same exact thing. But I couldn't see it. Besides, I hadn't done it in five years, so I figured I didn't have that problem anymore. Then she talked to me about rigidity around food. How I ate. Did I eat breakfast? Lunch? Dinner? It was very apparent to her—in fact it was loud and clear to her—that I had an eating disorder.

She asked me to come to an EDA meeting. It took me two or three months to actually go. I sat down and looked at everyone and thought to myself, *Oh, these people have eating disorders.* I would ask her, "I'm like a high bottom, right?" "No, you have a regular old eating disorder," was her reply. I would ask that many times and her answer was always the same, "You're actually worse than others." The words resonated with me. She was reaching out to me, trying to share her experience and help me.

One day I binged and purged and felt terrible. The energy levels and the imbalances in my body were horrible. Now that I have recovered and feel so well, I realize just how bad I was feeling. But that day was a bad one; it was my bottom and it was low.

I finally texted her and asked if she was going to the EDA meeting. She said no and asked me why. I told her I wanted to talk to her and wanted to know if she would be my EDA sponsor. She said yes. She told me to write my eating disorder log, so she could know the manifestations of my eating disorder and my history.

She really drove the point of mental obsession home with me. She reminded me that I needed an entire psychic change-—no human power, no doctor, no mother saying "please stop" would be able to help me. Unless I surrendered and admitted I had an eating disorder and worked the Twelve Steps of EDA, I would not get any better. I had done this in AA, so I knew the Steps worked. I decided to try EDA for six months, and if it didn't work, I was out the door.

She asked me to read the Preface and Forewords in the "Big Book" of Alcoholics Anonymous and to continue on to the Doctor's Opinion. She told me to replace the words "drinking" and "alcoholism" with the words "acting out" and "eating disorder." She told me it wasn't about the food, but about the feelings. She told me it is an obsession of the mind and an allergy of the body, that I needed to have a spiritual change, and that this would happen by working the Twelve Steps.

She also directed me to read Bill's Story in the "Big Book" and provide examples of how I am powerless over my eating disorder: how I have attempted to control or moderate it without success, and how I tried to stop the thoughts but was unable. We focused on the progression of the disease in Bill's story. She had me write about different areas of the unmanageability in my life and how my eating disorder was affecting the lives of everyone around me—my family, my child, my sponsees in the other fellowship, my personal and sexual relationships. Then we read "More About Alcoholism" and "There is a Solution" together. Again, there was a pattern of powerlessness and unmanageability, focusing on how the problem centers in my mind rather than in my body. Admitting I am powerless over my eating disorder and that I misuse food was just the beginning.

We talked about the concept of a Higher Power, and that I could believe whatever I wanted to believe, as long as I believed. We then read "We Agnostics." We discussed how in the Second Step we had "come to believe in a Power greater than ourselves." Now I could see and hope that God could restore me to sanity by removing the thoughts and obsessions of my eating disorder and stopping me from acting out. I wrote what restoring me to sanity would look like for me. Then I read "How it Works."

One of the tools I really loved was breaking down the Third Step Prayer into my own words: make it mine, talk about relieving the obsession of bingeing and acting out, take away the obsessive thoughts about my weight, my body. That prayer really started changing my thinking. I believe in the power of prayer. I remember my own version of the Third Step Prayer addressing my eating disorder went something like this: "God, I offer my eating disorder to you. I offer my bingeing to you, to build me and do with me as Thou wilt. Relieve me of the obsession of food, weight, and body, that I may better do Thy will. Take away my bingeing and restricting, that victory over it would bear witness to those I would help of Thy power, Thy love, and Thy way of life. May I do Thy will, always."

Then we got to the chapter "How it Works." We got on our knees and read the Third Step prayer together, and I made a decision to go on with the rest of the work. I was feeling better and had stopped bingeing. She suggested that I eat breakfast, lunch and dinner—balanced meals with snacks in between—if I was hungry, and I followed this suggestion. She told me to eat when I was hungry and stop when I felt full. She told me to listen to my stomach when I went to the refrigerator. If my stomach wasn't hungry, walk away. I had to a find balance in my eating, which I had not had in thirty years.

Then she had me write out my resentments: who I was resentful with and why. She was very thorough in this step. For each resentment, I had to clarify what it was affecting. I had to explain different aspects of each (self-esteem, ambition, etc.) and how they were affected. Also personal and sexual relationships and how they were affected. Before I started writing, I read the resentment prayer for each individual on my 4th Step. I would get on my knees and pray for them.

I then wrote about my part in the resentment and talked about how I was selfish, self-seeking, dishonest, and afraid—either before, during, or after the event had occurred. I could see how I acted out against others, because different people had caused me to have resentments against them. I had done that throughout my life.

One of the biggest things my sponsor talked to me about was how self-reliance had failed me. Time and time again, I could not handle this. She emphasized that no human power was ever going to help me: I had to work and live the Twelve Steps to be free, keep connected to, and trust God; and that I could not "manage" my eating disorder, just as I could not "manage" my alcoholism. They are the same exact type of disease. The obsession drives me to act out; and, once I act out, I cannot stop.

It took my sponsor quite a few months to get me into the rooms of Eating Disorders Anonymous. I am so grateful to her, because she has helped me change my life. She taught me how to rely on God instead of my eating disorder and to stop depending on time at the gym, what my mother said, what diet my friend was on, or what this or that person thinks I should do, because none of that worked. It didn't work because it wasn't a power greater than me—it was human reliance.

Then I did my sexual inventory and I realized how much my eating disorder has affected those relationships and how it had spread into my drug and alcohol addiction. I wanted to be pretty, I wanted to be thin, I wanted to be noticed, I wanted to succeed, and I wanted to be popular. I thought I had to be thin to be worthy of love and attention.

I realized through this work that I had never truly been myself in any sexual relationship.

I have always been in one addiction or another. Now, I am finally free. I am able to love my body without hiding it, to run down the beach without thinking everyone is looking at me, to be happy and accept and enjoy my life, my body, and whichever person is in my life. I no longer surround myself with people who care only for material or social media ideals that society says we need to meet. I don't need to meet them; they don't make me happy. I have written out my own standards and ideals (just for myself), and I check them regularly. I also refer to them before I go on a date with anyone and have been lucky enough to meet some wonderful men since I've been in EDA.

When we got to my character defects, I was taught that by building up my character assets, the defects would lessen. I loved that my sponsor had me going around doing random acts of kindness: cleaning up bathrooms, picking up trash, helping others, being aware of the environment around me, and being caring and kind to others. This I continue to do on a daily basis. Integrating this simple idea and doing positive affirmations daily have truly changed my life. I've made some big amends that were long overdue. I am healing and happy.

Steps Ten and Eleven are powerful tools. I do spot-check and nightly inventories to keep my mind clear of resentments and clutter. This keeps my channel to God clear, because I have to constantly look at myself; and in doing this, I have become even closer to God. My sponsor has taught me how to meditate, which I do on a regular basis. I am so grateful for this suggestion. It changes my whole way of thinking. I have worked hard on promptly admitting when I am wrong and I have gotten really good at it.

Once I completed the Twelve Steps of EDA, I immediately started helping others. I didn't think I could help anyone because I had only ten months in. But I have more time in now and am working with a handful of people. I find my own recovery is strengthened when I sponsor, continue to make my amends, and continue character building. I have had a spiritual awakening as a result of these steps. Carrying this message to others with eating disorders and "practicing these principles in all my affairs" is a way of life for me—and my life just keeps getting better and better!

(6)

OVERCOMING UNMANAGEABILITY

Taking responsibility for her commitment to balance and recovery led her to work through the layers...and find a life of richness and joy.

*I*f I am going to tell you my story about my eating disorder, I am going to need to start at the beginning. I am the youngest of four children, although by only two minutes. I have a twin sister who was born just before me. You wouldn't think two minutes could matter, but it did. You see, my parents planned for only three children. But the last pregnancy got them a pair of babies, instead of just one. And while most couples would be joyful, I think my mother was probably already struggling with postpartum depression, or just depression, or perhaps just overwhelmed. Two babies were too much for her. I clearly remember, as far back as I am able, that she would tell me (in as many words) that I wasn't wanted. I was a mistake they didn't plan for. I was a pain in her butt.

That started my desperation for approval. Early on, I learned that love in my world was conditional, and I started behaving to please, to earn love. Of course, I didn't know that was what I was doing; I just knew that perfectionism, people pleasing, and all that were things I needed to be doing all the time.

I suppose it didn't help that I was different. My siblings—and in particular my fraternal twin—were all very slender, tall, and lovely. Although I can see more clearly now that I wasn't ugly by any means, back then I really believed I was. My sister was the pretty one, I was the smart one; even our parents and grandparents told us that.

By the time I was five, I had an older cousin who was molesting me. I am sure my lack of self-esteem didn't help—probably made me the perfect target. That lasted a couple of years, and when I had finally had enough and found the courage to tell my mother, she basically said it must be my fault, that I was ruined, and brushed it under the rug.

Although no one knew it then, I suffered from depression by the time I was seven. My pre-teen and teen years were no better. I struggled, and because I struggled I am most certain I wasn't easy to live with.

Those years were filled with angst and heartache. I was tormented at home for what I ate, what I said or didn't say, even how I looked. I was tormented at school for being smart and got attention from the teachers for being that way—attention I was desperately seeking. I left home at the first available opportunity and never looked back. I thought everything would be better once I was out of there. I thought I would be better, but I was wrong.

Leaving home didn't change anything for me. Those feelings of being inadequate and "not enough" followed me all the way through my university years and into law school. They followed me through a failed engagement and a lost pregnancy. Eventually, they followed me right into my career, marriage, and parenthood.

I remember even in those days believing—really believing—I was fat and ugly. Not long ago, I looked back at a photo of myself then and honestly, I was gorgeous. Maybe not model gorgeous, but I was cute—healthy looking, great smile, nice hair.

About the time I was twenty-two, I developed a metabolic disorder: a real, true medical condition causing me to gain a lot of weight fast. I was told it was incurable. All of a sudden I was heavier than I had ever been, and my self-esteem plummeted.

I worked with doctors, I tinkered with diets and food modification, I upped the ante on exercise. I spent a fortune I didn't have on the next miracle program. Nothing gave. So I tried harder. And harder. And harder.

Each time my doctor would suggest something new, some new drug, some new diet, some new food to avoid, and I would do it with the dedication of a dying woman. I knew I looked terrible and I felt terrible—so whatever it took.

I became obsessive. I was so focused on sticking perfectly to whatever the plan-of-the-day was regarding food and exercise that I stopped being able to focus on life. I pushed myself at the gym like there was no tomorrow, sometimes to the point of throwing up.

I didn't really see it happening; I just knew I was obsessed with controlling the "clean food." I stopped agreeing to go out or attend any event where eating was required, unless I could be sure I was going to be able to stay on plan. And if I did go, I rarely enjoyed myself because I was so focused on what other people thought of me and what I ate. Or, I was focused on having to eat at all!

Inevitably, a social situation would break my perfect streak and I would blame myself for not being able to "stick to it," therefore explaining why I wasn't losing the weight, wasn't feeling better, wasn't in control of the metabolic disorder. I was a failure. It was my fault I couldn't do this.

I was in a vicious circle when my husband and I discovered this same disorder was going to cause us to struggle to get pregnant. Needless to say, I felt like even less of a woman than I already believed myself to be.

Five years of fertility treatments did nothing to help the situation. Doctors would say if I lost a certain amount of weight my chances of getting pregnant would go up. Didn't they know how hard I was trying to lose that weight? There was clearly something wrong with me. Despite a lot of ups and downs (and an eating disorder I didn't recognize spiraling out of control), we got pregnant. I was sure pregnancy would make me happy; after all, it was everything we had hoped and dreamed about.

Then came the news we were expecting twins, and I was likely to gain even more weight than normal (as with most multiple birth pregnancies). And *poof!* The joy of expecting was gone. All I knew was I couldn't gain *that* much—I had to figure out how not to. So, I obsessed some more.

Our babies were on their way, and I succeeded in keeping things somewhat in control during the pregnancy. It wasn't obvious to me then, but it sure is now, how ridiculous and unmanageable it was for me to "manage" my weight gain in pregnancy so obsessively. (I am actually surprised the doctor didn't notice the eating disorder behavior. However, I do wonder if medical professionals are even educated to look for it in pregnant women. The fact that I was actively orthorexic during that time was painfully obvious.)

The ensuing stress from having twins, a traveling husband, no family support to speak of, and not to mention my need to be perfect at everything finally came crashing down around me when the kids were about two.

I battled severe depression, but begged my doctors not to hospitalize me, because my husband would lose his job if he had to stop traveling to take care of the kids. Yet the crushing weight of my life and responsibilities was just too much. I felt like my life was spiraling completely out of control. It was a battle to even find the will to live.

The only thing I still had control of was the food and exercise. So I got serious with that because I would get a temporary relief through eating-disordered behaviors. For a few minutes, they would take the edge off.

Life continued that way: obsessing not only about what I ate and how I exercised, but also what the kids ate and how they exercised. My deepest bottom came the year we took the kids to Mexico for a family wedding at an all-inclusive resort where food and drink was everywhere...*all* the time. I also could not exercise because I had hurt my back and didn't have the equipment to accommodate my physical recovery. It was a perfect storm.

On the third day of the trip I couldn't leave the hotel room. I sent my husband off with the kids, but was in complete and utter fear they would eat ice cream (again) and end up like me—a metabolic mess. I tried to make myself leave the room to remind him not to let the kids eat junk, but I couldn't force myself out. It was too much.

At the time, I was blessed to have been working with a life coach who was also a recovery coach and recovering alcoholic herself. Several times she had suggested that I had a problem, but my answer was that I had to do *something*— there was obviously something wrong with me. I didn't recognize the program language that day, but I was so desperate to change that I did what she asked. I didn't want to be the mother who had two beautiful, healthy children, but couldn't see it for fear of what they might eat. We have to hit bottom before we are ready to change.

I emailed my coach. I never expected what it would mean to send that email, but, honestly, it was the best thing that ever happened to me. She responded and asked me to tell her why this wasn't working anymore, why it was so unmanageable.

I didn't want to miss a family wedding because I was terrified of the world outside. I didn't want to be the woman who couldn't look herself in the mirror. I didn't want to be the woman who judged herself for how she looked, instead of how big her heart was. I didn't want to feel bad all the time, because the control I got from the eating disorder wasn't making me feel better anymore. I was sick and tired of being a failure; I was sick and tired of being sick and tired. When I came home, my coach asked me if I wanted help. The most courageous answer I have ever given was, "Yes" at that moment. She told me I would need to be willing to go to any lengths to get well, and I told her I would.

We found EDA online and a meeting about three hours from home, so I got in the car on a January afternoon and took off. (A road trip on Canadian roads that time of year can be sketchy at best. But I know God was on my side, because it was an absolutely glorious, clear day.) My coach couldn't come with me, so I really had to do it alone. I went to the location only to find out that no meetings were held there anymore. I learned later that was my first step in being responsible for my recovery.

Initially, I was so discouraged. I wondered if it was a sign. But my coach, who had now turned into my pseudo-sponsor (there weren't EDA sponsors available at the time) talked to me on the phone in the car on the way home and said it wasn't about the meeting for me in that moment, but about understanding my willingness to go to any lengths.

I hung onto that courage. I started going to open AA meetings with her and attending the online meetings at EDA and a few phone meetings. I took the "Big Book" of

Alcoholics Anonymous and made it my business to study it. I wish I could show you my "Big Book" today—it is the most beautifully worn and marked-up book you have ever seen. And it gives me peace just to look at it. But things didn't switch off for me right away; I didn't have a sudden "spiritual awakening" by any means. It was meticulous, slow, steady work. Balance came a bit at a time. In some ways, it is still coming.

In order to get well, there were layers of recovery. My upbringing was a strict Catholic one, and the God I was raised with was punishing. Through working my first three Steps, I found a new and personal relationship with a God that is loving and forgiving. It had only taken some time with my sponsor and the "Big Book."

I believed He worked in other people's lives, so it was really the work of coming to trust (at first only because my sponsor told me so) that He would work in mine if I let Him. She told me I was worthy, and I knew I could trust that, because she was also in recovery and had had a similar belief about herself. I wanted what she had.

At first, that trust in Step Two—that God could and would if He were sought—was a leap of faith, the faith of a mustard seed for those of you with a faith upbringing. But it was enough.

Not long after those first meetings I found a willingness to surrender...*really* surrender. In the beginning, it was just surrender about the food and exercise. I had to let go to realize what was and wasn't working. Deep surrender is an active thing for me, an everyday thing, and that was scary for me. More than once, my fear of gaining weight was almost the end of my precarious recovery, but I persevered by reaching out to my sponsor, finding contacts in the program, and going to meetings—lots and lots of meetings!

Even those open AA meetings, where all I could do was listen, helped; they helped me see the similarities.

When I started working Step Four, I realized how much resentment I carried. Although I was perceived by those in my world as a peaceful and loving person, beneath the surface was a raging, angry child/teenager/adult. As I wrote out those resentments, I saw the pattern of control, perfectionism, and expectation. It was like someone slapped me upside the head! I could see it. I could see how I held on to the hurt and allowed myself to continue to be a victim to my abuse, to my health problems, and eventually to my eating disorder.

My Step Five—sharing with God and another living person—was terrifying but empowering. I told my sponsor all these ugly things about me and her response was one of love and acceptance. I will never forget her telling me there was nothing I could say that was worse than some of the things she had done in active addiction. Such genuine love and caring.

So, I dug in. It felt like we talked for weeks about my character defects, my willingness to let them go. But doing that meant letting go of control, and I already knew my ED was based on a need to control.

Finally, I was ready to ask God to remove my shortcomings in Step Seven. I found the humility necessary to see that God was at the helm, and all I needed was to ask for His help. At times, I have taken back control of some of those shortcomings, but knowing how beautiful surrender and joy in recovery has been for me has made it easier to ask Him to take them back again.

When I hit Step Eight, I was finally experiencing joy in my life: a contentedness I had never known. I was "seeing" my children for the first time. I was "hearing" their laughter in a part of my soul that had been closed off for so very long. Making the list of people I had harmed was a daunting task, but it was made easier by the reward of peace and joy in my life.

By then, I was fully committed to balance and recovery. Humility was my cloak as I made amends. I also began to live some amends to my family by showing my children a healthy and content mother who no longer judges herself, or others, by a standard of perfection about food or physical beauty.

I had learned about the Step Ten daily inventory long before I got there, but I made it my mission to never let a day go by without looking at my thinking and my choices, and making immediate amends. I had seen how resentment made and kept me sick, so today I keep a vigilant eye out for any sign of it in my daily affairs.

Every day I am living Steps Eleven and Twelve. Today, I know a loving God who, when I seek His presence, is *everywhere* in my life. He works in my business, He works in my family, and He has worked in my social circle to help me align with more like-minded people.

What does recovery look like for me? Today, it is days filled with the busy-ness of being a mom to small children and a wife to a husband who travels. Recovery has given me the gifts of peace of mind, of courage to face my problems, of always knowing that God is my first stop and the program is next. With these support systems I know I can stay balanced.

No day is perfect. Life happens. My kids get into trouble, my husband and I disagree, we have money struggles and friendship issues. But nothing is BIG anymore because with God I can surrender all and trust Him to let me live my recovery one day at a time. It is how I deal with life that is different. No longer do I need to numb or control to gain acceptance. I have also been blessed to continue having the same sponsor, and she has marked my life indelibly. I am so grateful for that.

I recently found the courage to test my recovery when I worked with a nutritionist and a naturopath to make amends to my body. The result of years of an eating disorder, fertility treatments, and depression was a body depleted of vital nutrients and in adrenal failure. Doing the next right thing meant I needed to work with these professionals to modify my foods, temporarily, to allow my body to heal.

As I started that program, I pulled close to my support network and slowly but surely I began the process of regulating those deficiencies. With that came the gifts of finding a weight that is healthy for me, and a return of my energy and clear head. Sometimes, it can be scary and challenging, but I have the tools to deal with difficult emotions in the healthiest way.

Today, thanks to EDA and my wonderful God, I have a life I could never dream of, one that is filled with joy and richness. What a gift of recovery that is!

(7)

RECOVERY IS A JOURNEY

Letting go of the need to be in control, she stopped judging herself and discovered self-acceptance, honesty, and the power of service.

For me, recovery hasn't happened overnight; it was, and still is, a journey. In my experience, recovery is ongoing, with twists, turns, peaks, valleys, and plateaus; but, on the whole, my life is improving. I owe this to the Twelve Steps and to God, and the more I follow the tenets of the Steps and rely on Him, the better I am able to see the improvements in my everyday life.

Growing up, I always felt different from my peers. I can distinctly remember being with other children and thinking I needed to keep the truth about me a secret, because it felt so overwhelmingly shameful. I was diagnosed with medical issues, and there was a lot of focus on treatment. By extension, there was a lot of focus on "fixing" or "improving" me. Somewhere along the way, I internalized that my feelings were not important, and that it was important to keep them inside. Although there was a lot of good in my childhood—I was extremely blessed with many opportunities and involved in many extracurricular activities, hobbies, and my childhood faith—I believe these may be the roots of my eating disorder.

My household was very structured, and we were allowed only "healthy" foods. I liked to eat as a child and was given large quantities of vegetables when I was hungry. I am forever grateful that I learned early about the benefits of eating these foods; however, when I had the opportunity to eat "unhealthy" snack food, I didn't stop until I got reprimanded or felt sick. This food had so much power over me that I would "sneak" it and lie about it to my parents. I even stole a dessert from a store once. My parents made me take it back in after eating part of it, apologize, and pay for it! Although I didn't know it yet, food was my "solution" to my problems from a very early age.

As I got older, I continued to lie about what I ate, and when stressed I would eat a lot of desserts and even steal them from other family members. I knew the importance of staying thin, so I ate dessert instead of other food. I began dieting for the first time in high school and was astonished at the high I got.

I was a really good student and went to another state for college. Entering as a freshman, I felt as though I could start over and be a different person. I made many friends and I felt free. I was very social. I joined a sorority and started drinking alcohol. At the beginning of "Bill's Story" in the "Big Book" of Alcoholics Anonymous, he talks about feeling as though he had "arrived." That is exactly how I felt when I got to college. All of the things I was concerned about suddenly became less of a concern. I still felt I needed to hide my true self, but I thought less about it. At the end of that freshman year, my grades suffered, and I gained weight.

I decided I needed to lose that weight and began restricting certain food groups, losing all of the infamous "freshman 15" I had gained over the first year. When I had surgery for my medical issues, I kept it a secret and managed to lose even more weight. When school started again,

I was very focused and stopped eating almost entirely. Obviously this wasn't sustainable, and I ended up hospitalized and quickly regained the weight (against my volition). Thus began a cycle of overeating (later bingeing), and then restricting. If I ate a lot of food, I would then decrease what I ate the day after to "balance out" the number of calories. I also began to restrict eating during the day, so I could drink and/or eat a big meal at night.

After experiencing more health problems, I was forced to withdraw from college and move home. There, my pattern of overeating and restricting became more entrenched. If I found I was gaining a few pounds, I would eat less; when I lost the weight again, I would eat more. It was a never-ending cycle.

I got a roommate who kept copious amounts of food from a bulk-supply store and I found myself unable to stop eating her food. I tried to come up with all sorts of different methods to keep myself from doing this (often in the middle of the night), but failed. I found myself "buying back" her food in the morning and trying to disguise the fact that I had eaten it. During the day, I would not eat and sometimes used chemicals to help decrease my appetite. Needless to say, that living situation did not work out.

I got my own place expressly so I could control what was and wasn't in my home. I thought that control would solve my problem. As you might already guess, that didn't work either. I began to calorie-count more than ever and weigh myself repeatedly. I would stick to the "healthy" foods I chose to buy for most of the day, but then go on mini-binges, counting each calorie. If I went above my calorie goal, my task was to exercise and consume as many energy drinks as necessary to burn the extra calories. *It was insanity.* There were many other eating-disordered behaviors, as well. I even counted my alcohol calories, trying to factor them in! If I failed to keep my calorie goal, or if my weight went up, it felt like my life was over. I would not leave my house because I was too ashamed of myself and how "fat" I felt. (If you haven't heard it already, you probably will soon: fat is not a feeling!)

The eating disorder I didn't think I had ruled my life. I thought people with eating disorders had to eat and throw up or starve themselves and be very thin with bones sticking out. I didn't fit either description: I was at a normal weight and could rarely make myself throw up (although I certainly tried).

My family convinced me to go to treatment for alcohol, anxiety, and food. *My life had become unmanageable.* I was not working or going to school, and lived only to obsess about what I ate and drank, and to compulsively spend money. I was introduced to Twelve-Step groups, but managed to continue my eating disorder while in treatment. Soon after, I attended a specialized program in another state.

In that program, I learned what it was to eat food in a healthy manner and what is often behind an eating disorder. I learned new, more adaptive ways to manage feelings. I got involved in a Twelve-Step program and went to meetings. Although I had been making a lot of progress, I began to struggle with my eating disorder again. After a "binge," I learned that I had "relapsed" and had to start the Step work over again. This became a constant battle—trying not to eat too much or too little.

I had a dietitian, but decided that I would listen to some of the "old-timers" in the Twelve-Step meeting I was attending and eliminate sugar from my diet. My life began to revolve around checking labels for any sugar content; and, if there was, how many ingredients were listed before the sugar. *Insanity!* And despite all the restricting of sugar, I still couldn't stop bingeing at all hours of the night. The frustration led me to relapse on alcohol after a period of sobriety.

I moved back to my hometown, desperate to stop bingeing and restricting. I found the nearby abstinence-based, Twelve-Step meetings were not supportive. One local EDA meeting had recently disbanded, but another girl wanted to start a new one. I love to plan, organize, and volunteer, and I was eager to help get a new group started— even though I didn't know a lot about the program.

Getting involved in EDA changed my life. It gave me a sense of purpose. I publicized meetings, printed out materials, and made contact with the church where the previous meeting had been held. I found friends who were also looking to recover; and, best of all, I found a supportive environment where I was not a failure when I overate. EDA encouraged me to focus on the milestones and the progress that I did make.

I found it hard that there weren't EDA sponsors. At first I got a buddy, but that didn't really work out. Luckily, the woman who had been leading the last meeting prior to its closure agreed to sponsor me, and we began working on the Steps. In completing my Fifth Step in another Twelve-Step program, I was able to be open and honest about things I had kept a secret for twenty-four years. As I took inventory of myself and was honest with others, I found my bingeing got better.

Despite this, I experienced a deep, deep depression that led me to restrict for about two months. I was able to work closely with my dietitian and remain involved in

EDA. Although I felt ashamed—because I was someone who *founded* the meeting and still was in such despair—I *kept showing up* anyway. It took me a while to realize I needed to stop judging myself, and that *it's ok to not be perfect.* I learned this is fairly normal (both the judging and the setbacks). I ended up getting another sponsor in another Twelve-Step program who helped me work the Steps both for my eating disorder *and* for alcohol. I completed working the Steps with her.

- I realized my life didn't work the way it had been going and that I couldn't control my eating disorder.

- I started to believe there was something outside of me, and greater than me, that had more power than I did.

- I turned my life over to that Higher Power, as things weren't working the way I was managing them. I found that creating my own Third Step Prayer (as in the EDA Step workbook) and the God-box (where I can offer my struggles to God) to be extremely powerful.

- I inventoried my relationships, resentments, fears, and harm done to others.

- I shared these with my sponsor.

- I became acquainted with the shortcomings within me that were causing many of my problems and became willing to have these removed. I learned shortcomings don't mean I am an inferior or bad person; it just means I could improve on some things.

- I humbly asked God to remove my shortcomings—I needed His help.

- I went back to Step Four and looked for those to whom I needed to make amends. This didn't mean I just had to say, "I'm sorry;" it meant I had to try to make things right.

- I actually made amends. I found it wasn't as hard or as painful as I thought it would be. I also discovered that not everyone wanted to hear or accept my amends—something with which I have had to make my own peace.

- I continue the process of Steps Four through Nine on a daily basis by observing my thoughts and actions, turning them over to God, and making things right with others if needed.

- I began to pray in the morning and at night. I ask Him for help with not acting out through my eating disorder and also for the well-being of others. This step also involves meditation. I tend to struggle with sitting still, so I try to reflect on a prayer or reading.

- This focus on helping others was something I was able to do right away by starting an EDA meeting with a friend. This also involved sponsorship and service work with EDA. I have discovered that helping others really helps me! As someone already familiar with Twelve-Step recovery, I knew it was very important to start "working" Steps Ten through Twelve right away, just as I had the other Steps (although I waited to start sponsoring until I was done with my 9th Step).

Today, my life has completely changed. When I was in my eating disorder, I stopped going to work and school and had unhealthy relationships. In recovery, I have been able to return to school for both my bachelor's and master's degrees and am now a licensed counselor. I have been able to be a good employee and support myself. I have had friends for many years. I just got married to the love of my life.

I struggle with health problems but am able to walk through the struggles. I have a wide array of feelings—happy, sad, angry, and ashamed—that I never used to feel before. My life no longer revolves around food. I don't eat a perfectly "healthy" diet, but that is not the end of the world. Sometimes I eat more than I am hungry for and feel full. Sometimes I make choices that I later regret. Sometimes I eat something sweet because I feel stressed. Sometimes I eat a balanced diet full of nutrients. Regardless of the choices I make, they do not have to determine my day anymore. Instead, I can look to God and those I trust for an alternate, more lasting solution.

My prayer is that you may find the same solution in the rooms of Eating Disorders Anonymous as I did. There is a solution. There is a way out.

PART II

THEY STOPPED IN TIME

AS SICK AS MY SECRETS

She showed up, did the work and, most importantly, told the truth. In return she was met with compassion, encouragement, and support that shaped her recovery.

$\mathcal{M}$any of us with eating disorders know about living with secrets, and I am no different. The biggest secrets, I kept—even from myself. I grew up in a house where "little white lies" to smooth over situations or feelings or imperfections were not only tolerated, but encouraged. I learned that honesty was rarely the best policy; that if I was honest with myself I wouldn't like what I saw. Recovery for me has been about practicing honesty, getting comfortable with discomfort, and speaking my truth.

At age nine what I wanted for Chanukah was a bunny; what I wanted at ten was anorexia. At nine I hit puberty, but at ten the only things bigger and more unruly than my frizzy, Ashkenazi hair were my breasts. I was the only ten-year-old in the women's section, often dressed more like my teachers than my peers. Baby-doll t-shirts and designer-labeled skirts eluded me.

I had seen the after school specials, the concern everyone felt for the willow-thin girls who always seemed to have a lot of friends and be very popular. They fit in at school and they fit into the cute clothes that lined the junior's section. I thought the key to having everything I wanted was my weight. Diet and weight management would solve not just my thinking problems, but *all* of my problems! Soon I began collecting evidence to support this. The most popular target for insults and bullying was my size. I watched the number of my friends dwindle as my body changed, getting bigger in what I thought were all the wrong places (read: everywhere). It started with exclusion. Suddenly, at recess I was playing by myself a lot more than I ever had before. Then it moved into name-calling: "fatso," "bucktooth beaver," "fatty," "tubby," etc. The worst was the subtle mockery of popular, thin girls being nice to me only to realize halfway through an interaction that they were actually laughing at me. Boys were cruel in their own way: it was a grade-wide pastime to ask me out and harass me until I finally said yes, then laugh about how I totally thought they were serious. There seemed to be no greater insult to a boy than for someone to say they liked me or was liked by me. I felt like a fat tub of industrial lard waste, which meant I was a fat tub of industrial lard waste! I just knew that if I could lose weight, if I could have an eating disorder like the girls on television, my life would be perfect. Everyone would care about me. People would care about me and feel bad that they had bullied me. I would have friends again. I'd never have to be alone at recess with just my imagination and resentments to keep me company. I'd stop crying after school. All of my cures lay in controlling my weight.

I remember being so proud of myself when I skipped my first meal that year. I took my seat at the girls' lunch table near a boy who had sat down at the boys' table. This was a boy I thought was cute, and he abruptly yelled, "No, you go sit over there." And I did, almost crying. He hadn't said anything about my weight, but I KNEW it had to be because I was fat and unlovable. I didn't eat anything at lunch that day because he was right. My best friend since preschool tried to convince me to eat, but I couldn't hear her healthy advice. No, I knew what I needed to do. I wanted to make the bullying stop and make my peers like me again. The only way I would ever make that happen was to lose weight. And the best way, the only way for me to lose weight was for me to do something drastic. I loved veggies, I ate healthy, I liked being outside, but my body shape had refused to change. Clearly, if I could get control of that, I could get control of my life!

I thought that if I could control my weight, my intake, my size, then I could control how people felt about me. If I could control how people felt about me, then I'd never have to feel any of the pain that lived inside of me. I didn't like me the way I was, and no one else seemed to like me the way I was either. While my slender friends could eat whatever they wanted and would demolish a box of cookies at my house, their parents would admonish me to "watch what I ate." I got nutrition lectures. They would forbid their daughters to play dress up with me, because I would stretch out their clothes. When I went to the pool with them, they would talk about how great swimming was for exercise when all I wanted to do was pretend to be a mermaid because I loved how free my body felt in the water.

Home wasn't a safe haven either. My mother agreed with her friends: I was heavy and just needed to eat right. My mother looked the opposite of me, straight where I had curves, flat where I had mountains on my chest. She hated how she looked, and I grew up hearing someone I thought was the ideal beauty compare her "bird legs" to my shapely ones. My mother talked about her own experiences with weight-related teasing, but it was hard for me to sympathize. After all, *everyone loved a skinny girl and no one loved fat me*, I thought as I dug deeper into my disorder. They'd love me when I hit the right size. *I'd* love myself when I hit the right size. I aspired to be anorexic, but didn't think I could do it. I hadn't skipped a meal after that one day in 5th grade. I wanted to, but I feared wasting food and would use it to soothe my feelings. In middle school my prayers were consumed with God making me anorexic or killing me in my sleep. I just wanted to get out of what I saw as an unending pit of misery, and the only way out was an eating disorder or death.

Then I turned fourteen, and a switch flipped. After a bad break-up with a long-time crush, I stopped eating. I threw the breakfasts my mom brought up to me into my bathroom trash. I gave away the lunches she packed for me to boys who didn't care enough to ask questions. I would sometimes eat dinner; but, given the option, I tended to throw it away. I began purging if I ate something. But the thing about starving myself was that my brain was too fo-cused on staying alive to let me feel anything, well…feel anything *except* for the anxiety that kept it going. I didn't talk a lot about it, making references to my "food issues" until it came out sideways and exploded. I wanted to tell everyone because I wanted them to worry. But I also didn't want to actually do anything about it. I wasn't skinny enough…or didn't think I was sick enough yet.

I kept that secret for four years or more. I told no one, hoping that I would get "better" at it and actually lose weight. I couldn't talk about it, because my behaviors felt necessary to my survival. But the thing about secrets is that they grow and absorb more parts of your life; you start keeping even more secrets so you can protect your big secret. I was consumed by my secrets in college. Freshman year might have been my rock bottom: purging multiple times a day for eating even "safe" foods, eating the bare minimum to keep my friends from bothering me, taking diet pills that made me so shaky it was hard to hold a pencil. I told myself that this was something I had to do, because if I didn't, the good things in my life (friends, a major I loved, a school I loved, my boyfriend) would disappear, and I would go back to being unlovable, bullied me. My most toxic thought was that I *needed* to do this. I wanted to be someone different— someone loveable—in college. I was going to reinvent myself into the person I had always wanted to be, and to do that I needed my eating disorder. But as much as I said I did it to be loveable to others, I was alone in my disorder. I separated myself from those around me, because while it felt too big to tell them, it was "not a big deal" to me.

After a doctor heard some irregularities in my heartbeat, I finally came clean to my friends and family about how I had been starving, throwing away food, and throwing up multiple times a day. I made it clear that I was not going to go to treatment, but was meeting every two weeks with the college counselor and, "No, you cannot point out how small my meal is." People knew about the disorder, but it was never something I let myself be held accountable for. I was not yet ready to give it up. I continued on that roller coaster, being "better" for a while and then sliding back. No matter where life took me, my eating disorder was there.

I met my husband-to-be during a "quiet period" of my eating disorder. While he knew about my history and showed a lot of understanding, it started to creep back in. First, it was expressing how much I hated my body or thought we were mismatched. Then I started eating less or eating erratically. I would sit at dinners and worry about what I was eating. By the time we were engaged, I had gained weight because of my yo-yo relationship with food, which sent me into a deep shame spiral throughout our entire engagement. For the first time, I realized I couldn't act out on behaviors when he was around. I couldn't purge if he was in the apartment. I would eat dinner if he was around. I had to have space to keep my secret, even if it was an open secret. These secrets ate at me; they followed me across an ocean to another country. They got worse; and while my weight dropped, I was even more unbelievably miserable than I had been. I added compulsive exercise to make it seem as though I was incredibly healthy. I would run until all I could do was lie on the couch, because standing up made me dizzy. I forgot things, I was flaky with my plans, I had massive mood swings. My husband and I fought about my food and my exercise regularly. I couldn't fake the energy during job interviews. My hair continued to thin, and my skin was riddled with bruises from minor bumps of daily life. I didn't even have the energy to cry anymore. I was disconnected from most of my friends, a living, one-way mirror in which they could tell me what was going on with them, but I couldn't allow myself to tell them I was even "a little blue."

One of our goals in Twelve-Step fellowships is to carry the message of hope to others, and I saw in a member of another fellowship something that I wanted—happiness, joy, and freedom from the burdens of addiction. We sat on a park bench on a summer day before I started my dream job, and they told me about how painful their life had been before they started a Twelve-Step program. In that moment, I felt a desire to connect, to tell them why I always "ate before I came" or "ate like a bird" around them. I shared that I was in recovery for an eating disorder and had been recovered for three years. They congratulated me, with all of their eight years of sobriety, and thanked me for sharing. It was all a lie. I had compulsively exercised and purged a few hours before the conversation happened. I lied to them and I lied to myself. I said it didn't count because it wasn't a long-term relapse (more self-deception!). I needed to deceive myself so I could stay in my eating disorder—a secret I kept even from myself. Their warm encouragement of my recovery made me uncomfortable with my secrets and lies. I turned it around and around in my head, that I was lying to everyone about my day-count, that I wasn't really better.

Seeing how much a Twelve-Step group had helped someone I admired, I decided to see if there was a local meeting of Eating Disorders Anonymous. I had tried what felt like everything, but I hadn't tried this. And I realized I was just so tired of living. I attended my first meeting online and the theme was "Show up, Do the Work, and Tell the Truth." In the chat room, I said "My name is _____, and I have an eating disorder." I shared, and while I don't remember exactly what I said, I think I talked about wanting a perfect recovery and realizing that it was a lie; that I hadn't been in recovery for an incredibly long time—if at all. I had finally spoken my secret to a room full of people who had lived my same secrets, and they were reaching out. They were tired of being as sick as the secrets they carried around with them. I realized, miraculously, that I was, too.

I started with my husband. Instead of being angry at me or disappointed, his reaction was different. He was compassionate and supportive, perhaps sensing that this time I was really committed to change. I told a few of my very close friends; none of them said, "I knew it" or "Duh." They thanked me for telling them, and asked what they could do to help. I then told my Twelve-Step friends, eventually owning up to lying to them about my disorder and years of behavior-free time. Once again, I was met with compassion, encouragement, and support. My secrets had lied to me; I didn't need to do this to keep all the good things I told myself I didn't deserve unless I was thin/loveable enough. In fact, those secrets had cut me off from seeing how truly loved I was, not because of my disorder, but just because. I started to realize I didn't have to understand why or feel worthy of love to be loved.

Diving into more honesty practice, I attended my first face-to-face meeting. I was running late and was tempted to skip it entirely. I'm glad I didn't, because being at that meeting gave me not only more practice at honesty, but also a great network of others. I ended up sitting next to the person who, months later, would become my sponsor. I wasn't always honest in group; I found it was easier for me to be open and honest when things were going well, which is common. I wanted the group to think I was doing great in my recovery!

One night I told my husband that I was not doing well, but had told everyone at meeting I was. He looked at me and plainly said, "What's the point in going to meetings if you're going to lie?" Now that I was being more honest about my past, I knew I had to start being more honest about my present, including when I was sinking in relapse quicksand. I started slowly trusting others, sharing even simple sentences like, "It's been a really hard week" or, "Everyone in my office is talking about diets and it's triggering." Those little steps, one foot in front of the other, helped me share bigger things, like speaking about my relapse after ninety-one days without behaviors.

I could start to see where I needed more help, at times being brutally honest about the parts of recovery that sucked, like trying to feed myself with no real nutritional experience. It opened me up to getting more help and honestly taught me to surrender, because I could finally admit that doing it alone had never ever worked in a meaningful way. And boy did I need all the help I could get when I got to Step Four! When you've been so self-deceptive, the idea of doing a fearless and searching moral inventory is anything but a fearless experience. As I did it, my own patterns started to emerge and I could see exactly what the stories I told myself looked like. In that knowledge, came freedom.

To stay honest with myself is a struggle; it's a challenge. To face down my character defects when they come up and see them for what they are, instead of an objective reality, isn't easy. But now I know I'm not alone in this fight: I'm no longer on a battlefield alone wearing the rusty armor of my eating disorder. I've got my Higher Power, my EDA network, my friends, and my family. I love the changes I've seen in my life, and the standout reason for that is a willingness to be honest with others and myself. As Mr. Rogers said, "Anything that is mentionable is manageable." By admitting how unmanageable my life was before I found EDA, working the Steps, and connecting with the sparks of my Higher Power and those around me, my life has started to become more manageable.

A TREATMENT PROFESSIONAL
SHARES HER STORY

When she began to communicate out loud, her eating disorder quieted; she became comfortable with being perfectly imperfect. Happy and free in recovery, she shares that surrender meant "joining the winning team."

I have been asked many times what caused my eating disorder: What was my family like? Did they have weird eating habits? Was I ever told I was fat? Trauma? Anything out of the ordinary? Honestly, I grew up in what I consider a fairly normal/healthy household. My parents had a solid marriage. My older brother and I had a fairly normal sibling relationship, outside of the usual rivalry. In the same way I view any other addiction, I consider eating disorders to be complex. There is not one cause. I feel like the right personality, social environment, and biological factors created the perfect storm for my eating disorder to thrive.

As a young child, I was extremely shy. Between my brother and me, I was the "quiet one." While he did all the talking and vocalizing, I kept to myself. I think my temperament alone was a factor in the development of my eating disorder. I internalized everything. And while I did have friends, I never had an abundance of them. My reservations and extreme introversion fueled fear surrounding new experiences and meeting new people.

As I entered middle school, my introverted side became detrimental to my confidence and consequently led to my insecurity about everything. I had friends, but I was never popular. I played sports, but I wasn't considered a "star player." I did my homework, but I didn't excel in any classes. Furthermore, like every other prepubescent girl, I went through what I can now say was a tremendously awkward stage. Weight gain, acne, limbs that were too long for my body, and still not hitting a growth spurt made me feel like I was an "ugly duckling." I remember looking at all the other girls, wishing I was as thin, petite, and "normal looking" as they were.

It wasn't until the summer going into high school that my eating disorder truly began to appear. A yearly physical was required, and as I stepped on the scale, the doctor called out my weight. My face turned bright red, and tears began to flood my eyes. I tried my best not to cry and remained silent for the rest of the appointment. This number has never left my brain. For my age and height, I was considered overweight. I remember that moment like it was yesterday. Driving home, I asked my mom her weight. I was shocked. She weighed less than I did. That was the very moment the obsession began. The eating disorder mentality ignited with fire. *How could I, a fourteen-year-old, be heavier than my mom? When did this happen? How did this happen?* I felt so ordinary in every other aspect of my life and now I considered myself "fat!" That day, I vowed to myself that I would no longer be average. I was not going to enter a new high school as ordinary. I wanted a new image for myself. I wanted to be perfect.

What started as a "healthy" change in eating habits, spiraled into a full-blown eating disorder. While other kids my age enjoyed their summer, hanging out with friends or going to the beach, I was in the gym running on treadmills or swimming lap after lap, measuring, portioning, body checking, restricting, and purging. Watching the number on the scale decrease day-by-day had never given me so much pride and what I thought was self-worth. I wasn't average anymore. Then came the compliments—by family, extended family, friends, and parents of friends. "What happened to that chubby kid?" they would ask, and commend me on my new body. I was finally happy. That "chubby kid" was gone. I hit my growth spurt and felt like I finally stood out. By the time the first day of high school approached, I had done it. I was pounds lighter and ready to make my debut.

Not surprisingly, the weight loss wasn't enough. That's the thing about eating disorders; you're never satisfied with that number on the scale. Obsessive thoughts and numbers filled my head every day: *What if I were to lose a few more pounds? Another couple here? A few there?* The goal was constantly changing. I would get to my "magic number," and be proud of myself for a day. Then the feeling would wear off and I was back to the drawing board: *How many more calories do I need to burn? What can I eliminate in my diet? What if I skip breakfast and have some fruit for a snack and swim for this amount of time? Then would I be okay? I have to eat dinner in front of my parents, but how much time can I spend at the gym after?* Those thoughts occupied my mind daily. It was exhausting. I was a prisoner in my own body. I was a prisoner in my own mind. While others had history facts, calculus equations, and vocabulary definitions floating through their minds, I had calories and numbers pertaining to sizes and exercise in mine.

Junior year was truly the worst year of my eating disorder. For my height and body type, I had become extremely gaunt. I had sustained a knee injury requiring surgery during swim season, which I now attribute to my weakened and sick body. I was depressed. I was constantly fighting with my family, lost friends, and found myself in a verbally abusive relationship with my first boyfriend. I was irritable, and my anxiety was the highest it had ever been. My eating disorder had morphed into the only aspect of control I had in my life. I was depressed, so I used behaviors. I was anxious, so I used behaviors. I was lonely, insecure, sad, and angry; my answer was to use behaviors. I had become stuck in the most destructive cycle imaginable and couldn't find a way out. It was a never-ending battle that was surely leading me toward death.

I remember getting called into the principal's office, feeling puzzled as to why. When I walked in, I saw a guidance counselor sitting next to the dean who expressed her concern for my health. I remember laughing out loud. The meeting was a blur, but I remember the counselor saying that she was in recovery from an eating disorder. Like any other individual struggling with an eating disorder, I became defensive and was in the true definition of denial. The counselor asked if I was dieting or not eating. I lied. "My family is thin and tall. I don't have a problem," I stated. Lies. "You don't know what you're talking about. I am at a healthy weight." Lies. "Ask my mom, she sees me eat every night!" Lies. (What my mom didn't know was that I was purging through self-induced vomiting or exhausting myself at the gym burning days' worth of calories). I left infuriated. *Who did they think they were? How could they think I was sick?!* I was not about to let them take away my eating disorder. It was my pride and joy, my friend, my comfort, and my way of communicating! At this point in time, it was just about the only thing I had left in my life. My grades had plummeted; I had no intention of going to college. I was getting D's in classes. I had lost everything: failing at life, but acing my eating disorder.

To this day, I can't blame my parents for not recognizing how unhealthy my eating habits were. To be in an eating disorder, you need to be a master manipulator and liar, and I had become both. I lied—A LOT. I lied about going to the gym. I lied about eating out. The web of lies became so excessive that I started lying about things that didn't even pertain to my eating disorder. I lied about where I was going out with my friends. I lied about being sick! I ditched classes and even full school days! I lied about a car accident that was *my* fault! I had turned into a monster. The more "attractive" I strived to be on the outside, the uglier and more unattractive I became on the inside.

The day my mom caught me purging, I felt so many emotions: shame, guilt, embarrassment, but also relief. I was relieved that she finally knew how bad it had become. I remember walking out of the bathroom and falling straight into her arms, sobbing and apologizing. The next day she made an appointment with a renowned psychologist who specialized in eating disorders. Although my mom had to practically drag me into that first appointment, I am so grateful that she did. I owe my life to my therapist. I had to come to terms with the fact that I was powerless over my disorder. My life had become unmanageable in every way, shape, and form. For the next three years I spent hours, sometimes multiple times a week in individual as well as group therapy, working on rebuilding myself. While all my friends went off to college, I had to sit back and work on picking up the wreckage that my eating disorder had created.

I took the recovery process a day at a time. Sometimes I took it an hour at a time, and in high stress, a minute at a time. I trusted my therapist and dietician, which was honestly one of the hardest, but most integral, parts of the process. Surrendering to the process is the only sustainable way through recovery. It wasn't easy, but the more I began to communicate aloud, the softer the eating disorder voice in my head became. The shy, introverted, shell of a human being I had once been transformed into an assertive, confident, young woman. I challenged beliefs about being perfect, and finally, after years, understood the idea of being "perfectly imperfect." As my behaviors subsided, my life began to thrive. I enrolled at a local junior college and began excelling in my classes. At the end of my second year, I had become an "A" student and had been accepted to two prestigious universities. Because of my experience of going through recovery, I majored in psychology and vowed to one day help other women facing the monster I had defeated.

Today, I am a therapist at an eating disorder treatment center. To say it was easy getting to this point would be another lie. It was hard! I had slips and relapses, but every one taught me something about myself. I became stronger.

Within my own recovery, as well as within my profession, using the Twelve Steps on a day-to-day basis has been a catalyst in my transformation. In meetings, I felt like I wasn't alone in this battle. I found a sanctuary where I could openly tell my story and feel not judged, scoffed at, or looked down upon, but understood. Others knew the hardships faced every day in recovery and the Steps provided relief from the insanity I endured.

Before being introduced to EDA, I struggled with admitting powerlessness and surrendering because I thought it meant weakness. It took another member of the Twelve-Step fellowship to reframe this skewed perception. She explained that instead of seeing surrender as weakness, I should think of it as joining the "winning team." That completely changed me: It gave me permission to finally let go of my disorder.

Even now, ten years into my recovery, surrender has to happen every single day for me. I continually recognize that in myself and I remind my clients who struggle, too. Working the Steps of EDA brought me from a place of captivity to a place of freedom and peace, and for that I am truly grateful. I know for certain I would not be writing this if it weren't for EDA.

When I have clients sitting in front of me, broken and hopeless, I recall where I came from and I try to encourage and reassure them about what can happen through recovery. With every ending of an eating disorder, there is a new beginning…a new life. And, believe me, it is so much sweeter.

(3)

AUTHENTICITY FREED ME TO FIND MY PURPOSE

Just as her connection to a Higher Power inspires her to pursue recovery every day, she inspires others to find their true worth.

I put off writing my story, because my perfectionist mind told me I needed to have all the answers and be unquestionably successful before "giving advice." But here I am, typing! That is the epitome of my recovery journey: challenging myself, my thoughts, my "Ed head," and doing everything in my power to go against it. When "Ed" (my eating disorder) tells me to not eat because I will get fat, I can now defy him! I can shout, "No" to all of Ed's rules, and I can stop the swirling anxiety inside my head. With each challenge, with each fulfilled human desire, I am made more aware of my humanness.

This scared me at first; and it still does, but not in the same way. Before, I let the fear of being myself express itself through starvation, bingeing, purging, and self-harming, because I utterly hated myself *that* much. I still have down days now, but nothing that compares to the insurmountable pain and shame that riddled me when active in my eating disorder. Sometimes I stop and remember the weight of those feelings and I can't even fathom how I survived such darkness. My head swam all day with thoughts of what I would eat, careful and precise planning always involved.

Then, when I did eat the so-called "planned" meal, I was not only full of food, but also full of regret.

Allowing my belly to be full removed my starving distraction, and I was faced with feelings that I didn't think I could bear. And even if I could, I didn't *want* to. I verbally abused the poor little girl inside me, constantly telling her she wasn't enough. I did this until I wanted to die. I did this until my obsession with avoiding my feelings of confusion and shame literally drove me to insanity. I did this until my pain broke me. It took looking into sunken-in eyes, dazed after being used and assaulted, to realize I could not go on like this. I would sit in my shower, empty after relieving my belly of that day's distress, and let the water drench my face. Heaving, panting, and shaking—at the brink of ending it all.

In the end, I called my mother. In that moment she was not the mother of an adult. I had thought of myself as an adult for several years, but at that point I was a broken, wingless, little bird—and I needed my mother. She came and she conquered, bringing me home from college after just three weeks and checking me into treatment.

I cried as I unpacked my bags at the treatment facility, realizing where Ed, my eating disorder, had taken me in life. Ed's desperate attempts to "save" and protect me ironically led to chaos that affected not only me, but also everyone who loved me. Ed made me blind to that love. No, my life had not been perfect, but people cared for me to the best of their abilities. I had been hurt, but I know now that we are all limited humans working through our own issues.

In treatment, I realized I had spent many years blaming myself for others' actions and things I could not control. Instead of seeing the vicious taunting I faced in middle school as a sign that my bully just hated himself, I was convinced that I had to hate *myself*. I would come home and look in the mirror and think that there was no possible way someone could look at another human being and tell them to die unless there was something wrong with them. But yes, people can be heartless. Through facing my own resentments, I have, uncomfortably, learned that. At first this made me angry, but anger is only toxic to the holder, so I began to look at everyone who had ever hurt me in my life with compassion, knowing that they only acted in such a desperate manner to soothe themselves. It seems we are all anxious and afraid. This doesn't excuse anything or anyone, but it has allowed me to begin practicing forgiveness, and this means with myself as well.

My recovery is about being kind to myself and allowing myself to feel. Connecting to my Higher Power has literally saved my life. I realize that I am a tiny speck in the universe, and that our world consists of billions of other little specks. I try to not let this make me feel insignificant. Instead, I use it as inspiration to overcome my circumstances, because in the grand scheme of things my issues are so small. The size of my soul matters more than the size of my belly, and the weight of my impact on this world is more important than my actual weight.

As I have become more comfortable with myself, I have seen that my passion for authenticity allows others to feel more comfortable with themselves as well. I am by no means perfect, and admitting that validates me more than any degree, job, size, or relationship ever could.

Acceptance to me means feeling my feelings, good and bad. The depths of the lows that I feel are in exact correlation with the intensity of joy and passion that I can also feel. This gives me appreciation and gratitude for my tougher emotions. I try to see them as a gift. And although living—truly living and feeling—is hard, it is also radiant and beautiful. Exploring myself as I go through life is the most overwhelming, daunting, playful, exciting, and exhilarating thing that I have ever done. Recovery has given me the blessing of this journey, and I have so much hope that I, and others, will make it through and achieve our purposes in life. Recovery from my eating disorder has allowed me to begin to see mine: advocating for self-love and helping others bridge the gap from the person they think they are supposed to be…to finding their authentic selves.

FAITH IN THE FELLOWSHIP

In her first meeting, she was amazed at the beautiful kindness and openness of the people who recovered; then, through working the Steps, she became one of them.

*B*efore coming to EDA, I didn't know how I could stop my obsession with food; all I was trying to do was control my weight and body image. I spent days and nights bingeing and purging in the bathroom or into trash bags in my bedroom, which later I would throw away in hopes that my dad would not find them. I exercised constantly and starved myself on the days following a binge. I was introduced to EDA by a friend who was in another Twelve-Step program. I didn't know then my life was about to change and the obsession and craving—the "allergy" which we speak of—was to be lifted. I was amazed by how much I related to these beautiful people who had recovered from their eating disorders. They shared their experiences of having worked the Twelve Steps of EDA with a sponsor, someone who has knowledge and experience with the Twelve Steps and has recovered from an eating disorder.

I sat and listened during my first meeting. In my second meeting, I heard a young woman speak who shared so much experience that I felt I had to ask her to sponsor me. She did become my sponsor, and far more, my spiritual advisor. Her struggles were so similar to mine, but there was something she had I could hardly conceive of back then.

She had hope, a practice of healthy eating, a sound body image, and a relationship with God. After starting the Steps in EDA, I didn't stop acting out, but there was something different this time: I had someone to call who understood what I was going through and who helped me reach out to God instead of the eating disorder. By the time we got to Step Three, I was very acquainted with how the "allergy" was both a mental and physical obsession. My sponsor received my 4th and 5th Steps with grace. She listened to all my angry rants about fast-food restaurants and Hollywood's model perfection image—resentments I had harbored and been obsessed with since I was eleven years old. I still remember the feeling of sitting with her that day, and after leaving, finding so much relief from these emotions that I had held in for years. *My secrets had been brought out into the open and shared with someone who understood.*

It was the season of the Girl Scouts. I decided to buy some things, thinking this time would be different. Once again, I was down on my knees and called my sponsor for help. But something different happened this time: I didn't purge. She reminded me that in EDA "We eat what we want, when we want it. We don't try to control—that is not our method. Pray. Ask God to help you. You can rely on Him every time," she said. And so I did. I began my relationship with Him that day and I haven't binged or purged since. In working my 8th and 9th Steps, I had to admit the truth to family and friends, and to people from whom I had stolen food; my secrets had to come out to the open. I offered money to make amends for the food I stole and shared the exact nature of my condition with my family. I didn't have to do this alone. I had a fellowship of people, and God's love and support the whole way through.

Today, I have a new sponsor whose faith in God restores me in my darkest moments when I want to binge or restrict, or my false body image ideas start to creep in. I am always redirected to a Higher Power and commitment to not binge for the next hour. It will always be "One Day at a Time" for me and countless others who have recovered from their malady.

I am grateful for my journey through EDA. By working the Steps with a sponsor and with the fellowship and community of Eating Disorders Anonymous, having faith in God, and taking part in service work with others who are struggling, I was able to recover from this deadly disorder. I hope all who are reading this will stay committed to their program and give back to others what was given to them. I have a brand new life, and each morning I awaken excited to live in this world thanks to the fellowship and program of EDA.

FREEDOM BEYOND MEASURE

When her obsession with numbers lifted and she became mindful of her inherent worth, she was inspired to help others…and became a clinical psychologist.

$\mathcal{M}$y life has been ruled by numbers. From an early age, I used numerical values of all sorts to measure my worth as a person.

I was a high achiever—this is where my perfectionism developed. Working hard in school and being recognized for my academic accomplishments (through high test scores and grade-point averages) were the defining markers of my identity.

Meanwhile, growing up, I was often teased about my weight. I was a chubbier child and vividly remember negative comments from others about my body: "Be careful not to get fat," a teacher once told me. Yet, I was part of a culture that revolved around extravagant dishes and desserts—if my grandparents offered me something to eat, I could not decline it or I would be looked at with disappointment and shame. I became a "refuse-not" eater.

If I wasn't feeling great about my body or appearance, I'd fall back on the fact that I was smart; this validated my self-worth. My academic performance became a reflection of my value and a concrete measure of my identity. I put everything I had into enhancing these numbers, fearing I would lose approval and become insignificant were I to get a lower grade on an exam, or if my GPA dropped—even a little bit.

Living in a toxic environment further reinforced my need for perfection. My parents' marriage has been chaotic for as long as I can remember, and my dad has struggled with depression for decades. In addition, the cultural community I have been a part of values privacy and focuses on keeping up appearances to avoid judgment. Looking back, I can see that the powerlessness I felt within my family and community dynamics motivated me to pay even more attention to what I could control at the time: the numerical values that supposedly measured my intelligence and value.

Around the time I started college, my own depression started to creep in. I was burnt out and felt rather unmotivated regarding my studies. I was no longer the perfect, top student, and so my sense of self-worth diminished. *If I'm not the smartest,* I would ask myself, *then what do I have to offer? What good am I?* I began using relationships as the next way to prove my worth. On and off through almost all of college, I was in a psychologically abusive relationship. When my boyfriend ended it against my pleas, efforts, and bargains, I again felt utterly powerless and worthless. I felt I had nothing validating that I had worth.

My emotions post-breakup were highly unstable. Now that I was single, I was spending more time with my girlfriends and naturally I compared my body to theirs, feeling inferior that most of them were thinner than me. I combined these two uncomfortable experiences to cope with my breakup and overwhelming emotions. I decided I was going to take "control" of my life and "work" on myself by getting into shape; this would solve all of my problems. Thus, I put myself on a very unrealistic, restrictive diet that eliminated complete food groups. I began exercising. I lost weight and received a ton of positive feedback. I felt incredibly accomplished and actually liked what I saw in the mirror. I had never experienced the sensation of liking my body, nor had I heard such positive comments about my figure, so this was a new and very exciting feeling for me. I was hooked. I felt powerful and in control. I was confident. My relationship grief diminished. I felt like my depression had lifted, and my new body was now my positive identifying feature. I had worth again.

I took a year off after college graduation to apply for graduate school. Without academics or relationships to absorb my energy, I felt severely empty and depressed. Subsequently, I found solace in a new "friend," which at the time I didn't realize was an eating disorder.

My diet and exercise habits were my new "project" that gradually became an obsession. I started weighing myself and noticed the number slowly creeping back up again. I equated this shift with failure and a lack of willpower. I realized I had no idea how or what to eat to be "healthy," so I went to a nutritionist with the intention of losing weight. When she gave me a low-calorie meal plan to follow, I took it and ran with it. I became obsessed. I followed the meal plan compulsively, precisely measuring and recording everything I ate. I was glued to my phone, constantly searching online for nutrition facts to determine what I could give myself permission to eat. I allotted myself a certain number of calories per day, so if I went over this limit, I would keep track of how many I would have to subtract from the following day(s) to compensate for eating too much. I forbade myself from eating "bad" foods and constantly made ridiculous substitutions when I would go out to eat. As I continued losing weight, I was still receiving positive feedback about my body, "healthy" eating habits, unwavering willpower, and commitment to fitness. These labels substantiated my significance as a human being, so I had to keep them going to maintain my identity and sense of self.

My family and friends constantly had to accommodate my new "healthy" lifestyle. My so-called life, once again, was dictated by numbers: calories consumed, calories burned, serving sizes, hours spent exercising, the speed and intensity at which I would exercise on machines, miles ran, grams of macronutrients, clothing sizes, and most significantly, the number on the scale. This number, which is merely a measure of the force of gravity, became the sole determinant of my self-worth, confidence, happiness, actions, and goals. This single value, which I measured multiple times a day, dictated whether or not I would have a good day, socialize with certain people, or feel worthy of love and attention. I was a slave to this number.

I was never at an unhealthy weight, so I didn't think I had a problem. I was used to having an obsessive, perfectionist personality and living my life rigidly. I just thought I was being health conscious. When people asked how I had kept the weight off, I would tell them that I had adopted a new lifestyle.

My behaviors and obsessions weren't really getting "in the way" of my functioning or responsibilities—or so I thought. But in order to make more space for them, I started sacrificing different parts of my life. I began to isolate to avoid stressful situations around food and to hide when I was facing intense body insecurity. When I did have intimate relationships, I was barely present and constantly worried about what I was eating on a date, or if the other person was judging my body. I also exercised excessively, multiple times a day. The few times I actually took a step back to feel my feelings, I was definitely aware that I was very depressed. I was seeing a therapist and psychiatrist, but didn't feel the need to divulge my eating and exercise habits, thinking they were healthy, normal, and even respectable. Although I did start discussing some underlying issues, I would still use these behaviors to control my body, and subsequently and unknowingly try to control what I was feeling.

A few months before I started graduate school, I started overeating regularly. At the time, I strongly believed it was a matter of willpower—and not a result of the low-calorie diet and excessive exercise I was taking part in—that was leaving me ravenous. My weight began to fluctuate; I felt incredibly out of control. I also felt like a failure for not being able to successfully monitor and manipulate my body in the way I wanted. I was miserable. I took a month to travel abroad and spent my vacation time looking up calories online, trying to keep track of my food, taking only stairs instead of escalators, and feeling anxious about whether or not the amount of walking I was doing counted as "exercise" to help me lose weight. The worst part was I didn't have access to a scale to decide if I was "okay." This madness continued into graduate school, which is when my downward spiral really took place.

Being a full-time graduate student, I was nervous about how I would lose or maintain my weight while in school. I wouldn't have the same amount of time to devote to exercise, and I wouldn't be home as much to "control" my eating. I was also living away from my family for the first time and felt loneliness. Looking back, I realize I subconsciously used my disordered habits to deal with all of this change, which included a graduate program that I wasn't passionate about.

Every weekend, my classmates would prepare for an intense few days of lecture and clinical work, while I would plan a new, restrictive diet and exercise regimen for the upcoming week. I had started plugging my food intake and exercise into online fitness trackers and obsessively counted calories. I did many juice cleanses and took diet pills. I put so much time and effort (and money!) into losing weight. However, my efforts would backfire, because I would end up bingeing at the end of the day. I was constantly at war with myself, trying to compensate for what I ate. I was consumed by this vicious binge-shame-restrict cycle.

As my clothes got tighter and tighter, school inevitably became a lower and lower priority, and my body became my main focus. I would leave class to exercise, obsessively look up nutritional facts during lecture, isolate from my peers, and have a hard time participating in school events that involved food. I didn't want anyone to see me, notice my weight gain, or make a negative body comment that would devastate me to my core.

My perceived sense of control was slipping away and I was in despair. I loathed myself. I couldn't look at myself in the mirror and would shower in the dark so I wouldn't have to see what I had done to my body (which in retrospect wasn't that drastic of a change). When I would catch a glimpse of myself, I would sob and scream in agony and blame myself for "ruining" my body. I told myself that I would never resort to purging, but I attempted it many, many times.

After a night of bingeing, I would feel so much shame, guilt, disgust, and sadness that I wouldn't attend school that day. One day absent would turn into three. This went on for months. My grades suffered to the point that my class evaluator met with me to express her concern.

I analyzed my life and realized I could not function: my obsession with food and weight had made my life unmanageable. I had lost everything that was once important to me. My only goal in life was to be thin.

I knew something was definitely not working, but couldn't convince myself I had an eating disorder. I remembered first learning about eating disorders in high school health class, seeing pictures of emaciated girls, or reading about people who would run to the bathroom after each meal to throw up. I wasn't emaciated, I thought. In fact, I kept gaining weight. I did eat—a lot. I wasn't fainting. Since I was now struggling with overeating, I definitely didn't think I fit the classic definition of having an eating disorder. I tried to intellectualize things—looking at facts, online checklists used to diagnose individuals, pictures of people with eating disorders—to see whether I actually had an issue. I really felt I had to have a certain body type, medical consequences, or be on the verge of death to be diagnosed with an eating disorder.

But then I looked at the condition my life was in. I had truly checked out for the past couple of years. I was no longer a participant. I really had to take a good look at how I was living and feeling, and how unhealthy and unmanageable my life had become, to admit to myself that I might have an eating disorder. I thought about how I would pray at night to die or had urges to hurt myself, all because I felt out of control around food and hated my body. These were definitely not healthy reactions. Oddly enough, my motivation for seeking help was eating disorder related—I wanted to stop bingeing...so I could lose weight.

After going to a couple of ED support groups and being more open with my therapist and psychiatrist about my distress around food and my body, I was introduced to a local eating disorder treatment center.

Looking back at this one defining moment, I wonder how my life would have played out were I not introduced to this recovery center, and didn't make the decision to go. I had a couple of weeks off for summer and decided to enroll in the treatment program to gain some skills and insight about my ED, and then leave, cured and ready to begin my fall semester at school. But it turned out that my eating disorder was much more complex and needed further unraveling before I could go back into the real world as a functioning human being. Long story short, I took a leave of absence from graduate school and continued treatment for a total of ten months. It was during treatment that I was introduced to EDA meetings and started attending regularly.

In both treatment and EDA, I became familiar with the concept of "It's not about the food." I had convinced myself that the source of my problems—and misery—was my obsession with my body and what I was eating or not eating. In meetings, I was often surprised and found it odd that EDA members didn't focus on their weight, food patterns, and exercise regimen in their group shares—they discussed their relationships, trauma, mental health issues, important life decisions, work and school challenges, and anything else that was distressing in their lives.

From these experiences and upon thorough self-examination, I soon learned the behaviors and obsessions of my eating disorder were symptoms of similar challenges going on in my life: depression, family turmoil, low self-worth and self-esteem, relationship grief, perfectionism, and dependence on external validation. I used these behaviors to cope with whatever I was struggling with internally.

Until I resolved my inner turmoil, my eating disorder would not go away. I began to speak my truth through EDA meetings, therapy, and other support groups. It felt like a relief to not have to suffer alone and in silence anymore. However, I definitely could not ignore the fact that I did have to look at "the food" in order to recover. I wasn't eating to nourish my body. I wasn't exercising to gain strength and uplift my mood. With the help of a dietician and therapist, I gradually learned how to eat intuitively by being in tune with my body's physical—not emotional—needs, and exercise because I love—rather than hate—my body.

I began envisioning the ED thoughts and voices to be a separate entity from the true self that I wanted to reconnect with. When faced with a thought or urge, I practiced taking a moment to analyze whether my ED voice or recovery voice was trying to dictate my actions and decisions, and I would act in accordance with the latter.

I have also been working the steps with an EDA sponsor. My perfectionist self could look at this process as another opportunity to obsess over numbers—the higher the Step I was working on, the more worthy I was. However, my work in recovery helped me reframe these thoughts. First off, working the Steps would not be a one-time task. I would not be "done" and recovered once I finished Step Twelve. These Steps (including surrendering to a Higher Power, making amends, and being of service) would have to be ongoing processes in my life. I would have to continually incorporate them into my life to keep strengthening my recovery. Sometimes they will overlap, or I may work through them in a different order. The point is, EDA and recovery are not about the "quantity" of the Steps I work through. They are about the quality of the time, effort, and willingness I put into the program in order to recover, and then help others on the same journey.

One day, I came to the realization that there is no such thing as a "perfect recovery." In fact, recovery must be imperfect to last. My eating disorder (and life in general) has been about rigidity and perfection. But, what I eat will never be "perfect." My weight and size can never be "perfect." The way I feel or express my feelings will never be "perfect." For me, there is no "perfect" number that can reflect how I am doing in recovery, which is exactly what I need. This is why I cherish EDA: this program is not about keeping track of numbers as reflections of my progress in recovery. It is about being mindful of the quality of my life—my health, relationships, passions, hobbies, and service to others.

Having my own experience with an ED and recovery, I have decided to attend a different graduate program to pursue becoming an eating disorder clinical psychologist. Recovery has helped me uncover my own worth, which inspires me to help others find their inherent value—one that no number could ever measure.

(6)

FREEDOM THROUGH WORKING
THE STEPS

*The Steps transformed her life, and now she feels beauty
not as something to be found in a mirror, but from the light she
sees in and shares with others.*

My story starts when I was a young girl, around seven years old, sitting in church staring at my thighs. I remember thinking, *If I only had skinnier thighs I would like myself.* From that moment on, I pretty much tried everything to change who I was on the outside, thinking it would automatically change how I felt about myself on the inside. How wrong I was.

From then on, when I saw other girls at school or out in public, all I could see was their outer self. I was comparing my insides with their outsides. Nothing about my body was okay with me. I was constantly uncomfortable with myself. I remember desperately praying for God to make me skinnier or taller or other impossible things.

I quickly found drugs and alcohol to mask my feelings of being "insufficient." That worked for many years—until it did not. My teenage years were filled with treatments, detoxes, and hospitalizations. In my early twenties, I developed diabetes, and the low blood sugars I would experience jolted me into bingeing until I would feel stable. I truly believe that is what set off the physical allergy that they explain in the "Big Book" of Alcoholics Anonymous. Bingeing literally made me physically okay. It went from happening every once in a while to daily occurrences.

After I could see the significant amount of weight I was putting on, I quickly went back to using drugs, telling myself, *Once I lose the weight, I'll try again to get sober.* When I was using, I had no desire for food and I also wasn't concerned with the way I looked since I knew I was losing weight. This went on for years, with both diseases progressing intensely.

By the time I was twenty-seven, I had lost everything, including my two children. I had no other option but to surrender to a new way of life. I got sober from drugs and alcohol and stayed sober for a year. Through that time I was still very concerned with my weight and body image. I was going on diet after diet, fast after fast, and cleanse after cleanse, thinking I had poor self-control because I couldn't stick to any of them. I believed that if I were down to a certain number then I would be complete.

My eating disorder progressed as time went on—as they always do. Every single day I woke up with a plan to eat three healthy meals, keep them all down, and be active and especially to not binge and purge at night. Every day the time between that commitment and the time I gave in to the obsession got shorter and shorter. I couldn't leave the house without trying on every outfit I owned, making me late anywhere I was going. I couldn't go grocery shopping without spending hours in the store reading labels and going back and forth through the junk food aisles.

I began purging at work, because the guilt and shame of eating breakfast was so intense. I was either stuck looking in a mirror picking out everything wrong with me, or I was avoiding mirrors knowing I would hate the reflection.

One night I was bingeing and purging, leaving the house many times to get more junk food (this had become a regular scenario). Due to my diabetes I began to feel sick from the extreme lows and highs in my blood sugar levels over such short periods of time. I thought about calling 911 a few times, because I was sure I wasn't going to make it. I remember dropping to the floor and begging God for help. That was the last time I purged.

Let me share with you what happened that made such a complete transformation possible. I decided to take the suggestion of my AA sponsor and call a woman she knew in EDA. She invited me to a meeting. It was bittersweet inside that room. I felt as though I was genuinely understood by other people for the first time in my life. I found out they were thinking and feeling the same exact thoughts as me! On the other hand, my ED wanted me to suffer more: I felt completely paralyzed. I felt I couldn't get up or talk or I would be judged. It was all about me and my feelings of being inadequate. After a while that feeling lessened and I asked the woman my AA sponsor knew to be my EDA sponsor. I began my journey, meeting her every week and going through the Twelve Steps with her.

I took my sponsor's suggestions, which included going to all the EDA meetings there were at the time (two a week), eating three balanced meals a day, and staying in constant contact with God. Every day would start with a prayer, "God, please take away this obsession." And when I started getting thoughts to eat when I wasn't hungry, weigh myself, purge, or restrict, I would reach out to my sponsor or someone in EDA. Nine times out of ten, the first thing they told me to do was to get on my knees and pray.

I used prayer before I ate, after, and sometimes during! When I would look in the mirror and start thinking negatively, I would ask, "God, please help me love and accept my body exactly the way it is at this moment." After reading my Fifth Step to another person, I began to see my part in life and in all the situations that bothered me. In the past, being uncomfortable gave me an excuse to use food or act out to cope with my feelings. Now I could see the truth in those situations and use the tools that were given to me to get through them. In Steps Six and Seven, I learned how to be less selfish and more selfless. I learned my shortcomings were a direct path to God. I did what I could to live in my assets and trust that going to Him—and not food—would fix my character defects. Steps Eight and Nine gave me the gift of forgiving others and myself, taking responsibility for the wrongs I had done.

It was in Step Ten that I really experienced release from the nightly torment. Instead of going home to binge, I used that time to review my day in writing, seeing where I had fallen short and where I had done well, and meditating on what God would have me do tomorrow.

By the time I got to Step Twelve I was on fire! I was so passionate about what this program offered me. The transformation that took place on the inside of me was astounding! I couldn't wait to share it with others so they could have freedom too! Today, I no longer feel beauty solely from my reflection in the mirror. I feel beauty from the light I see in others, and from feeling loved and wanted by God. I was shown that He can and will restore you to sanity, and free you from the hell of an eating disorder. All I had to do was to believe—and act!

A LIFE WORTH LIVING

Once her eating disorder had taken its toll, this accomplished veteran's unhappiness finally drove her to find a solution. Today, she finds joy through living authentically—comfortable in her own skin.

Looking back, I can say my eating disorder began well before I could have been diagnosed by clinical standards. My parents were both professors, and (as it happened) tenure was hard to come by. So we moved—from Oregon to Washington and then on to Kentucky, Alaska, Hawaii, and eventually Utah. With an ever-rotating scene of classmates, teachers, and friends, I strove to fit in but found it difficult, if not impossible. Early on, I had an instinct to eat to console myself. I remember hiding in pantries and inhaling whole packages of sweets.

It was as though the food and secrecy (the forbiddenness of it) were a bulwark against a world that seemed to reject me—a world I could not understand.

At some point, in about the 3rd grade, I realized that I was unusual looking—plump, redheaded, and sullen—and began to attribute my unhappiness and social isolation to the form of my body. Whereas other young girls seemed naturally thin and unencumbered by their bodies, I was morbidly self-conscious. I fantasized about slipping into a pair of shorts without having to think of the sweaty width of my thighs. Never did I consider the possibility that my social difficulties might stem from constantly moving between schools, or that I was unusually bright and somewhat socially awkward. My body became the sole source of unhappiness. Then the thought came, *If I could just make my body look like the bodies of other girls, I would be happy.*

Years passed in an entranced state of self-loathing. I felt desperately out of control, as I continued to medicate myself by bingeing on food, and eventually alcohol and drugs. Then, in the 11th grade, my parents sent me on a month-long wilderness excursion. The experience taught me the joy of living *in* my body without mirrors, without constantly appraising myself from outside. I felt the burn and ache of my thighs when they carried me up the steep back of a mountain, and I did not care what I looked like as I stood atop a 14,059 ft. peak and soaked in what seemed to be the whole world—all its jagged lines and greens and the sun so clear and bright over my head.

Upon coming home, I learned that I had lost a significant amount of weight. Neighbors and classmates all commented approvingly, and I even began to get some attention from boys. I reveled in this thinner body, but it was not to last. I still did not know how to cope with life on life's terms, and when I felt bored or rejected, I turned again to food to quell my unmanageable feelings. It was still the only means by which I knew how to control the chaos of my inner world.

I began exercising obsessively to get rid of the excess calories I consumed. I was unwilling to sacrifice my "new" body. But management of my food and exercise turned out to be an exhausting, full time job. At seventeen, I decided to join the Army, in part because I thought the enforced exercise and discipline would help me stay in command of my size. Within a year of joining, I ran my first marathon. My commanders and peers commended my pursuit of athletic excellence and rewarded me with leadership positions. Little did they know, I depended on all those training runs to burn off the loads of sweets I ate secretly in my barracks room. I was caught in a desperate loop of addiction, shame, self-punishment, and social reward.

In short time, I began stealing food and alcohol from my roommate. She was naturally frustrated and reported me to the commander. I was deeply ashamed, but didn't know how to stop. Often I would binge on her food and immediately drive to the commissary to buy replacements. I would then calculate how many calories I had consumed and exercise them off. My knees started giving out, and my body suffered from the constant battering of extremes: high, jolting doses of sugar, followed by long, punishing runs. I willed myself to ignore my body's pleas for rest. The ritual was so grueling that it wasn't long before I couldn't keep up with it.

One night, after inhaling a large quantity food, I knew that I could not endure another run. In a fit of panic, I reached for my black, plastic trash can and did my best to induce vomiting. I was unable to puke that night and was insane with anxiety over the mound of sugar digesting in my stomach. But the next time I binged, I tried it again, and that time it worked—or at least that's what I thought at the time: *this could work.* I was twenty-three, and far from being a solution to my problems, bulimia became a fast road to internal hell.

These were the "Dr. Jekyll and Mr. Hyde" years. On the one hand, I was good at my job and one of the top athletes in our unit. On the other, I was desperately sick— mentally, physically, and spiritually. I could think of no one but myself, my pain, my war against myself and my body. Every meal and snack was a battleground of the will. Would I be "good" and eat only "healthy" food? Or would I be weak-willed and eat "less healthy" food, which I would later throw up? And if I was going to throw up anyway, I might as well have "forbidden" food—and so it went. From time to time, I felt as though I had emerged from the chaos and figured out the right diet or formula to control my body and its appetites. But I always sank back into bingeing and purging. The more I restricted as a means of regaining control, the more I actually lost control. I was insane; there's no other way to describe it.

Over the years, without realizing it, I sacrificed jobs, friendships, romantic relationships, and my health at the altar of my eating disorder. I was so self-obsessed that I was incapable of being a good partner; so filled with shame, I would not, could not, let anyone emotionally near; so totally under the thumb of my eating disorder that I was flakey and irresponsible (canceling on friends at the last minute in order to go for a run or avoid food). And I was often too sick and depressed to get up for work. Then, at the age of twenty-five, I was admitted for the first (but not last) time to a hospital for heart problems related to bulimia.

Although my eating disorder subtly, insidiously worked its life-destroying tendrils into nearly every corner of my life, I still clung to it as to a buoy. I believed that if only I could figure out how to be in control of my food and body, I would be happy. At that point, I reasoned, I would be able to love and be loved; I would be fully human and could walk around the earth without shame.

I went to counselors and psychiatrists. I read self-help and diet books. The message always seemed to be: self-knowledge will set you free. But none of it worked for me. In fact, I often left my counselor's office feeling more desperate and full of self-pity than when I arrived.

It wasn't until I was twenty-six and nearly homeless from alcoholism that I decided to try AA. Over the course of many years and alcoholic relapses, I began to learn what it might mean to surrender my will and my life over to the care of a Higher Power. I also began to see that as long as I continued to engage in disordered eating behavior— whether bingeing, purging, over-exercising, or restricting—the spiritual life and all its rewards would elude me.

After a few months, I started looking for a Twelve-Step program that would help me with food in the same way AA had helped me with alcohol. There appeared to be an abundance of programs offering different visions of "sobriety." But I knew that, for me, eating sobriety could not be restrictive in any way, because restriction had been a central dimension of my disease. So when I stumbled across EDA's website, I nearly cried with joy. Here was a program that offered an understanding of the disease that matched my experience and a vision of recovery that seemed both real and unimaginable.

I began a small EDA meeting at a church in our town. Only a few men and women from AA attended at first, but eventually it grew to include people outside the AA community. We found a wonderful freedom in speaking openly about our problems and solidarity as we began to stumble towards recovery, hand in hand.

But willpower and camaraderie were not enough. Eventually, I suffered another severe, bulimic relapse and sank even more deeply into despair over the apparent hopelessness of my situation. I was at the end of my rope. I felt that I had tried every conventional remedy to no avail. Then one day a thought—one I do not attribute to myself—entered my head: *You say you have tried every available remedy, but have you really? Have you ever been entirely willing to surrender this disease?* Then I realized the truth: I had been unwilling or unable to work the Steps and continued to engage in the same old self-centered thinking and behaviors. I was hoping for something akin to a magical bolt of lightening to zap the insanity out of me. In truth, though I hated the misery of bulimia, I had also been a little in love with my disease and had been unwilling to let it go completely. I wanted to "have my cake and eat it, too."

With all the humility I could muster, I checked myself into an outpatient treatment program. This time, I knew I would have to do things differently. Clearly, no one could help me without my willing participation, so I did what was suggested: no exercise for as long as my doctor ordered, four meals a day, therapy, and much uncomfortable, honest talk of emotions. I was willing, and this time it worked. Or, I should say, *I* worked. Although the treatment program was the first step along the road of willingness, it certainly could not (and did not) provide me with tools sufficient for enduring sobriety.

Recovery has not been an easy or smooth road. I relapsed many times after that first EDA meeting. Looking back, I can say that early on I was unwilling to completely surrender my body size and shape over to the care of my Higher Power. I still didn't trust that I was essentially, irrevocably loveable—no matter my body fat percentage or the size of my pants. I was afraid and clung (consciously or not) to the belief that I needed to secure my portion of love through demonstrations of self-denial and willpower. But it turns out that fear was poison to me. Every time I relied on my *own* power to manipulate my body and food, I cut out the sunlight of the spirit—the only power by which I have ever been freed from this disease.

So, on a daily basis, I pray and commit myself to listening to my body's cues. I eat when hungry and stop when moderately full. When I exercise, it's for the pure, animal joy of it, not to undo the food I've consumed or perfect my physique. I don't have rules about when, or where, or how much I'm allowed to eat. I don't have rules about how much I need to exercise. When unmanageable feelings and cravings arise (as they inevitably will), I know that with the help of my Higher Power, I can bear them—and that they will pass. It sounds unbelievable that I get to write this. It sounds almost too good to be true, but it's not. By following the simple guidelines of this program, I have been free of disordered eating for over two years, which is nothing short of a miracle.

Where self-knowledge and will power could not save me, the Twelve Steps of EDA have given me freedom from an obsession so deep and old I thought it was one of the foundational pillars of my personality. I am so grateful today to have learned that it was not. Each day, as I grow in sobriety, I am restored to a state of usefulness to the people around me and to my God. There is no greater satisfaction in life than this. Today, I get to live a life that is rich with love and purpose—a life absolutely worth living. I believe it is what I was meant for all along.

8

HE USED TO WORK FOR HIS ED;
NOW HE WORKS FOR JOY

*His biggest blessing was being ready to change. He worked
the Steps and learned self-compassion and understanding.*

I started emotional and binge eating as a child, and it
continued through my early twenties. There are probably a number of causes and conditions that brought this on,
but in therapy I was able to identify that I used food and
the activity of bingeing primarily as a way to soothe and
numb myself from a turbulent—and often intoxicated—
childhood home environment. This comfort was induced
by food and bingeing, and offered an escape from both the
instability and aggression going on around me and the fears
and vulnerability I felt inside.

I functioned relatively well through my mid-twenties
and hadn't turned to any extreme, constant behaviors, but
my emotional reliance on food was alive and would come
up at times of stress—as well as bingeing. My extreme ED
behavior first developed in my late twenties, when I turned
to restricting. I had started a new and demanding job and
had gotten into a very challenging relationship. I began to
feel shame from thoughts that I was too lazy and inadequate for my job, and my emotional reliance on food really
began to stand out to me. But rather than work with my

thoughts and emotional patterns, I started restricting as a way to "cure" this reliance on food.

The restricting served many functions. The numbness and high that comes from starving could block out the feelings I associated with laziness—which at that point equaled failure—and it also gave me a sense that I was on the right side of things. I also used it to feel a superiority that I relied on in my relationship to push away my partner and stay in control.

As the years went by, the job and relationship ended and restricting started serving other functions. My weight loss and nutritional deficiency made routine living very hard. I had no energy and getting through the day was a real slog. The emotional abuse I was inflicting on myself by denying basic and natural needs for nourishment, pleasure, joy, and so forth was much heavier than my physical weight; I had become more and more isolating, paranoid, fearful of humiliation, and even fearful of pleasure and happiness itself.

Life was very bleak and strenuous, even though somehow I was still getting great jobs and living in beautiful places. It was a terrible struggle. After a few years, confessional thoughts to myself started bubbling up. These were my first moments of real self-acknowledgement and acceptance that I had a problem. Shortly after, I told my best friend. He said he could see I was obviously suffering and at times wanted to help, but he didn't know what he could do or what was going on with me. I was so sick at the time I actually confessed to him that my problem was eating too much—while I was clearly anorexic and very underweight.

I sought out therapy with someone who was trained in ED recovery. It was my first time in therapy, and I was working through and uncovering a heap of traumas and emotions that I hadn't faced until then. I later moved to a new town and didn't have the money or insurance for a new therapist, but fortunately there was an EDA group where I was living. I started going and found a kind and generous sponsor who helped me work through the first five Steps.

The first time I did the 4th and 5th Step was very powerful. A huge weight was lifted after I began my inventory and was left with more compassion and understanding towards myself. My demons were feeling like allies in a way. They hadn't killed me, luckily, and by having a more honest and fearless relationship with them, they turned into a source of compassion and courage. I had a deeper sense of how I *didn't* want to behave (after learning the hard way of course), and could better see the process that causes those behaviors in the first place. I could see for myself how we all can fall into these patterns as we search for any way to cope with our pain and confusion.

I made amends to those I had harmed, but didn't continue on through Steps Ten through Twelve, which in hindsight could have helped keep my recovery grounded and actively being lived. Unfortunately, I found myself facing similar external circumstances as when I first started restricting, and my ED symptoms came back. I was again fearful, restricting, anxious, and depressed. I had a new relationship and new job; both were very inconvenient for my ED, and vice versa. The basic things of life that I valued and loved to do when not gripped by my ED, couldn't really happen. Life became hard once again.

The relationship ended, as did the job situation, and I was again in a new city that had EDA. I rejoined the program, but at that point I was so conditioned in my restricting behaviors, that I didn't know how to eat. I knew I couldn't work this out on my own; I had too many fear foods, deep misconceptions about how much I needed to eat, and a complicated and entrenched set of beliefs and values about eating food that was absolutely crazy. I sought an intensive treatment program to get extra professional support, and my recovery team included a therapist, a dietician that specialized in ED recovery, a psychiatrist, and a process group of struggling peers.

I was very fortunate to find a good EDA group and an amazing treatment center, but I believe the biggest blessing I had was a mind that was really ready to change. I had given up, I was exhausted, and I wanted to get better. I sought help from those who could guide me back into sanity and good physical health. I had trust in the process (though it was very uncomfortable at times) and began creating new habits with eating that would support a healthy and happy body and mind. I had worked hard to create my disorder—it didn't fall out of the sky onto me—and there was no reason I couldn't also work hard to create the causes for sanity.

I found with exposure as well as guidance from professionals that my fears were untrue: Eating an "unhealthy" food wasn't going to ruin me. A small quantity of a binge food was plenty enough to enjoy and feel content. By practicing mindfulness while eating I could overcome compulsiveness and rid myself of the fear of being overtaken by urges. What I ate did not actually matter to my self-worth. Eating was not a real solution to non-food-related issues.

Now when I eat, it is because my body is hungry, or I eat to spend time with friends and share something with others. I eat things I enjoy because that is a normal thing humans do. I trust and value mindful eating and find that the more I am present while eating, the more the compulsions and thoughts die down and lose power. Taste is taste, whether sweet, sour, bland, intense, whatever. Taste doesn't mean anything beyond the sensation and no matter how good it feels at first it's not going to save me or change my life. I'll still be there when the meal is over with my same life. Being present also makes enjoyment much more simple and not a big deal.

I don't eat to avoid my anger, I don't eat to balance my checkbook, I don't eat to get rest. Napping and relaxing is for rest. Balancing my budget needs paper or a spreadsheet, not binge food. A conflict with my partner doesn't go away by eating something; it is resolved with kind and honest communication. It's humbling (and encouraging) to see that sobriety and a happy life is mostly about following common sense.

With a ton of support and willingness and work, I have created new habits of eating in a balanced way, without black-and-white extreme thinking. The high that comes from hunger is not attractive anymore. I am baffled that I valued the pain of starvation as something worthwhile (though I know I used it to try and help myself). The restricting mentality that was once precious to me is repulsive now. If it ever comes up, I look at it and remember it is a cause for pain and trouble. It leads nowhere else!

Even though I don't act destructively with food these days, I recognize the causes of my behaviors were not about the food; they were mental, emotional, and spiritual in nature. I don't want to make the same mistake again by abandoning the Steps and the support of a recovery community. I go to meetings to get a boost, to spend an hour contemplating and discussing the insanity of an ED and the causes for recovery and happiness. I'm working on my second round of amends to others and try to keep myself grounded with daily inventory, meditation, service, using acronyms like H.A.L.T. (Hungry, Angry, Lonely, Tired), and reflection.

I do believe that over time I can completely remove the ED from my system, but there is no end to challenges in life. To me, the principles of recovery are just principles of our humanity. I use them to support living my values of love, compassion, and inspiration on a daily basis.

9

I AM *JOIE DE VIVRE*

When she chose EDA, she found a source of strength that brought the light back to her eyes.

I believe I am strong. I believe I am unworthy. I believe I am disgusting. I believe I am resilient. I hate my body. I feel alone. I am in love. I am afraid to lose the people I love. I will never be enough. I am restless. I can't tolerate my body. I want to crawl out of my skin. These intense thoughts brought up emotions that, at times, seemed to control every decision in my life. At other times, these thoughts triggered responses within me that kept me safe and protected.

I was always the girl smiling. From a young age, I was always outgoing, gregarious, positive, surrounded by friends with a *joie de vivre* that lit up a room. I was always joking and the first to make a silly face or charge headfirst into an embarrassing situation with a brave and unashamed freedom. I would occasionally make disparaging comments about my body or how much I ate, because it was a central part of my comedy routine; however, I never put much weight into these comments, or felt that I really took them to heart, or struggled with body image. This is why I never saw my eating disorder coming. Anorexia is literally the antithesis of everything that I am. My anorexia was about deprivation, punishment, and isolation. My anorexia kept me from singing and dancing. My anorexia stole the light from my eyes. My anorexia tried to destroy the spirit I carried and the body that acts as the suitcase for my soul.

It all began my junior year of high school, which sometimes I see as a blessing because I am still able to remember a time when food didn't control my life. This was when I couldn't tell you where to find a serving size on a box of food and I certainly didn't understand what the ever-ambiguous and looming "carb" really was. From my perspective carbs could have been a high profile gang the way that society warned us: "Stay away from carbs," "No carbs is the answer," and "No carbs after dark." It wasn't until the summer before my junior year that my life took a 180-degree turn—one that would forever alter my ways of thinking.

The summer before my junior year of high school I had my first real relationship—not one of my previous "group date, give you a hug after school" relationships. When it became physical I didn't appear to be extremely bothered, but I knew that something didn't feel right. I wondered if other girls felt a nauseous feeling deep in the pit of their stomach after their boyfriends left their houses. I slowly distanced myself, which inevitably caused my boyfriend to end things. I was so relieved, and yet for some reason furious at the same time, because not more than two days after we broke up he had a date with another girl. I am an independent person and I was always surrounded by strong friendships, so I tried to put it out of my mind. But the physical triggers and nauseous fear that had been a constant facet of our relationship would not leave me. I didn't think much of it, but after the fall cross-country season started I began to run a little bit—for fun.

Running for fun turned into more exercise, which turned into eating healthier, which snowballed into the

Catholic season of Lent. I decided to give up desserts because, of course, that is what God would want. Fast-forward to the summer and the snowball was officially on the move, collecting speed every day. My friends and family began to comment on my weight change and worried about my isolating behaviors surrounding exercise. I calmed these fears by reminding them that I was always the girl who would take the last serving or be the first to order a dessert. I made excuses, denied my clearly disordered behaviors, and became furious at the mention of an eating disorder. I was not some vain, skinny, mean girl who was crazy about her appearance—which up until this point had been my only perception of someone with an eating disorder. All I knew was what the media had told me, and having always been the girl with "joie de vivre," I was not about to trade in that title for psychotic, skinny b----.

It wasn't until the first time I tried to explain to the doctor what my behaviors had been over the past year that I suddenly saw how insane my day-to-day life had become. Speaking my reality aloud made me aware of the irrational lengths I was going through to suppress some fear that I couldn't fully explain. At this point I began an outpatient journey that would lead to uncovering a history of trauma and sexual abuse that had subconsciously resurfaced with the physical interactions of my relationship in the summer. I began to feel freedom; the weight of these secret memories lifted when I shared them. My therapist had inquired about any history of sexual abuse, and when I recalled one of my vague memories that I had tried to convince myself was a dream, my therapist informed me that the event I remembered had actually happened. My parents had revealed this to her in confidence, because they thought I had forgotten the incident. The shame that I had carried for years, and my fears surrounding physical intimacy, suddenly made sense. However, the journey of working through this and other contributing factors led me through what seemed a revolving door of treatment centers.

My freshman year of college lasted all of two months before I was sent to treatment. I tried to restart the following fall and again left for treatment. The following fall I decided to conquer my struggles in outpatient treatment instead of another residential center; and, yet again, I was able to tread water for about a year until I entered a partial hospitalization program (PHP) the spring of my junior year. I felt like nothing worked. I felt like I had uncovered the reasons I needed my eating disorder to protect me, but I also felt like I was making a choice to give in to that false sense of safety, which always led to another relapse. I *knew* I knew better. I knew that it was my choice to manage my disorder, and I knew it would be the hardest journey of my life.

The minute I realized I needed to change was the same minute I realized I couldn't do it alone. The fact that I wanted to fight led me to find the rooms of EDA. If I was going to fight, I needed to see the soldiers who were standing with me. The rooms of EDA have brought a constant strength that I have not found in any other treatment center, support group, or eating disorder workbook.

Today, I know my constant efforts to fight and my conscious decisions to look at the defects in my character that pull me back into my eating disorder will test me every day. It doesn't matter *when* my eating disorder started, it doesn't matter *how* my eating disorder started, it doesn't matter *why* my eating disorder still likes to tell me lies and steal my light. What matters is what I choose to do now;

how I choose to live in the moment now, just now; and how just for today I choose recovery. I didn't cause it, I can't cure it, but I can be sure it will not steal my *joie de vivre* ever again. EDA is a program that involves choice and surrender every day. EDA is a program that provides a guide to change that can be worked every day. EDA is a program that reminds me of the *joie de vivre*—the joy of life.

I am self-conscious. I am a survivor. I am weak. I am strong. I am afraid. I am brave. I have support. I am love. I am powerless. I am the courage to change.

10

IN GOD'S HANDS

As a result of surrendering to the program, she became the woman that she believes God intended her to be, gaining peace, freedom, and an ability to connect with others.

My eating disorder started out casually: I just wanted to lose a little weight. I was in 8th grade and fourteen years old. I noticed another girl in my middle school was also my height (I'm a tall girl), and she was a little thinner than me. She looked great! I even overheard her say her exact weight in the gym locker room one day, and I realized I was not even that far away from that number. I only needed to lose a few pounds or so. So that's what I set out to do.

I started cutting out a few higher calorie options from my daily food intake and began to see results. I realized quickly that if I cut out even more foods from my diet, then I would achieve more rapid weight loss. I loved getting results and encouraged my friends to also lose weight. They attempted, but no one could cut out or cut down foods as well as I could (I have since realized this was a symptom of my disease that made my life unmanageable—not something to be "proud" of). I had the self-discipline that my friends didn't; it felt powerful.

But it became an obsession. I became very rigid in what I would or wouldn't eat. I had an exercise regimen I made myself stick to. I had little time for doing activities with friends, because they might try to get me to eat, and that didn't work in with my plans. I was more concerned with exercise and finding ways to avoid eating.

Family dinners were a nightmare as I refused to eat more and more foods. I was so particular. I stopped eating just about everything my mom cooked in order to stick to the foods that I allowed myself to eat. It was only a few months after I started my "diet" that my parents had me start seeing a professional therapist, psychiatrist, and nutritionist, and thus started my struggle to hang on to my eating disorder.

I was angry at everyone for butting into my business. I didn't see the problem with my way of living. I got results! I loved the feeling of being thin. I had gotten to the point that I had no social life, but I didn't care. I felt safe. I abused the knowledge given to me by the nutritionist and restricted even further.

During my 9th grade year, my heavy restricting caught up with me; I became extremely sick and ended up in the hospital due to a simple flu. My thin body couldn't handle the illness, and I needed to be given extra nutrients intravenously. I think being in the hospital scared me. I don't know why, but something seemed to switch for me in my eating after that. I got out of the hospital and allowed myself to eat again!

And I mean eat! Somehow the girl that was so afraid of eating any type of variety of foods began to overeat freely. Everyone appeared happy, and I felt somewhat normal again. Yet I was obsessed with eating food. I would come home from school and snack for hours until my parents came home. I didn't care about the weight gain for quite a few months. When I did start to feel somewhat uncomfortable with my body, I made an attempt to purge one of my binges; but it didn't work, and I quickly moved on. A few months later, I tried it again and found more "success." Thus started my full-fledged bulimic career.

Much like I had prided myself on my ability to restrict, my bulimia also gave me some pride in that I figured I had beaten the game of life. Acting out in bulimia seemed to be the solution to all my problems. I felt deviously accomplished. Finally I could eat all I wanted— participate in social functions if needed (where I would be required to eat)—and not gain weight. Bingeing and purging became my love. I didn't necessarily like the purging part so much, but it came with the territory.

Also like the anorexia, bulimia took me down a dark hole of depression and isolation. My "solution" led me to misery. I pushed away people and things that might have interfered with my acting out process. As much as I didn't want to be, I was constantly obsessed with eating-disordered thinking: planning my next binge, beating myself up in my head, and sizing myself up in comparison to every other body around me.

My parents found out about my bulimia, because my excessive purging ended up causing damage to the plumbing in our home. So I started seeing the mental health professionals again. I hated this. I couldn't see why people didn't just leave me alone; this was my body! I lied and tried to hide the bingeing and purging behavior, becoming even sneakier and going to even stranger lengths to hide what I was doing.

At some point in my high school career, I came to the realization that I was dejected. And I knew it was because of my eating disorder. I hadn't minded being obsessed with food, weight, and body image in the beginning, but I recognized it was costing me any enjoyment in life outside of the superficial pleasure I received from bingeing. But this "pleasure" was uncomfortable, and I felt out of control and extremely depressed. I had a relationship with God and frequently went to church and youth group activities, but my eating disorder ruled me. I began to wish and pray it away. I claimed a Bible verse for my life: Psalms 142:7a, which states "Set me free from my prison that I may praise Your name." By "prison" I meant my eating disorder. Even as a seventeen-year-old girl, I knew my life and future would be desolate. My eating disorder was my master. I couldn't escape.

I had the idea that a change of scenery would help and that going away to college was the solution. I assumed it would be reasonably difficult to find ways to purge in the communal-style living in the dormitory hall. Needless to say, I managed to find ways to continue my eating disorder.

Having always been a pretty good kid and a good student, it was as though my eating disorder was my one black cloud. Not everyone knew about it, so I had become quite accustomed to living a double life. I was the sweet Christian girl on the outside, yet those who knew me knew that I had a monster of an eating disorder. I had gotten used to living one way in private and attempting to portray quite a different picture to the world. That's why when I got introduced to drugs, I had little problem living the lie that I was the "good Christian girl" attending Christian college—even while secretly adopting a drug habit.

Drugs seemed to be the new solution; they seemed to solve all my problems with food simply because I was rarely hungry! When I ran hard with using drugs, I didn't eat; but when I wasn't using, my bulimia was still my "go to." Regardless, I was relieved to have found at least *some* level of escape from my eating disorder.

My parents found out about the drug use and sent me to eating disorder treatment. It's my belief they chose this instead of drug treatment, because they had difficulty facing that their "sweet girl" was using drugs (and they'd known about the eating disorder for years). While at the inpatient facility, I played along with what they wanted me to do, but I was angry that I was there. I told the staff, "I'm just going to do drugs with my boyfriend when I get out of here." And I did. The treatment wasn't a complete waste, but I just wasn't ready to face my most deep-seated demons at that time. I went home and did drugs—just as I said I would—and my relationship with my family got worse.

The boyfriend I mentioned was also my drug dealer; he was not a good man and I suffered a lot of emotional and some physical pain due to that relationship. We eventually broke up, and I started dating someone new who didn't like that I did drugs. He encouraged me to stop and to drink alcohol instead. I didn't like alcohol at this time, but eventually gave up the drugs and instead picked up the bottle. After all, this was legal! And normal!

There were times during my drinking career I didn't act out in bulimia. This was usually during times I felt I had something "exciting" going on in my life, such as a new boyfriend or some other positive event. During bad times, like break-ups or any other emotional disturbance, bulimia was faithfully there for me.

Again, never having dealt with what was going on inside of me, the alcohol also became a problem. At one point, I tried to stop drinking, but my eating disorder took over at an insane level. I knew I'd rather be drinking while bingeing and purging instead of being solely left with bulimia! Bulimia was a full-time job when I didn't allow myself alcohol.

The magnitude of my drinking increased, and I started to have difficulty functioning in my daily work life due to my hands shaking from withdrawals. This led me to drinking in the morning to still my nerves, and I bowed down before the bottle. I knew this had to stop, so I finally went to substance abuse treatment. It was there that I was finally able to separate from drugs and alcohol. Yet once again, my "friend" the eating disorder remained faithfully there for me.

I attempted to adopt the Twelve-Step way of life, proclaiming rigorous honesty and amazing willingness to change. Yet I continued to live dishonestly by way of stealing my roommates' food and lying about purging in our apartment. I stayed sober from substances, but it seemed as though my eating disorder had exploded. Taking away the drink and the drug left me with my original vice—my eating disorder. I hated this one most of all. Yes, for many people an eating disorder may not lead to such severe consequences as legal problems, severe relationship issues, financial ruin, and some of the other negative consequences often associated with a substance abuse problem. But my eating disorder has proven to be ten times more shameful and lonely than my drinking/drugging career ever appeared to be.

I had been attending EDA meetings since early in my recovery from other substances, but didn't fully surrender to the EDA process. I listened to people in meetings, yet wondered whether or not they were going home afterwards to secretly binge and purge. The people that claimed to have recovered from an eating disorder seemed to be happy, but I couldn't imagine life without one and didn't believe recovery in this area of my life could happen for me. I had been eating disordered for over half my life. Out of desperation and misery I finally asked an EDA sponsor to take me through the Twelve Steps. She introduced me to a peace and a freedom I had never known.

Though I was raised in the church and at times prayed incessantly for my eating disorder to be removed, I didn't previously have any action to go along with that. Yes, I'd had therapists, psychiatrists, nutritionists, parents, and others working with me to try to help me get better; but, to be honest, I hadn't surrendered. Though I had been praying to God for years, He did not reach down and miraculously heal my eating disorder. Truthfully, I hadn't totally wanted Him to do so; it was a part of me, and at some level I wanted to hang on to it with full force.

Yet at other times I prayed fervently for God to take away my eating disorder. I would make these prayers as I stuffed my face with binge food, fully intending to purge. I was expecting Him to change my thinking and actions without me doing anything. I do believe that God is fully capable of miraculous healing, yet without my participation I don't think I would have truly found long-term recovery and a way of living more satisfying than any I had ever known. I hadn't been giving God much to work with in order for Him to transform me.

Coming to EDA was the first exposure I had to my need to take action. Prayer was certainly part of it: prayer for the removal of my eating disorder, specifically my obsession with food, weight, and body image. I realized I needed to take certain actions, and EDA was the first time that I was given clear-cut directions and suggestions, as well as the support of others who had gone through the same thing. In EDA, I was introduced to people who had recovered—people who had suffered like me but had gotten better. Historically, my eating disorder had been something I protected, done solely by myself, and I didn't let people in.

Truly being authentic about my eating disorder was a new experience for me. Yet, as it states in the AA "Big Book," "one (*eating-disordered*) could affect another as no (*non-eating-disordered*) could."[1] The eating-disordered individual understands the weird twist in the minds of those would steal food, or do all these crazy things, just to support their illness. Furthermore, the AA "Big Book" states, "But the ex-problem (*eating-disordered*) who has found this solution, who is properly armed with facts about himself, can generally win the entire confidence of another (*eating-disordered*) in a few hours."[2] For me it certainly took more than a few hours, but it still worked!

It was liberating to hear people who had walked in my shoes freely share about the insidious nature of eating disorders. They stated they got better and were willing to show me exactly what they did to recover. They said I needed regular support and suggested I get a sponsor and reach out to people in the rooms of EDA. I needed to develop a healthy relationship with food and see it as a mechanism to nourish my body rather than something to control my weight, feelings, mood, or anything else.

Slowly my actions changed, and it *was* slow! Yet, I had the support of other people in EDA sharing that this is what they had gone through, too—that it can be slow and painful, but recovery is a process. If it wasn't for their continual reassurance, I probably would not have stayed on course. I thank God for the rooms of EDA, for the fellowship, for joining people together with this common disease. Having that revolutionary change in my way of thinking

---

[1] *Alcoholics Anonymous.* (2001) New York, NY: AA World Services, Inc., xvi-xvii. Replaced "alcoholic" with "eating-disordered," as the same concept applies. This was done by early sponsors in EDA.
[2] Ibid., 18. Replaced "drinker" and "alcoholic" with "eating-disordered."

took effort, consistent prayer, and support. At times I didn't think anything was working or any changes were taking place. Looking back, it was more like, *Oh my gosh, I didn't binge or purge today* or *It's been a few days together,* and then much later on it was *Wow! I went through a whole day and I was completely not focusing on my eating disorder.*

Notably, there was a time after having found recovery that I relapsed in my eating disorder. I had the insane thought that I could act out once: that I could have one binge/purge episode and move on from there. Clearly that wasn't well thought out; yet I acted on it, which sent me into some of the most miserable of times with my eating disorder. Having a brief sense of what freedom could be like and then handing that gift back to God was incredibly painful. It took me a long time to come back into the rooms of EDA out of my own stubbornness and pride. I didn't want to admit to a relapse. I didn't want to have to start over in my Steps. I wanted to fix this on my own, yet I had the very real knowledge that I would be unable to do so. After succumbing to enough emotional pain, I asked a woman who worked a very strong program of recovery to sponsor me and I surrendered to God, the program, and finally to my own powerlessness and the unmanageability of living outside of the Twelve-Step way of life.

My recovery the second time was that much stronger. I also felt the disease was much stronger, and it took me quite a while to free myself from the intrusive eating-disordered thoughts. As mentioned, the disease came back with a vengeance; I worked for recovery that much harder the second time. Yet I did learn from the experience. Never again do I want to get even close to a relapse. It's too painful and hard to come back (though not impossible). I hold on to my eating disorder recovery like a precious gift, because that's what it is. Never in a million years did I expect that one day I would have the freedom from worrying about weight, food, and body image. Today, I eat what I want to eat, and food serves its intended purpose: as a means of fueling my body for life's activities. During my recovery, I earned a master's degree and often thought about how, during the grueling process of school, I never could have been diligent in my responsibilities had the eating disorder still been wreaking havoc on my life. My life is free today. I am free to travel, and my eating disorder no longer holds me back. I am able to be a friend and family member without constant thoughts of myself invading all conversations.

It's a beautiful thing to be so dependent upon God and a Twelve-Step fellowship; my need to have a healthy relationship with food and my body keeps me working with others and active in working my own program of recovery. I notice that if I slack, my thoughts start to get somewhat haywire. I am glad I've learned my lesson. God willing, I will always be an active member of EDA and I will continue to seek God to gain lasting release from the prison of my faulty thinking.

"When we look back, we realize that the things which came to us when we put ourselves in God's hands were better than anything we could have planned."[3]

---

[3] *Alcoholics Anonymous.* (2001) New York, NY: AA World Services, Inc., 100.

11

LIFE SENTENCE LIFTED

She earned her freedom when she stopped trying to be perfect and accepted life on life's terms.

Surely freedom from restricting, bingeing, or purging behaviors for twenty-four years had made a good life possible: a loving marriage, wide circle of friends and pursuits, meeting serious life challenges of my own and others. Thanks to Twelve-Step rooms, gratefully, I'd been sober for even longer. Yet, eating-disordered thinking and stealth rigidity around eating and food persisted.

I finally decided I'd received all the grace I deserved. The shadow of my eating disorder would be there for life, and I just had to be vigilant and derail any out-of-control anxiety and depression. I cycled through various Twelve-Step programs to address over- or under-eating, but I heard only what was said about abstinence. I had worked the Steps only to curtail behavior.

I believed my number-rules about weight and calories had kept me safe from feelings greater than I could handle. I'd had therapy all along and my psychologist admired what hurdles I had overcome. I told myself, *What's wrong with some preoccupation with numbers? After all, it's typical for middle-aged and older women. It's nothing compared to a gaunt body, exorbitant weight gain or loss, institutions, and fearful self-harm.*

This was so wrong! My dishonesty had led me to construct a functioning façade, which I sternly kept reworking. The authentic joy and sorrow that come with acceptance of life on life's terms were stunted. Relapse remained an unacknowledged option.

Finding EDA on the web has been a turning point. I wept when I read the brochure on Balance. It seemed as though I had finally found a tribe that spoke a language I could understand. The tools, Step-work, and insights I have learned through the years are valuable supports. With EDA, the Twelve Steps, and hearing the hope and experience of others, I am ceasing the attempts to be perfect in a perfectly artificial semblance of recovery, which, in fact, is a prison cell.

I feel I am returning to the eleven-year-old who went to the library and found an insurance table of desirable weights. That was the pivotal year in which I put on a form-fitting mental straight jacket, and sadly, it was so easy.

It has taken many, many years to come home to the truth that living by numbers, judgments, and comparisons is useless and spirit-throttling. At any age, the key of willingness can open the door to the surprise—the fulsome serendipity—of real life.

(12)

RECOVERY AFTER 42 YEARS OF BULIMIA

Willingness, commitment, and perseverance transformed a tennis pro's resignation—that she would always have an eating disorder—into a durable recovery.

I remember how important my food was to me as far back as when I was four years old. I would sit in my Dad's big chair in the living room waiting for him to come home, listening to Peter and the Wolf and eating my favorite comfort food. It reminded me of how secure I felt when he was home with us. I was getting my needs met. This feeling became a recurrent theme in my life as I grew into a teenager.

I was part of a family of seven children, and both parents came from good "Southern stock." My dad was a doctor and my mother a nurse. Surely they could be wonderful and take good care of me. But my dad was a sweet and loving man who would turn into a controlling, raging alcoholic. He loved to drink, play tennis with his buddies, and stay out until the wee hours of the morning, only to put the fear of God into me about what he would do when he got home, wanting his dinner on the table at 3:30 am. He also believed his children should excel in one thing, and they should know what it was and be pursuing it by the age of twelve. Mine was tennis, and my dad was my coach. I was molded into his clone and the prodigy he wished he had been as a young boy. I was "like a son" to him, because

I was very athletic and he lived vicariously through me; my brothers were artists and didn't fit the bill.

On the other hand, my mother was a stay-at-home mom who was quite subservient and weak. She was intelligent, but an emotionally unavailable, depressed woman who spent her time either trying to take care of us, painting, or hiding in her closet crying. I often wondered how she could take care of her children when she struggled to take care of herself. She never stood up to my father and never protected me from him. She allowed emotional and verbal abuse, both of which can be worse than any other kind. She and I would wait up together at night for my father to come home, terrified of what he would do when he arrived. One night I stood in the kitchen with my mother while my father pulled a knife on my Mom; I stepped in front of her.

I thought that if he hurt me I could handle it, while my mother could not. She was close to the artists and dancers in the family. I was the family scapegoat and spoke my mind when I could, until I realized that I still had to be the perfect child. My mother studied the Eastern philosophies when I was a teenager and became a vegetarian to keep her body in its best health. She also developed an eating disorder and probably died early as a result (she was diagnosed with cirrhosis of the liver, although she was not a drinker). She became an Episcopal priest, and to the world she was a saint. To me she was cold and devoid of emotion.

When I was fifteen, I was a very angry and controlled teenager and developed an eating disorder one day after a guy I had a crush on told me I looked pregnant. This comment hit me like a dagger in my heart. To me, I was not okay being who I was, and this struck a chord in me. Now, two men, my teenage crush and my father had given me the message that I was not good enough. At least this was my interpretation. I decided to go on a diet and become some- one I could accept. No one would ever control me again.

During this time my sister taught me about bulimia, and I thought I had found a secret I could have to myself that no one could take away from me. Two months later, when she died in a car accident, I found out she had been drinking. I blamed myself because I knew she drank and I never told anyone about it. I believe I held onto my eating disorder for so long because I thought it kept me connected to her.

With my eating disorder firmly entrenched, I felt I was finally in charge of my life. *No one was going to tell me what to do!* As sick as I was, no one knew. I hid my secret and still spent endless hours on the court with my father. I played a lot of tournaments and secured national rank- ing. When I graduated from high school at seventeen, I left home to tour on the Women's Pro Circuit. There was no discussion of college; I didn't want to go anyway, because I didn't know how to handle my eating disorder in a dorm. I thought I was finally free, but my eating disorder followed me. My childhood felt like a lie. The family secrets were no more than a dysfunctional family hiding behind a façade of over-achieving puppets. It was all about how it looked on the outside.

My anorexia and bulimia controlled my life for the next thirty-eight years.

To further cut ties with my father, I ran away and got married at nineteen to a pro tennis player. I lost a lot of weight, and when my parents sent me for some tests on my stomach they found nothing. Then they sent me to a psy- chiatrist, and it was suggested that I move as far away from my father as possible, so I could find out who I was. So my husband and I moved to Vermont to teach tennis. I went into therapy for the first time and continued playing tennis even though I was burned out and wanted to quit. I never told a soul about my eating disorder, but I believed others knew something was going on. I kept thinking I could beat it if I just used more willpower. I had so much shame and guilt that I could not face the truth. I was living a life of denial. No one questioned me and no one showed any concern, so I kept at it in hope that someone would care enough to notice something was wrong. I even told my husband and he said nothing. I began to think I was crazy. I suffered from depression, went on antidepressants, and then had two children.

I wanted to get help so badly, but no one really knew about eating disorders back then. Nothing changed. I was miserable in a marriage that was devoid of intimacy because of my eating disorder. I thought it was his fault, so I decided to get a divorce.

I quickly found a new love and moved to Montreal six months later to be with him. He had four children and I had two: six kids total. This set me off on a roller coaster ride, but we decided to get married anyway. I was convinced having two more kids would be the cure. But at thirty years of age, with two more children, I felt smothered and controlled and began drinking heavily. I felt I had married my father and after eleven years of marriage wanted out. He threatened to take my children from me if I didn't get my eating disorder and drinking under control. I had a better idea: I would leave him, but not until we moved to Florida where my family lived—he was retiring and we thought Florida was the place to do that.

I got sober from alcohol, but the real issue was my eating disorder, and I needed help because I was still hiding it. I decided to go into treatment, which gave me a good break. However, my eating disorder told me to get out of my marriage, because the control I felt under my husband was killing me.

What I didn't realize was that I would never begin to heal until I stopped acting out. Again, I didn't have the tools to change my behaviors and felt I needed to be out of my marriage in order to work on myself. I got a divorce, leaving me alone with my four children. At this time I stopped drinking and stopped the eating-disordered behaviors. This was the toughest year of my life...getting a divorce, getting sober, and trying to use the 12-Steps of AA to relieve me of my eating disorder. I took that time to really *be* with my children while working on myself. I was not in a committed relationship for the next ten years; I wanted to focus on my children and my recovery. I stayed sober, but my eating disorder had become active again. I realized I could not beat it on my own, but still wouldn't be honest with myself about how it kept me sick and out of intimate relationships.

By the time my two oldest kids were in college and my two younger boys were eleven and thirteen, I had met a wonderful man who loved me unconditionally. My children adored him and he was great to them. I began to feel so much better about myself, yet my eating disorder continued. I had never really had any consequences from my behaviors, so nothing scared me enough to stop. I had resigned myself to this being my life. After a year, my new husband realized my eating behaviors were strange. He couldn't understand and felt as though I were cheating on him. He felt my first love was my disorder. I had been found out and felt more guilt and shame than ever. *How could I do this while he was so wonderful to my family and me?* He didn't deserve that. I was so entitled and felt I couldn't stop. My disease had such a strong hold on me that I continued to ignore the truth and hid it even more. When was all of this denial going to have some consequences for me?

I felt a lot of pressure and knew I would have to stop if I wanted to be in a healthy relationship with my husband. When all of my children were gone, we moved into a new house to downsize. It was great to be alone with him, but there was so much focus on us I got really scared about his catching me as I acted out. My husband is British and takes baths. He later told me that when he would go take a bath, he knew I would go in and take a barf. He confronted me about it, but I always lied. This would enrage him; he felt cheated on and no longer trusted me. Then he began to wonder what else I lied about and felt very distant to me. He is such an honest and loyal person that he was very disappointed in me and he thought our relationship was failing. We argued about my behaviors, but I loved him so much that I knew that I had to change.

A year later, I was losing a lot of weight due to the stress of my eating disorder and my fears around my failing relationship. I was also stressed about my job and how miserable I was there. A good friend from AA approached me and my husband and told me I was really sick and in bad shape. At this time I was fifty-seven and finally ready to truly deal with my eating disorder. My husband had been doing research online and found EDA. He told me that there were local meetings and that he would go with me to my first one. I felt *so* supported. We went on a Tuesday night and I saw someone I knew. This was even more comforting. I loved the meeting and felt I had finally found home, a place where I could feel unconditional love—no judgment and people who understood me. I didn't share, I just listened. I wanted to take it all in. After a few meetings I shared and let the others know I had had an eating disorder for forty-two years. This was crazy to me. I made a decision to do whatever it took to beat this. There were people there who had recovered, and I thought this was amazing! I had resigned myself to the fact that I would be acting out until the day I died. I found hope and began to believe that I could recover as I had with my alcoholism. I committed to getting a sponsor and working the Steps. I was so happy and excited that I saw a possibility. I felt happy to be alive!

I immediately stopped purging and worked as hard as I could to learn as much as I could. This was the beginning of a life I had never dreamed of. The last time I felt this good was when I was fifteen, before my eating disorder began. I had my whole life ahead of me then, and I realized I was at that same place now. At fifteen, my eating disorder began, and when I found EDA, I felt I was back home with the support I never had. My EDA supports were like sisters to me.

Today, my life is awesome! I have great relationships and have healed the relationships with my children. I can be with them today in a way I was not able to while they were growing up. They are healthy, happy, successful adults, and I am very proud of them. I have gone back to school to study addiction and have a job working in the recovery field. I feel so blessed to give back to the community that has nurtured me back to health. I can now pursue hobbies and dreams I never believed possible while I was in my eating disorder. I work the Steps, and have a sponsor and strong sober supports. I also sponsor others in order to help those that are still suffering with this disease. This is so rewarding to me and helps keep me focused and happy in recovery, remembering where I come from.

Today, I take care of my mind, body, and spirit by exercising, praying, meditating, doing yoga, and nurturing myself in other ways. I know I am no good to others if I don't first take care of myself. I feel a quality of peace and happiness I never knew in my eating disorder. I have been able to give up the many unproductive ways I used to cope with life. I have found new and healthier ways to comfort myself, deal with my problems, and no longer hold secrets because I live an honest life. I no longer live in the problems of my eating disorder; I live in the solution. I use the Steps and tools I have learned in the program of EDA. They remind me to live my life with integrity and practice the principles in all of my affairs.

I feel a responsibility to share my experience, strength and hope to carry the message that it is possible to recover from an eating disorder, and to thank those who have been a powerful example to me, those who gave me hope and the belief I could recover and my Higher Power, for making my recovery possible. I really believe anyone can recover from an eating disorder. The promises can come true for you too. Willingness, commitment, and perseverance have been the keys to my freedom!

(13)

RECOVERY OPENED A WHOLE
NEW WORLD

When she began to trust people, she discovered her voice and experienced the joy of sharing with others on a deep and meaningful level.

The history of my eating disorder begins around age seven. My parents had divorced, and my mom had a new boyfriend. We would sit together and eat dinner with my older sister. There were a lot of rules at the table such as how to eat, what noises not to make, finishing all your food, and more. If we didn't like the food or eat all of it, we would be having it for breakfast, lunch, and dinner again until it was all gone. There were a lot of meals I disliked but knew I had to force down, somehow doing my best to not taste what I was eating. If we made certain sounds at the table (the fork scratching the plate, chewing too loudly, or teeth touching the fork) or didn't say "Sir" or Ma'am" we would be punished. I vividly remember the night when I was informed that I was swallowing too loudly. My mom's boyfriend said since I was eating like a dog, then I might as well eat with them. I had to take my dinner plate and eat my food on the floor of the kitchen next to the dog's food while my family ate at the table. I was humiliated. My fear of eating "wrong" in front of others became deeply ingrained in my head.

I would continue to avoid eating in front other others, or I would eat very little in fear of criticism for how I was doing it. I feared the humiliation of eating "wrong" and felt like everyone around me could surely see how bad I was. I became concerned about my body from a young age. I received criticism from my mom's boyfriend about my body: he said my butt was too big, my stomach stuck out, and I was chubby. My sister added criticism about my appearance. I was called "ugly," "fat," and "disgusting" more times than I could count, and at an after-school program, a peer called me similar names. This experience was the first time someone outside my family called me fat. I decided to tell the leader, and her response was, "Well you are kinda chubby." I never told anyone about this experience, because I was too humiliated.

I learned a lot about body image and dieting from my mom. I witnessed her calling herself "fat," putting herself down, asking us if she was as big as someone else and always criticizing her body. I thought she was beautiful. She was perfect in my eyes when I was a little girl. *If she saw those things were wrong with her, did she notice those same flaws in me?* She would talk about the times when she was very skinny and how she would eat almost nothing for dinner. I saw pictures of her at an unhealthy weight with her bones protruding. If that was beauty, I wanted to strive for that. My mom tried numerous fad diets and her weight fluctuated up and down. As I began to get older, I became concerned that if I didn't lose the weight now I would be in a constant struggle with weight later on, or end up overweight like my mom.

I was a very sensitive child and adult; I had a lot of anxiety and fear. I experienced physical, emotional, and sexual abuse during my life. I didn't express how I was feeling and was a people pleaser, always trying to do things "right." I developed a protective shell around me, so I could keep people away from my inner feelings and thoughts and prevent them from connecting with me. Movement was the one outlet for expression where I felt safe. I started dance at age four and continued dancing competitively through high school. I spent four years on my high school cheer squad and dance team, and also danced outside of school. Practices and performances gave me an opportunity to express myself. Dance and cheerleading focused a lot on our bodies and sizes. During measurement days for costumes, I wanted mine to be smaller than those of the other girls. I would cringe if a number that sounded "large" was shouted to the person writing down our measurements. I felt self-conscious and was always comparing my body to those of the better dancers. They were skinnier, taller, and had longer lines. In high school, I was shorter, had no long lines, and was more stout than slender. I was extremely critical of myself and always strived to be "good enough."

At age fifteen, I started to diet. I began by eating less and being cautious of the foods I was consuming. Later it progressed into restricting certain foods, drinking meal supplements instead of eating, and recording how much I ate daily. By my senior year in high school I was eating so little that I was passing out during classes and after performances. I was sent to the school nurse who asked about my eating patterns. This was the first time anyone had ever asked me about them. She wanted me to keep a record of what I ate for three days and bring it back to her. Instead, I avoided her the rest of the year and didn't let other people know what happened.

In college, I continued to go in and out of my eating disorder. It had become my "go to" when things were stressful. I would overeat at times, mostly when I was sad, and then try to compensate later on. I tried several different diet plans and fitness regimes over the years. I delved into calorie counting, daily weighing, graphing my progress, using laxatives, and purging. In my mind, I was engaging in all of this to get the ideal body—the body that would make me smarter, prettier, more popular, more successful. What I didn't realize was that I was focusing on my outer appearance because I had so much pain and anguish on the inside.

Straight from college, I went into teaching, which had always been a dream of mine. My eating disorder followed me, and not far behind it were new ways I'd come across to help me cope. I found drinking was the magic cure to turn me from that shy girl into a social butterfly at parties or clubs. After a few drinks, I could forget about any of my emotions that had come up—and push them further down inside. Unfortunately, my emotions started sneaking out through panic attacks and severe anxiety.

At age twenty-six, I finally sought treatment, because although I could teach without eating much, I couldn't manage the panic attacks. Having to talk to a therapist about what was going on was nearly impossible for me. I didn't express myself openly or say what was going on inside to anyone. During sessions, I would have panic attacks that led the therapist to refer me to a psychiatrist. I was prescribed medications for both depression and anxiety. By taking the anxiety medication prior to an appointment, I could begin to share a little bit more in sessions. Weekly therapy does not stay at a surface level for very long. Soon we were delving into deeper issues, and the past was brought up. This led to nightmares between sessions, more anxiety attacks, an increase in my eating disorder behaviors, drinking, pill abuse, and self-injury.

It wasn't until I was really involved in therapy that I realized how much of life I had been missing. While other people were able to be present in the moment and enjoy normal events, I was stuck in my head worrying about everything from body image to peoples' thoughts, so much that I could barely remember details from key life experiences. I had become so closed off that I could not talk to my closest friends about my struggles. I was exhausted from always putting on a facade that everything was okay. Instead of building connections, I felt lonelier every day. Instead of starting to climb out of this and open up, I developed yet another coping mechanism, which was to overwork.

I focused all my energy on my job both while I was at work and during my time off. I was always creating things, talking about classroom experiences, writing lesson plans and reports. When I did take time to go out with friends, I would panic. I worried I wouldn't know what to say; that I'd be judged, not fit in, not be talkative enough, and, of course, worried about my body image, too. There were countless times I canceled, making up some excuse, because I felt I looked too fat after tearing up my closet. I would end up on the floor crying; I thought I never had a chance of having that "normal," "happy" life other people seemed to have. Other times, when I did follow through and go out with my friends, I would first stress about what to wear, and then worry about what I ate, how much I ate, and how I ate. I would be in my head the whole night while trying to engage in small conversation. I would come home completely exhausted from the experience, immediately want to purge because I felt fat, and then self-injure to punish myself for not being good enough.

On the outside, my life as a thirty-year-old woman looked ideal. I had a successful teaching job, a new car, a small house on the bay, friends, and a cute dog, to top it all off. It was inside—the part nobody saw—that was completely crashing down. I was exhausted with life. I had lost hope that things would ever get better. I was discouraged, confused, and ready to give up. There was that determined part of me, though, that held on to hope that I could find even a glimpse of something better. I turned in an application to an eating disorder treatment center, truly feeling this was my last chance. I knew I had come to a breaking point and if I wanted anything to get better I would have to give it my all. With the tiny bit of hopefulness I had for a better life, I quit my job, packed up my classroom, ended my lease early, and moved all my stuff into storage.

I entered treatment completely terrified and having no idea what to expect. I was out of my comfort zone. I didn't have my work to hide behind, my behaviors to comfort me, or my house to hide in. I felt exposed, raw, and overwhelmed with fear. From being a fully independent woman, I now had to follow house rules, was being served food, had to ask to go to the bathroom, and couldn't flush or take medication without observation. I was very guarded and unsure of everyone around me. These people wanted to know me and help me, but my wall had been built up over so many years that allowing even one person in (besides my previous therapist) was an enormous struggle. The treatment team remained patient with me. I continued trying to open up and allow them to help me explore the "purpose" of my eating disorder, but this task was far from easy. In fact, it was a very painful time for me. Slowly, layer upon layer was being torn off and exposed to the light. Things I had never talked about or dealt with were coming up. I would panic and resort to using familiar behaviors to cope. I began to see that my eating disorder was the way I handled the difficulties of life, but it was only a temporary fix. Just like a drink, pill, or self-injury, it only masks the pain until you stop using it.

I was at the same treatment center for a year and a half between residential care, partial hospitalization, and intensive outpatient. I learned how much of my eating disorder was not really about the food. I learned how to cope with life in a healthy way, how to create boundaries, and how to use my voice. For the first time, I found I actually *had* a voice to use. We were taught about nutrition, healthy exercise, portions, and how to fuel our bodies appropriately. The phrase that will always stick with me is "All food is good in variety, balance, and moderation." My beliefs about "good" foods and "bad" foods were challenged. I learned to sit with the feeling of fullness, as uncomfortable as that was.

The biggest hurdle I had was learning to trust, and luckily, my treatment team gave me no reason to not trust them. They wanted to help and were always there in a very supportive, non-threatening, and non-judgmental way. Slowly, very slowly, I opened up a little more. I gradually let people into my life in an intimate, authentic way that I had never done before. I allowed them to see the real me— all of me. Eventually, they could see my emotions as I was able to truly feel them. I could cry about things and learned how to tolerate vulnerable feelings. I had to be taught, and personally experience, that they couldn't hurt me. One therapist told me that if you are numbing out one emotion, it isn't truly possible to feel the rest. By numbing out my sadness and fear, I had never truly experienced happiness, love, or joy at the level I now do. It took over twenty-three years of food issues and an eating disorder to find that out.

Life in recovery is better than anything I could have ever imagined. Today, I have courage, I have a voice, and I have an array of emotions that I feel and express in healthy ways. I also have people that I truly trust in life. I allow them to see the real me. Connecting with people at this new level allows me to experience what love really feels like. I have a new freedom. My days aren't focused around food, calories, body image, and worrying about being good enough. I can see beyond myself and relate to other people in a way that lets me be helpful. During treatment I was introduced to the Twelve Steps and I continue to work through them. I have the help of a sponsor and I attend meetings. Working through the Twelve Steps, with the guidance of both my sponsor and therapist, has helped me stay grounded in my recovery and has become my foundation and way of life. I connect with God, my Higher Power, on a much more intimate level than I ever have. I am able to move away from the driver's seat and give control of my life to Him, where it belongs. No longer am I chained down or burdened with all I let life put upon me. I can give those burdens to God and allow Him to shape me into the person He intends me to be.

Every day is a day in recovery for me. I still have negative thoughts about food, my body, and self-criticism, although they are fading. I can challenge these thoughts much more easily, though, because I have become so accustomed to practicing counteracting them. I have a toolbox of ways to handle any life situation that comes my way without using my eating disorder, a substance, or another behavior. I know now that I have a choice to *not* cause myself emotional pain by inflicting physical pain upon my body. I have so much hope for life! I am excited about everything it has to offer. I can be present in special moments with family and friends. I can enjoy life, and I do! Recovery from an eating disorder has opened a whole new world for me, one that is better than I ever imagined.

WELCOMING LIFE WITH OPEN ARMS

She graduated college with high honors and helped with multiple social justice campaigns, yet it wasn't until she let go of rigidity that she found her own kind and compassionate heart. Surrender—humility—turned out to be the gateway to freedom.

*W*ould it be possible to bring a little bit of compassion to yourself right now? *Ugh, here we go again. I am trying so hard to dredge up and eradicate all of the horrendously unlovable parts of myself and my therapist is just getting in my way again. The idea of loving myself repulses me. How could I possibly love someone so selfish, so pathetic, so weak, so intrinsically unlovable? What good would it do me anyway? There has to be another way to find freedom from this eating disorder hell. I'll do anything to get out of this cycle of suffering—anything but love myself. I just can't do that...*

That was me three years ago, before I started working the Twelve Steps of EDA. Since then, things have changed dramatically, and I have uncovered something beautiful—a lotus has grown from the dark, murky pond of my suffering. This is my story.

From the time I was a little girl, I believed that in order to survive, I needed other people to love me. I wanted so badly to be seen and held with care, to have my specialness appreciated and celebrated by the caregivers and role models in my life whom I looked up to. They seemed to have something essential that I lacked, and I needed them to give it to me. Holding tightly to this belief as one would a life raft, I spent my days chasing after the security promised by love, believing that if I just got a little bit more, maybe I would finally be safe and live happily ever after.

All children need love and care to survive, and I was no exception. Unfortunately, my parents usually seemed to fall short of my expectations of them. When I needed emotional connection and understanding, they couldn't give it to me. When I wanted them to empathize with my suffering, they told me I was too much and pushed me away. As someone who believed the love I needed to survive would come from outside of me, these refusals threatened my very existence. I needed to come up with some other strategy to take care of myself, to feel I was in control of my world, that I could keep my head above water when all other measures failed.

When I turned eighteen and went away to college, all of my strategies for finding love began to slip through my fingers. Suddenly I was lonely, afraid, disconnected, and depressed—desperate to find a way to cope with how difficult my inner life had become. Relief finally came when one night when I found myself curled up on the floor of my apartment gulping down spoonful after spoonful of sweet oblivion, unable to stop. Finally, I had found something that reliably provided a momentary reprieve from the struggle of being human. Each bite promised the love and sweetness I had yet been unable to find inside myself. And I could have as much as I wanted, whenever I wanted it. This fantasy did not last but a few brief minutes; it was immediately followed by a belly full of ache and a mind full of shame and regret. With swift determination, I began hatching elaborate plans to fix my new problem, and thus I entered into a seven-year binge-starve-compulsive exercise cycle that nearly cost me my life.

I binged to indulge in self-pity and victimhood, starved to feel powerful and in control, and exercised to reprimand my body for putting on weight. When I was starving, I obsessed about what vegetables I could get from the farmers market to make the perfect dinner. When I was planning a binge, I wandered about the grocery store in an unconscious haze searching for the right combination of desserts that might soothe whatever pain was in my heart. Whenever I was not thinking about food, I felt overwhelmingly imprisoned in a body that refused to cooperate with my desires for "perfection" and thinness. Given that I spent so much time thinking about myself and my food, there was not a whole lot of bandwidth remaining to consider other people. I kept a few close friends, but was constantly plagued by a sense of alternating deficiency and superiority that separated me from everyone. I dated, fell in love, and had many exciting experiences, but all of my relationships were plagued by co-dependence and self-centeredness. Outwardly, I accomplished many things: I graduated from college with high honors, helped win multiple social justice campaigns, started a local non-profit, and lived in a radical cooperative community. But on the inside, I was exhausted from the constant struggle of manipulating everything around me to be exactly as I wanted it to be—so I could feel ok.

Though I was starting to realize that what I was doing wasn't working, I didn't hit bottom until several years later. Before finally coming to Eating Disorders Anonymous, I tried EVERYTHING else I possibly could to get rid of my eating disorder, once and for all. I tried cutting out certain foods, following special diets, drinking more water, exercising on my lunch breaks at work to avoid eating too much, and all kinds of other misguided strategies. Eventually, after a lot of group and individual therapy geared specifically toward addressing the underlying causes of my eating disorder, I started to become willing to heal. I also started meditating regularly which allowed me to become more intimate with both the simple pleasures of being alive and bring sincere compassion to the direct experience of despair that plagued my mind, body and heart. However, after a while, it became clear I needed something much greater than this hodgepodge of support systems to help me recover what I had lost to the eating disorder.

A few months after I started attending EDA meetings and working the Steps with a sponsor, I entered an intensive outpatient treatment program, determined to turn my life and my will over to the care of the treatment team. I humbly realized I did not know how to recover and required the guidance of people whose job it was to help people like me. It wasn't fun, it wasn't easy, but it was exactly what I needed. I let myself feel angry with them for limiting my access to disordered eating behaviors. I let myself express my discontent and irritation without shame. I just let my experience be exactly as it was, period. I reached out to fellow EDA's who had been through treatment themselves and asked for their advice; they all said the same exact thing—just surrender and do everything they tell you to do. Surrender your will completely, and if by the end of the program you want to go back to doing things the way you did them before, go ahead. To my surprise, by the end of the program, I had begun to relax into humility—there was something comforting about not knowing how to solve my eating disorder. I did not have to force it into submission or do anything to push it away. When I came to terms with my powerlessness over it, believed something greater than myself could restore me to sanity, and surrendered to the process of recovery, it began to let go of me.

Now each time there is a sense of rigidity—be it a tightness in my mind around an idea of how I think things should be or a contraction in my body from stress or fear— I trust that if I let go, I will be ok. Through my experience, I have found surrender is the most consistent and reliable gateway to love and freedom. In working the Steps, I have had the opportunity to become intimate with my fears, shortcomings, and the impact of my actions not only on myself, but also on other people. I am more in touch with myself and how challenging it is to be alive, which has naturally awoken a sincere compassion for myself and everyone around me.

When I first began this life-long journey of recovery, I did not have any interest in being kind or compassionate to myself. But through this process of touching the most tender parts of my heart with patience, acceptance and openness, these have arisen on their own. Even after all this time of being free from eating-disordered behaviors, I still have to face the myriad challenges life inevitably brings. The difference is that now I am willing to learn and grow from the full spectrum of experiences on this path, from the 10,000 joys to the 10,000 sorrows. I welcome life with open arms, unconditionally. May courage and curiosity in the face of difficulty serve to awaken us all to our own compassionate hearts, and may we all find the love we long for. It is already right here.

(15)

WHAT DOESN'T KILL YOU...

Through perseverance and research, she discovered a residential program where she learned priceless lessons. She is now aware of her worth and mindful of her many blessings.

What doesn't kill you makes your stronger. I believe in that old saying (pretty good song, too!). For me, the "what" was a twenty-five-year-old eating disorder, but with the help of my faith, an amazing family, supportive friends, treatment, and EDA, I'm alive and getting stronger.

Since the age of seventeen, I've been through constant bouts of anorexia, binge eating, food restriction, over-exercise, and orthorexia. Maybe you or someone you know is also suffering from one of these disorders. While they do include a genetic component, anyone who is predisposed can develop an eating disorder. Young or old, male or female, rich or poor, no category is excluded. My eating disorder, which I now un-affectionately refer to as "Ed," took on many faces. I found you don't have to be skin and bones or overweight to have an eating disorder.

I can remember being seven years old and telling a friend of my parents that my thighs were too big (who sets that standard, anyway?). I remember thinking if I didn't make all A's, it wasn't good enough. I remember feeling very self-conscious. I remember my grandmother dying. And I remember discovering among all these fears and out-of-control feelings that there was something I could control: how much I ate and how much I exercised. Body manipulation became my comfort.

What followed was years of mind games, getting up at obscene hours to exercise, entire days with little to no food, and the deterioration of not only a body, but also the spirit of a girl and a woman with much to give.

Miraculously enough, amidst the chaos in my mind and body, I got married to the smartest, most fantastic husband ever; adopted two amazing, beautiful kids; started a business; built close friendships; and gave back to my community. But it was only by the grace of God that any of that happened, because with all these wonderful life events comes stress, and my perfectionist, people-pleasing personality created inner confusion, over-functioning, and fear. In my journal, I described it like this: "It feels like I'm standing in the middle of a circle with my life—work, home, community, kids, husband, activities—swirling around me, and I'm just grabbing at them, hoping nothing falls and breaks."

The only things that seemed to give me relief were controlling my food intake and isolating myself through exercise. As can only be expected, the years of unhealthy behaviors were catching up, destroying not only my physical health, but also the health of my family relationships.

One evening in March I got up the guts to take myself to an eating disorder conference. I heard the same ideas I had heard before, but this time something was different. This time something hit me like a ton of bricks— what I now consider to be the Holy Spirit moving me to take action. The next week, my very supportive husband (who, by the way, spent many years trying to help me) and I consulted a trusted therapist in the field who shared some scary, but necessary news. "You have to go away, and for a long while. You need to be somewhere you can get comprehensive, 24-hour treatment. This can't be done at home," she said. "If you had cancer or diabetes, you wouldn't question the need for treatment, and this disease is no different."

After researching facilities around the country, I found a residential program right in my own backyard. I got intensive therapy and nutrition education. I learned to enjoy food again and how to plan meals. I learned I am worthy. And I learned to live again. My time there was indescribable; what I discovered there was priceless. The people, staff, and fellow residents, they were my lifesavers. After seven weeks of residential and five weeks of day program, I came home ready to face the real world.

About a year ago, I was introduced to EDA. A close friend of mine who also struggles wanted to get a group started in our community. I was very excited about it, because I really wanted a Twelve-Step program, one that encouraged faith, hope, and trust in God. Since we started, I have developed an even deeper understanding of myself and God, who is there for me always, ready to make my recovery process easier. When I am having a tough week, my EDA meeting centers me and helps me deal with the issues at hand. Having the support of the EDA program and the people in my group has added tremendously to my recovery journey, and I am forever grateful.

Don't get me wrong, none of the life stressors are gone: the housework still waits, as does my job and a society where diets and competitive exercise are the norm. But today, I am different. I am healthy, not just in my body, but in my mind. I have an outpatient team behind me, coping skills, EDA, and most importantly, I have a family that loves me, friends that support me, and my spirit—the one that was buried so many years ago.

Please let me be clear that I am no poster child for recovery. This is a struggle every day. Lapses happen, but I no longer beat myself up. All I can do—all any of us can do—is take it one day at a time, mindful of our blessings and aware of our own worth.

So whatever type of eating disorder keeps your spirit from coming alive, don't let it kill you. Use it to make you stronger. In the end, it is worth the fight.

PART III

THEY LOST NEARLY ALL

A MAN FINDS HOPE AND MEANING IN RECOVERY FROM ANOREXIA

He once believed his purpose in life was to have an eating disorder; now, his purpose is to recover so he can reach out and help others.

It is hard to believe that in comparison to where I was just one year ago, I'm writing down and sharing this story. Never in my wildest dreams did I imagine there would come a day when I could take the necessary steps to improve my life while living with this horrible disease, or being in a state of mind where I would genuinely want to share my experience by reaching out to others who also may be suffering. I lived with my eating disorder for thirteen years, roughly half of my life. It's made living miserable at best, and nearly unbearable the rest of the time. There were three or four years in particular that felt as though nothing ever made a difference. Remembering how lonely and hopeless that felt, I couldn't be happier that the last year has proven me completely wrong.

For the sake of brevity, I'll share with you the highlights of my life with my disorder up until its climax a few years ago, which lead to my last round of treatment. I first started developing disordered-eating behaviors at the age of fifteen. I hadn't been a happy child for a long time, but entering high school my depression began to take a stronger hold of me: I began engaging in self-harming behaviors. However, once restriction came into the mix, I felt so at ease all of a sudden. To me, it was the perfect solution to everything I felt about myself and it became a daily go-to outlet for my depression, frustration, and poor self-image. I committed to it as much as I possibly could—right from the start. Admittedly, my behaviors never exactly went unnoticed, but being a teenage boy kept the majority of my peers and family from jumping to the assumption that I actually had anorexia. To some, it was just a phase. Others just assumed I was one of the many other skinny teenage boys that would surely bulk up within the next few years when my metabolism changed.

It's weird looking back at those first couple of years and realizing how little I understood, or even knowingly engaged in, a lot of these routines I created for myself. There's something really cunning about an eating disorder. It has a way of keeping the severity of your actions entirely at bay. I can remember purposely going through the days with as little food as possible, sitting down to meals, barely picking at anything on my plate and obsessing over how I looked and what my weight was. But not once did the thought that I might be sick cross my mind. I was acting without thinking, and if anyone brought the subject up, I would become overly defensive, affirming that I did in fact eat. I'd insist that I ate consistently throughout the day, and I would believe every word I said. To me, I was eating more than enough, and no one else knew what they were talking about. This disease truly has its own survival instincts, and, right from the beginning, I fell victim to it.

By the age of twenty-three, I had been hospitalized twice, once my senior year of high school and again two years later. Both times I just went through the motions of weight restoration, and after coming to terms with the fact that I actually did have a problem, would attempt to find a way to move on with my life. But in both cases, after a certain weight was reached and the doctors pushed me to do some serious soul-searching to discover what the root cause of all of this was, I retaliated. I became aggressively defensive, argumentative, and after my release I decided to go about recovery my own way. I wanted to rid myself of my behaviors without acknowledging where they came from. And I wouldn't let anyone convince me to do otherwise.

I developed a routine of doing fairly well for a few weeks, restricting a couple after that, getting back in the habit of eating more regularly, and so on. Never was my eating disorder voice gone completely, even during periods of eating moderately well. I would only eat because I knew I had to, and every time I would hate myself more and more because, deep down, I just wanted to give in and use my behaviors once again. My disorder would tear me apart each time I went against what it wanted me to do. This went on for years until I moved out on my own, to another state, and began to spiral out of control entirely.

Once I was left alone to my own devices, my anorexia finally had the chance to take total control, in spite of my best efforts. I would try to go food shopping, which one way or another, would be a disaster. I would either spend forever in the store, trying and failing to decide what I wanted to buy, or be in and out in five minutes, just grabbing my safe foods—and anything else I happened to see. I usually ended up throwing away half of what I bought, because I'd realize I would never actually eat it. This only furthered my constant sense of shame and guilt for behaving this way and wasting so much food and money. There would be days when I would be utterly starving; but all I could do was stare at my pantry on the verge of tears, because I couldn't allow myself to have anything. I developed very particular safe foods and scheduled times I could eat. What I ate one day affected what I could eat the rest of the week; nearly every waking thought I had was what I would consume and when. I would obsess over it for hours, to the point I felt I was having a panic attack that kept me up more than half of the night; nothing could keep the thoughts from racing. In spite of all of this, I couldn't bring myself to get any help. I always thought, *I could be worse, so why bother?* Obviously, I was having a hard time, but I never thought for a second I was in a bad enough state, physically, to require help.

Eventually, I saw a doctor and couldn't believe what I was hearing. Apparently I was back to my lowest weight and I should go to an in-patient facility as soon as possible. This was so hard to wrap my head around, because when I looked in the mirror, I thought I looked completely normal. *How could it really be that bad?* I'll admit part of me screamed that I should agree to treatment right away; I desperately wanted help. But my disorder wouldn't let me. I had to make myself suffer at all costs, and getting treatment would undo everything I had worked for.

The months that followed pushed me to my utmost breaking point. Alcohol abuse had been a common occurrence for a while, but it became my main coping skill during this time. Many times a week I would get black-out drunk, which only led to bingeing. Then I would take laxatives to undo the "damage." After a few weeks of this routine, my body was a mess; and, with my health at such a horrible point, my dependency on alcohol only got worse. I started regularly going to work drunk and then going through withdrawals before my shift was over. Every day I would try—and fail—to break the habit, but without even thinking about it I would already be on my third drink and wouldn't stop until I passed out. I lost all will to take care of myself. While the idea of suicide had always been a passive thought, it then became a near certainty. I have never been so scared of what I was going to do to myself. Every night I would cry, because there didn't seem to be any hope at all. I would think about how easy it would be to end it all, and how little there was preventing me from doing so. I can honestly say if it weren't for my family, I probably wouldn't be here today.

When I broke down and asked for help, my parents bought a plane ticket for me and I was back in a treatment facility within a few days. I swore to myself that I wouldn't take it for granted. From day one, I ate everything that was put in front of me. I opened up to every doctor about my thought processes and struggles, even going as far as to warn them how I would previously hit a wall and resist treatment. I didn't want to give myself any room to budge this time. I wanted to finish this once and for all.

In no way was any of it easy. There were countless times I fought back, arguing and rationalizing, trying to do things my way and not theirs. But somehow I managed to push myself further than ever, going through every step of the program. At first, when it felt like too much to handle or pried too insistently into my past, I resentfully came to believe that recovery was worth all of the struggles. But over time, I began to *embrace* the idea of a new life without this disease. I shared more about myself than ever before, addressing behaviors I had never discussed with anyone and events from my past I never thought another soul would ever hear. Every breakthrough only made my ability to fight for recovery stronger, and I couldn't be more grateful to have been surrounded by such an understanding treatment team to help guide me through it all. I wish I could say things have been perfect since I left, but when I discharged I went right back to my old apartment and friends and fell back into some old habits. Once again, alcohol became a real struggle, but I'm proud to say that I'm finally moving past all of my self-destructive behaviors. I want to live and enjoy life for once and I'm taking every necessary step I can to make that happen. I'm attending AA meetings, no longer surrounding myself with unhealthy company, keeping in regular contact with family, and being completely honest with them about how I'm doing. I honestly love it.

It's so freeing to live without the constant torture of an eating disorder: no longer obsessing over every calorie I ingest, being able to tag along with coworkers to grab dinner regardless of where they're going. I can finally eat "treats" for the first time in almost eight years, which may not seem like much to some, but it's huge for me and I hope you can understand. I'm finally comfortable making sure I eat consistently throughout the day, even if I have to carry snacks with me everywhere I go and eat even if no one else is having something. Sure, there are days when my body image is terrible and I can't imagine being any heavier, but I trust those thoughts are not the truth. They're simply the start of a downward spiral I know I won't have the strength to pull myself out of again. Nothing about recovery is going to be perfect, and that's okay. If I struggle, I forgive myself and pick up where I left off, so I can continue to improve and ensure that the same mistake won't happen again. You can't be too hard on yourself when you're trying to beat something like this.

When it comes down to it, I think the best part of all of this is the possibility of what else is to come. I finally have goals in my life. I would love to become more involved in the EDA movement and even have goals to start my own EDA meeting in the city I live. For as long as I can remember, I've believed it was my purpose in life to have an eating disorder; I just misunderstood to what end. Maybe it's not to die from and be another statistic, but to struggle and survive in order to reach out to and help others. That thought gives me so much hope.

BREAK THE RULES AND ENJOY
THE PROMISES

Living with an eating disorder is not truly living. Moving from self-loathing to self-love, she is at peace through her sustaining relationship with her Higher Power.

*L*iving with my eating disorder was not really living. For years, I competed in numerous athletic events, because I thought a medal or trophy would make me feel better about myself. I surrounded myself with people who placed extreme importance on outward appearance and I purged and starved myself, because I thought I would be happy if I lost more weight. I felt good when others commented on my "self-discipline" and "motivation," but the effects were short-lived. Even at my lowest weight, I hated my body and was still convinced changing it would make me happy. My eating disorder progressed when I developed a diet and exercise plan that combined a lifetime of coaches' advice, articles, cleanses, and weight-loss challenges—all of which became "The Rules." I set myself up for failure by adopting The Rules as a way of living. Each time I failed, I binged and purged and I swore I would never break The Rules again. I sought self-love in my eating disorder, which, in turn, only produced self-loathing.

At the lowest point in my eating disorder, I had over two years of abstinence in another Twelve-Step program, but my eating disorder was negatively affecting my health, work, family, and relationships. I was passing out while driving due to lack of nourishment and exhaustion from intense workouts. Even abnormal lab results did nothing to curb my self-destructive behaviors. I was insanely immersed in my eating disorder instead of performing at work or engaging with loved ones. My life was completely unmanageable. I started working the Steps a second time with my sponsor, and we focused solely on my eating disorder. I was at a local diner having coffee with her when my Higher Power led me to the conclusion that I needed to seek help through a residential treatment program.

Recovering for my seven-year-old daughter was a huge motivation for me, because I did not wish for her to follow my example and encounter what I was experiencing. Ironically, I learned from her how to live a balanced life with food and exercise. After years of punishing myself, I allowed myself to eat all foods in moderation and enjoy movement. One of my favorite milestones was when I went on a lunch outing with my husband and daughter during my stay at the treatment center. I challenged my eating disorder by asking my family to choose a restaurant, and we ate a meal most children enjoy. For the first time in my daughter's life, I shared the same meal as her and I was proud of myself.

My stay in treatment was difficult, primarily because my family was allowed only a single three-hour visit per week. The three of us shared tears over painful telephone calls while my husband heroically managed the household and his work schedule. But these temporary difficulties resulted in long-lasting benefits. Both mine and my family's lives are so much better today that I have no regrets about my decision to enter and remain in treatment as long as the center's staff recommended.

Today, The Rules are being replaced by The Promises in my life. I am almost nine months free from bulimia and I am amazed that I am free from the obsession about my body, food, and exercise! Although being honest with myself and taking the necessary steps was painstaking, life in recovery is better than I ever imagined. Today, I am at peace with food and exercise. Also, I practice gratitude for my body, because it allowed me to bring a child into this world and it lets me hike and rock climb San Diego's trails and beaches. I am no longer in bondage, instead, "(I) know a new freedom and a new happiness," as The Promises state.

I sought recovery from my eating disorder because I wanted to stop obsessing about food and exercise, but my journey has led me on a path of developing self-love. I discovered that while the greatest gift in recovery is giving back, I have to love myself before I can truly love others. I started an EDA meeting a couple months ago and began sponsoring women. I also intentionally seek and develop skills to be a better wife and mother. Today, I am of service to others seeking recovery and to my family, because I actively work on myself.

For me, remaining in recovery requires attending Twelve-Step meetings, appointments with my therapist and psychiatrist, working the Steps with my sponsor, and working with other women in recovery. Incorporating these tasks can seem overwhelming, especially with family and work schedules, but I make it a priority because of The Promises that have already come true during my short time in recovery. Every day, I surrender to my Higher Power and ask for the willingness, strength, and courage to do what He wants me to do. As a result, my Higher Power relieved me of my struggle and allows me to help others. My feelings of self-loathing are transforming into self-love and I am at peace. God is doing for me what I could not do for myself.

(3)

DANCING FROM DARKNESS
TO DAYLIGHT

Recovery is about honesty and willingness to grow—and experiencing that growth. Her life today wouldn't be possible if she hadn't stepped onto the road of recovery.

My eating disorder began when I was twelve years old. I was a compulsive overeater, and at the time did not know it. I was young and having a love affair with food. It was my best friend and my worst enemy. I ate as a reward and I ate as a punishment. Despite my father's relentless teasing about the pounds added on, I continued to torturously eat (or non-torturously as the case may have been). I had already been self-mutilating since the age of nine, but at that age I didn't know that's what it was; I just knew what I was doing made me feel better after I did it. Little did I know I was in a downward spiral that would last through my teen years and into adulthood. I would go on diets, only to fail and beat myself up because of my failure. I didn't realize that my compulsive overeating was the start of something big—bigger than me, bigger than the food, bigger than anything. I was out of control and I hated it.

I don't know what happened, but one day something snapped, and I went on a diet with a friend. We decided we were going to rollerblade after school every day and we were only going to eat certain foods. I don't know what made this time different, but it was. I stuck to my regimen, and the pounds started dropping off of me. It was the best feeling in the world. People started complimenting me on my weight loss, and on my gaining control. I was on top of the world. I realized I could eat less than I already was, up my exercise, and still survive just fine—so that's what I did. As time progressed, my friend dropped out of our diet, realizing that she didn't need to lose any more weight. But not me. I was almost down to "normal" weight and people were telling me it was time to stop. *Were these people absolutely insane?* I was having the time of my life! For once I *had* something. I was in control. I was doing something amazing, and I felt really awesome about myself. It was powerful and exhilarating. I didn't listen when they told me to slow down my dieting. I did the complete opposite. I continued to cut calories and fat. I became a vegetarian. I restricted even more. As I lost more and more weight, my diet turned into something I couldn't control anymore. It became an obsession. I was exercising many hours a day and I was becoming worn down. Thinner wasn't ever thin enough and people were very concerned, but I was still on a rush. I was also very hungry. One day I binged on Chinese food and I told myself I was going to purge, just this once. And I did. It was the most awful thing I had ever done, and at the same time provided such relief. But I swore I would never do it again.

The next six years of my life were filled with compulsive exercising, starving for weeks at a time, bingeing and purging (sometimes many times a day), abusing drugs and alcohol, self-mutilation, and low self-esteem. On the outside I tried to be perfect and I lost myself in the midst of all of the things I was doing. I was a high-functioning anorexic/bulimic/alcoholic/addict, or so I thought. I had finished high school and left for college, but dropped out because "it was for the best." I really just couldn't admit I dropped out because I was sick and I couldn't handle it. I was holding down a full-time job, supporting myself financially, and living with my boyfriend, and… I was lost in a whirlwind of addictions. I hit rock bottom at the age of twenty. I had developed knee problems that sometimes didn't allow me to even walk (due to malnutrition and over-exercise), I had a borderline-to-mild heart attack, my teeth were in horrible shape, and my hair wasn't so hot either. At times I lost the ability to control my bowels. I had rectal bleeding that sent me to the ER more than once. Physically I was knocking on death's door. The prognosis wasn't looking great—unless I was willing to recover.

My eating disorder doctor looked me in the eye and told me I was going to die the next time I had a heart attack. My electrolytes were all screwy, which triggered the first episode. At that point, I was referred to a residential treatment facility for eating disorders and women's issues. I had already been in therapy for years prior to this, and my therapist (whom I still see once a week and love tremendously) said it was time for me to get the foundation built. Outpatient therapy was only doing so much for me and it would be much more meaningful once I was in aftercare.

So I went to treatment for several months. The whole process was NOT easy, but it was well worth it; and, to be honest, I would go back there in a heartbeat. It was the best thing I could have done for myself. I regained my self-esteem and I learned how to live. I learned so much about myself and my feelings. First, I had to learn I actually HAD feelings. I learned about my thought patterns, as well as my eating disorder, and about the dynamics of why I was doing what I was doing. I can hardly describe everything that I learned about myself. I highly recommend a good residential program to anyone considering it.

Things haven't been easy since I have been back, either. While I am glad my experiences in treatment prepared me for the struggles I would face, inpatient care is just the foundation: aftercare is where the real work happens. Right now, I am just taking things one day at a time. I go to therapy once a week, attend three AA meetings a week, and started an EDA meeting where I live. For me it's about perseverance and realizing that I am only human. It's hard not to want to rush things, but recovery is a process, not an event. It is about honesty and willingness to grow, and experiencing that growth. I am happy to remember to enjoy life, because this is a life I wouldn't have had if I didn't step onto the road of recovery. And for that I am truly grateful.

(4)

DUAL DIAGNOSIS

By learning to be comfortable with change, she allows herself to be guided by her Higher Power and the principles of EDA. And life is just amazing!

My story has a dual aspect. On one hand, I was fully and completely immersed in my eating disorder that began when I was thirteen. On the other, I had given myself over to drugs and alcohol to quiet the shame and guilt from my eating disorder as well as numb myself to the depression and constant berating in my head. From the time I began experimenting with purging until the day I fully surrendered to my Higher Power, I floated between these two addictions. Sometimes I was sober, but engaged in eating-disordered behaviors; sometimes I was using chemicals heavily, but my eating was more stable; and other times I was simultaneously using both in an attempt to escape from a life that felt unbearable.

I couldn't tell you when I started to hate myself. Some of my earliest memories include feeling fat, or stupid, or "not good enough." That isn't to say I had a terrible childhood. For the most part, I was a completely normal kid. My parents were still married and I had a little sister I usually got along with (when I wasn't being mean to her). I loved to play soccer, climb trees, sing, read, and eat normal food. But inside, I think I always knew something was different about me. I always felt an incessant need to show people I was smart and a good kid. Although I constantly sought the praise of my parents, coaches, and friends, I never felt like anything I did was ever good enough. I always compared myself to my friends; this friend was a faster swimmer, that one had better toys, and another was skinnier than me. Kindergarten was the first time I decided I was fat. My best friend's family was all naturally very tall and slender, and I felt inadequate next to her. I would battle the thoughts of "coming up short" to my friends for years afterwards.

But I couldn't ever put a name to the "disease" I was feeling until the end of seventh grade. That year I first attempted suicide, and my life was forever changed. By the middle of eighth grade, I was chronically suicidal and kept copies of suicide notes in my desk drawers. I started self-injuring and got curious about drugs. I went on and off psychiatric medications during this time, often refusing to take them because they made me feel numb. I continued to see different therapists, but nothing seemed to help me break free of the depression controlling my life.

During this time, I also started experimenting with dieting and various methods of weight control. I hated my body and wanted it to suffer the way I was suffering inside. I vividly remember the first time I tried to make myself vomit after eating dinner with my family. I heaved and gagged, but nothing came up. Eventually, my insides hurt so bad that I gave up and cried myself to sleep because I thought I would always be fat.

Next, I discovered drugs. They were easy enough to get and made me feel less hungry during the day. They also gave me a rush of energy and level of focus I had never experienced. I began to take them daily and always carried them with me in my bag. I believe now the drugs served a dual purpose in my eating disorder. First, they gave me a sense of control over food and my body, and second, they introduced me to the intoxicating feeling of an altered state of mind. Granted it was mild, but something changed in my brain, and I figured out that external substances could make me feel the way I couldn't feel on my own.

As I entered high school, my world became a dark haze as I looked at it through the lenses of depression. I began to experiment with more drugs to give me the high I wanted. I continued to play around with purging off and on, but on the outside I looked fairly normal. All of that changed when I reached my junior year. At that point, I had begun a slow transition towards more alternative life-styles and clothing. I traded in my jeans and t-shirts for baggy pants and oversized trucker shirts. I started a punk band and began dying my hair different colors and wearing black makeup. I wanted to exude an air of confidence and standoffish-ness. I used this as a protection to keep every-one at arm's length and as a way to start making friends who thought and acted more like me.

My drug use became significantly heavier. I started to rely completely on chemicals to take me away from the feel-ings of loneliness and sadness that consumed me. I dropped from an honor roll student the first semester of my junior year, to failing almost all my classes the second. In order to graduate on time, I was forced to transfer to an alterna-tive school, but there my pattern just continued; the only change was that my classes were easy enough I could pass without attending much. So, instead of going to school, I went to friends' houses and used drugs or alcohol. My life became a constant search for drugs. At this time, my eating was stable enough that my weight did not change much, and I didn't put too much effort into changing it. I was still consumed by moments of hatred for my body and wishing

I could lose weight; but I had found that as long as I was on drugs, I didn't have to think about it.

Complications with my eating disorder didn't begin until I decided to take my uncle up on an offer to live with him in Manhattan for a few months to care for my cousin while he was in school. Coincidently, just before leaving, I stepped on a pay-scale at the mall. To my horror, I found I weighed a great deal more than I thought. Then and there I decided that while I was in New York, I was going to lose weight by whatever means necessary. I didn't tell anyone about my plan, but got on the plane dreaming about how much better my life was going to be when I weighed less.

From then on, it was a downward spiral. I began cutting my daily intake to dangerously low levels. I started exercising more by walking around the city and going to a gym that was nearby. I purged when I felt I had eaten too much and began, once again, to use drugs to quell my appetite. Much of my time in NYC was marked by the pant sizes I dropped and the sense of accomplishment I felt as each size grew too big on me. I also developed a taste for alcohol. I acquired a fake ID and began drinking profusely to escape the knowledge that what I was doing was wrong. The entire time, I was lying to my aunt and uncle about what I was doing and how I was feeling.

Returning home did not mean really changing my thoughts and behavior, though my habits changed a bit to accommodate being around more people who might ask questions. I started exercising in secret, usually leaving work early so I could get a run in before I was expected anywhere. I added yet another drug habit to the mix and fell further into the pit. Each day was measured by the numbers on the scale: good if it went down, bad if it went up. I'd make multiple trips to the bathroom to see if I had lost any more weight. I became obsessed with other measures to see if I had lost weight. To me, anorexia was the answer to all my problems. As long as I could lose weight, everything else in the world didn't matter. For months, I lived in the denial, thinking I had control over my eating disorder and my drug addiction, that I could stop when I wanted to...I thought I just didn't want to.

The realization that my beliefs about the eating disorder were all a façade came harshly one day, and in a matter of minutes my ignorance was shattered. I was at work and felt the familiar hunger pangs in my stomach and the light-headedness that came along with restriction. I quickly tallied up the calories I had consumed that day and decided I could eat something. I walked down to the cafeteria, my mind racing with thoughts of what I should or should not eat when I got there. But when I stepped into the cafeteria, the entire room seemed to close in on me. My heart seemed desperate to break out of my chest as I walked from station to station looking at the food and wondering if I could eat it. As I circled for the third or fourth time, I realized I wasn't the one in control anymore. I had to ask permission from my eating disorder to let me eat—and the eating disorder always told me no. There were *no* foods that were safe anymore; each time I put something in my mouth I was a failure, and the eating disorder was sure to make that clear to me.

Within a few months, I checked myself into a hospital-based treatment program. But my desire to recover quickly subsided as the eating disorder convinced me that I would be losing ground if I let go of it and gained weight. My journal from the time I spent inpatient is filled with self-hatred and anger at myself, my body, and everyone around me. When I gave in to the eating disorder, I began to do anything I could to subvert the treatment I was receiving. I hid food, found ways to purge, and would lie in my bed at night doing leg-lifts or sit-ups. I knew when I got out I wasn't going to mess around anymore. My low weight going into the hospital wasn't good enough; I needed to go below it. I didn't need to delude myself anymore with thoughts of stopping my weight loss; rather, I was going to lose weight until there was no more weight to lose. At this point, I couldn't even be distracted by drugs and alcohol; I decided to quit chemicals in order to devote all my focus to the eating disorder.

The next year-and-a-half of my life was a blur of hunger pains, vomit, and food. I resorted to methods I would have previously found appalling to avoid eating, to steal food, and to purge. As my body reached a critical point of starvation, the primal instincts of survival took over, and I began to binge and purge—many times a day. Because my denial about my condition was obliterated, self-loathing and disgust now consumed my mind; each time I binged and purged was a simultaneous accomplishment and punishment. I pulled away from everyone and soon had no friends left. I had alienated myself from my family. My ability to have emotions other than sadness, hatred, and anger disappeared, and I spent most of my time numb to the world.

Eventually I wanted out. I was so filled with hatred for the eating disorder that I wanted to cast it off, but the fear of gaining weight kept me chained. As much as I hated what was happening, I still loved the eating disorder in some sick way. I loved feeling light-headed. I loved the bruises and pains. I loved being small. In truth, the eating disorder had me convinced that I loved these things; what was really happening was that these were the times my mental anguish subsided, because the eating disorder stopped berating me for a few minutes when I had accomplished a goal it wanted. However, my desperation to escape the disorder continued to grow, so I tried what I thought would be the key to getting away from it: I was going to relocate myself to college, and everything would be okay. I would stop the cycle and get on with my life… but I was still going to control what I ate enough to stay thin.

What happened was the exact opposite. My cycles of bingeing and purging grew worse, and I became more miserable than ever. A few weeks into my first semester, I overdosed and had to take a medical leave. I was out of school for over a month. The saddest part about the experience was that by this point I was so disconnected from everyone, including my roommates, that I had to walk myself to the emergency room. But I returned to school and finished the semester, doing exceptionally well in all my classes. I found I loved school, but with the eating disorder I couldn't put my energy towards it. So, next, I tried moving into my own apartment for the summer to regain my footing. What I hadn't realized at that point, though, was I could never move away from my problems as long as I was "taking myself with me." Drugs began to sneak back into my life, and I started to steal medications. But I told myself that I wasn't a drug addict because I was only stealing medications to help me focus on things, and I wasn't using them because I needed a chemical to alter my mood.

I reentered treatment that summer when I finally hit my first bottom. My bingeing and purging had escalated even more, because I was living alone and my weight continued to drop. I had received blood work from my doctor saying that my electrolytes were off, and I was in danger of a heart attack each time I purged. I couldn't lie to myself anymore that I would be okay doing this. I knew I had to go back to treatment or I was going to die. While I prayed every evening for my heart to give out in my sleep, something in me wasn't about to let me die. I believe now that my Higher Power ultimately stepped in when I couldn't do it alone. I realized I finally had something more important to me than my eating disorder, and that was school. Having to take the medical leave and almost not finishing the semester felt terrible to me. I returned to the hospital and was determined to get past my eating disorder and move on with my life.

Treatment this time went great—too great. I took everything seriously and fought through my bad days. I regained weight, and my body stabilized itself. I worked with the treatment team and was completely honest. I thought everything was going to be great from then on. I returned to school that fall and began to reconnect with a friend from elementary school. I told her about my struggles and how hard I was working on getting better, and she supported me through it all. Life seemed brand new. Everything was glorious as I awoke each day with my new resolve to be healthy and have a "normal" life. Unfortunately, my "normal life" included drinking like a college student, or at least how I thought a college student was supposed to drink.

Within a month, I was drinking almost daily. I would get drunk when my roommate wasn't home and buy new bottles so she couldn't tell. I would drink with her and her friends on the weekends and spent many mornings very hung over. Two months into the semester, I was raped twice while intoxicated. The rapes were exactly one week apart and were completely unrelated—except for the fact that I had been drinking and blacked out.

My idea of the world being perfect and the sense all would be okay was shattered. Almost immediately, I began to focus on food again in order to avoid thinking about what had happened. The eating disorder happily came back into my life and settled into my head. This time, I was convinced I was going to do it right. I would lose weight through eating less and exercising more. I would control food and my body, but I wouldn't go "too far." I didn't want to end up like I had last year, so I'd just take it a little easier.

The next year was a series of bouts with the eating disorder and chemical use. I spent the summer exercising, restricting, purging, and losing weight. I had sworn off alcohol at this point, but still made a few exceptions (not seeing anything wrong with resuming my pilfering of drugs in order to help me study). In the back of my head, I always knew it couldn't last forever and I tried many times to stop my destructive patterns. I'd last one or two days, but ultimately I'd return to the eating disorder. What I didn't realize was I was trying to give up parts of the eating disorder and keep others. I thought I could give up bingeing and purging, but keep restricting and my low weight. I wasn't fully ready to completely surrender to recovery; the eating disorder still had me convinced my life would fall apart if I did.

I hit a bottom again when I realized my credit card was nearly maxed out from buying binge food. I had heard about the Twelve Steps from some friends who were in Alcoholics Anonymous and thought maybe I could apply those to my eating disorder. I started doing research and found Eating Disorders Anonymous on the web, but there were no meetings in my state. Disappointed, but not dissuaded, I resolved to do the Twelve Steps by myself. I printed off the worksheets and began to do more reading. But my commitment quickly diminished as I had no one to share it with and was easily beaten back into submission by the eating disorder.

About a month later, I wandered back to the EDA site to try to learn more. To my surprise the first meeting in my state was starting that weekend, and it wasn't too far from where I was living! A new feeling came over me. For the first time in a very long time, I felt hopeful that something might be the solution. Although I was scared, I mustered up my courage and went to that first meeting.

What I found was amazing, and it carried me through the next difficult months. The people I encountered fully understood me. They knew my struggles and my desire to recover. They accepted me despite the tearfulness and fear I displayed those first few meetings. These same people that suggested I take a look at my chemical use. They pointed out recovery can't come in certain parts of our life and be excluded from others. If I wanted to live by the principles of the Twelve Steps—honesty, open-mindedness and willingness—I had to look at my entire life.

I wish I could say that my behaviors stopped right then and there, but they didn't. The process of letting go of my eating disorder took a long time, but what mattered most was that I never gave up. I held on to hope that I could recover and did what I could each day to move forward. In my persistence, my life slowly began to change. I started doing what members of the group told me to do in order to better my life, and I started taking tips from AA and applying them to my eating disorder. Finally, as my thinking changed, my behavior slowly started to follow.

After about nine months of trying recovery on my own, I made the decision to go back to intensive outpatient treatment. I felt I had stalled and even hit a point where I teetered on the brink of full relapse when my cousin went through a terrible accident and almost didn't survive. During this time I continued to attend EDA meetings and was living in a sober program at my school, surrounded with students who were also in recovery from chemical dependency.

I believe the precursor to stopping my behavior was the moment I started getting fully honest with myself and with others. I opened up to staff and peers in my sober program about my eating disorder and my attempts to recover. I asked for help with accountability and support when I was struggling. To my surprise my peers responded splendidly. Many had also struggled with food and understood where I was coming from, and those that hadn't were still supportive and wanted to help in any way they could.

I didn't even realize I had stopped engaging in my eating disorder until the end of the fourth day of abstaining. I was attending a Monday session of intensive outpatient, and we were supposed to report on how our weekend went. As I sat on the couch listening to the others in my group, I started thinking about my weekend and was surprised to recognize I had been behavior free. *I had been so immersed in my life outside of my eating disorder that it hadn't crossed my mind.* At that moment I felt genuinely happy.

Recovery hasn't been easy. At first, I had to take things day by day. I worked with a sponsor, kept close contact with my Higher Power, and did my best to live the Twelve Steps; the support I kept close around me helped me persevere. The moment I reached thirty days was one of the proudest moments in my life and I knew at that point, by the grace of God, I wasn't willing to give up my recovery for anything.

Slowly, I started to live a normal life again. As I began consistently nourishing my body, I found I could think more clearly. I began to make friends and learn how to have meaningful relationships. I also started to tackle my fear of men that had resulted from my rapes and I eventually fumbled my way into a wonderful relationship with a man whom I love deeply.

The hardest part about recovery has been learning to be comfortable with change. Life stops when we are immersed in our eating disorder, and to fully recover we have to realize change is inevitable—even desirable. The person I was becoming through my work with the Twelve Steps was beautiful, inside and out. The going was tough. Learning to experience and understand my emotions and life situations was terrifying, but each situation I made it through showed me more clearly that living a full life meant keeping the eating disorder out.

I now see when I try to control my life, whether through food or chemicals, I end up unhappy and sick. But when I surrender fully to my Higher Power and live life the way God wants me to, things are better—and life is beautiful. When I was in the middle of my eating disorder it didn't matter if things were good or bad, life still sucked. But when I live under the guidance of my Higher Power and the principles of EDA, it doesn't matter if circumstances are good or bad. Life is just amazing. For that I am truly grateful.

(5)

FOLLOWING THE LIGHT OF RECOVERY

After twenty-six years with an eating disorder, she wanted to lead a normal life. Recovery was about faith, hope, and a willingness to accept and love herself—inside and out.

*T*hank you for reading my story of recovery and discovery. To those of you who have an eating disorder, an addiction, or some other form of self-harm or abuse: just under three years ago, I was in the very same spot you are in right now. I was weak, frail, hiding, using symptoms excessively, getting away with shoplifting, stealing, lying, manipulating, and entrenched in a disease in which I felt helpless, misunderstood, and a lost cause. I firmly believed that I was meant to live in suffering, completely hopeless. At the age of thirty, I was certain one of three things would happen: that I would live my life in a residential home for the mentally ill, that I would be committed to a state hospital, or that I would die.

I felt like I had nowhere to go, that there was no way out. And frankly, all I wanted to do was continue using the symptoms that kept me imprisoned, stuck, selfish, and sick—even though there were some fleeting moments where I did want something different. But those moments never lasted, and before long I was again face to face with avoiding food, bingeing, purging, self-mutilating, and then repeating the whole cycle over again. I was constantly suicidal. I wrote letters to those I wanted to say goodbye to, and I was even planning my own funeral.

Today, thinking of each of you who may be feeling hopeless, I can honestly tell you that having an eating disorder is not a death sentence. While I am well aware that it is an incredibly powerful disease to overcome, I know firsthand that it is possible to lead a different life.

Being in recovery for the past three years has been the most fulfilling, wondrous, adventurous, and remarkable story I could ever tell. What has happened in the past couple years isn't anything that I could have ever comprehended when I was sick. There wasn't even a small part of me that could have imagined it or dreamt it, and yet it has become my life. The real me has emerged. I can now handle life on life's terms without resorting to using symptoms to cope. Even with so many incredibly wonderful things happening, there are still difficulties that I face. Life is hard, it is challenging, and living the life of a responsible adult, well, comes with real responsibilities.

I'm sure everyone has already heard, probably numerous times, that "Being in recovery takes work and dedication." But even though it is a constant job, I wouldn't trade it in for anything. I would never choose to go back to the darkness in which I fell asleep in a never-ending nightmare that became my life. Those days were ruthless. They were torturous. But at the time they were the only thing I knew. I became a pro at my eating disorder and I became a master at a lot of negative things even though I never wanted to be that way. Despite how good I became at living the secret life of an eating-disordered woman, I can look back and tell you that being healthy and in recovery is ten times more gratifying in terms of feeling accomplished.

I now feel worthy, I have self-love, I am loved by others in positive and fulfilling relationships, and I'm independent—all in a way I've never experienced before. When you have an eating disorder that rules your every thought, decision, and action, there is very little time for anything else. There's no time to be happy or sad, there's no time to care about yourself, or care about others, and there's no time for a real job or relationships.

Eating disorders are all consuming and all powerful. Today, in recovery, I am not a prisoner any longer. I have the freedom to live, to choose, and to be. Most of my time, I don't think about the obsession that I once could not escape. I don't constantly think about food, calories, my weight, my shape, the extra fat on my body, my stomach, my thighs, the impression others see of me, or have time to think about what others may think of me. My mind is clear and productive. My body is well nourished. I am not starving, and therefore I am free to live without the fears and angst and obsessions that once ruled every second of my life.

Maybe you're reading this right now and thinking, *She couldn't possibly have been sick like me,* or *She wasn't really on her death bed,* or *She didn't cut herself like I have,* or *Her hair wasn't falling out like mine.* But I was doing all of those things, experiencing all those things—and more. I was desperate for things I could not figure out; I was ashamed, lonely, and waiting for my life to end. The toilet bowl filled up with vomit when I swore the previous time was my last; my body bled from me cutting it; my fingernails and lips were blue, and I was constantly cold; I spent days and months inside the hospital, inside treatment facilities, and inside therapists' offices. I screamed and scared even myself when I didn't have the words to express my frustrations and anger. I cheated my way through many systems, planned my own suicide, planned my funeral, and said my goodbyes.

But today I am here to tell you that it doesn't have to be that way. Your story doesn't have to end like that, with an eating disorder, living within the walls of a treatment center or a hospital, trying to learn how to eat, how to care and love yourself, and how to self-soothe and cope. It just doesn't.

I firmly believe that no matter how young or old you are, how few years or how many years you have suffered, *everyone is completely capable of a full recovery.* I'm sure you have told yourself many times before, *Others may be able to, but I sure can't,* or maybe you've heard that message indirectly from others. I did too. Everyone under the sun, at one point along that hellish journey, told that me I couldn't recover. My message to you is that no matter what you currently think or what others may think, I say, "Yes, you can recover!"

After twenty-six years of having my eating disorder, which began when I was seven, I found my recovery because of the determination I had for a different life. I wanted it to be done once and for all. I had to make that choice and I had to "do life" differently. I wanted real friendships and relationships in which I didn't have to tell them I was going back to the hospital or treatment again. I didn't want to disappear from life any longer. I wanted a job I felt good about and my own place that I could call home. Those desires are what helped me find my way to recovery and stay there. The change did not happen overnight. It was like a teeter-totter of good and bad days, with fewer instances of bad hours, and then the food obsessions became less frequent, until I was riding my own bike and the training wheels came off.

People always ask me about the one thing that helped me find my way to recovery. I can't say it was only one thing, but I do know of two very powerful things that happened that helped me step onto the path to recovery—and stay there. First, I remember looking out the window so many times while I was in treatment and in the hospital. I would watch cars driving by on the road below my window; I would see people crossing the street; I would watch people walking their dogs, people talking on their cell phones, and couples holding hands taking a walk. I longed for that normalcy. I would think to myself, *I want to be able to lead a normal life. I want to drive my car and not use symptoms on my way from one destination to the next. I want to find my soul mate and hold hands walking down the street. I want to stroll leisurely on the sidewalk without thinking about food and my body. I want to drive to work as the sun rises and drive home at night when the sun is setting.* I desperately wanted to experience what that life was like, what others seemed to be doing so effortlessly, while I could only watch from my hospital window. I was miserable.

The second thing that helped me tremendously was attending Eating Disorder Anonymous groups, reading Twelve-Step literature, and working the Twelve Steps of the EDA program. The first step of EDA *(admitting I was powerless over my eating disorder—that my life had become unmanageable)* was something I could not deny any longer. My life *was* completely unmanageable and I *was* powerless. My eating disorder had a hold on me and the grip was stronger than I could release on my own. That's when I started to realize that only *a power greater than myself could truly restore me to sanity* (Step Two) and that I had to put my trust in "God" to help me through. I had to reframe my mindset and reset my beliefs, from *God is making me suffer,* to *God wants me to heal and recover. So I turned my will and my life over to God's care* (Step Three) and I remember feeling relief. It was as though a weight had been lifted. I was no longer fighting against myself or fighting with my eating disorder. I gave it to God, and He gave me strength I never knew I had. As I worked Steps Four through Twelve, I came to terms with all the wrongs I had committed and all the people I had hurt. It was painful at times and yet, as I worked the Steps, I uncovered my true self. I came to believe I was a good human being, and that I deserved a life worth living. Attending EDA groups helped me to stay motivated, to be honest and authentic, to remain symptom free, and to face the new realities of daily life. Early on I remember counting the days that I abstained from symptom use. One day, then two days, and later three days, everyone at the group congratulated me and was so happy for me. Months later I lost track of the days that I was symptom free, and it was as though I was truly standing on my own two feet. That was an incredible feeling I will never forget.

When I found my new self in recovery, the label of "disabled" that the State of Minnesota gave me was thrown away, the food stamps were stopped, the food charts and the food plans were ditched, the scales were destroyed, my binge shopping bags were shredded and put into the dumpster, my jobless existence was over, my social security benefits fell by the way side, and my commitment was dismissed. I never have to be escorted by the police or see the inside of the courthouse again. All that was left was *me*, completely exposed and in plain sight, to live each day head on and fight for my recovery in each moment.

I want to switch gears a bit and give you a few lists that I have jotted down. I would like to remind you that what works for me, or for any one person, is not the same recipe that will work for someone else. Remember your recovery is your own journey of self-discovery, and it may look very different.

First, a list of challenges I faced:

- Comparisons of all varieties have always been a huge trigger for me and very difficult to stop. I really needed to work hard on not comparing myself to others.

- For me, one of the hardest things that I had to stop was comparing my body to others who were thinner, thinking that I should be that thin, without hips, or thighs.

- Boredom

- Transitions during the day, life transitions, and seasons

- Holding back my feelings

- Not sharing my honest thoughts

- When other people are telling me what to do or making decisions for me

- Inappropriate boundaries

- When feeling like using symptoms, I needed to remind myself that by using symptoms I would decrease the amount of time I had to spend with people, and that spending quality time with others was what I really wanted

Second, how I went from my eating disorder mindset to a recovery mindset:

- Disconnecting from people who viewed my chances of recovery negatively or who reinforced eating-disordered thinking

- Limiting mirror time

- Getting rid of small clothes (some I donated, others I cut up and threw away)

- Buying appropriate-sized clothing

- Knowing my performance in life does not depend on my weight

- Reducing my time on social media

- Surrounding myself with normal eaters

- Participating in life

- Staying on a schedule

- Asking for help

- Looking for patterns, such as triggers, hard conversations, questions, and times of day that are more challenging (when I am most prone to challenges and symptom use)

- Finding a therapist

- Refusing to refer to myself as unable, eating-disordered, and hopeless

- Realizing it is okay to be on medication: it does not mean I am a failure or any less capable than others who are not on medications

- Expressing emotions instead of burying them, neglecting them, or telling myself they are not important
- Being with people who are respectful of me and nonjudgmental
- Embracing my worthiness, and letting go of old negative mindsets and belief systems
- Being in charge of my own life and my own decisions

Third, the benefits of being in recovery and living fully:

- Being present in the moment—in my own life and in the lives of those around me
- Traveling
- Having my own home: I look forward to coming home at the end of the day
- Living with a man I love, who loves me back, and building a life together
- The ability to work again and maintain a full-time job
- Getting off disability and food stamps
- Not being irritable, dysregulated, or constantly triggered
- Rebuilding friendships and making new friendships
- Realizing my confidence and my own light that I have to shine out onto the world

So with all of that, let me tell you what has happened in the past three years, as a result of making that life-changing decision to work the Steps and get better:

- I have achieved a healthy weight for myself, which allows me to be active, explore, and engage in adventures like I have always wanted.

- I am the Director of Nursing at a home care agency, a position in which I am respected and for which I have great responsibility.

- I have fallen in love with a man who shares the same interests and passions for life that I do: I have blessed his life and he has blessed mine.

- I have traveled to Hawaii and hiked.

- I have camped and canoed in the boundary waters.

- I have jumped off cliffs into the Temperance River.

- I have set appropriate boundaries with people who were emotionally abusing me.

- I have spoken at eating disorder recovery rallies in Minneapolis.

- I have taken and responded to phone calls and emails from people seeking help with their eating disorders, as well as from parents looking for guidance for their kids: I have been able to help others as a result of my experiences.

- I am happy, smiling, full of laughter, and stable for the first time in my life.

- I am engaged to be married!

I want to reiterate that although my life today is better than I would have ever thought possible, it was not so long ago that I saw no hope for myself. I told myself I had been living with the eating disorder too long, that there was no alternative, and that I had no choice but to live at the bottom. And yet, I have come to live on the other side of it all and I am in full recovery. I believe this is possible for anyone who is still struggling—no matter the circumstances or where you are along your journey.

Full recovery is possible. It is worth it, it is incredible, and life is and can be a remarkable story of triumph and success that each one of you is capable of living and sharing with the world. I hope you each will join me in the adventure of living!

(6)

MAKING THE MOST OF EVERY MOMENT

Her dedication to therapy, determination to stop binge-ing, and EDA support have given her a life of love today. No longer dependent on an eating disorder, she shares her "Steps to Happiness I Now Know."

I would like to share with everyone a part of what I've learned about myself in the past year. I've lived with bulimia for over twenty years. It began when I was only fourteen years old. I had a period of recovery, but relapsed. When this happened, I found out that having insurance coverage doesn't mean you can receive the care you need. I was denied coverage for treatment in an inpatient facility. I fought with my insurance company for six long months and got nowhere. By the time I reached the end of those six months, I was emaciated and knew I had to do something to get back on track.

One evening, I spent the entire night on the internet searching for self-help books. I was determined to find one that would help me help myself. The one I decided on had a chapter on how to stop bingeing and I'm here to tell you this book honestly saved my life. It also made recovery—through therapy and EDA—possible.

Not long after I discovered that book, I began therapy, grateful that the Expanded Psychiatric Services in my insurance contract covered every penny of my outpatient care. I also began following the advice in the book and was able to stop bingeing completely. My dedication to my therapy, my determination to stop bingeing, and the EDA support I rely on have paid off.

I want to share with all of you what I've learned about myself. I hope it will help you to start on, or remain on, your journey to recovery.

Steps to Happiness I Now Know

I can't be all things to all people.
I can't do all things at once.
I can't do all things equally well.
I can't do all things better than everyone else.
My humanity is showing just like everyone else's.

So:

I have to find out who I am and be that.
I have to decide what comes first and do that.
I have to discover my strengths and use them.
I have to learn to not compete with others
Because no one else is in the contest of "being me."

Then:

I will have to learn to accept my own uniqueness.
I will have to learn to set priorities and make decisions.
I will have to learn to live with my limitations.
I will have to learn to give myself the respect that is due.
And I'll be a most vital mortal.

Dare To Believe:

That I am a wonderful, unique person.
That I am a once-in-all-history event.
That it's more than a right, it's my duty to be who I am.

That life is not a problem to be solved, but a gift to be cherished.

And I'll be able to stay one up on what used to get me down.

I'm now almost a year into my recovery from binge-ing, bulimia, and anorexia. I'm reading more than ever and worrying less. I am now able to sit in the yard and admire the view without fussing about the weeds in the flowerbeds. I'm spending more time with my new friends in EDA and less time working.

Whenever possible, life should be a pattern of expe-riences to savor, not to endure. I'm learning to recognize and appreciate and cherish the moments. I'm not "saving" anything; we use the "good" dinnerware every day. I wear my big smile to the market. My thought is, *If I look at binge foods and not put them in my shopping cart, I can shell out the same money for a bag of healthy groceries.* Also, I'm not sav-ing my good perfume for special occasions either—I wear it every day.

I'm learning that if something is worth seeing or hear-ing or doing, I want to see and hear and do it—now. I used to take so much for granted. Now I feel like every day is new adventure. Life may not be the party I had hoped for, but I might as well dance while I am here.

I think about what those who lost their lives to their eating disorders would have done if they had known this day was their last. I think they would have called family members and a few close friends. They might have called a few former friends to apologize and mend fences. I like to think they would have gone out for whatever their fa-vorite food was and, just maybe, enjoyed it. It's those little things left undone that would make me angry if I knew my hours were limited; angry because of all those letters I had intended to write and sorry that I didn't tell my family and friends often enough how much I truly loved them. Now I have a chance at really living. I'm trying very hard not to put off, hold back, or save anything that would add laughter and luster to my life today. Every morning when I open my eyes, I tell myself my recovery process is a special journey. Every day, every minute, every breath truly is a gift from God.

I treasure my EDA friends, because their hands are always ready to reach out to the newcomer. I want everyone to have a miracle of recovery like I have found. I don't believe in miracles: I know I *am* one!

OFF TO THE RACES

She thought the mirror, scale, and measuring tape were her Holy Grail to becoming happy, joyous, and free. But when she got to EDA, she learned that she had it all wrong—and started living in the solution.

At a very young age, I developed a sense of entitlement. I began to think, act, and treat people in my life like they owed me something. I had the belief that I deserved special treatment. I strived for perfection and expected to be rewarded for it. The many honor roll awards, trophies from dance and athletics, and playbooks highlighting my name as the school star were all living proof. I set very high standards for myself and was quite competitive.

Perfection became the theme of my youth. I felt powerful knowing that I could control my flaws and shape them into assets. The furthest back that I can remember feeling powerless is when I was six years old. My father went missing in a boating accident. I was in first grade and already feeling different than my classmates. I recall people having sympathy for me and being overly kind. I took comfort in protecting my feelings of despair in solitude. The hole in my heart was just too big to share with anyone.

I constantly had my head in a book and excelled in my studies as well as my elementary school acting career. Being on stage took me out of myself; it seemed like the perfect cure to my broken heart. I could not bear to feel a thing. Acting made me temporarily forget who I was and enabled me to be a completely different character. My family and friends gave me unconditional love and support.

I can recall being thirteen years old and sitting on my bedroom floor reading a story on eating disorders. The story outlined various types with comments from the youth in our nation who were acting out. I can remember a feeling of what I thought was hope wash over me. I had also recently discovered alcohol and the effects that it had on my psyche. Alcohol had made me feel in control of my feelings. It enabled me to successfully numb them out. I decided to take my experimentation to the next level.

Memories of my first purge still haunt me from time to time. I distinctly remember the feeling of control that I felt: like I could fly. My home life was becoming more and more abnormal and it made me feel lost, empty, and alone. My bulimia won every time in allowing me to numb these feelings of despair. I dreamt of running away and finding my father. I was stuck in a home filled with little joy and lots of anger. I did not feel important. My eating disorder gave me the comfort that I craved. I no longer felt that I needed attention from my loved ones.

I like to think that I hid my relationship with bulimia from the outside world. I had a nice year-long run with my eating disorder before it started to ruin my life. I began to feel dizzy and, quite often, weak. I lost color in my face and my weight was dropping drastically. A routine yearly physical revealed that my electrolytes were low, and that I was severely dehydrated. My doctor warned me of what my teeth might look like if I continued purging. Naturally, I started using whitening toothpaste and disregarded the true meaning behind her concern.

I was medically directed to take calcium chews and drink electrolyte-packed drinks. I told my mother that I was on my way to being "cured," but secretly kept engaging in my eating disorder behaviors. I experimented with laxatives—they seemed to work just fine too! I was only fourteen when I began drinking with the intention of blacking out. I started feeling too hung-over in the mornings to eat anything, so skipping meals sounded like the sensible solution.

In the middle of my high school years, my family moved from New York to Florida. This was entirely too much for me to handle. Within a short time, I began to implement drugs into my daily routine. They were love at first sight for my anorexia. I felt thin, looked thin, and strived desperately to be invisible. I would go days on end without eating. I became depressed and anxious. I sought medical treatment for magic pills that helped me get through my days of misery.

When confronted by others about my weight and how sick they thought I looked, I became very angry. I was defensive, because, by this time, my body dysmorphia had completely taken over my mind. I was obsessed with my shape and the way that I thought I could redesign the way I looked. I honestly thought that the mirror, the scale, and the measuring tape were my Holy Grail to becoming happy, joyous, and free.

I somehow managed to graduate high school while in the midst of becoming an alcoholic, a drug addict, and an anorexic. Nevertheless, I went off to college to become a fashion mogul. I protected my anorexia by lying to the people I love. I did everything in my power to ensure that my eating disorder was taken care of. If hungry in the morning, I would make hot tea. If dizzy in the afternoon, I would have a cigarette. Alcohol was typically on the menu for dinner and, in the end, for breakfast and lunch as well.

When I drank enough, I became full. When I became full and continued drinking…well, that was the real
treat—I threw up automatically. I started incorporating a
few small snacks into my daily routine and drinking more
to rid myself of the shame. I thought about how invincible
I was and decided to take my eating disorder back to New
York City with me. I had out-lived Orlando and was in dire
need of a geographical cure.

I landed my dream career in the fashion industry. At
the time, I thought that a requirement of getting hired was
how thin I was. I worked through lunch while eating small
snacks at my desk so nobody would question me. I drank
lattes for lunch and had champagne for dinner. I was just
another twenty-something living the dream in the big city.
I worked all day and partied all night.

From the outside, my life seemed to be completely
glamorous. On the inside, I was broken, tired, and extremely sick. I felt as though my world was falling apart.
I began toying with the idea of overdosing. I did not yet
think that I was powerless—that came a few years later.
I moved out to California. I traveled frequently and ate
around other people, because I was ashamed for them to
know about my struggles. My weight began to fluctuate
and I fell into another deep depression. Thoughts of suicide
were becoming more frequent. I did not know where to
turn to for relief anymore. I had exhausted all my options.

The last time I ran my life on self-will, I woke up in
the emergency room from an overdose. It was not the way
I had imagined it would happen: my daydreams of overdosing ended with me not waking up. This was not the
first overdose that unexpectedly left me very much alive.
I had my first spiritual experience in that New York City
hospital. I had nothing left in me to give to my eating dis-

order. But I didn't have the willingness or honesty to seek treatment either. Something intervened with my pain and hopelessness that night.

The next morning, I hopped on a flight to Florida to enter a detox facility for a few days. I went with the intentions of fighting off all of my demons. I had no idea that my eating disorder was planning on coming along to sabotage my experience. Without alcohol or drugs to help me stay numb and thin, I was left with my destructive and progressive eating disorder. My thirteen-year struggle was at its highest peak.

I began to feel weak and hopeless again—feelings that were way too familiar. With no other way to cope while in rehab, I slipped deep into my disordered thinking. I was being hospitalized for dehydration like it was going out of style, and it became clear to me that being this dehydrated affected me mentally, spiritually, and emotionally. Nothing in the world gave me less pleasure than walking into an emergency room asking desperately for fluids to stabilize me.

Upon completion of my treatment program, I was referred to an eating disorder treatment center to work on my core issues. This was in South Florida, where I had just discovered Eating Disorders Anonymous. I struggled with the idea of surrendering to my eating disorder. I did not understand how life could possibly be better without it. It comforted me in times of need and ensured that I was never too alone, too fat, or too ugly. It made me feel great; my identity as a human being was solely based on what it told me.

I met my sponsor at an EDA meeting while I was still in rehab. It amazed me how much we had in common. I used to choose friends based on their social status, but I was able to connect with my sponsor on a much differ-ent level. Not only is she a member of EDA, but she also carries the message of recovery to me for my Alcoholics Anonymous program. She is a true gift in my life today, as I feel I am right where I am supposed to be. I was so desperate to recover, and the people I met at meetings in both fellowships had this *je ne sais quoi* about them that I craved.

I listened in meetings, I raised my hand frequently to carry the message of recovery, and I worked the Twelve Steps of EDA and AA with my sponsor. I engaged in service work and I recently started sponsoring. I did everything that was suggested to me; and, today, I am in the best place I have ever been in my life. The first story I read in the AA "Big Book" was "Acceptance Was the Answer," which helped me understand the extent of my alcoholism and dis-ordered mind. It also helped me to understand that before I dive into my program head-on, I have to accept certain things first.

Honesty has been a major part of the solid founda-tion that I have built in my recovery. Before I came into the rooms, I did not know how to be honest. Through lis-tening, connecting, and identifying, I was able to let go of everything that was keeping me sick. It suggests in our literature that we be fearless and thorough from the very start, so that is exactly what I did. As I mentioned earlier, I had exhausted all of my options, so I figured, *Why not try a way that seems to work?*

The first thing I surrendered to was my ego-driven mind. I continue to do this on a daily basis, because I need to remind myself that I am completely powerless over my eating disorder. Looking back on my experiences over the past thirteen years, I am able to see that my life was, in fact, unmanageable. When I got to EDA, I was so broken that I would do anything that was asked of me. I had a complete willingness and open-mindedness about me that enabled me to take the Twelve Steps with honesty and integrity.

With that being said, the idea of trusting in a Power greater than myself was a bit difficult. I grew up with religion and lost it during my years of active addiction. My sponsor suggested I write a list of ideals of what I would want my Higher Power to look like. I listed endearing qualities that I thought would help me have more faith. I do not recall at what point in my recovery I actually started to believe in my Higher Power. The beauty of it was that I just came to believe. I ceased fighting everything and everyone, and the channel of spirituality and divine greatness just happened—with a lot of prayer and patience!

Once I began to have faith, I next had to turn it over. By reciting the 3rd Step prayer, I become free. I have to remind myself every day that I can no longer run life on self-will. When I give my questions, concerns, thoughts, and troubles to my Higher Power, the result is so much more rewarding. My second spiritual experience came after completing Steps Four and Five. I was told in early recovery that our secrets keep us sick. This is a great reminder for me that I am no longer running the show and that I need to stay consistent in holding myself accountable. I took pen to paper and did a thorough housecleaning. This was indeed an eye-opening experience for me, especially after I completed Step Five with my sponsor. I was able to sit back and truly take a look at my life: how having an eating disorder for so many years had affected me and the people, places, and things I care for.

Before I found EDA and AA, I did not know the true meaning behind gratitude. My entitlement and self-will-driven life up until this point had made me feel restless, irritable, and discontent. For me, it helps to bring gratitude to light by jotting down a few things I am grateful for on an ongoing list that I have kept since early recovery. It is truly amazing how long this list has come to be! Today, to be able to feel my feelings is a blessing in itself.

Through working the Twelve Steps, I have learned how to identify and embrace my shortcomings, make amends to those I believe I have hurt, and develop a tremendous relationship with my Higher Power—all while staying free from alcohol, drugs, and my eating disorder. I consider Steps Ten through Twelve to be my maintenance steps. These are things I do daily to ensure my recovery stays strong. Early recovery was no walk in the park for me. I have experienced a lot of trial and error, pain, and insanity in the past year. The silver lining, however, is that I walked through all of that fear without acting out or picking up a drink or drug.

After treatment, I decided the next best thing for my recovery would be to stay in Florida, close to my family. I am the most grounded I have ever been in my life. I am able to be fully present today. I used to feel confused when people in the rooms would mention that they were living a life beyond their wildest dreams. Now, I can whole-heartedly say that I, too, am living that same life. I have freedom from the bondage of self. I am free from all of my disordered thinking that kept me sick.

It is significant to my recovery that I carry the message of recovery to others with eating disorders; this is how I keep my freedom. I started an EDA meeting in my town here in North Florida. The feeling of lending a hand to someone in need is the most rewarding emotion I have ever felt. My unhealthy obsession with being thin is something that lives in my past. Today, I know how to honor my body and my feelings—and take care of myself. I practice loving myself one day at a time.

8

OWNING MY STORY

Instead of letting an eating disorder speak for her, she now uses her voice to carry the message of recovery.

There is nothing remarkably special or earth shattering about this story. It's really not that different from others about people with eating disorders and it's not unique in any way other than it is MY story and I own it—good and bad.

For as long as I can remember, food has been the answer to everything. Growing up in the South meant it was all about food, all the time. There were family dinners at my grandmother's house with generations and generations of relatives, and food always at the ready for whoever wanted what at any given moment. Food was an expression of love...for fun events, sad events, and every event in between. I grew up in the generation of eating everything on your plate, because "Children in Africa are starving." It took many years of clean plates to realize one thing had little to do with the other. Why didn't we just donate food to the other countries?

I started working at only fourteen. Our town was experiencing an economic boom thanks to the oil industry and had a serious lack of available labor, so, with a work release signed by my parents, I got a job at a national, fast food restaurant. While there, one of the managers would occasionally call me "thunder thighs." I had a serious crush on him and let all the comments slide (obviously, in today's world his comments would never be tolerated). This only added to my struggling, teenage body image.

In high school I had a large group of friends. I got good grades, but wasn't a "brain." I was pretty good at sports, but wasn't a "jock." I never tried drugs, but truly tried to not judge the friends that did. I was in the band, but not really a "band-geek." I got along well with and knew many of the popular kids, but didn't really hang out with them. I developed my own primary circle of friends, but could float around the periphery of all the other cliques. It felt good to be included by almost every group of people—something that is rare in the world of high school. The big turning point of those years was that I had my first real boyfriend, who happened to be a cross-country runner and so had a naturally thin build.

All my friends wore single-digit size clothes and then there was me—barely squeezing into a size that was more than twice that. It didn't matter that I was anywhere from four to six inches taller than all of them, I just knew I never fit into single-digit size ANYTHING. Between this reality and the new thin boyfriend, my self-image and subsequent insecurities finally frustrated him so much that he ended our relationship, which devastated me. I know now my jealousy and neediness had to have been exhausting. I had seen pictures of old girlfriends who were curvy like me, so I shouldn't have been so insecure. But I just couldn't get past the fact that I was bigger than him.

In my early twenties, I began a two-year relationship with a man sixteen years my senior and completely, terribly, horrifically wrong for me—oh, and he was married. Again, my insecurities led me down the wrong path, because I didn't feel I deserved any better, and no one else wanted me. I was flattered, all the while knowing it was absolutely wrong. In the midst of this fiasco, I admitted to myself that part of the reason I was willing to go against all of my moral foundations was that this man lived directly across the street from the same first boyfriend who had broken my heart. I wanted to show him I had moved on like him, as twisted as that may sound.

About this time I developed bulimic behaviors as an outlet for my disappointments in myself and my life. I had never been one for self-induced vomiting, but I started abusing laxatives to make up for the comfort I found through food. Off and on for the next twenty years, these actions, coupled with heavy exercising, helped ease my anxiety, self-loathing, and fears—but never truly affected my weight. After I stopped the bulimic behavior on my own, I became a compulsive over-eater, and my weight skyrocketed. Several years later, I had gastric bypass and dropped an extreme amount of weight in a very short time. People sometimes ask me if I think the surgery contributed to or caused my eating disorder, and I unequivocally say no. I had surgery over five years before my eating disorder came screaming back to unprecedented levels.

Perhaps surprisingly, there were many highly stressful events in my life when I *didn't* use my eating disorder to cope. In a time frame of only six months: we moved; my sister died; my grandmother died on the EXACT same day as my sister; my mother-in-law, step-daughter, and her boyfriend all moved in with us; I lost my job; started a new one; my wife lost her job and decided to start her own business; and I had to put my wonderful and much loved cat down because of kidney failure. Between all this and my parent's premature deaths, I had A LOT of unresolved grief. When this was pointed out in treatment I was like,

"Ya think?!" On any other day, my grandmother's death would have been really hard, but she was 95 and had dementia. Her passing paled in comparison to that of my sister, who was only 43 and left behind a grieving husband and four-year-old daughter.

As a way to cope with the stress and anxiety of a new job that was beyond my ability, I started walking A LOT. It was a great way to decompress and kept me from obsessing over work so much. At first, it started as only a nice, reasonable walk and gradually morphed into spending hours "on my journey," as my therapist would say. This was my routine five to six days a week, on top of working at least sixty hours and driving over an hour each way. It wasn't like I simply decided one day that I was going to go on a diet, develop an eating disorder, or walk forever. In fact, I didn't even recognize what was happening. I knew I seriously did not want to regain any weight I had lost; but, again, I didn't see that as an eating disorder characteristic. The staff at my first treatment program told me I had an exercise addiction, which I didn't even realize was something that could exist. I purchased a new pair of shoes and literally walked the treads off of them in six weeks.

After I had dropped a significant amount, I talked to a really good friend who is also a marriage and family therapist. One of the main things he asked was if I could accept being in a weight *range*. I said that I was not ok with that idea, and his response back to me was "Houston, we have a problem." I had a low and very specific number in my head and was close to it when I started treatment that year at a part-time, cross-diagnosis, outpatient day program. I had to take a leave of absence from work for ten weeks.

I hadn't yet met the clinical director of that program when one day a woman walked toward me with an uneaten lunch container that had my name on it and asked me if I was going to eat—and I said no. I had been weighed that morning by the nurse and freaked out over the number. Clearly, not a great first impression! Two things happened because of that incident: I started having to do "blind weigh-ins," where I had to turn around or the readout was covered so I couldn't see it. Only an hour later, my group therapist told me I had to keep my body mass index and weight up or I would be referred to a higher level of care. Because I was so resistant to gaining weight in the program, the medical director started talking about "Plan B," which I knew meant a specialized eating disorder program. "Plan B" scared me to death. In one conversation with him he asked me how I felt about my weight, and I told him I wasn't exactly looking to gain any.

I was discharged from that program just two weeks before Thanksgiving, because it was the only way to keep my job. Not even six weeks later, I completely relapsed—losing all the ground I had gained in the ten weeks of the program.

I officially resigned from my job and had every intention of going back to the same treatment program, but the medical director wouldn't readmit me. He enforced his "Plan B," and that's when I entered a residential program about an hour-and-a-half from home. I would be there for nine months through three levels of care: residential, partial hospitalization, and intensive outpatient. These months would be some of the best and worst times of my life. I met women whom I will always consider friends, while at the same time I had to face the reasons I was there and learn how to deal with negative emotions in a way that did not include starving and exercising. I never thought we could afford private care, but fortunately insurance covered a large portion of the costs. And I sure couldn't complain about the location—it was a multi-million dollar house on a world-renowned golf course in southern California. In the end, the expense was completely worth it...that program saved my life.

When I was in treatment the first time, I developed a "Don't Ask, Don't Tell" policy (if you didn't ask, I didn't tell). I carried it with me to residential; my therapist learned to hate it. Like many people with eating disorders, I had food rituals and a case of OCD that had actually started in my teens. I weighed myself constantly and counted calories to the extent of including my gummy vitamins in the total. I also did NOT like eating in front of people one-on-one, but in a restaurant I was fine, as I felt no one was truly watching me. I also had "fear foods." I've managed to work through most of them, leaving only one at this point. My dietitian would ask me why I let that particular thing have so much power and I just shrugged...I genuinely didn't know.

It's always said that eating disorders are not about food, but about the underlying, driving issues—as are all types of addictions. They are often used as your "voice." I couldn't talk about my self-doubt and feelings of failure, anxiety, and depression. Eating disorders also often come with significant perfectionism, which is a fundamental part of my personality that has been with me as long as I can remember. The more my negative feelings about myself increased over time, the more I engaged in my eating disorder. It made me feel safe and accomplished; I was good at it. The hard thing for me to accept is that a central reality of being human means making mistakes, and my perfectionism goes completely against that.

One thing that took place during my stay at treatment included a family intensive weekend when friends and family come to learn more about eating disorders and ask questions. I had to leave the room during the medical portion of the presentation, because the topic was about necessary caloric intake. I started doing the math and calculated the number of calories and intended amount of weight gain expected each week. This number scared me to death! I had restricted for so long I couldn't even tell what a normal-size meal or caloric intake was anymore.

Another thing was I started hiding my medications. It was very easy to fake taking them, and then pocket them. I had collected a couple of weeks' worth of medications before telling the psychiatrist and explained how easy it was to do. In reality, I had only stashed enough to make myself sick, but it was still an embarrassing thing to admit. The psychiatrist was really calm about it, but right after our session he went to the rest of the staff and told them what was happening. Later that day at dinner, the head nurse came in and told all of us that there had been a medication policy change that made mouth checks mandatory—effective immediately. Supposedly, they had been discussing it, but hadn't implemented it yet. I knew without a doubt it was because of me...I felt so proud!

One of the last things that happened was when I stepped-down from residential to partial hospitalization. I took control of my medications, because at that level you are considered to be in transitional living. But when they handed me a brown grocery bag half filled with all my meds, I got completely overwhelmed. Because of my high levels of suicidal ideation, the next time I saw the doctor I asked him, given my history, if I was really the best person to be given all those meds? I also said that I had already looked up the toxic levels of one of them and was being handed twice that amount. It's well known that anorexia has the highest mortality rate of any mental health issue. One third of those deaths are from suicide. Obviously, the doctor was not happy with what had happened. The staff promptly took back the medications and had me start going to the main house every morning to get them.

I'm not exactly what you would call a humble person. I struggle with willingness to *not* rely on my eating disorder to navigate things that happen in my life. While there have been really stressful times when I didn't cope by using behaviors, other things that I think should be easier sometimes send me into a complete spiral. I struggle with surrender. I frequently think I only need to give up "this" part or "that" part and not every piece of the disorder. I am still resistant, thanks to my trust and control issues that started in my teens. I even want to control my surrender. I want surrender on my terms and, obviously, it doesn't work that way! Many times I feel my disorder defines who I have become. Eating disorders are loyal enigmas; they don't leave you, you have to leave them.

I am currently working on my third round of the Steps and I am now on Step Six. It talks about insanity, and the second time I was in residential treatment for what my therapist friend called a "reset," I found myself doing completely insane things such as stealing food and even picking the lock to the bathroom that was attached to my bedroom. Neither of these are things I would have ever imagined myself doing, just like I never would have imagined myself hiding medication.

I was lucky enough to find a wonderful sponsor through the EDA online meetings. She is strong in her recovery and very good at helping me see things in a different light. She truly inspires me to work towards something more productive than living in the turmoil of my disorder. When I had the opportunity to meet her in person, all I could see was a confident, secure, powerful young woman; I wanted that for myself.

I was encouraged to start service work to help strengthen my recovery. I took the advice and not only started the first face-to-face EDA group in my area, but also began helping the EDA General Service Board with literature development. All of this has helped me stay focused on the right things and keeps me from being so self-absorbed; I have discovered life really isn't all about me.

I want recovery and I am willing to trust that I can have more peace and freedom—if I just keep doing the work.

9

RECOVER OR DIE: SICK OF SUFFERING

Now a sponsor, she accepted that perfection doesn't equal happiness and she regained her purpose and spirit through EDA.

I was sick of suffering. *Recover or die,* I told myself. My eating disorder wanted me dead, but the truth is it wants *everyone* dead. I try to remind myself of that fact every day. But for almost twenty-five years I held onto my eating disorder tightly. It was mine. I never thought I would be able to let it go....but I did. And so can you. Through EDA, a relationship with a Higher Power, a support group, sponsor, and faith, you can recover too!

My eating disorder was the first layer, the foundation, of all of my addictions. It was my baby. I started acting out at the age of ten. I felt like an alien as a child. Overweight and shy, I never really knew how to express myself, or cope with life. I used food to "fill." I come from a large European family, and food is the center of everything. I learned to eat when I was happy and when I was sad. It made things better for a brief time. It became my coping mechanism.

By fourteen, I hated that I was "fat" and not very outgoing. My older sister was thin, athletic, and had a lot of friends. She seemed comfortable with life, while I always felt like I wanted to crawl out of my skin. I wanted to be like my sister and didn't understand why I wasn't skinny or happy like her. I didn't like myself, or the way I looked. Over the next two decades, I struggled with several ways of acting out trying to get outside of myself: bingeing, purging, over-exercising, anorexia, laxative and diet pill abuse, alcoholism, drug addiction, addiction to love and men, perfectionism, adrenaline addiction, poor body image and low self-worth, and several suicide attempts. Maybe you have suffered or do suffer from one of these. If you do, you are not alone.

For years, I covered up my eating disorder with a horrendous alcohol and drug problem. These two addictions allowed me to keep my weight very low: I barely ate. I was distracted by bad relationships, too busy doing drugs, and being in and out of jail to notice my eating disorder under it all. I was in complete denial.

In my late twenties, when I did get off the drugs, the eating disorder began progressing. I used to spend hours working out, counting calories, and planning meals. I thought I could "control" the eating disorder and I liked that. I lost a lot of weight, and people began to notice me for my great body and commend me for being so disciplined. But I was thin—too thin. It was hard to keep it up. This phase of my eating disorder was when I really felt the insanity. I was so strict: eating maybe once a day and killing myself at the gym. I was irritable, not sharp. My employer at the time even noticed how rigid I was with food and meal schedules. Nothing came before my eating disorder. It was number one.

I began passing out because my calorie intake and my blood sugar were always so low. One time I stood up too quickly and fainted, hitting my head on the dishwasher. Thankfully I was okay. I would pass out, then convulse. (I always thought it might have been a stroke.) *Who would find me?* I didn't care. I hated life. It was exhausting and uncomfortable. The only time I felt safe and in control was when I was acting out.

The eating disorder demanded so much time. It destroyed any soul or spirit I had left. I was still drinking and this, combined with my ED, robbed me of becoming a woman. I didn't know *who* I was. I destroyed several relationships. I could only "let others in" to a certain point, always afraid they would discover I had an eating disorder. I was dating someone, and we were supposed to go to Mexico together. But I ended up breaking up with him, because I didn't know how I would obsessively exercise—or not eat—with him around all of the time. If I went away with him he would find out how sick I was, and I just couldn't let him know that. Later, when I was working my EDA Steps and made amends to him, he told me how hurt he was, because on that trip he was going to propose to me. My eating disorder blocked me from a wonderful life. I had a miscarriage that was directly related to it—and alcoholism. I was incapable of starting a family or having a healthy relationship, because I put my eating disorder ahead of *everything*.

I caused so much stress in my family. I was always difficult about where we ate and what was served at holidays or parties. I was selfish, and if the world didn't revolve around me, you heard about it. I strived for perfection. I often wouldn't leave the house if my nails were chipped, or I wouldn't walk down the hall to put my laundry in if I wasn't dressed just right. I was insane and thought I would die that way. I couldn't see how I could ever let any of these disorders go. I was so ashamed. I thought death was the answer.

In March two years ago, by the grace of God I got sober from my alcohol and drug addictions. That was when

I began to see God was capable of saving me from a life of insanity. It was surreal. I began to love life. I found my Warrior Spirit again. I craved light instead of darkness. I knew God kept me alive and allowed me to recover in order to help other women. It was a gift, and I wanted to give it away.

I had made wonderful friends in AA—and was in recovery from drugs and alcohol—but I was still acting out and hiding in my eating disorder. I continued to think that as long as I held onto it, I was going to be okay. But deep down I knew that if I *didn't* give it up, it could lead me back to the drugs and booze—and that scared me. I didn't want to be sick anymore.

A friend I met through AA was also a member of EDA and I began attending a Sunday meeting with her. I didn't know what EDA was, but I was still drawn to it—she led me to this wonderful program. All I had to have was an open mind and hope.

When I first began attending EDA meetings, I was skeptical. *What do you mean these people are recovered?* I thought it was a lie. But the more I went, the more I listened. They were feeling and experiencing the same things I was feeling and experiencing! I didn't feel so alone. I was still bingeing and over-exercising, so I decided to get a sponsor. I wanted to commit to letting go of this disease. I was convinced that if others could recover, so could I.

With my sponsor, I began working the Twelve Steps. This is when the miracles started happening. I learned to truly get honest and trust my sponsor with my deepest eating disorder-related secrets. She shared similar stories, and I didn't feel so ashamed anymore. I knew I had to stop acting out. She taught me balance, not abstinence. I ate when I was hungry and stopped when I was full. I committed to eating three meals a day. I reached out when I felt like acting out and you know what? The urges passed. I began to spend less time at the gym or in the bathroom and more time with people. When I struggled with comparing, my sponsor would tell me perfection doesn't equal happiness… and she was right. I was becoming a whole, NEW woman. I had to put fear aside. I was willing to do anything to stay in recovery from my eating disorder.

Today, I know that I don't ever have to go back to that life of insanity. I don't have to punish myself or stay sick. I am now sponsoring other women. I'm sharing the gift that was so freely given to me. Just for today, I don't have to suffer. Because for me, it was *recover or die*. And today, I choose life. I'm living a life beyond my wildest dreams. I'm free, and you can be, too.

10

WICKED, HOT MESS TO ALIVE AND FREE

She was in a halfway house when she finally found the help she needed to put her life back together. Her love for God now allows her to make use of her experiences to help others in similar circumstances.

I grew up in a small, rural town. The first few years of my life were fairly normal, until my dad cheated on my mom and left with her best friend (taking her kids with them). Her son was my best friend. I was four at the time, I was daddy's little girl, and this left me feeling abandoned. I began to act out, seeking attention in any way that I could.

When I was eight years old, I was raped for the first time by my mom's half-brother. When she found out, she called my dad, thinking that he would come to the rescue and kill her brother. Instead, he came over and started yelling at my mom, my brother, and myself, saying to us that it was our fault that it happened. During this time, I remember clearly making the decision to start acting out in eating-disordered behavior and begin bingeing as a means of protecting myself. I thought that if I was fat and ugly, no one would ever want to touch me again. I look back now at that poor eight-year-old and realize how sad that was, but at the time, no one noticed what I was doing. My mom was a binge eater, so it just went unnoticed when I started putting on the weight. People wrote it off as genetics. I also started self-mutilation around this time. I would do things that would distract me from the emotional pain going on inside of me. Less than a year later, when I was nine, I was raped again, this time by my mom's boyfriend. This drove me deeper into a pit with food and other behaviors.

I hated myself, and no one else liked me either. I had no real friends. Being a child of a single mom meant that we had no money and stood out in school. I was made fun of on a daily basis for not wearing the "right" clothes or shoes. Since I couldn't make human friends, food became my best friend.

Throughout my childhood, I attended a local church with my neighbors and found real peace in the idea of a relationship with God—even though I could not fully grasp it. I was raped again at sixteen; this time I became pregnant. I chose to abort the baby; and, in the end, hated myself for that decision. I felt that I had murdered the child that God had given me, instead of allowing someone else to raise it. Those feelings drove me away from the church and further into the eating disorder and self-mutilation. I didn't think that anyone could understand what I was thinking or feeling at the time, so I bottled it up as best as I could and tried to soldier on—like the rest of my family did with their problems. I didn't see that they, too, were using unhealthy coping mechanisms, like alcohol, drugs, and eating disorders, to deal with all the things that they weren't talking about or dealing with.

After I left for college the first time, a friend of mine and I were attacked in our dorm by a guy who was high on PCP. The school covered it up and gave us no support. I left shortly after on academic suspension. I couldn't handle life on life's terms anymore. I returned home and started a career. As I look back, I can see a change in the eating disorder around this time. I started to restrict during the day while at work, and binge at night. I became a workaholic, working more than ninety hours a week. I was also back in church and running three church ministries in my "spare" time. Part of the reason for restricting during the day was that I didn't want people to see me eat and judge me. Another was that I didn't want to stop working and take the chance that someone else would pick up where I left off and get it wrong. My perfectionism was at the worst it had ever been. I did this for almost fifteen years before something catastrophic happened and I walked away from my church again; and eventually, without a connection to my Higher Power (God), I was lost.

A year later I was a wicked, hot mess! I was told by my pain management doctor that I needed a gastric bypass, which equated to death to me, since my mom had recently had one and nearly died due to complications. My primary care doctor was also telling me that everything that went wrong with me lately was due to my depression. And so, that same day, when I went in with a viral infection in my throat that was causing it to bleed and I got the same response—the problem was due to my depression—I lost it. I went home and stopped eating or drinking altogether. To me, it was a slow way of dying. I truly had no clue what I was doing at the time. I told everyone around me that I just couldn't keep anything down, and they believed me. I quickly noticed the weight dropping off. I had hated myself for the damage I had done to my body, and here was a solution to that problem! Diets had never worked before. I could never stay on them, but this was working. A month in, I told my doctor about the massive weight loss. Her only response was that I "could afford to lose more." So I kept going. I was also in and out of psychiatric units at this time, but they had no clue what I was doing to myself. They continued to rehydrate me, but did nothing about trying to get me to eat. No one cared because I was "overweight" and "could afford to lose more." I eventually attempted suicide three times and was sent to a drug and alcohol treatment center in Florida. I didn't struggle with those issues, but because the treatment center also dealt with depression, my family felt it was the only way to keep me alive.

The treatment center also did not know what to do with the eating-disordered behavior or cutting and therefore did not address those issues either. I left thirty days later and moved into a halfway house in Delray Beach. After about two weeks, I finally came clean with one of my housemates about not eating. She gave me two options: (1) Go downstairs and eat, or (2) She was calling the house manager. I asked for a third. She called the house manager. I started getting help that day. I found out that God was doing for me what I could not do for myself: I had chosen the one halfway house in town that specialized in eating disorders. I was again given two options: getting help by being honest with my therapist, starting to see a nutritionist, and going to EDA—or finding a new place to live. Thankfully I chose the first option.

I remained a wicked, hot mess until I finally got a sponsor and started to work the program to the best of my ability. This was a hard thing for me to do. I had never been really honest with anyone before, and I did not feel like I could be at that time either. I met my EDA sponsor at an in-house EDA meeting. We immediately started the Steps. She asked me to write my eating disorder history. This was eye opening for me. I had not realized that the behaviors that I had been doing since I was eight were actually eating-disordered! As I said, bingeing was normal in my family. I had very little trouble seeing and believing Step One, because I was obviously powerless over *everything* that I did, and my life was definitely unmanageable because of it. I was intrigued with the idea that I had a three-part disease: physical, mental, and spiritual.

I had a spiritual malady. I had a hole in my soul, which I tried to fill with everything *except* what it was made for: God. And when I tried to fill it with other things, I kicked off a physical allergy that made me crave more of it. When I put down those behaviors I obsessed about them. It was insanity! Next I did Step Two, which was also easy for me. I knew I needed God back in my life, and that He was the only answer for me. But Step Three was a bit harder. I believed in who He was, but to give up the control that I thought I had in my life was not easy. I still sometimes struggle with taking it back, so this is a daily and sometimes moment-by-moment action for me.

My first 4th and 5th Steps were the hardest for me. I could not believe that God wanted me to share all the dirt in my life with someone else. I held some stuff back that I did not dare to share for fear of not being loved anymore once they found out who I REALLY was. I felt guilty for holding back and I was still suicidal, so I finally opened up. After I became thorough and honest, I found I had a new freedom. I was no longer hiding who I was and found God's complete forgiveness for my sins. The people that I shared with still loved me and did not judge me. I was amazed! They also helped me to unload all that extra baggage I had been carrying around for so long that was keeping me from God's true forgiveness. I was now able to see both sides of the street and begin to clean up the wreckage of my past. There was so much healing in this process.

Next I took Steps Six and Seven. By this point I start-ed to see who I truly was, as well as all the shortcomings that made up who I was—and no longer wanted to be. I wanted (and still want) God to have all of that nasty stuff and mold me into the woman He wanted me to be. Next were Steps Eight and Nine. I kinda balked at this point. I was afraid of what people were going to think or say (one of my character defects). I made the easy amends quickly so that I could move on, but left the harder, more personal ones until last—until I had no other choice—because I was going to act out again if I didn't do them. I became miser-able, which was worse than the fear of doing them. I found great relief when I finally spoke to my father and mother, because I finally was the adult and willing to face the real issues in these relationships. I also made amends to my stepmother, which I definitely was not going to do, but felt called by God to do it. We had a great conversation, and since then I have actually been able to spend time with her and laugh, not to mention the fact that I am now welcome in her house. That hadn't been the case for the fifteen years, since she and my father first got married.

After that, I worked the remainder of the Steps. Some people like to refer to them as the "maintenance Steps," but I like to call them the "growing Steps." They all grow my relationship with God, not maintain it. I need to live in them every day or I get miserable. First off is Step Ten, where I have to pay attention to things throughout the day, and take care of things as they crop up. Sometimes my character defects come out, and I may need to make an immediate amends to someone. Other times I start to get resentful at something or someone, and I need to see why that is—usually a character defect driven by self-centered fear. Next is Step Eleven, which calls me to spend time dedicated to prayer and time in meditation every day. It is very noticeable to me when I skip this Step. My day usually goes much crazier than if I take the time in the morning and devote it to God. Then, last—but certainly not least— is Step Twelve, where I practice these principles in all my affairs. That means I need to live in honesty, equality, accountability, love, trust, and humility. I also need to take the message of hope and recovery to those who are still suffering. I've done this by sponsoring women, volunteering for an eating disorder awareness organization in West Palm Beach, working in a transitional living facility, and starting a new EDA meeting in the town where I currently reside. God is using me in mighty ways. I have found that He will recycle my pain to help others who have been through similar circumstances. For this I am truly grateful. All of this is happening because I took my eating disorder off the throne and put Him back on.

I have had bumps and turns along the way, but one of the lessons I have learned from them is that my path doesn't have to be perfectly straight. I may stray some and come back to the path, but I never go back to the beginning because I don't forget what I have learned on my previous journeys. I just keep learning more each time, no matter how far off the path I stray. I just need to keep coming back!

Another lesson has been that in order to maintain my recovery, it is important for me to keep balance in all areas of my life, not just in the areas of food. I need to be careful to keep my workaholism and perfectionism in check, and I can only do this by staying in fit spiritual condition. When I let any area slip, I tend to start to let the others slip as well.

The last and most important lesson that I have learned is that *recovery is possible!* It is amazing to live without "Ed" whispering/screaming in your head constantly. The first time I realized that I wasn't obsessing over whether or not I was going to eat or how much I weighed, I freaked out! At first (I will be honest) I thought it was too quiet and had to play some noise in the background. But after that, I got used to just being able to think about other things and be present in the moment. It is amazing to actually "be there" during special events. Without "Ed"—his judgment, his negativity, and his misery—riding on my shoulder, I am free to create the life I've always wanted. I hope everyone has this opportunity. Good luck to you in your journey!

APPENDICES

Appendix A:
The Twelve Steps and Twelve Traditions of EDA

Appendix B:
A Perspective on Balance

Appendix C:
An EDA Member Works the Steps

Appendix D:
Example 4th Step Inventory

Appendix E:
Contacting EDA

Appendix A:

THE TWELVE STEPS AND
TWELVE TRADITIONS OF EDA

The Twelve Steps of EDA[1]
(also known as the "Keep It Simple" or "Long Form")

1. **We admitted we were powerless over our eating disorders—that our lives had become unmanageable.** We finally had to admit that what we were doing wasn't working.

2. **Came to believe that a Power greater than ourselves could restore us to sanity.** We started to believe that we could get better, and that there was a fundamental healing power upon which we could rely for recovery.

3. **Made a decision to turn our will and our lives over to the care of God** *as we understood God.*[2] We decided to trust that, as we let go of rigidity, we would not fall. As we took (and continue to take) careful risks, our trust grew—in God, in ourselves, and in others.

---

[1] EDA's Twelve Steps and Twelve Traditions are reprinted and adapted from the first 164 pages of the "Big Book," *Alcoholics Anonymous,* with permission from Alcoholics Anonymous World Services, Inc. Permission to reprint and adapt this material does not mean that AA has reviewed or approved this or any other EDA material. AA is a program for recovery from alcoholism only. Use of AA material in the program of EDA, which is patterned after that of AA but which addresses other issues, does not constitute endorsement by, or affiliation with, AA.

[2] "God" in EDA literature can mean the Deity, a deity, a spiritual entity of one's own understanding (a Higher Power), or a non-spiritual conception (a higher purpose). Reliance on any of these conceptions confers a perspective that transcends our immediate physical, social, and emotional circumstances and allows us to "keep calm and carry on" with what really matters.

4. **Made a searching and fearless moral inventory of ourselves.** We looked at why we had gotten stuck, so we would be less likely to get stuck again. We looked at our fears and why we were afraid, our lies and why we had told them, our shame and guilt and why we had them. (This Step is the searchlight that reveals the blockages in our connection to God.)

5. **Admitted to God, to ourselves, and to another human being the exact nature of our wrongs.** We shared our shortcomings. We held ourselves accountable to others for our past thoughts and actions, and discussed what we ought to have thought and done instead. This established our authority as responsible people; we began to feel like we belonged to the human race. (This Step is the bulldozer that clears the blockages in our connection to God.)

6. **Were entirely ready to have God remove all these defects of character.** We began to accept ourselves as we really were and take responsibility for our actions. We realized we couldn't "fix" ourselves. We had to be patient and focus on our efforts instead of results. We realized that the results were not ours to control.

7. **Humbly asked God to remove our shortcomings.** We asked God to help us accept our imperfect efforts. We made a conscious effort to take care of our own basic needs, so we could be of better service to God and those around us. Character-building exercises helped us build strength from weakness. We began to notice what we were doing right. As we did so, the "right" things began to increase.

8. **Made a list of all persons we had harmed and be-came willing to make amends to them all.** We made a list of people we had treated badly, no matter how they treated us. We accepted responsibility for our part and made an effort to forgive them for their part.

9. **Made direct amends to such people wherever possible, except when to do so would injure them or others.** After counsel with a sponsor, or an EDA (or other Twelve-Step group member who has worked the Twelve Steps), we went to the people we had injured and admitted our fault and regret. Our statements were simple, sincere, and without blame. We set right the wrongs as best we could and expected nothing in return. Accountability set us free.

10. **Continued to take personal inventory and when we were wrong, promptly admitted it.** We continued (and continue) to listen to our conscience. When troubled, we get honest, make amends, and change our thinking or behavior. We continue to notice what we do right, and we are grateful when engaged in right thinking and positive action.

11. **Sought through prayer and meditation to improve our conscious contact with God *as we understood God*, praying only for knowledge of God's will for us and the power to carry that out.** We earnestly and consciously seek to understand and to do whatever will best serve our God or higher purpose every day. When we take care of our basic needs and place ourselves in service to our Higher Power or higher purpose, we gain the peace and perspective needed for recovery.

12. **Having had a spiritual awakening[3] as the result of these steps, we tried to carry this message to others with eating disorders, and to practice these principles in all our affairs.** If we have been patient and persistent in working these Steps, we have experienced a transformation that enables us to live at peace with ourselves and the world around us. We consciously bring our new way of thinking into everything we do, for it is a pattern for living that works in all contexts. We readily share our experience, strength, and hope with those who suffer with eating disorders as we once did, glad that even our worst experiences can now serve some good purpose. Carrying the message of recovery reinforces gratitude, solidifies new habits of thought and action, and fills us with purpose and joy.

[3] The term "spiritual awakening" can refer to an event—a vital spiritual experience—or to a gradual change. Those of us who are atheists also experience a transformation, enabling us to place service before selfishness.

The Twelve Traditions of EDA[4]

1. **Our common welfare should come first; personal recovery depends upon EDA unity. Eating Disorders Anonymous is a "we" program.** United we stand; divided we fall. EDA groups are effective in carrying the message of recovery to individual EDA members because we are united in our commitment to our common purpose, consistent in our use of the Twelve-Step program of recovery, and allied in adhering to our common Traditions. Without the support of EDA, many would not have found recovery at all, and many more would have died. We want the hand of fellowship and support to be there whenever anyone needs it.

2. **For our group purpose there is but one ultimate authority—a loving God[5] as God may be expressed in our group conscience. Our leaders are but trusted servants; they do not govern.** When making decisions that affect an EDA group or EDA as a whole, EDA's servant leaders use a democratic process called

[4] EDA's Twelve Steps and Twelve Traditions are reprinted and adapted from the first 164 pages of the "Big Book," *Alcoholics Anonymous,* with permission from Alcoholics Anonymous World Services, Inc. Permission to reprint and adapt this material does not mean that AA has reviewed or approved this or any other EDA material. AA is a program for recovery from alcoholism only. Use of AA material in the program of EDA, which is patterned after that of AA but which addresses other issues, does not constitute endorsement by, or affiliation with, AA.

[5] "God" in EDA literature can mean the Deity, a deity, a spiritual entity of one's own understanding (a Higher Power), or a non-spiritual conception (a higher purpose). Reliance on any of these conceptions confers a perspective that transcends our immediate physical, social, and emotional circumstances and allows us to "keep calm and carry on" with what really matters.

a group conscience. In a group conscience, each participant consults his or her own conscience and votes as he or she thinks will best serve EDA's primary purpose: to carry the message of recovery to those who still suffer.

3. **The only requirement for EDA membership is a desire to recover from an eating disorder.** To deny EDA membership to anyone could be to pronounce their death sentence. Hence, the only prerequisite for EDA membership is the individual's desire for recovery. We never turn anyone away who is trying to recover from an eating disorder.

4. **Each group should be autonomous except in matters affecting other groups or EDA as a whole.** Each EDA group manages its own affairs, but every group is part of the EDA fellowship. Each group must be careful to not cause harm to EDA as a whole. Thus, special consideration must be taken in matters beyond the scope of the immediate group. We work together, while remaining separate.

5. **Each group has but one primary purpose—to carry its message of recovery to others with eating disorders.** We freely give away what others have given to us. People struggling with eating disorders need hope to be able to make any progress in recovery. EDA members strengthen and build recovery by sharing their experience, strength, and hope with others who still suffer. Each EDA group serves as a channel for the message of recovery, helping newcomers and "old-timers" alike.

6. **An EDA group ought never endorse, finance, or lend the EDA name to any related facility or outside enterprise, lest problems of money, property, or prestige divert us from our primary purpose.** To involve our fellowship in issues outside the direct scope of our primary purpose is to distract us from carrying the EDA message to those who still suffer. To best serve our primary purpose, we hold no affiliation to external organizations or activities.

7. **Every EDA group ought to be fully self-supporting, declining outside contributions.** EDA subsists solely on voluntary donations from its members. Financial contributions from outside our fellowship would distract from our primary purpose and undermine group autonomy. Each EDA group is responsible for its own expenses, while carrying a prudent reserve.

8. **EDA should remain forever nonprofessional, but our service centers may employ special workers.** We do not give or receive payment for Twelve-Step work. While we support EDA members in their individual pursuit of professional help, we are not a professional organization. EDA employs workers when necessary to maintain the essential functions that support our fellowship.

9. **EDA, as such, ought never be organized; but we may create service boards or committees directly responsible to those they serve.** The EDA fellowship is grounded in guidance based on experience. We avoid giving directions or ultimatums lest we risk defiance and competition between members and groups. Since our experience proves that service work is essential for

recovery, we extend opportunities for our members to be of service within the EDA fellowship.

10. **EDA has no opinion on outside issues; hence the EDA name ought never be drawn into public controversy.** EDA does not take sides in any debate. A foundation of neutrality and acceptance allows us to remain focused entirely on our primary purpose.

11. **Our public relations policy is based on attraction rather than promotion; we need to maintain personal anonymity at the level of press, radio, film, and web.** Our fellowship gains membership by demonstrating EDA principles in our daily lives and by sharing our message of recovery within our groups. We focus on the EDA program rather than on individual members. Each member serves as an active guardian of our fellowship.

12. **Anonymity is the spiritual foundation of all our Traditions, ever reminding us to place principles before personalities.** Our fellowship is grounded on a foundation of tolerance and love. Personal distinction does not interest us. We gather with the single goal of carrying the EDA message of recovery, irrespective of our personal opinions. True humility is achieved through the principle of anonymous service. We place priority on principles, not personalities.

Appendix B

A PERSPECTIVE ON BALANCE

When members of the original EDA group in Phoenix first thought about how to define recovery from an eating disorder, we initially considered abstinence as the logical equivalent of sobriety. After all, other Twelve-Step groups had done the same thing—why should EDA be any different? Yet, when we focused on abstinence as the measure of recovery, we found ourselves sidelined by small errors in judgment as we discovered what we needed to do to get and stay free of ill thinking and behavior. This was not helpful at all. Having a negative goal (abstinence), in which people seemed fixated on *not* bingeing, *not* purging, and *not* restricting just felt wrong. An "abstinence is recovery" mindset can be rigid and uncompromising. We decided that any definition of recovery that depended on specific ideas about food, weight, and body image meant defining the solution in terms of the symptoms of the problem. This made no sense to us: focusing on what we *didn't* want drew our attention away from what we *did* want. And when we considered alternatives to abstinence as the hallmark of recovery, the idea of "balance" just felt right.

We wanted to feel safe and happy, free to be ourselves. We wanted to be able to express ourselves without fear of hurting ourselves, or others. We wanted to love and to be loved, to feel and express joy, to sing and dance and shout, unencumbered by our eating disorders. Peace and freedom were what we were really after, but at first this seemed too much to ask! We settled on the idea of balance because it expressed key ideas concisely. When we are in balance, we can push a few limits yet remain safe; we can be calm yet passionate; we can be efficient yet unhurried; we can be at peace while effecting real change in the world. When we realized that maintaining perspective enabled us to achieve balance, we knew we were on the right track. We found it did not matter whether we acquired perspective through reliance on God or on ideas that gave shape and meaning to our lives.

Newcomers to EDA are often confused about the idea of balance. For people like us, it is not always an easy concept to grasp or apply! Below we offer one person's perspective, but this is by no means a prescriptive definition. We urge every EDA member to search within and consult with others, taking inspiration, guidance, and example from wherever it may present itself in order to come up with their own working definition of balance.

In EDA's early days, I knew "balance" was a reasonable goal, but I wasn't too sure what "being in balance" would feel like. I was still in and out of eating-disordered patterns, and being in balance seemed to require a lot of focus and attention, like walking a tightrope or a balance beam. At the time, I was still emotionally raw, easily upset by all I thought was problematic about myself and about others. Yet I knew that when I focused on what was wrong, I was more likely to seek solace in old behaviors. So I did my best to stay positive and pay attention to what was right and good. As I did so, I found I could deal much more effectively with whatever happened. I began to feel like I could respond with dignity to most situations and provocations. And I loved living free of my eating disorder. It was amazing to realize I was starting to feel safe and strong, able to live life on life's terms.

As I kept my focus on positive things—love and appreciation for everyone and everything—I started to see tremendous changes in myself, and, perhaps surprisingly, in those around me. Other people weren't changing all that much, but my understanding and empathy—my attitude—surely was. After about a year, I no longer felt triggered by external circumstances. I lost interest in old patterns of thought and behavior. And the more of life I experienced in recovery, the more resilient I became. Before long, years had passed without any reminders of my old ways of coping: full recovery. Yet, as I've gone along, I've tripped myself up a few times and discovered that taking recovery for granted isn't all that safe. Through trial and error, I've learned I need to do a few things to maintain my balance every day. No surprises there—Steps Ten, Eleven, and Twelve keep me safe and protected.

In full recovery, finding and maintaining balance no longer feels like running along a narrow ledge in the semi-dark. Although there is great exhilaration in early recovery, being in balance nowadays feels more like moving easily along a wide, sunlit trail. I am able to take in the grandness of the journey and appreciate the wit and wisdom of fellow travelers. I find joy in the depth and breadth of life without serious risk of tripping over the edge into old insanity.

Just like trail running, maintaining balance sometimes presents challenges. I like feeling safe, but I am not happy when I am not taking any emotional, social, or intellectual risks. Balance means taking enough risk so I continue to grow, but not so many or such large risks that I become overwhelmed: I need to maintain enough perspective that I reliably take care of basics no matter what.

Happily, I have come to understand that I do not have to be "perfect" in any, let alone all, aspects of my life to be in balance. All I need is a modicum of strength and stability in four areas: physical, mental/intellectual, emotional/social, and spiritual/purpose-oriented. Like the legs of a chair, as soon as any one of these areas gets weak or compromised, I am at risk of falling on my rear. I've found it isn't so hard to spend a little time each day maintaining the "legs of my chair." A blessing of recovery is that I have come to enjoy the process!

Physical:

In recovery, I generally find it easy to take care of the physical basics (food, shelter, sleep, exercise, and physical intimacy), because I know these are essential to maintaining balance. In early recovery I took care of physical needs primarily because doing so was a means to an end: when I addressed basic needs, I could (finally!) turn my attention to things that provided perspective and meaning. But over time, I've become much more appreciative of my physical senses and my physical being; I find genuine delight in being fully human. Physical touch and intimacy, and caring for another person are more fulfilling than I could have imagined decades ago. Hugging friends and family brings a flood of emotion I don't remember feeling with such intensity and depth in earlier years. Seeing the faces of those most dear to me fills me with joy, and my heart quickens when I hear the voices of those I love. My favorite tracks of music often give me goose bumps, and ok, I'll admit, I get great pleasure belting out songs in my car with the windows rolled up. Sunlight on my face and a warm breeze on my arms make me happy. I feel peaceful awareness and love of nature when I hike, taking in sights, sounds, and smells both familiar and new. I've come to appreciate the rush of adrenaline when I've accomplished something difficult. And I love feeling strong and healthy: it is just so much dang fun!

Of course, I sometimes make mistakes. When I work too much, sleep too little, or eat in a way that sends up red flags, I've learned to be gentle with myself and make sure I address the underlying emotional issues by working my 10th Step. One thing I don't do is focus on food or weight: these are just distractions, and heaven knows I have spent enough time in my life obsessively focused on those!

One of the greatest freedoms of recovery is that I enjoy food for what it is. But when I'm not eating I don't spend much time thinking about it unless I'm preparing some kind of fancy dinner, which happens about four times a year. Then, I'm thinking about the process and logistics of preparation and delivery, not about food as an object of desire. During times of the month when hormones make things somewhat unpredictable, I tend to eat from the "use sparingly" section of the USDA Food Pyramid. I have learned to accept this rather than question it. My body is a lot smarter than I used to think! I eat when hungry and stop when moderately full, regardless of whether I am eating "healthy" or "junk" food. If I have eaten too much, sleep works best to reset my equilibrium.

Though I am happier when exercising regularly, too much physical activity can interfere with getting a better perspective on whatever is going on in my life that I need to address. Doing my 10th Step is the best way for me to restore peace and balance, but anything that brings me gratitude is a boon to my recovery. At a physical level there is much that brings me joy!

Mental/Intellectual:

When I am in balance, I am grateful to have a calm mind that can focus on the things that are important to me. In part, this includes intellectual stimulation, which takes many forms: reading, working, keeping up with the news, technological investigation and innovation, learning new things that pertain to my work, organizing and packing for hiking treks and family outings, and making presentations to volunteer groups.

I generally love activities that stimulate my mind, so if I am having trouble focusing or getting motivated it is usually because I didn't get enough sleep (physical), or because I am resentful or fearful about something (emotional).

It is helpful to take a closer look and identify the real issue that is holding me back. Through working the Steps regularly, this has become relatively easy. I know I will feel better immediately if I seek to understand the issue (4th or 10th Step), admit my error (5th or 10th Step), let go of the situation and my feelings about it (6th and 7th Step), make amends if necessary (8th, 9th, or 10th Step), and turn my attention to whatever I can reasonably and responsibly do at that moment (11th and 12th Step). Sometimes an awful lot of mental energy is required just to keep myself emotionally balanced, but I figure that it is as good a use of my capabilities as any!

Emotional/Social:

As a recovering alcoholic and bulimic—even with many years of recovery—I am usually most vulnerable and awkward in the social and emotional realm. Admitting that I can easily become self-pitying and angry is embarrassing, but I can honestly say I spend very little time hanging out in that space; to do so means embracing danger, and that no longer feels good to me. I am aware that it is silly and arrogant to get frustrated with those who do not share my perspectives; I am grateful I can usually laugh at myself!

Yet, even after all these years, my first response to practically everything life presents is still some form of fear. Luckily, there is always a clear solution: *perspective* that comes from humility and *gratitude* for the opportunity I now have to be of service to my family, friends, community, and humanity. My emotions, whatever they may be, exist to ensure that I take reasonable care of myself and am attentive and compassionate with others—all so I may be of service.

I have learned to be grateful for my emotional nature even if I still do not like some of my innate responses to the natural provocations of life. I have learned to love and trust. I have learned to be patient and tolerant—most of the time. I have learned to be quiet and flexible, though I am not always graceful. I am still very much a work in progress, but there is joy and humor in being fully human. I am grateful for and delighted with the relationships that recovery has made possible with my spouse, my children, friends, colleagues, and fellow volunteers. Today, I am gratefully free to feel and express the depth and breadth of all the emotions of which I am capable. I am unafraid to feel and unafraid to express myself, because I now trust I can do so without causing pain and suffering. Also, much of what I feel is now positive: sharing love and joy with passion and delight—what could be more amazing?

Spiritual/Purpose-oriented:

For me, balance means organizing my thoughts and actions around the idea that I am here to serve the greater good. I am happy that my long-standing difficulty with the idea of spirituality has turned out to be a non-issue in my recovery; I decided that I do not *need* to make it an issue. Like everyone else, I am just a human being here on Earth for a very short time. My limited ability to accept much on faith need not stand in the way of my understanding of what I am here to do. I cannot bring myself to believe that a Higher Power has any personal interest in me, my family, or even humanity as a whole—except as expressed in and through me and through those I see around me. Praying a certain way or believing any particular credo does not seem to be required, but I do sincerely and firmly believe (as stated on page 77 in AA's "Big Book," *Alcoholics Anonymous)* that, "Our real purpose is to fit ourselves to be of maximum service to God and the people about us." To me, service to God means service to the ideals of truth, justice, fairness, and equality for all; service to EDA; and carrying the message of recovery. My belief in the power of these ideas, and my commitment to upholding them, is enough to reel me back from lapses into self-pity, resentment, and fear. I am here to serve as best I can, and that is all I really need to know. When I remember my place, I am simply grateful to be here. When I remember my purpose, I am restored to sanity, and my equilibrium returns.

All I need is to stay accountable for what I am thinking and feeling, address my basic needs, and find gratitude for what I have. I do this when I spend a few minutes on Steps Ten and Eleven every day. It's that simple!

To take Step Ten, I jot down the *events* that happened in my life over the last twenty-four hours. Then I write about the *issues:* areas where I've made a mistake, feel upset, or anticipate that I may encounter difficulty. Usually, I don't focus too much on these because, thanks to my 4th Step, I already know what I should do. But when life gets to be a tough slog, I take the time to write about each issue specifically: the source of the disturbance, the cause, what it affects or threatens, my part in the situation (my errors in thinking), and my resolution (what I am willing to do about it that day). This process is amazingly quick and effective. And the more often I follow it, the more effective it is: practice is such a key idea! I don't spend *too* much time on issues, however, because rebalancing by finding gratitude is so important.

So next, I write about what I am grateful for that day. This can be a challenge when my basic needs haven't been met, so I always re-check these when I am feeling out of sorts. But usually, once I've spent a few minutes thinking about what I am going to *do* to address my issues, it is pretty easy to let my heart fill up with love as I write about who and what I appreciate. I can breathe again. I feel hope and excitement when I consider how lucky I am to have the awesome opportunity each day to do things that matter in the long run, and to do them authentically—as myself. Although I am not an exceedingly graceful person, I can laugh and I can behave with integrity and dignity. That feels terrific.

After writing about gratitude, I spend a few minutes on Step Eleven, thinking about and jotting down a couple of goals: little things that could make a difference in someone else's day, as well as an action I can take that day that could affect the bigger picture. I try to think of something

I can say or do (anonymously) that would make me proud to be a human being. Setting out with a perspective that embraces humility not only gives me peace, but also frees me to bring energy and focus to what I think really matters. It's a great way to start the day!

Appendix C

AN EDA MEMBER WORKS THE STEPS

A brief note on what follows: Please take what you can use and leave the rest. My experience working the Twelve Steps of EDA may not align well with what you have experienced or hope to experience. What I am offering is only a point of reference, not a tutorial or form of instruction. Do not be discouraged. I have always been—and probably always will be—a flawed person. I hope that you will not struggle as I did with what has been correctly described as a "simple program of action." If, however, you *are* struggling with the Steps, perhaps you will find something of your own experience in the following pages. My hope is that you will find courage to keep going, for if I can work the Twelve Steps successfully, surely anyone can do it!

Step One: *We admitted we were powerless over our eating disorders—that our lives had become unmanageable.*

At first, I found the word "powerless" difficult to reconcile with my experience, so getting past semantics was critical for me. So here's how I had to think about it: If my car gets stuck in the sand, it is not without power, and I am not without power, but my power and my car's power are clearly insufficient to get out of the trap. I cannot fool myself; however much power I may have, I need help (people, resources, or both). I live in Arizona, where getting stuck miles from anywhere in the desert means you stick with your car (it provides shade and shelter and is easy to spot from the air). You also hope you were smart enough to have brought a LOT of water with you, and to have told people where you were going and when you would return. If you *are* stuck, you will need help getting out alive, even if you have what my son calls "mad survival skills."

Having an eating disorder is a lot like getting stuck in the desert miles from anywhere; it is an emergency, and you can die. Even if you don't die, you are bound to be scared, lonely, and miserable. Life doesn't have to be like that. I have learned that the quicker I am to recognize when I am stuck, the faster I can get unstuck by taking Step One.

I also had a major problem with the word "unmanageable." It seems that no matter how bad things get, my life never "feels" completely unmanageable. When I first started working the Steps, I had recently graduated from college and was in a stable relationship. That doesn't sound completely unmanageable, does it? But I was doing a lot of behaviors to prevent myself from feeling much of anything at all, my boss had just eliminated my job position (because he was so "done" with me and my defiant attitude), and I was so weak I could barely walk. I was having panic attacks and felt like I was about to pass out a lot of the time. In that condition, trying to find another job was almost impossible. I felt defeated and humiliated and lived in terror that I would pass out behind the wheel of my car and end up killing people. But did my life *feel* unmanageable? No, it did not.

I had to think of it this way: Rational people do not—except perhaps in war and childbearing—knowingly choose to jeopardize their own lives or the lives of others. But I was doing exactly that, every single day, without fail. No matter how many times I made a decision to cease and desist, I was simply unable to stop doing behaviors that were putting me and other people in harm's way. Not one rational person I could think of would knowingly do what I was doing. Even though I did not feel insane, I had to admit my behavior was insane. My life, as I was living it, *was* unmanageable.

These days, I am conscious of when I pick up old patterns, but I am constantly amazed at the new and different ways I can get myself stuck. I don't get stuck all that often, but when I do, I break out my whole Twelve-Step toolkit and start with Step One. Even though my life has never again become as unmanageable as it was before my first Step One, I know that when resentment, fear, or self-pity start to cloud my vision, unmanageability is just around the corner. I am grateful I now recognize that when these emotions start to rise up in me, I have lost my perspective and balance. I need to be still, feel deeply how miserable I have let myself become, and admit defeat. Step One is an admission of defeat, of powerlessness. And it is not as hard for me as it used to be, because now I am confident that a solution lies ahead in the rest of the Steps.

Step Two: *Came to believe that a Power greater than ourselves could restore us to sanity.*

In Step One, I admitted that what I was doing wasn't sane, even if I didn't feel crazy. That was humbling—a good first step—but I still had enormous difficulty with the idea that any external force could "restore" me to "sanity." I struggled mightily until I realized that the same forces that enable life to exist on Earth also allow me to wake up and want to live each day. I found it helpful to think of my "Higher Power" as the creative and life-engendering forces of the natural world. I could trust these without fully understanding them, and there was no question that these forces were more powerful than I was, spanning the universe throughout time.

I got and stayed sober in AA and was initially freed from my eating disorder on the basis of exactly this conception of a Higher Power. Then, after four years of peace and freedom, I turned back to bulimic behaviors to deal with an insanely trivial but persistent emotional provocation. This did not happen overnight. I could see it coming and feverishly worked the Steps to prevent that outcome, but by the time I understood the danger I was in, it was too late. I was caught in a deep and growing resentment that I could not and would not shake.

Soon after the return of my eating disorder, I decided that the idea that I could be freed from my pernicious insanity by "forces of nature" (forces that clearly coexisted with my wretched condition) had been ill-conceived. Nature, after all, permits innocent young creatures to die horrible deaths all the time. Others may argue the point, but there does not seem to be any individual caring presence involved when a lioness slaughters a gazelle to feed herself and her cubs.

In any case, I determined I must try what was working for others who seemed to be more successful in their recoveries. I attempted religious practices: I prayed, I read the Bible, I went to Bible study, I talked to one pastor, and then others. When, after a few years of earnest effort, nothing seemed to take hold, I took a different tack: I attended sweat lodge ceremonies, I started a drumming group, and I took up yoga. Throughout all of this, I prayed daily, asking only for God's will and the power to carry it out. I spent a *decade* working the Steps of AA, mentoring newcomers, trying another Twelve-Step program, and working with a sponsor (through the Steps of that program) to try and achieve abstinence. When that failed, I tried still other programs and self-help groups, different sponsors, different meditations, medication, a treatment center, and different therapists. I am sorry to have to tell you I miserably worked my Step One most days of those ten-plus years, but lasting relief eluded me.

Cut to the chase: I was obviously still quite insane despite my continuous efforts to get well. At the heart of it, I had lost all perspective. When I picked up my eating disorder after four years of peace and freedom, I had broken trust with myself and lost faith in the power of my Higher Power to restore me to sanity. After a decade of trying to badger myself into surrendering to various alternative Higher Powers, I had to admit a new and different kind of defeat. I knew there wasn't anything fundamentally wrong with Twelve-Step programs, though my eating disorder was still present, and I felt hopeless about it. I was still happily sober in AA, and for the most part I had a wonderful life: a husband whom I loved and who loved me, and two healthy, amazing, and delightful children. I had friends and good relationships with my family of origin. How could I still be engaged in an eating disorder when I so desperately needed to be sane, if not for myself, then for the other people in my life?

What was my problem? I was looking in the wrong direction: searching for something "out there" that I could trust to restore me to sanity. But for me, as I think for everyone, *sanity requires taking care of basics first*. Once I discovered this, I felt so stupid, but it is true. Throughout most of those difficult years, except when pregnant and nursing, I did not truly understand what it was to put "first things first." Most of my basic needs were covered, but *I had not really accepted the responsibility for meeting my basic needs was mine and mine alone.* Every person needs water, sleep, food, shelter, clothes, and primary relationships. Every person needs to feel safe. Well, I wasn't exactly creating a safe environment for myself. As long as I was not taking full responsibility for getting my needs met, I was doomed in working Step Two because I was unable to trust. Once I realized this and took action to deliberately address the gaps, things began to turn around. I began to make real progress in my ED recovery. When EDA members say recovery is a process, not an event, they are not joking! It took the better part of a year for me to say goodbye to my eating-disordered behaviors, and for several years there were regular reminders when I failed to pay sufficient attention to basics or to working my Steps.

So, what about Step Two? What about "came to believe that a Power greater than ourselves could restore us to sanity?" My Higher Power has to be a force I can believe in for all time and it has to be a power that can restore me to sanity. For most people in EDA, perspective and balance come directly from their connection to God—a God of their own understanding. As someone honestly lacking any innate concept of God, this approach just did not work for me. To this day, I have not been able to achieve anything like the spiritual connection to a personal God that others in recovery enjoy. I had to find a different way and I discovered it wasn't that hard.

I had been sober in AA all along and was limping along in my eating disorder recovery, because I was (mostly) already living in surrender to a higher purpose: *service to the greater good.* When I realized this concept of a "higher purpose" was actually working for me and could serve as a solid foundation for my recovery, I felt indescribable relief and hope. *My truth set me free.*

I no longer struggle with the old behaviors as long as I continue to make a daily commitment to, and practice of, working to serve the greater good. This work brings me both peace and perspective. I still believe in the power of a life-engendering creative force that pervades the universe, that enables me to wake up and want to live each day, that brought me into early recovery thirty years ago. But the power that gives me perspective to "keep calm and carry on" is the power of surrender to the principles of truth, equality, justice, and love, and to the process of equipping myself to be of useful service to the greater good: a higher purpose.

Step Three: *Made a decision to turn our will and our lives over to the care of God* as we understood God.

I was scared of Step Three at first, because it seemed to require me to somehow give myself up, abandon myself, and become less than I was—or thought I was. In any case I wasn't really sure I understood what it meant. What was "my will?" What was "my life?" What was "the care of God?" And what did it mean to "turn over?" When I asked these questions in meetings, I learned that "our will" meant our thoughts and "our lives" meant our actions. I also heard that "G.O.D." could mean "Good Orderly Direction." I learned that "to turn over" meant something like "to hand over" and "to let go."

Back in Step Two, I trusted in a fundamental healing power and a higher purpose that had the capacity to restore me to sanity. In Step Three, I decided to let God (reliance on a higher purpose) guide my thoughts and actions. I realized I wasn't fundamentally "giving myself up" to anything I didn't believe in or fully trust. *I was giving up on what hadn't worked, and giving in to sound principles, logic, and reason I could trust.* In Twelve-Step programs, one often hears the first three steps interpreted as "I can't, God can, and I think I'll let Him." I struggled mightily with that slogan, but the basic idea—that my old ways didn't work and other ways did, and that I'd better trust the ideas that work *for me*—well, that really *did* and *does* work.

When I first took Step Three, I barely understood it, but working the rest of the Steps illuminated it for me. By letting go of "my way," I was opening myself up to a happy and purposeful life of love and service that "my way" had not previously permitted. I have never regretted that decision! Today, I turn back to Step Three whenever I realize I am struggling to impose "my way" on others or even on myself; I know how that story turns out, and it isn't pretty. These days I want a new story—one with a less predictable ending. When I am doing my best to take care of myself and serve others, I can be happy regardless of my current circumstances. Today, I am joyous and free in my recovery. I am fully and gratefully surrendered to the ideal of serving a higher purpose. I can maintain recovery easily, without struggle, because I am here to serve something greater than myself. This puts my life into perspective and makes it possible for me to care for myself, which I must do to be as aware and effective as possible.

Step Four: *Made a searching and fearless moral inventory of ourselves* (and)

Step Five: *Admitted to God, to ourselves, and to another human being the exact nature of our wrongs.*

My first 4th Step was a simple list of everything I had done wrong up to that point: the things I stole, the lies I told, and the miserable way I had treated people. As soon as I understood that I needed to tell someone all this in order to stay sober, I confided in a friend from my AA meetings. I was unhesitating and as thorough as I could possibly be. These were perfectly effective 4th and 5th Steps that kept me sane and sober for a long time, even though my inventory took only minutes to compile and not much longer to tell. I left my first 5th Step feeling accomplished, connected to the program and to the person I had talked with, and at peace with myself. After a few more months in AA, I started to wonder if I had done my 4th and 5th Steps "correctly," as I had not followed the prescription laid out in the "Big Book."[6] I vowed to "do it right" the next time.

My second 4th Step, however, was done under duress. I had developed resentment against a co-worker whom I felt was getting attention that should have gone to me. I was plunging headfirst into that toxic combination of resentment and self-pity that seemed to presage every slide back into my old behaviors. I filled three journals, trying again and again to "get it right," because I knew my sanity, sobriety, and peace with food were all at stake. First, I followed an "official" 4th Step Guide, and then I tried to follow the format set out in the "Big Book"[7] where I listed (for each resentment) whom I was upset with, the cause, what was threatened in each situation, and where I had been selfish, dishonest, self-seeking, and/or frightened. I listed my fears and why I had them. I created a guilt and sex inventory where I listed (for each person) where I had been selfish, dishonest, and/or inconsiderate; who had been hurt; where I had unjustifiably aroused jealousy, suspicion, and/or bitterness; and what I should have done instead if I had been at fault in any way.

When I reached the point where I had written all I could and was "ready" to take the 5th Step, I was so filled with emotional pain that I was completely unable to hear the gist of what my sponsor (upon suffering through my interminable 5th Step) was telling me. I thought admitting the exact nature of my wrongs would set everything right again. But my expectations were out of line. *A 5th Step only "works" if we take responsibility for our thoughts and actions.* It does no good to admit what we did, only to blame something or someone else for our actions.

After that second 5th Step, I felt indescribably horrible, as though the program had failed me, and I had failed the program. *What the heck was wrong with me?* Was I one of those people who are "constitutionally incapable of being honest with themselves"[8] and thus incapable of benefiting from the Twelve-Step process? Overwhelmed by anger, shame, and fear, it wasn't long before I returned to bingeing and purging.

In those long years before EDA, I continued attending AA meetings and eventually got honest with people about what I was doing. I was directed to other programs that were available at the time. I dutifully went to A LOT of Twelve-Step meetings, trying every version of abstinence I could in an attempt to arrest a return to full-blown bulimia. Finally, after three more failed attempts at Steps Four and Five, the person hearing my 5th Step grabbed my shoulders and practically yelled at me, "Stop playing the victim!" *Why had I not heard that before?* Others, earlier, had surely said something like this to me, but somehow I did not fully

---

[8] Ibid., 58.

understand what they were talking about. I certainly never *thought* of myself as a victim! But on closer inspection, I could see I was dramatically affected by what other people said and did. I did, in fact, feel victimized.

I left that 5th Step meeting feeling stupid and hopelessly stuck. Although angry that "the program" had left me in the dark for so long, I also saw that the issue was with me, not with the program or the people in the program. *There was hope*. Once again, reluctantly and miserably, I started over with Step One. But now I was on more solid footing. My next 4th Step looked at why so many of my waking hours were spent reacting to life, what was wrong about my reactions, and why I was avoiding taking deliberate action when I could. I was finally starting to ask myself—sometimes hourly—why I felt like a victim and what I was going to do about it. I had long understood that everything I *did* was my free choice, whether I knew it or not, but I hadn't really considered that *what I chose to think was my free choice,* as well. When I gave my next 5th Step, I again found that incredibly powerful feeling of being one with all humanity, finding deep joy and delight in the knowledge that everything was going to be all right—whatever happened.

Step Six: *Were entirely ready to have God remove all these defects of character.*

With my very first Step One, I began to accept myself for who I really was. At that point I was an alcoholic and a bulimic with a riot of uncontrolled emotions. With Steps Two and Three, I committed myself to follow a program of action I trusted, having faith this could change everything so long as I was taking care of getting my basic needs met. With Steps Four and Five, I began to recognize my responsibility for my actions and understand the damage I had caused. Fear, pride, selfishness, stubbornness, and anger always crop up in my 4th and 5th Steps, as do self-pity and resentment. Step Six reminds me that I cannot "fix" my character defects directly; that would be like performing brain surgery on myself.

By the time I am done with my 5th Step, I am usually quite ready to be done with my defects and the damage I do as a result of hanging onto them. Step Six is about being entirely ready to have God remove all these defects of character. For me, this just means I am entirely ready to recognize that *my shortcomings get in the way of service to a higher purpose.* I cannot serve the greater good or those around me very well if I am all caught up in my own self-centered ideas about how things ought to be. My efforts to understand and contribute to the flow of life will be crippled if I am wallowing in anger or self-pity. I have to get rid of these, and I cannot do it by focusing on anger or self-pity: I have to take care of basics, and focus on service to the greater good. This is when I find relief from my defects!

The Twelve-Step approach provides a way to live a wonderfully useful life. I trust that as long as I work my program, completely and without reservation, there is no need to engage in any of my defects of character. When I do engage in them, my daily practice of Step Ten helps me set right the wrongs. As a result, they gradually become smaller and fewer, at least until something new comes up that reminds me how very, very human I am. When this happens, I am grateful to know that right feelings will eventually follow right action. I am grateful that I have the opportunity to choose to think, and then act, differently in each situation that formerly caused pain and suffering. Step Six lets me move ahead with remedial action while eliminating unnecessary and harmful hand-wringing and self-judgment.

Step Seven: *Humbly asked God to remove our shortcomings.*

When I first started working the Steps and got to this point, I was overcome with relief at being sober and happy, and amazed to be completely free of any bulimic behavior. I was so grateful that the Twelve-Step process (my idea of Higher Power at that point) had restored me to sanity. I followed directions. I humbly thanked AA for enabling me to live, asked for continued help and strength to stay sober and sane with food, and launched into Step Eight. That approach worked marvelously for my first four years. The gratitude and humility I felt were sincere, and I was healthy.

My next several times through the Steps, worked while I was intermittently active in my eating disorder, were almost comical. I went through the motions, trying hard to be humble and grateful, but believing little and feeling almost nothing—except a deep longing for the peace I had once enjoyed and frustration at not being able to find it. Knowing I needed to work the remaining Steps, I did my best and moved on. This was a mistake.

In Step Two, I agreed that my Higher Power had the ability to relieve my insanity, but in Step Seven, I found I could not find faith that my Higher Power would remove my shortcomings so long as I was active in my eating disorder. Turns out, my real issue was way back in Step Two, but it was on Step Seven that I regularly got stuck.

Eventually, I learned I couldn't be humble or grateful until I achieved a basic level of safety, trust, and security. Today, I am willing to do the hard work of taking care of myself as best I can, even when miserable, disappointed, frustrated, and hopeless. *If I do the work to keep myself safe regardless of how I feel, I regain humility and gratitude and can turn my attention to what really matters.* It is that simple. I take care of basics[9] as doing so makes taking care of everything else possible. I do it so I can be of service to others. I do not have a relationship with a God or Higher Power that can remove my shortcomings, but when I focus on humble service to the greater good, my defects based on selfish desires get very little play. It is not that I do not *have* deficiencies; it is that I do not have to exercise them. And when I do not exercise them, I am free: it is as if they are removed, at least for a while. I find that the longer I can live without my defects, the more unappealing they are, and the more grateful I am that they are gone.

Frankly, I try not to worry too much about my shortcomings or those of others; such concerns lead me right back to self-pity and resentment. Today, I have faith that if I take care of my own basic needs and do my level best every day to make myself cheerfully useful to family, friends, work, and community, I need not worry about my shortcomings. Today, I am in awe of how much my life has changed. Nothing miraculous has eliminated my fears and angers. I still experience them, but today I am convinced I have everything I need to live in peace and freedom. And, as I focus more on what we are all doing right, instead of belaboring what is wrong, the more correct and hopeful everything seems to be.

---

[9] Reference Appendix B: "A Perspective on Balance" in this volume.

Step Eight: *Made a list of all persons we had harmed and became willing to make amends to them all.*

My first 8th Step list was very short. It included the owner of a car I had sideswiped, the owners of a store from which I had (repeatedly) stolen, three former roommates, my parents, and all of my former boyfriends. I didn't even *think* of my current boyfriend, my sister, employers, or any of my friends. My next 8th Step list—one that came out of a 4th Step where I had tried to "do it right" and failed—included over 120 people, most of whom I felt, at best, ambivalent about. In no way did I want to make amends to all these people! As things turned out, I really did not have to: my sponsor reminded me that I was to focus on the top ten first: the co-worker with whom I'd had that resentment, my ex-husband, my current husband, a former employer, a former friend, a client, a former sponsor, and two former roommates to whom I had never made amends. I did not have to become willing all at once, as I had done (easily) the first time through. This time, I had to take each situation and person independently. This approach to Step Eight really worked for me.

In recent years when I work Step Eight, I focus on just one person at a time from the current top ten on my list. When quiet and alone, I think long and hard about their situation and challenges. I try to imagine their pains and fears and how my own attitudes and actions have contributed to their burden. I earnestly wish them happiness, peace, and freedom with all the heart I can muster. I try to think of things I can do that would be kind or helpful if done anonymously. I must admit, I find this step hardest to do with those closest to me: it can be really hard to wish someone profound and abundant joy when I am hurt and disappointed. Nevertheless, I try to imagine that whatever they urgently need is being supplied, and that they are able to move forward with a clear mind and an untroubled heart, knowing they are much loved and needed. When I feel at peace with my willingness to set right my wrongs, I move immediately to Step Nine.

Step Nine: *Made direct amends to such people wherever possible, except when to do so would injure them or others.*

My first 9th Step really scared me. I didn't have any idea how to make amends. I had barely ever apologized to anyone about anything in my life. I also knew that some of the amends would be really big, expensive, and humiliating. Finding the person who owned the parked car I'd sideswiped proved impossible. I thought I knew when and where the incident had occurred and what type of car I had hit, but my search of police records revealed nothing. I talked with my sponsor about the situation, and she suggested determining the amount of money the repair would have cost and donating the money to M.A.D.D. (Mothers Against Drunk Drivers). After talking the situation over with my husband (since he would be affected by the loss of income), I did exactly that.

The store from which I had stolen had been bought out by another chain. Again, I was unsure how to proceed. My sponsor suggested figuring the monetary value of what I had taken, contacting the current store managers (who might be the same people), and asking them for guidance on how to repay the debt. This was embarrassing and difficult. I would much rather have just sent a money order to a corporate office somewhere, but I did as my sponsor suggested. I spoke with a store manager, who thoughtfully suggested I donate to a charity he thought the former owners would have cared about. I gratefully did so. For the room-mates, I made an effort to see each in person, but they had scattered. I wrote short, sincere letters of apology and sent one to the last known address that I was able to find. I never found addresses for the rest. I was only able to find one former boyfriend. I met him over coffee and apologized for putting him and his interests in jeopardy, for creating chaos in his life, and for failing to be the trustworthy friend and partner he deserved. This was one of my hardest amends, since I no longer had a relationship with this fellow and really did not want one. I did not think I owed him any money, but I certainly did owe him an apology: I had been awful. I suspected my apology was not likely to be accepted gracefully, and in truth it was not. I felt even sadder about my behavior than before we sat down, but I also felt cleaner and more accomplished for having undertaken this difficult encounter.

Apologizing to my parents was also hard, but less dif-ficult than I thought it would be. Before talking with my sponsor, I had thought I was going to have to atone for each time I had disappointed and hurt my parents, but this was not the case. A detailed litany could only have hurt them more. I was to stick to those activities they knew about or suspected, and focus primarily on how I intended to straighten things out with them. My main hope was to be as humble as possible and to accept anything they had to say graciously, without judgment or defensiveness. I sat down with my folks at the next opportunity and explained what I was about to do. My father did not want to hear me out. He told me to talk to my mother and left us sitting at the table. That hurt, but I went ahead with my Mom. She was understanding and far more gracious than I could have imagined possible. After that talk, I resolved never to lie to or evade contact with my parents ever again. I was really lucky I still had them, and for perhaps the first time I *felt* lucky, too. In time, I tried again with my father, who stopped me at the second sentence and said, "Apology accepted. I don't want to hear any more about it." I won't lie: it still hurt, but I was grateful.

Since my first 9th Step, I have had to make amends (and am still making amends) that were far harder and more complex, but in each case I have learned to review my plan with someone before acting, to keep apologies short and simple, to define a plan for restitution I am confident I can keep, and to expect nothing in return. A great burden is lifted when I am able to admit my wrongs sincerely without blaming anyone, and I feel hopeful and happy to be free of self-pity and resentment, for that is exactly what happens! Accountability has set me free.

Step Ten: *Continued to take personal inventory and when we were wrong, promptly admitted it.*

It is often said that Steps Ten through Twelve are the "maintenance" Steps. That makes them sound easy, and they do almost seem effortless after working Steps One through Nine. But when Steps Ten, Eleven, and Twelve become drudgery and a chore, it is time for me to formally work *all* the Steps again.

In EDA, working all the Steps is essential in establishing balance. That said, Steps Ten through Twelve are the most critical in *maintaining* balance. With Step Ten, I spend about twenty to thirty minutes each day reviewing the prior day and planning the day ahead. For me, writing things down in the morning works best, though I know many people complete their Step Ten work at night.

I start by outlining the major events of the past twenty-four hours. Then, I list both the issues that came up over the past day and any that I anticipate in the course of the day ahead. If I have determined what to do about an issue, I write that down, too. This is similar to the part of the 4th Step where we ask ourselves what we should think and do instead of reacting out of fear, pride, selfishness, and anger. If I have hurt someone and haven't properly apologized, I make a plan to right the wrong. When I have been wrong in other correctable ways, I make a plan to correct the deficiencies. When really upset, I find it helpful to list out all the columns from the 4th Step Inventory: the source, the reason, what is affected or threatened, my part, and my resolution. Otherwise I let the issues go, knowing that I will soon focus on making the most of the day.

I do not dwell on things. Reflection is an excellent practice, but rumination is not. I gave up my character defects in Step Seven; my job each day is to recognize how my issues reflect my character defects and let them go, so I can focus on character-building activities instead.

Next, I write down what I am grateful for that day. By the time I am done, I am often overwhelmed by love. I am so grateful for my family, for EDA, for recovery, for my friends, and for my co-workers. Sometimes I cry, which would have seemed weird to me a few years ago, but I am not ashamed. I am sincerely grateful to be able to think and feel clearly. I have so much for which to be grateful that I will never run out of things to write! Finally, I list out my goals for the day—whatever comes to mind. I have a separate process for managing daily tasks, so the goal-writing is not intended to be task-oriented (although sometimes tasks creep in edgewise). I try to be specific: committing to say something kind to a person who is often ill tempered, staying out of the fray of some particular office maneuverings, or connecting with someone who may be feeling lonely. Often, my goals include quick and easy slogans one hears in Twelve-Step programs: "First Things First," "One Thing at A Time," "Easy Does It," "Act, Don't React."

My Step Ten practice has evolved over the years, but is in no way "perfect." Although my reflection on my issues is never complete and my Step Ten never really feels "thorough," I am happy and comfortable with my approach. It is good enough. My best advice for those starting out on Step Ten is to do what feels right, do the best you can, and be open to change. You will change over the years, and your Step Ten process will likely change, too.

Alas, so far we have covered only the first part of Step Ten: there is more to go! The heart of this Step is about addressing hot emotions and missteps we take in the course of daily life.

When I am really agitated about something in the course of the day, I desperately need perspective. Journaling is a good option, but is usually not convenient when things feel like they are breaking all around me. I require a clearer head for journaling than I am likely to have under challenging circumstances. If I am at home, I try to get outside and do something that calms me down, or I try to nap. It is amazing what a good nap will do! If at work, I make the rounds, looking for ways to help and encourage people. I set aside whatever hurt or fear I am feeling and focus on what I can do that is useful. I know I will address my emotional upset when in a setting where I can be safe, because it is dangerous to avoid dealing with hot emotions for very long. However, if I have done something wrong, I find it is best to address the error as soon as possible to prevent making a bad situation worse. Sometimes, I really do make things worse, but I don't worry too much about it. I just keep trying to do the next right thing and hope I learn from my mistakes.

Whenever things go sideways, I usually find that my expectations have been thwarted in some way and I have to examine why I have these expectations. I find I often think other people should want the same things I do, but they do not. Sometimes I don't even realize I have unspoken expectations—until they aren't met. At other times I know I have them, but don't think I should have to express them, which is silly. Or I am embarrassed to express them, which frequently points to unreasonableness on my part. Sometimes, my expectations are rational and clearly expressed, but I don't always get what I want. I can even get more upset when the very person who has just disappointed me has the temerity to be disrespectful as well! When that happens, I usually discover that I became judgmental and critical as a result of some disappointment; I can behave badly without even recognizing it. Even now, at thirty years sober and with many years of solid recovery from my eating disorder, I catch myself trying to "direct the show," which can be exasperating. But at least I know what is the matter and what to do about it.

Much of the time, however, my expectations and disappointments are entirely internal. Maybe I was not amusing enough, inquisitive enough, or polite enough in conversation with others. Often, I don't accomplish all the goals and tasks I set for myself in any given twenty-four hour period. Maybe I evaded something important or took offense when I should have laughed. In each case, I have to ask myself, *What am I willing to do?* Sometimes the answers are obvious, and I need to take action promptly. Sometimes just acknowledging my feelings and moving on is best.

When I am making the daily effort to "name it, claim it, and dump it," and something comes up repeatedly, Step

Ten gives me the option to make a plan to do things differently. I can then see how each alternative works out, or I can keep doing the same thing. I know resentment and self-pity are waiting patiently for such an opportunity, so I usually make an effort to change my thinking and behavior.

Part of Step Ten is to continue to take personal inventory, *not only of what is wrong, but also what is right.* I do this for myself throughout the day, which is a wonderful boon to gratitude and to my recovery. It is really quite a useful practice! The more comfortable I become with what is going right with me, the more compassion I find I have for others. When I focus and comment on what others are doing well, the happier and more purposeful everyone seems to be.

Step Eleven: *Sought through prayer and meditation to improve our conscious contact with God as we understood God, praying only for knowledge of God's will for us and the power to carry that out.*

While Step Ten is like taking a daily dose of Steps Four through Nine, Step Eleven builds on Steps Three, Six, and Seven. I surrender to the principles in which I have faith, knowing that my commitment to serve a higher purpose means I need to clean up my act without any hand-wringing about my defects of character. I renew my commitment to serve as best I can for the current day. I do this every day—or nearly every day—after my 10th Step journaling.

Step Eleven reminds me daily that my life is not all about me—which is a good thing! This perspective helps me move past my ups and downs to why I am here at all. The "Big Book" of AA, *Alcoholics Anonymous,* states on page 77 that, "Our primary purpose is to fit ourselves to be of maximum service to God and our fellows." I believe that everything I experience in life helps prepare me to be of better and more useful service, provided I let go of my expectations and allow myself to be shaped and molded into something better than I was before. I surrender to this process every day, looking for what is good and right about the people I live and work with, and what is good and right about how I choose to respond to whatever comes up. I am often somewhat (and sometimes very) disappointed in myself and others, but this does not diminish my faith in the process or my commitment to serving a greater purpose.

In my search for truth and meaning, I have found much that is good and right, delightful and awe-inspiring. My conscious contact with my Higher Power/higher purpose is my daily commitment to do my best to be of useful service to others, and to seek truth, justice, fairness, and equality for all. I am profoundly grateful for the opportunity, even when it frightens me. I know I am safe from the ravages of the hideous "four horsemen" described on page 151 of *Alcoholics Anonymous (4th edition)*—Terror, Bewilderment, Frustration and Despair—so long as I maintain this daily commitment.

Step Twelve: *Having had a spiritual awakening as the result of these steps, we tried to carry this message to others, and to practice these principles in all our affairs.*

I have never been a spiritual person, and my awakening has not been of a spiritual nature. As one of my sponsors in another Twelve-Step program, Tessie, was fond of saying about herself, "My spiritual awakening is that I am not a spiritual person." You can see why I asked her to sponsor me! All the same, as a result of working the Steps of EDA, my life has been transformed. I am genuinely happy. I am solid in my recovery from my eating disorder and I am solid in my recovery, period. I have had an awakening to a truth, happiness, and freedom I never knew existed.

I get a daily reprieve from my eating disorder, contingent on my daily practice of reliance on my higher purpose to provide peace and perspective. Perspective, developed through working the Steps, makes dealing with my issues much more rewarding than running from them. When I turn my will and my life over to serving the greater good, I can more readily see my day-to-day issues for what they really are:

- *impediments* to fully serving others in the here and now

- *reminders* of my humanity

- *signals* that I am neglecting something that needs to be dealt with first

- *challenges* to my commitment to place service to the greater good ahead of my self-generated emotional states

- *opportunities* to build bridges of empathy and understanding with others who suffer the same issues

- *means* through which I grow more resilient, strong, and flexible in my recovery

I know from experience that I am perfectly capable of "falling asleep at the wheel" when I do not work the Steps on a daily basis. I am also still capable of lapses into self-pity, resentment, and fear whenever I fail to remind myself of who

I am, where I came from, and what I am here to do. *Step Twelve provides me an easy way to be reminded: I can share my experience, strength, and hope with others.* Perhaps they will be able to take something useful from my story and insights, perhaps not. But in any case, I do my level best to turn my most awful experiences to good purpose. In working with sponsees, I get deep satisfaction from establishing authentic bonds with other human beings based on the truths of our lives. Often these bonds turn into durable connections with people who inspire me with their warmth, compassion, energy, and determination to "do the next right thing," no matter what. I am humbled and awed by what simple reliance on a higher purpose can do, and I am intensely grateful to feel connected to so many amazing people.

Although I am far from perfect and sometimes doubt that I am a great role model for working the Steps, I am amazed at the difference between how I felt about my life before recovery and how I feel about it now. Today, practicing the principles of the program in everything I do—however imperfectly—makes it possible for me to be in recovery and continue to carry a message of hope for others like me. If I can make service to the greater good more important than my personal desires—one day at a time—anyone can.

Thanks to the honesty, open-mindedness, and willingness of AA and EDA members, and to the simplicity of these programs, I am free at last. I am happy and grateful to have the opportunity to help carry the message of recovery to those who still suffer and to practice the principles of the Twelve Steps of EDA in all my affairs.

I sincerely hope that everyone who wants to recover from an eating disorder has the opportunity I have had. May you find peace, freedom, and joy!

Appendix D

EXAMPLE 4TH STEP INVENTORY

Resentment: people and institutions that made or make me angry

Source	Reason/Cause	At Risk/Affects My
My spouse	Judges me. Makes me feel inadequate. Is losing patience with my issues. I resent him/her for how I feel about myself.	Love and intimacy, self-esteem, family relationships (I experience fear, anger)
My spouse	Wants more variety in sex. I am frightened he/she will look elsewhere. I resent feeling like I am not enough.	Love and intimacy, self-esteem, family relationships (I experience fear, anger)
My child	Won't follow directions or accept guidance. Doesn't appreciate me. Acts like he/she hates me. Hurts my feelings. I don't want to be angry but I am.	Fear, self-esteem (pride), family relationships, ambition for others (I am scared for him/her, and I feel hurt, anguish, despair)
The person who molested me	Destroyed my trust in self and others. Affected how I see myself and my place in the world. Damaged my self-esteem and understanding of sex.	Love and intimacy, self-esteem, family relationships (I experience fear, anger)

My Error/My Part	Resolution
Fear and selfishness: I've not been a good partner in many respects. My expectations may be out of line. I need to focus on what I can do, instead of on what he/she is or isn't doing.	Focus on what I can do, instead of what he/she does. Seek the peace and power to be the partner my spouse needs. Admit my mistakes and fix them promptly.
Fear of losing what I have and selfishness: of course I will feel inadequate if I am not agreeing to legitimate and reasonable requests. Why feel so vulnerable (afraid)? What would make me feel safe? Where is my sense of adventure?	Seek the peace and power to address inhibitions (fear). Outside counseling might be appropriate if reasonable requests seem impossible. Fears exist for a reason, and need to be addressed calmly. Be authentic. Make time for love and play. Find the good and the humorous.
Fear for him/her, and also dishonesty: blaming my child for my emotional state. I need to be the adult. Selfishness: I am not seeing life through his/her eyes because I want him/her to see things my way. My child is hurt by my rejection of his/her point of view.	Get outside help. Seek the peace and power to let go of the negative feelings that stand in the way of being useful to him/her. Understand and empathize with his/her views. Be grateful for what is right. Find the positive. Talk to friends. Be the parent he/she needs. Set reasonable expectations.
Blaming my current attitudes and limitations on damage suffered long ago. Failing to take responsibility for my recovery. I was a victim, but I do not need to stay one.	Consider discussing the situation with authorities: use anger to serve the greater good and work to protect others, especially if there is still risk of harm to children or others. Amends can be made to those who have been silenced by abuse, rather than to the abuser, since amends made to an abuser may be taken as condoning the abuse.

Fear: things that frightened or still frighten me

Source	Reason/Cause	At Risk/Affects My
Death	I don't feel done with life yet. Others depend upon me.	Life itself
Abandonment	I think my family and friends may desert me.	Self-esteem, family relationships
Self-betrayal/ Loss of self	I have failed myself so many times.	Peace, freedom, happiness, purpose
Gaining (or losing) weight	I think if I eat whatever I want I will gain (or lose) an excessive amount of weight. It has happened before!	Self-esteem, ability to work program, health, life, sexual and other relationships
Sexual intimacy and/ or overactive sex drive (loss of control)	Sometimes I don't even like being with myself. At other times, I worry that my life might turn into a hedonistic nightmare: I might injure those I love.	Self-esteem, integrity, relationships with others

My Error/My Part	Resolution
Selfishness: Not making the most of the time I have here. Not being grateful for the opportunity to make a positive difference.	Seek a perspective that will help me take care of myself: rest, eat, drive safely, and do the right things. Act with love.
Dishonesty (drama and hand-wringing): I can only control what I do, not what happens to me. Worrying instead of being useful.	Ensure that I do not abandon them. I cannot control whether anyone else abandons me.
If this happens, it will be because I have lost perspective. The more I practice a positive perspective the stronger I will be.	Keep working the Steps and daily practices to create and maintain a calm outlook and balanced perspective.
Lack of trust in myself, my body, and my God, Higher Power or higher purpose: I know my body may not be perfect, but I realize it is working hard to keep me healthy.	I will trust that keeping my emotional life free of obstacles (so I can better serve my Higher Power/higher purpose) enables me to find and keep in balance with food. I will trust that my body will let me know what it needs, and I will listen to it without fear, judgment, or second-guessing. I will live authentically.
Dishonesty: Basic human needs include physical intimacy and release. Restriction and rigidity are hallmarks of fear: signs of that I do not trust my Higher Power/higher purpose to keep me (and those I love) safe.	As I continue to live up to my Step 3 commitment, I will lose my fear of self and others. It is important to my health that I can be safe in, and enjoy, intimate relationships. I can behave with integrity and authenticity without harming anyone.

Fear: things that frightened or still frighten me (continued)

Source	Reason/Cause	At Risk/Affects My
Exercise (either too much or too little)	I have hurt myself before. Now I am concerned that I may go too far in the other direction. It is confusing!	Self-esteem, ability to work program, health, life, relationships with others
Letting go of my eating disorder/ loss of control	I think if I let go of my eating disorder, my whole life may run amok. What will I do with all those unmanageable emotions? I might injure myself, or others, in novel and horrifying ways. At least the eating disorder is "safe." I want to feel in control. It does not feel safe to let go of control.	Self-esteem, ability to work the program of EDA, health, life, financial security, sexual and other relationships
Letting go of excess food	I am scared that I will be miserable if I have to restrict my food to recover. I have always been miserable when I try to eat healthily. I don't want to be miserable.	Hope of recovery, willingness and ability to work the program of EDA, self-esteem, health, life, relationships

My Error/My Part	Resolution
Dishonesty: Basic human needs include physical exercise. Excess exercise and exercise avoidance both signal that I need more perspective to guide my thinking.	Listen to my body and talk with medical professionals to define a sane approach to exercise. Watch out for rigidity. Focus on service.
Dishonesty: Although I may feel in control, I know it is an illusion. My eating disorder is not safe at all, and I now trust that if I follow the suggestions and examples of people in recovery, *I can be free and safe.* If I choose to follow suggestions, I am still in the driver's seat. I may be surrendering to a new perspective, but I am the only one who can do this. The choice is mine alone, and I can choose to return to my eating disorder any time it looks like a better option than recovery.	I resolve to rely on the bigger picture (Higher Power/higher purpose) to provide context for my life and my struggles, so that they do not overwhelm me. I know I can turn to the peace that my new perspective brings at any time; it is with me always and can remove my fear of mismanaging my food, weight, body, relationships, work, and life. I can tell the truth, live my truth, and let go of the outcomes.
Dishonesty: I am already miserable! Life is better without having an eating disorder. I can see that in people who have recovered. I can find comfort, soothing, and safety in food, when I know I can find comfort, soothing, and safety in reliance on a Higher Power/higher purpose. Also, I know I do not have to "restrict"—I can eat whatever I want, whenever I want, so long as I *eat only when hungry, and stop when moderately full.*	Even though I am frightened, and I know there will be a transitional period that will be difficult while I am learning to what to do to stay safe, I made a decision to take the Twelve Steps, because *I want to be free.* I am willing to go through being miserable for a while if it means I get to live in peace and freedom. I want to be happy. And I can be happy. Excess food does not make me happy in the long run.

Self-pity: reasons I felt or feel sorry for myself

Source	Reason/Cause	At Risk/Affects My
Lousy role models	Don't like—but feel doomed to repeat—patterns from family of origin. Same with spouse: his/her examples are no better.	Self-esteem, family relationships (I feel fear)
Health	Impacts from past behaviors now limit what I can do physically.	Ambition, pride, self-esteem, family and social relationships (I feel remorse)
Burden of past	I have so much to make up for, I don't think I'll ever feel like a good parent or spouse.	Self-esteem, love and intimacy, family relationships (I feel remorse)
Crappy job	I don't like my job but I need it.	Self-esteem, pride, finances, ambition, family relationships (I feel anger, fear)
Feel like a terrible parent	My kids don't confide in me very much.	Self-esteem (pride), ambition to be an excellent mother/father, family relationships

My Error/My Part	Resolution
Fear: Hand-wringing instead of action. My actions are the product of my thinking and my choices. These are not written in my genes.	Remember no one is doomed to repeat the past. Every day is an opportunity to change everything. Act deliberately, not from fear.
Fear: Focusing on, and worrying about, "what is not" instead of being grateful for "what is." Hand-wringing.	Remember none of us get out alive, and many "normal" people have health issues. Be grateful for what I have, instead of worrying about what I lack.
Fear and losing perspective: worrying about how I will feel, instead of concentrating on and seeking power to do what I need to do.	Rely more on greater purpose, and focus on today. Be of cheerful service. Be grateful for what I have. Find the positive in everyone.
Self-seeking: Instead of making the most of what I have, I complain about what I don't have.	Look for new job opportunities. Consider additional training. Make the most of what I have. Be the best I can be given the current circumstances. Work on finding the good and the humorous.
Self-seeking: Thinking my kids need to behave in any specific way for me to feel validated as a parent. Dishonesty/drama: I have done a lot wrong, but I am the best parent I know how to be.	Keep working the Steps and look for ways to build and maintain calm and balanced perspective. Be the parent I would have wanted and the parent they need.

Shame: things for which I felt or feel ashamed, though I am not responsible for them

Be sure to include situations where you were bullied or abused, and anything for which you felt or feel embarrassed such as: childhood poverty, your personality (i.e. too introverted/extroverted), your gender, race, ethnicity, sexual orientation, or other people's problems.

Source	Reason/Cause	At Risk/ Affects My
The rape	I did not "ask for it" and I did not deserve it, but I still feel dirty and ashamed at times.	Love and intimacy, self-esteem, trust (I experience fear, anger, revulsion)
My children	Poor performance in school and in social relationships. I feel at fault even though I have done everything I could to help them.	Self-esteem, family relationships, social relationships, pride
My sexual orientation	Sometimes the voice in my head echoes the judgment I hear from others. I experience sadness and pain.	Emotional and financial security, self-esteem, social relationships
My ethnicity	I feel excluded/ discriminated against because of my ethnicity.	Self-esteem, pride, social relationships

My Error/My Part	Resolution
Fear: Thinking that I am fundamentally different from others who have been spared this experience. Failing to forgive myself for lapsing into victimhood occasionally, and for not taking full responsibility for my recovery.	Expect that I will still feel trauma at times. Use my experience to help others. Find my voice and advocate for victims' rights.
Selfishness: expecting validation through my children. Fear: Worrying, instead of resolving to do what I can to help them. Worrying too much, period; there is only so much I can do. And actually they are fine, probably more graceful than I was at their ages.	Love them exactly as they are. Continue to focus on what is right. Support them because this isn't about me! Seek counseling for them and for myself if others see issues.
Fear: Thinking ill of myself and others just because key people in my life were unreasonable and judgmental, not because there is anything fundamentally wrong.	Seek the peace and perspective that allows me to accept life on life's terms. I cannot change who I am and I cannot change what others think, but I can change my own judgmental and critical thinking.
Fear: Worrying about how I feel instead of what I can do to change the here and now for the better.	No one is doomed by association. Be the best person I can be. Find the courage to fight for peace and justice.

Guilt: wrongs I have done or am doing to others

Be sure to include lies, cheating (including infidelity), theft (including non-payment of taxes), property damage, and any emotional or physical damage done to others.

Source	Reason/Cause	At Risk/ Affects My
Spouse	I don't prioritize time with him/her. He/she suffers and feels un-loved. I blamed him/her for my emotional states.	Love and intimacy (I feel fear), family relationships, spouse's emotional health
Children	I judge them harshly and overreact to fears regarding what they do and don't do. I set a bad example. I lose my temper. I yell. I whine and complain. I with-draw. I do the wrong things. I blame them for my emotional states.	Children's health, fam-ily relationships, my self-esteem
Ex-spouse	I cheated on him/her, and then did not honor a renewed com-mitment to respect our marriage vows once he/she knew of the affair.	Love and intimacy (I feel fear), self-trust, trust with current spouse

My Error/My Part	Resolution
Fear and selfishness, drama: All-or-nothing thinking. Expecting that if I spend time with my spouse he/she will come to demand it, and I will not feel good about myself because I already feel so guilty. I fear I will not want to spend more time with him/her. Fear of change and of losing what I have prevents me from doing the right things.	Seek the peace and power to turn this around. Plan to spend time with spouse. Be kind, loving, grateful for what we have. I love his/her sense of humor and perspective. Take responsibility for my own thoughts and actions: how I feel is the result of how I think. What I think is my choice. His/her choices are his/her business.
Dishonesty, fear, and selfishness: I demand better behavior from my children than I was capable of at their ages. I have been unreasonable and judgmental. Fear and dishonesty, drama: Behaving erratically because I lose sight of what matters. For my children, that is safety, dependability, love, and acceptance.	Seek the peace and perspective to stop judging. Focus on what is good. Love them where they are now, and be grateful. Try to see things from their perspective. Be honest about my failings, apologize, and resolve to correct my mistakes. Keep doing the next right thing. Find the positive. Cut the drama.
Dishonesty: Any clandestine relationship is based on deceit. Allowed my need for validation, and my libido, to overwhelm the conscious commitment I made to my ex-spouse. Unrealistic expectations of spouse, and unwillingness to admit the truth about myself. Arrogance: Did not seek therapy to understand what was behind my error.	Resolve not to take current spouse for granted. Be grateful for the intimacy we have. Do not allow any friendships or fantasies to come between us: our relationship is paramount. Respect my physical needs. Make an effort to give more than I get. *If tempted, work all the harder with others, for it quiets the imperious urge, when to yield would mean heartache.*[1]

[1] *Alcoholics Anonymous.* (2001) New York, NY: AA World Services, Inc., 70.

Confusion: situations where I felt or still feel abandoned or bewildered

Source	Reason/Cause	At Risk/Affects My
Parents	Did not believe me when I told them of the abuse. Did not protect me from my molester.	Love and intimacy, self-esteem, ability to trust, family relationships (I experience fear, anger)
Sibling(s)	Humiliated and belittled me. Scared me for fun. Told on me.	Self-esteem, ability to trust, family relationships
Spouse	Can't help me, despite his/her love and willingness to do so. Sometimes gets angry with me. Sometimes doesn't pay attention to me.	Love and intimacy, family relationships
Self	Tried to follow directions (of sponsors, therapists treatment programs, pastors, mentor and Twelve Steps,) but failed utterly. I abandoned myself.	Life itself, self-esteem, ambition for usefulness, happiness, peace, freedom (the Promises)

My Error/My Part	Resolution
I expected and deserved something better than I got. Expected my parents, especially my mother, to understand and empathize with me. Blamed them for my troubles. I cannot change the past, nor change the mistakes that others made—or are still making. I can, however, make use of my experience to help others.	Imagine what I would have wanted my parents to do when I told them I had been abused. Then do those things, one thing at a time, with as much dignity as I can find. Be the parent I needed and did not have. Get outside support to work through the anger and grief. Forgive. Commit not to abandon myself now.
Selfishness: Expected my sibling(s) to come to my defense and aid, mostly because they usually did so. We are all only human and even the best among us sometimes fail.	Forgive. Sibling(s) were suffering, too, and they did the best they could. I have no right to judge. I don't need sibling(s) to provide for me now. Instead, I commit not to abandon my family members.
Selfishness, self-seeking, and dishonesty: Depending on my spouse to solve my problems. He/she has plenty of his/her own, and my attitudes and behavior are among them. Depending too much on others for things I should take care of myself.	My spouse loves me and is doing his/her level best to show me every day. I am grateful. None of us are perfect. I commit to forgive his/her imperfections, to forgive myself for expecting perfection, and to do my best to show my love for my spouse every day.
Dishonesty: Black-and-white, all-or-nothing thinking. It was rational not to trust when there was no basis for it, but now there is a new basis. Now I trust in the power that active reliance on a higher purpose provides, and I don't have to stay stuck and confused.	I am on a surer footing, relying on a purpose greater than myself to help me build and keep perspective, so I can be at peace and do the next right thing. I have the power to be the peace I want to see in the world.

Frustration: things that made or make me angry, even if I had or have no resentment in connection to them

Source	Reason/Cause	At Risk/Affects My
Self	I often do not do what I know I should.	Self-esteem, self-trust, family relationships, social relationships
Others	Other people often refuse to see things my way.	Self-esteem, family and social relationships, ambition
Inability to understand what I am feeling when I am first feeling it	When I first feel an uncomfortable emotion, I don't know what it is or why I am feeling it. I certainly cannot express myself.	Pride, self-esteem, family relations, ambition (fear of not being able to express myself at work, with loved ones)

My Error/My Part	Resolution
Dishonesty (perfectionism) and focus on the negative: Rather than being grateful for what I can do and how well I do it, I get hung up on what I have not done "correctly."	Be grateful to be able to do what I do and for what I do well. Accept that I will not always do as well as I would like. Tell the truth and admit my errors. Find humor. Turn thoughts to how to be more helpful to others.
Selfishness and dishonesty (dependency): My life and happiness should not hinge on what others think. Depending heavily on others for validation is unreasonable and sets me up for frustration.	Let go of expectations of others. Let service to the greater good provide the validation I need. I can show up, do the work, tell the truth, and let go of the outcomes.
Dishonesty (pride): Thinking this is abnormal or wrong. Usually I've neglected something basic: hunger, anger, loneliness, tiredness (HALT).	Build trust with myself to get and stay safe until I can process my emotions. If I take care of basics, reason will return.

Despair: reasons for hopelessness, past and present

Source	Reason/Cause	At Risk/Affects My
Eating disorder	Kept failing at recovery, despite doing everything I thought I needed to do.	Life itself, self-esteem, ambition for usefulness, happiness, peace, freedom (the Promises)
Self	Spent much of my life looking at things from a narrow and constrained context. How can I now think I will be able to change in such a fundamental way?	Life itself (fear), self-esteem, ambition for usefulness, happiness, peace, freedom (the Promises)
Children	Sure I did so many wrong things and passed on so many terrible genetic and attitudinal issues that my children are doomed to be miserable.	Self-esteem, family relationships, children's emotional health

My Error/My Part	Resolution
Dishonesty: Not willing to be completely honest with myself about what was and wasn't working for me. "Bring the body and the mind will follow" did not work. The Steps do not work through osmosis!	I cannot change the past, but I can change today. Rely on higher purpose to help me commit to honor my truth and take care of myself, so that I may serve those around me and the greater good to the best of my ability.
Dishonesty (drama): Still thinking from such a limited context, and hand-wringing (drama). Black-and-white thinking. Should think instead of how much of my life is still ahead of me. I have choices each and every day to think and act differently.	Seek the peace and power to live each day carefully and deliberately, being grateful for the opportunity to be of cheerful service to the greater good and those around me. Take care of the basics. Work to stay in balance so I can be of service without drama.
Fear and dishonesty (judgmental and untrusting): Failing to see and respect the strength, goodwill, and good sense in my children.	Share my joy and appreciation for life with them. Share what is working for me. Live each day grateful for and respectful of my children and their choices. Their lives are up to them, and they have the exact same opportunity to find peace and joy that I have.

Completing the 4th Step Inventory does not mean that we are "done" with Step Four. Please refer back to Chapter 5 for guidance.

Appendix E

CONTACTING EDA

Detailed information about
Eating Disorders Anonymous (EDA) is available at:

www.4EDA.org

also, *www.eatingdisordersanonymous.org*

- Lists of face-to-face, online, phone, and Skype meetings of EDA
- Literature and free brochures
- Answers to frequently asked questions
- The EDA concept of balance
- Procedures for getting a meeting started
- Information about the General Service Board of EDA, including conference call details and meeting times

For specific questions or concerns, please write to EDA at *info@eatingdisordersanonymous.org.* Note that email is answered by volunteers: response times may vary.

Book Orders

This text, *Eating Disorders Anonymous,* may be ordered from most bookstores and online booksellers.